ARCHAEOLOGICAL EXCAVATION
NICHOLAS AND WINETAVERN S

ARCHAEOLOGICAL
EXCAVATIONS

~ AT ~

PATRICK, NICHOLAS & WINETAVERN STREETS

DUBLIN

C LAIRE W ALSH

BRANDON

First published in 1997 by
Brandon Book Publishers Ltd
Dingle, Co. Kerry, Ireland
in association with Dublin Corporation

British Library Cataloguing-in-Publication Data is available for this book.

ISBN 0 86322 222 7

Front cover shows a bracteate from Patrick Street.

Cover photography by Barry Murphy, Tralee, Co. Kerry
Cover design by Peter Staunton, Tralee, Co. Kerry
Typeset by Koinonia, Bury, Lancashire
Printed by ColourBooks Ltd, Dublin

PREFACE

In the late 1980s, Dublin Corporation undertook major drainage improvements in the general area of Patrick St, Nicholas St and Winetavern St in order to facilitate the redevelopment and regeneration of the area as a thriving business and residential centre. Given the sensitivity of the location, which stands in the medieval core of the city, and the extent of the works proposed, it was recognised from the very outset that there would be significant archaeological implications and that extensive archaeological excavations would be required.

The Corporation engaged the services of Claire Walsh Archaeological Projects Ltd to conduct a series of archaeological excavations, and this work was carried out between March and July 1990. It is generally recognised that the publication of the results of such excavation is a vital part of the whole process: the knowledge gained and evidence uncovered needs to be documented, interpreted and made available in an accessible format. I am delighted to see the fruits of this excavation finally brought to a successful conclusion by the publication of this book.

Annalistic references point to a settlement in Dublin in the 9th century, and the available archaeological evidence suggests that the earliest settlement occurred in the area of Fishamble St and along the natural moraine ridge of present day Christchurch Place. The focus of the early medieval town was centred around Christ Church Cathedral. It is particularly significant that this area of the city is once more the focus of new building, civic authority and population growth. It is also appropriate that work to facilitate this latter development has provided so much valuable information on the earliest settlements in the area.

I would like to thank the National Monuments Service and the National Museum of Ireland for their help and assistance, as well as Claire Walsh and the variety of specialist contributors who have worked together to bring the results of these excavations to publication. A special word of thanks is due to the staff of the Corporation's Main Drainage Division and to the City Archaeologist, Daire O'Rourke.

John Fitzgerald
City Manager
Dublin

FOREWORD

This report describes an excavation along the defences and periphery of medieval Dublin. The excavated areas extended from the junction of Dean St/Kevin St to the town defences at Nicholas St, and from the pre-Norman defences north of Christ Church Cathedral to the Liffey quays at the foot of Winetavern St.

The excavation of the Poddle river bed at Patrick St broke new ground in more than one sense: it was the first major archaeological excavation to have taken place outside the southern walls of the medieval town. The survey includes the first excavated example in this country of an Anglo-Norman mill, which adds new and important evidence to the Irish archaeological record, and the recording of some 125m. of well-preserved medieval waterside structures in the Poddle river at Patrick St indicates the enormous archaeological potential of sites outside the town walls of Dublin. The results of the excavations at Patrick St are combined with new historical research on the area to reinterpret the dating and the reasons for the artificial channelling of the Poddle river at this point.

Evidence for other industrial activity along the banks of the Poddle was also recovered, as was the base of a late 12th-century limekiln. Part of the defences of the town were excavated – the Anglo-Norman town ditch at Nicholas St and the pre-Norman town wall at Winetavern St – while timber structures relating to the late 12th and early 13th century Liffey docksides were uncovered at the northern limit of the excavation.

An excavation of this scope could not have been completed without the input of very many people. Jack Keyes, Niall Kerrigan and Jim Hill (Divisional Engineer), all formerly of Dublin Corporation's Main Drainage Division, initiated the archaeological work, and their vision and courage in doing so is unprecedented. The work was made possible by the Department of the Environment and Dublin Corporation, who jointly funded the project.

My thanks to Tom Kinirons of Dublin Corporation, who facilitated the archaeological element during construction work, and also to the Corporation construction crews on both lines, who were co-operative and pleasant to work alongside. Eddie Dowling of Dublin Corporation Roads Department facilitated the excavation at Site G. Particular thanks is due to John Barrett for his supervision of building works.

Over thirty people worked extremely hard on site, ensuring that all schedules were met. My sincere thanks to them all, not only for their excellent work, but for their enduring good spirits.

Many archaeologists contributed to this report. For supervision of the sites along the route and preparation of the stratigraphic reports, thanks to Edward Bourke (Sites D and I), Kieran Campbell (Sites C and J), Alan Hayden (Site K), Finola O'Carroll (Site B), Georgina Scally (Sites E and F) and Andrew Shelley (Site H). Linzi Simpson monitored the construction work on Patrick St, and Alan Hayden and Frank Myles at Winetavern St. Aoife Daly and Conor McDermott identified and reported on wood *in situ*. Finds were processed under the supervision of Eileen Whyte, who also carried out the cataloguing of the pottery, assisted by Sylvia Desmond.

I wish to record my gratitude to all the contributors of specialist reports. Four persons in particular worked on the completion of this report. The finished plans are the work of Georgina Scally, excepting Fig. 6 (C. Walsh), Fig. 16 (E. Bourke), Fig. 38 (A. Hayden) and Figs 34 and 35 (C. Rynne). The finds drawings were undertaken by Alan Hayden, excepting Figs 72, 73, 78, 80, 81 (M. Keane) and Figs 102-104 (C. Power), and most of the finds catalogue is his work. For her exhaustive documentary research on the Patrick St area, my thanks to Linzi Simpson, who also compiled the data for the woodworking section. Jeannette D'Arcy lifted most of the burden of administrative duties from me, both during fieldwork and the preparation of this report.

For access to N.M.I. plans, thanks to Dr P. F. Wallace and Debbie Caulfield. Conservation of metal and fabric finds was undertaken by Adrian Kennedy, who also commented on several of the objects. Wood and leather conservation was facilitated by Rose Cleary of U.C.C.

Cyril Meehan, Dublin Corporation, and Martin Walsh proofread the first draft, while Brian Curtis, Dublin Corporation Drainage Department, and Michael Walsh of U.C.D. Computing Services, assisted in the production of the report. The last word must go to Jeannette D'Arcy, who typed the entire manuscript.

Claire Walsh
Dublin

CONTENTS

LIST OF ILLUSTRATIONS

Photographs

1. Possible tanning pit, Site B
2. Wattle revetment of River Poddle, Site C
3. Baseplates of early 13th-century revetment, Site D
4. Level 1 mill: inlet
5. Level 2 mill, Site E
6. Detail of timbers 1128 and 1125, level 1 mill
7. Late 12th-century jetty or boardwalk, Site J
8. Base of early 13th-century pier, Site K

INTRODUCTION

Background to the excavation programme

In June 1989 the Drainage Division of Dublin Corporation drew up design proposals detailing the construction of a 700m. long, 1.5m. diameter replacement sewer. The pipe was to be laid in an open cut trench along the west side of Patrick St, in a tunnel beneath St Michael's Hill, and to continue down the west side of Winetavern St in an open cut trench to meet with existing pipes on Wood Quay.

The archaeological implications of the construction work were realised by the divisional engineers at an early stage, and a consultant archaeologist, Mary McMahon, was appointed to monitor boreholes along the route of the pipe. Her report formed the basis for evaluating the depth and nature of the archaeological deposits, particularly in Patrick St, where no previous archaeological excavation had taken place.

In consultation with the National Parks and Monuments Branch of the Office of Public Works, nine sites along the route were initially selected for excavation (Figs 1, 2, 3). The contract was advertised as a public tender in September 1989, with funding provided jointly by Dublin Corporation and the Department of the Environment. Excavation work began in late March 1990 and continued into July 1990. Monitoring of the construction trenching for the sewage pipe was completed in November 1990.

A further excavation, Site G, was undertaken in October 1991, when the original site of the tunnel reception shaft at Nicholas St was moved *c*. 20m further to the north. The results of continuous archaeological monitoring of relocated service trenches during the summer of 1991 are also integrated into the report. Large-scale clearance of deposits for the construction of road-widening took place in autumn 1991. The final archaeological site work, Site A, was carried out in October 1992.

The excavated areas

The designated areas for excavation were revised somewhat when excavation began, and a more extensive area of the pipe route was covered by excavation than initially proposed.

Similarly, Site H at the top of Winetavern St had little or no remains of archaeological significance, and resources were diverted elsewhere along the line. Of the 125m. length of the line on Winetavern St, 51.5m. was excavated, while of the 240m. long length of open trenching at Patrick St, 71.5m. was excavated. The intervening areas were archaeologically monitored until construction was completed in November 1991.

All the sites were opened under archaeological supervision by Atlas 1604 tracked machine. All modern red-brick rubble was mechanically removed. Shoring was in all cases, excepting Site G, immediately installed by Dublin Corporation direct labour crew. The type of shoring used – metal trenchboxes with expandable braces, with timber or metal bulkheads at the short axes of the site – resulted in the loss of a complete site section. The shoring at Site G consisted of interlocking steel sheeting, retained behind a rigid timber frame, suitable for deep excavation and tunnelling. As the excavation here progressed, the sheeting was mechanically driven deeper, and a continuous site section was maintained. Where complete site sections or profiles are presented from the other sites in the excavation report, these were compiled from rapid measurements taken during clearance, and alternatively, sections were generated from overlaying principal features that had been recorded on the horizontal plane.

Recording methods

Each site, numbered from A to K (Figs 2, 3), was supervised by an archaeologist, who was responsible for the maintenance of the site records. Batches of numbers – in hundreds – were allocated to each site and given to the various features. These numbers have been retained throughout the report and are included in the text in brackets. Each feature – layer, wall, structure – was recorded in a standard field sheet. Timbers were also described in detail, using a standardised timber sheet based on that used by the Urban Archaeology Department of the Museum of London (Milne 1982, 14). When the timbers were planned and photographed *in situ*, they were lifted (generally with the aid of a machine) to dry ground and recorded in full detail. Many timbers were then drawn at a scale of 1:10 when lifted.

Surveying was generally done at a scale of 1:20, and section drawings or elevations at a scale of 1:10. All Ordnance Datum points are relative to Poolbeg. All measurements in the report are given in metres (m.), unless otherwise stated. The common English names of woods are given in the main report.

Numbering of finds

Each find and sherd of pottery is numbered accordingly:
  National Museum Site registration number: E543
  Layer or feature number: 5, 343, etc.
  Find accession number (repeated for each layer): 1- ...
These numbers are maintained throughout the report.

Layout of the report

The section of the report pertaining to Patrick St follows the route from south (Site A) to north (Site G). Each site is individually described, and, where relevant, the evidence is integrated with that of its neighbours. The dating evidence for the different levels is derived in the main from the series of dendrochronological dates received from Queen's University, and this is integrated with the ceramic evidence. Because of the nature of the soft riverine deposits, the river silts cannot be considered securely stratified. There exists also the likelihood that the bed of the river was periodically scoured out during the medieval period, which factor would not be apparent on examination of the silts during excavation. The levels of occupation on each site are specific only to that particular site, and are correlated with the other sites in Table 1.

The relative dating of the stratigraphy on the sites at Winetavern St is much more straightforward, resulting mainly from the evidence recovered from the extensive waterfront excavations at Wood Quay (Wallace 1981, 103). The dating evidence is summarised in Table 2. A list of the layers/features of each site, by phase, is given in Appendix 1.

Table 1. Relative dating of sites, Patrick Street

Site	A	B	C	D	E	F	G	Date
		L5	L3	L4	L3	L6	L7	1750
							L6	1650
							L5	1590
							L4	1550
							L3	1500
		L4	L2		L2	L5	L2	1370
		L3						1300
				L3		L4		1250
	L1				L1			1240
		L2		L2		L3		1202
			L1	L1		L2		1185
		L1				L1	L1	1180

Table 2. Relative dating of sites, Winetavern Street

Site	I	J	K	Date
	L3	L3	L4	1692
			L3	1500
		L2	L2	1300
			L1	1204
		L1		1189
	L2			1100
	L1			950

PART ONE
THE SITES

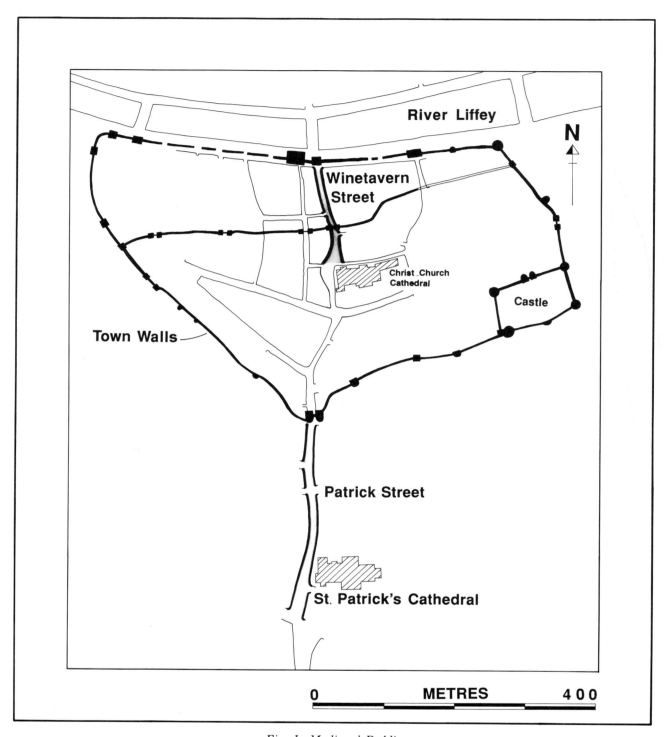

Fig. 1. Medieval Dublin

HISTORICAL BACKGROUND TO THE PATRICK STREET EXCAVATION

Linzi Simpson

Introduction

The history of Patrick St and the surrounding area has an important contribution to make to our understanding of medieval settlement patterns outside the city of Dublin. Patrick St, the main access route to Dublin from the south, lay beyond the city wall and played little part in the urbanisation of the early town (Fig. 1). However, there are indications that settlement had begun in this area long before the arrival of the Vikings in the 9th century.

Early Dublin

Documentary sources, although somewhat dubious, record the names of bishops at Dublin from the 7th century onwards, suggesting the existence of a pre-Viking ecclesiastical settlement at Dublin (Clarke 1977, 40). More reliable evidence, however, is found in the form of annalistic sources which refer to abbots of Dublin in the 7th and 8th centuries (ibid.). The exact location of this early centre is not known. However, the outline of a possible oval enclosure, often associated with early church sites, may be preserved in the street alignment at Peter's Row, Whitefriar St, Upper and Lower Stephen St and the eastern boundary of Mercer St (ibid., 39).

Alternatively, the church site at St Michael le Pole, to the east of Patrick St, may be the location of the early centre. Excavations there exposed the remains of a stone church with a round tower which is known from documentary sources to have survived until the late 18th century (Gowen, forthcoming). In addition, a large cemetery, which stretched as far west as Bride St, was associated with the early church (McMahon, forthcoming).

The documentary sources also record a scatter of small churches with early Irish dedications in the area around Patrick St. These were the churches of St Brigid, St Kevin, St Patrick and possibly St Michael le Pole (Little 1957, 109-10). Although these churches appear in the documentary sources after the Anglo-Norman invasion of 1170, the survival of native dedications suggests, at least, their existence on the eve of the invasion, perhaps serving a settled Viking community, on this side of the town.

Viking expansion

The Vikings first settled in Dublin in the 9th century, quickly establishing a flourishing port surrounded by earthen defences. By *c.* 1100 the early defences had been replaced by a substantial city wall (Wallace 1981, 109-54). However, there was expansion beyond the line of this wall, on the south-east side of the town. Documentary sources record that Asculf Mac Turcaill, the last Viking king of Dublin, held lands in the early 12th century around Bride St, which he granted to the Priory of the Holy Trinity (Christ Church). In addition, he held a garden outside the Pole Gate, one of the mural gates into the city (McNeill 1950, 29).

The Anglo-Normans at Dublin

In 1170 Dublin was taken by the Anglo-Normans, who immediately began to refortify the town's defences. This included rebuilding the western mural gate, digging a city fosse on the south side, and probably repairing the existing city wall. The 13th century saw a period of expansion outside the line of the Viking wall. By the mid-13th century an extension to the city wall had to be added on the northern side of the town to accommodate a growing population and to protect the quays. Expansion also took place to the south and west of the town. Thus by the 13th century, documentary sources record property plots along Thomas St, Francis St, Patrick St, and Kevin St.

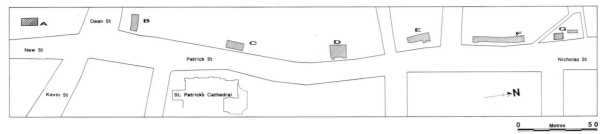

Fig. 2. Patrick Street: location of sites

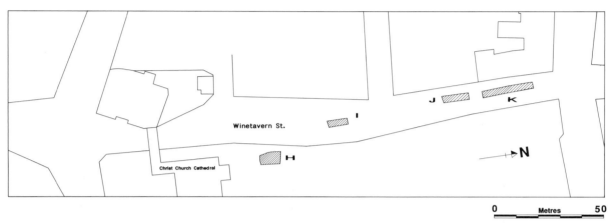

Fig. 3. Winetavern Street: location of sites

The Poddle river

The plain to the south of the walled town was dominated by the presence of a river which had a major influence on the subsequent development of the area. The Poddle, rising in Greenhills in Tallaght (Fig. 4), approached Patrick St from the south and, because it was subject to flooding, rendered the plain wet and marshy (Clarke 1977, 39). The river probably meandered, in many different channels, across the valley before discharging into the Liffey (Simms 1978, 29). Cross Poddle, at the south end of Patrick St, preserved an old crossing point where the river, on joining with a stream from the Coombe valley, was most easily forded. The importance of this crossing may be reflected in the junction of three of the four great roads in early Ireland at Cross Poddle. Although scholars are divided on this issue (Ryan 1949, 68) the Slighe Midluachra from Ulster, the Slighe Dála from Munster and the Slighe Cualann from Leinster may have intersected south of St Patrick's Cathedral (Clarke 1977, 35).

St Patrick's Church

St Patrick's *in Insula*, destined to become a cathedral, must have been one of the most important of the small churches in the area. The church was sited on the low-lying plain (Fig. 5) overlooked from the north by the long narrow gravel bluff of St Michael's Hill. As the name suggests, the church was sited on an island with the Poddle river flowing around either side (McNeill 1950, 4). Monck-Mason records, rather dubiously, that Gregory, king of Scotland, reputedly visited St Patrick's in 890 (Monck-Mason 1818, 1). The next known reference is in a poem dated possibly to 1121 in which the churches of St Patrick and St Brigid are mentioned (H. Clarke, pers. comm.). In 1179, after the Anglo-Norman invasion, a confirmation of the possessions of the diocese of Dublin refers to the church of St Patrick *in Insula,* as well as the churches of St Thomas, St Nicholas and St Werburgh (McNeill 1950, 3).

18

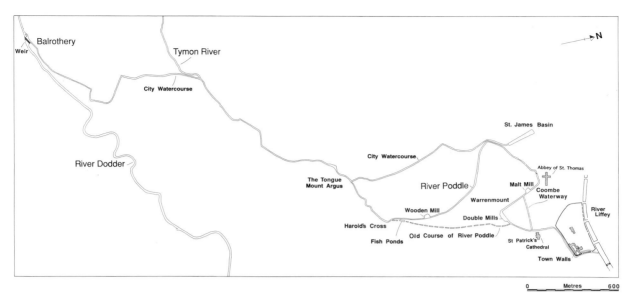

Fig. 4. Route of Poddle

In 1902, during renovations carried out along the old culverted line of the Poddle, which ran north in front of the west end of the cathedral, the site of St Patrick's Well was re-located. The well was originally marked by a granite stone inscribed with two crosses (Drew 1891, 426). Four early grave slabs and three skeletons oriented east/west were also found in the area, associated perhaps with a cemetery attached to the church (Lawlor 1930, 10).

The historian and architect Thomas Drew suggested that there was some architectural evidence of a small aisleless building on the same line of the present nave, completely transformed by subsequent rebuilding and Victorian restoration. He further suggested that Archbishop Comyn, the first Anglo-Norman archbishop, found at St Patrick's 'a community which lived monastic-fashion around a cloister garth of usual plan, the foundations of which remain and the lines of which may yet be discerned on the Ordnance Survey' (Drew 1891, 426).

Sources

Alen's Register

One of the most important sources for Anglo-Norman Patrick St is *Archbishop Alen's Register*. It contains many land-grants and confirmation charters and covers an extensive period, from 1172 to 1534. Although it is mostly concerned with the property of the church, it also records copies of the early charters of Dublin. In addition, it also contains invaluable information about the possessions of the Manor of St Sepulchre and St Patrick's Cathedral. It must be considered the most important source for the See of Dublin during this period.

Register of St John the Baptist

A second important source is the *Register of St John the Baptist Without the New Gate*. This register, compiled from the original charters of the hospital, is thought to be in a complete state and contains a compilation of various deeds dating from the 13th to the 15th centuries, and grouped according to locality. Under the Dublin section, there are details of lands held in the parish of St Patrick's and St Kevin's.

The White Book of Dublin

The White Book of Dublin supplies details of civic transactions in transcripts of various documents, dating from the 13th to the 17th centuries. Thus we get information about municipal property, municipal duties, the mural defences and the water supply, as well as information about private ownership. It also supplies details about the various liberties and accounts of the custom of 'Riding the Franchises of the City'.

19

There are other various sources which add details to our knowledge of the topography of the city of Dublin and the surrounding lands. An attempt is made here to use some of these sources in an effort to understand what the excavations in Patrick St have revealed.

Religious houses

In the aftermath of the Anglo-Norman invasion of Ireland, the lands conquered were quickly carved into large estates and granted out, many to prominent Anglo-Norman individuals. The town of Dublin and the surrounding area, however, was initially reserved by King Henry II. As ruler of Dublin, he confirmed the possessions of the existing religious houses which had held lands prior to the invasion. He also granted them new lands on both sides of the Liffey. Thus St Mary's Abbey received confirmation of the land they held before the invasion, as did the archbishop of Dublin and the Priory of the Holy Trinity. The years that followed saw the introduction of different religious orders and the establishment of a series of monastic houses, all of which received land and possessions from the new inhabitants of Dublin.

One of the largest of these was the Augustinian abbey dedicated to St Thomas. Located south of Thomas St, the abbey was founded in 1177 by William fitzAudelin, on behalf of Henry II (Gilbert 1889, xi). The following year the king granted one carucate (approx. 240 modern acres) of land called Dunore with 'mills, meadows and other appurtenances' (Gwynn and Hadcock 1970, 172; Elliot 1990, 64). The foundation was a royal abbey enjoying special favour from the king. They held their lands as a 'liberty', free from the city laws and regulations (Gilbert 1870, 212). When the abbey was surrendered after the Dissolution in 1539, the holdings in Dublin included fifty messuages, four mills, eight orchards and thirty acres of wood (Cal. Close R. Hen. VIII, 134).

The Hospital of St John the Baptist was another important religious house in the area. It lay just outside Newgate at the western end of the city. Founded by Ailred the Palmer sometime between 1185-88, the complex of buildings included two chapels, three watermills and a hospital with fifty beds for the sick (Gwynn and Hadcock 1970, 212).

Directly west of St Patrick's Cathedral lay St Francis's Friary, founded in 1233. Its holdings were never extensive and the valuation of its property after the Dissolution was very low. The house only held a two-acre site in Francis St, which by the 16th century was in a very bad state of repair (Cal. Close R. Hen. VIII, 89).

The Manor of St Sepulchre

The extensive holdings of the archbishop of Dublin had the greatest impact on the development of lands south of the city, especially in the Patrick St area. The archbishop accounted for 53,000 acres of land in the medieval county of Dublin, both north and south of the city (Jackson 1975, 83). This huge acreage was divided into manorial centres which could administer the lands most effectively and profitably. The Manor of St Sepulchre, which encompassed lands both within the city as well as in the outskirts, was one of nine such manors in the Vale of Dublin (McNeill 1950, 179-96). With an area of over 3070 acres, it was the most important of all the manors since it housed the archiepiscopal palace, on Kevin St, and was the administrative centre which controlled all the possessions (Jackson 1975, 83). The manor was formerly known as Colonia, a name which still survives in the placename 'Cullenswood' today, but a 13th century seal matrix, bearing the inscription *'Sigullum Sancti Sepulchre'* on one side with the seal of the archbishop on the reverse, indicates that the manor was known as St Sepulchre at that date (ibid., 84). The official changeover did not take place until the early 14th century (Court Lib. viii).

The manor was held as a separate liberty, similar to St Thomas's Abbey, and was not subject to the laws and regulations laid down by the mayor and commonalty of Dublin. Thus the location of the palace was very favourable since it was beyond the jurisdiction of the civil and military authorities. The archbishop exercised temporal control and ruled as a feudal lord, with his own courts and gallows (Wood 1930, 1). Similarly, Patrick St, which was also within the Manor of St Sepulchre, was ruled directly by the archbishop.

St Patrick's Cathedral

It was from the Manor of St Sepulchre that Archbishop Comyn, the first Anglo-Norman arch-bishop, dissatisfied, perhaps, with his level of control over the Priory of the Holy Trinity (Christ Church), decided to establish a college of 'approved life and learning' in 1191 (McNeill 1950, 11). He chose the Church of St Patrick *in Insula* as a place of special veneration.

The small church was elevated to prebendal status and the archbishop granted 'eight plots about the graveyard to build on' (McNeill 1950, 18). The grant included the tithes (church tax) of the demesne land of St Kevin's and the land of St Patrick's. Twenty-eight years later, in 1219, Arch-bishop Henry de London elevated the church a second time, to cathedral status (ibid., 42). Thus by the early 13th century, there were two rival cathedral chapters in Dublin, one within the walled city and one outside. In addition, the lands and grounds attached to the new cathedral chapter were held as a separate liberty.

Speed's map of Dublin

Speed's map of Dublin, dated 1610, depicts the cathedral and the surrounding precinct (Andrews 1983, 207). The palace of St Sepulchre, the only private residence shown under its original name, is surrounded by a wall intersected by small gates. The cathedral of St Patrick is shown as the largest building in Dublin at this date (ibid., 222). It was surrounded by a wall which opened directly west of the cathedral on to Patrick St. The Kendrick survey of the Patrick St area, dated to *c.* 1749, illustrates the location of individual property plots around the cathedral. In addition, it contains handwritten accounts of lands held in the area from 1647 onwards. From it we learn that the cathedral was enclosed by an 'ample wall' which had at least two fortified gates. At the south end stood St Paul's Gate, while St Patrick's Gate, which stood on the west side of the cathedral, was said to be 'very lofty' (Monck-Mason 1818, 17). Within the walls stood the archdeacon's manse, treas-urer's manse, the vicar's halls and various other administrative and domestic buildings. Around these were gardens and orchards belonging to the prebendaries.

The boundary between the Manor of St Sepulchre and St Patrick's bisected Patrick St as far as Walker's Alley, which ran east/west through the modern St Patrick's Park (Drew 1891, 426-28). This effectively divided lower Patrick St in two, the east side belonging to St Patrick's, while the west remained in the Manor of St Sepulchre. However, there was a small narrow strip of land containing one house and a garden on the west side of the street. This belonged to the Prebendary of Clonmethan, one of the 13 churches granted to the cathedral (Monck-Mason 1818, 48).

The Liberties

The city of Dublin was held as a liberty, granted by Henry II to 'his men of Bristol' in 1172 (Curtis and McDowell 1943, 24). Thus the mayor and commonalty exercised full judicial and administrative control, within the boundaries or franchise of the city. The limits were well-known and extended some distance beyond the walled town. In 1192 the boundary was recorded as running east along Kevin St as far as Donnybrook and west along the Coombe as far as Kilmainham (McNeill 1950, 21). On the north side of the river the boundary extended as far as Clonliffe and the Tolka river (ibid.). The boundaries were known by topographical features and local landmarks, but the circuit was ridden every three years, by the mayor and commonalty, to reinforce their claims to the land (ibid., 233, 272, 302). Despite the great pageantry which accompanied each Riding of the Franchise, the custom, in fact, had a practical purpose, since it served to prevent encroachment of city property.

By the mid-13th century there were three separate liberties, the Liberty of St Patrick's, St Thomas's, and the Manor of St Sepulchre, which were all operating within the city liberty (ibid., 302). This caused a great deal of tension and confusion, both in the judicial system and in property ownership. Thus there were various legal disputes which were not easily resolved. Attempts were made to deal with these problems by agreements made between the archbishop and the citizens (ibid., 46). However, disputes still arose. In some cases, tenants of the archbishop living in the Manor of St Sepulchre committed crimes within the walls of the city. This resulted in legal wrangling between the mayor of the city and the archbishop as to who exercised judicial control. There was also direct conflict between the various ecclesiastical establishments about similar issues.

In addition, although the various liberty boundaries were relatively well-known, there were small pockets of land which always remained in dispute.

In 1225 an agreement was made between the archbishop and the citizens of Dublin in an attempt to prevent tenants' manipulating the system. It was decided that the archbishop's tenants, who 'wished to be free of the city', would not pay murage tolls, for fortifying and defending the city, unless by command of the king. If this occurred it would be implemented by the archbishop's bailiff. However, the archbishop's tenants would not be liable for compensation if the citizens lost some of their property (ibid., 46). The reverse was also true. Even if a tenant lived in the Manor of St Sepulchre, he could place himself within the city jurisdiction by simply paying the murage and paving tolls: 'they had a choice of jurisdiction they might prefer' (Lynch 1831, 43).

The Poddle and City Watercourse

The Poddle river originally encircled St Patrick's Church (McNeill 1950, 4) (Fig. 5). At an early date, however, it was channelled into two artificially created watercourses, running northwards along either side of Patrick St. On reaching St Nicholas Gate, it turned sharply east into the city fosse and thus constituted an important part of the city's defences.

Speed's map of Dublin of 1610 fails to show the course of the Poddle along Patrick St, but this is probably due to an engraver's ignorance concerning the depiction of watercourses which ran close to or under houses (Andrews 1983, 219). There are no known documentary sources concerning the rechannelling of the Poddle, but excavation yielded a date of 1202 for the earliest timber revetments (Site D, level 2). The wooden revetments were constructed on almost 1m. of silt, and artefacts recovered suggest that the diversion of the watercourse dates, in all likelihood, to the late 12th century. Bearing this early date in mind, the question arises as to who initiated the works and why. In order to investigate the possibilities satisfactorily, the history of the Poddle watercourse must be explored in greater detail.

There is no doubt that the inhabitants of the suburbs of Dublin in the Patrick St area depended heavily on the Poddle for their water supply. As the river approached the city wall, however, and entered the fosse, it must have become contaminated by the salty tidal water of the Liffey. Although the river ran along the perimeter wall of Dublin Castle, the castle itself depended on the internal well for its supply and so possibly did the rest of the city (C.D.I. I, 187).

It was against this background that the justiciar, Maurice fitzGerald, in April 1244, issued a writ commanding the sheriff of Dublin 'without delay, by twelve free and lawful men of his country, to make inquisition, with advice of the Mayor and Citizens, as to whence water can be best and most conveniently taken from its course and conducted to the King's city of Dublin, for the benefit of the city, and at the cost of the citizens, who have undertaken to pay the amount. By the same twelve men the sheriff is to enquire whether any damage can arise by thus taking and bringing the water. The sheriff under his seal, and the seals of the jurors, is to return the inquisition to the justiciar so that the damage, if any, may be repaired at the cost of the King...' (C.A.R.D. I, 92). There are no documentary references stating when this was carried out, but in 1245 a mandate was issued instructing the justiciar to have the King's Hall (at Dublin Castle) completed with a pipe supplied by the city conduit (C.D.I. I, 417). From this we can infer that the works were either complete or nearing completion.

The supply of water, for the City Watercourse, was drawn from the combined Poddle and Dodder rivers. The Dodder, rising in the Glenasmole valley, was diverted at Balrothery near Firhouse, Tallaght, by a stone weir. Shortly after this it was joined by the Poddle coming from Tymon, and together they flowed until they reached Mount Argus, where at a place known as 'the Tongue' they separated, one third going to supply the City Watercourse (Fig. 4). This watercourse, taking the shortest route possible but skirting the western boundary of St Thomas's Abbey, fed into the city cistern near St John's Church (Dick 1974, 42).

The watercourse of St Thomas's Abbey

The remaining two thirds of the water continued through the lands of the Abbey of St Thomas. The historian Myles Ronan points out that the course of the river from Harold's Cross on is at variance with the general topography and suggests that it was artificially channelled to deliberately meander

22

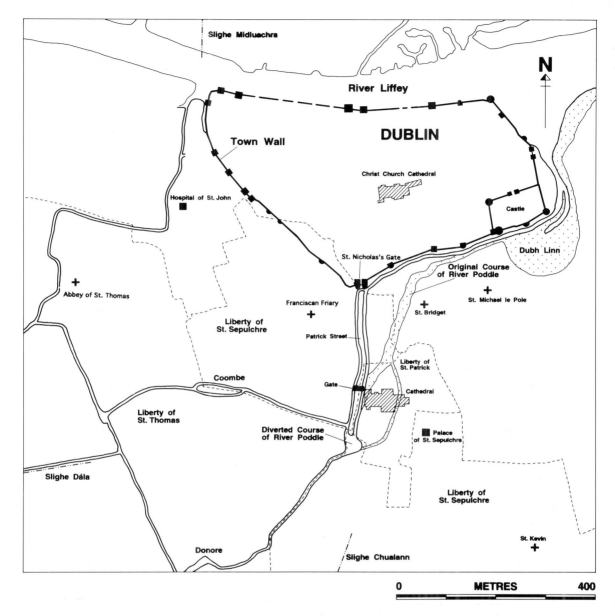

Fig. 5. Dublin, south city, with course of Poddle (after Clarke 1978)

by a winding route to service a series of mills erected along the course (Ronan 1927, 40). There are strong indications that this was in fact the case. The course of the river as it travels across the abbey lands was never referred to as the Poddle river but as the Abbey Millstream until the suppression of the abbey in 1539 (ibid.). In addition, the line of an old river bed is preserved in an estate map of Lord Meath's estate, where it is called the 'course of ancient water'. This course runs in a northerly direction from Harold's Cross through Blackpitts to rejoin the Poddle proper at Warrenmount (Fig. 4). It follows a far more direct route than the Abbey stream and may represent the original course of the Poddle, before it was deflected at Harold's Cross. Finally, one might note that in a decree dated 1544, it was stated that the Abbey stream was brought through the abbey lands for the purpose of the mills erected along the course (ibid.).

The new watercourse was constructed to run along the western boundary of the abbey lands in a curving three-mile stretch, which involved considerable engineering works. Mill ponds were created, and suitable falls, needed to generate power, were constructed for each individual mill. Ronan dates this new watercourse to some time after 1244 and suggests that it was constructed in direct imitation of the new City Watercourse. However, there is evidence to suggest that the monks proved adept at manipulating the water supply at a much earlier date.

The Woodenmill at Donore

In 1185, Prince John granted a property plot beside St Kevin's Church 'and the site of a mill' there, to the Priory of the Holy Trinity, as well as a carucate of land (approx. 240 modern acres) in the general vicinity (McNeill 1950, 11). The reference states that the land had previously been in the hands of Richard del Tuit, one of Hugh de Lacy's followers. Prince John revoked the grant, as he did with many other de Lacy grants, and replaced the powerful magnate del Tuit with the archbishop of Dublin. The site of the mill had previously been in the hands of another Anglo-Norman by the name of Marcel. The exact location of the mill subsequently built is not specified, but it has been generally accepted that it was close by the Church of St Kevin despite the absence of a suitable watercourse in this area (Fig. 5).

In 1191, however, with the establishment of the collegiate college of St Patrick, a grant was made by the archbishop of Dublin of the demesne lands of St Kevin's and 'all tithes of the mills he has now or will acquire hereafter' (ibid., 19). This must have included the tithes of the new mill built by the priory. In 1215 there is a confirmation of this (ibid., 37, 41). In a grant in which the king is confirming the church of Crumlin to St Patrick's, Archbishop Alen has added 'and half a burgage before the gate of St Kevin's and a mill near Dunnor' (ibid., 37). A second reference to St Patrick's, dated to between 1213-16, includes 'half a burgage before the gate of St Kevin's, and a mill by Donowre' (ibid., 41). These sound suspiciously similar to the grant of a tenement beside St Kevin's Church and the site of a mill, granted to the priory in 1185. However, the location of the mill is now given as Donore. Donore was to the west of St Kevin's Church and formed part of the Liberty of St Thomas's Abbey, an unlikely location for a mill belonging to the Priory of the Holy Trinity.

Confirmation that this was the location of the mill is received in an account of the Manor of St Sepulchre, dated 1326 (ibid., 172). This records a mill named as 'Woodmylle' for which the prior paid four marks a year. Woodenmill was within the Liberty of Donore, on the Abbey stream watercourse, the site of which survived until the early 20th century. The mill of the priory was therefore on the artificial watercourse constructed by the monks, within the Liberty of Donore. This must be the same mill, since Archbishop Alen has added in a footnote '... a mill of St Thomas which is called Woodmylle' (ibid., 172).

This evidence for the location of the mill is further supported in a rental of the Manor of St Sepulchre, dated 1386, in which the priory is recorded as holding one mill to which they 'were accustomed to paying 4 marks rent' (Mills 1889, 119). Although not named as Woodenmill in the rental, the rent recorded in the 1326 extent was also four marks and is evidently the same.

The documentary sources suggest, therefore, that the Woodenmill was constructed shortly after 1185 and was located on the Abbey stream watercourse. It should be noted that although the Priory of the Holy Trinity owned the mill, St Thomas's Abbey rented it. Thus after the Dissolution, the abbey is described as having four mills, including the Woodenmill (Cal. Close R. Hen VIII, 134). However, Archbishop Alen records that the priory was still holding the mill in his time, in the mid-16th century (McNeill 1950, 11).

A second mill, the Malt Mill, was also located on the new watercourse, serviced by a large mill pond. Because the pond is not mentioned in an account of Riding the Franchise in 1191, Ronan infers that it was not in existence at this date, the earliest reference being in 1324 (Ronan 1927, 41). However, the mill pond may have existed as early as 1181 since in a reference dated to between 1181 and 1212, a pond is mentioned as a topographical landmark, '... as far as the pond below St Thomas's' (McNeill 1950, 32).

Dispute between St Patrick's and St Thomas's

A dispute arose between St Patrick's and St Thomas's Abbey between 1243 and 1244, concerning tithes of mills 'situated within St Patrick's parish' (Gilbert 1889, 295). Ronan cites this dispute as evidence that the Abbey stream watercourse must have dated to after 1244. He states that the dispute could not have concerned the four mills known to have been on the Abbey stream watercourse, since they were situated well within the abbey boundary and their locations could not have been open to dispute. The mills referred to, he concluded, must have been positioned along the original line of the Poddle marked on the Earl of Meath's estate map. This positioning of the mills, because it was a boundary line between the archbishop's land and the lands of St Thomas's Abbey, was a far more likely location for a clash of interest concerning tithes of mills. These mills, he suggests, became obsolete and disappeared after the monks created the Abbey stream sometime after 1244.

But the dispute did not concern the boundaries between the archbishop's land and the lands of the abbey. It referred specifically to mills situated within the parish of St Patrick. The original grant to St Patrick's in 1191 included the tithes of mills that the archbishop held or was to hold in the future, including land in St Patrick's parish (McNeill 1950, 19). Donore was in the parish of St Patrick (Brooks 1936, 96), and the dispute may have concerned any of the mills situated there.

A reference dated to between 1181 and 1212, in which the archbishop granted St James's Church to the canons of St Thomas, may represent the bone of contention between both parties. He fixed the parish boundaries of St James's Church as stretching from the New Gate (the western city gate) as far west as Kilmainham. However, Donour Street, which led to St Thomas's Abbey, was exempted since it was within the parish of St Patrick, '... saving Donour Street as far as the pond below St Thomas Court in which St Patrick's Church should have parochial rights; saving, however, to the canons all tithes of their mills and arable lands, and should they wish to let their arable land they may [still] have parish rights in it' (McNeill 1950, 32-33). The dispute, therefore, probably did concern the mills on the Abbey stream watercourse. By the 16th century there were at least four, the Double Mills, the Malt Mill, and the Woodenmill, with a fifth mill on Patrick St in the Manor of St Sepulchre. St Patrick's may have attempted to claim tithes of the mills belonging to the abbey. The dispute ended amicably and probably in favour of St Thomas's Abbey (Ronan 1927, 42).

The location of Woodenmill, on the Abbey stream watercourse, the site of which was granted in 1185, suggests that the latter dated to a similar period. Prince John, perhaps unscrupulously taking advantage of the royal association with St Thomas's Abbey, granted the site of the mill to the Priory of the Holy Trinity, even though the abbey had received Donore in an earlier grant. The land was seized from Marcel, who possibly held it prior to St Thomas's Abbey. Prince John granted the mill site there because it was probably the only suitable watercourse in the area. The fact that only a mill site rather than a mill was granted may suggest that the watercourse had just been completed.

The Balrothery-Kimmage watercourse

The Abbey stream watercourse may then have been in existence as early as 1185, but the volume of water required by the monks could hardly have been supplied by the Poddle river alone. The section of water from Balrothery to Kimmage, connecting the Dodder water with the Poddle, is generally considered to be part of the City Watercourse of 1244. However, an inquisition of 1259 discovered by Berry and later examined by Jackson (1990) throws further light on the terms under which the City Watercourse was constructed (Berry 1904, 40). The inquisition reveals details of an agreement between the monks of St Thomas and the citizens of Dublin, concerning the diversion at Balrothery, made some time before 1259: 'It was formerly agreed between the Abbot of St Thomas and the Mayor and Commonalty they should take running water of the Dodder belonging to the Priory ... the Citizens are bound to make a stone wall on the Dodder at their expense ... the Abbot was bound to maintain the said wall ...' (Jackson 1990, 131).

The inquisition makes it clear that the citizens had failed to keep the agreement, that they had not constructed the wall at Balrothery and had drawn off considerably more water than the stipulated quantity. They had also sold water to various religious houses and had not paid the agreed rent (Berry 1904, 40, 41).

Jackson (1990, 128) examined the wording of the inquisition in detail. The water of the Dodder is referred to as the property of the monks, although the Dodder never came closer than within two miles of their property. The abbey received most of the water at the Tongue, a peculiar arrangement considering the jealously guarded municipal riverine rights which were usually in operation. Why were the monks left effectively in charge of maintaining the weir at Balrothery? Jackson concluded that the monks must have been responsible for the initial diversion at Balrothery. From there they channelled the increased volume of water as far as Harold's Cross, where the Poddle was diverted for the second time. The citizens had agreed to build a weir at Balrothery because the deflection of the water at the Tongue to the City Watercourse would undoubtedly have impaired the powering of the abbey mills already in existence on the artificial Abbey stream. A weir at Templeogue would redress the balance of water. The documentary sources suggest that the Abbey stream was constructed sometime in the late 12th century; the diversion at Balrothery was probably of a similar date.

The mandate of 1244, therefore, did not initiate the Dodder/Poddle union, but solely the City Watercourse, which tapped into a watercourse already in existence. Although the shortest route would have been to siphon a supply from the course near Marrowbone Lane, the city's high prominence had to be taken into consideration. A suitable fall was needed to run the water as far as the city conduit in High St. In addition, it is doubtful that the abbey would have allowed access to the water at this point. The necessary damming and ponding of water in a millrace would also have interfered with the continuous supply of water to the city. The Tongue was an ideal location and utilised as such.

The municipal riverine rights

Although the Abbey of St Thomas undoubtedly had a claim to the water of the Dodder, the riverine rights remained the citizens' prerogative. They had prior claim not only to the section from the Tongue to the city cistern but stretching as far back as Balrothery and the initial diversion. There were constant disputes between the citizens and the monks. Finally, in 1547, it was agreed that the mayor and commonalty should have control of the water, with the monks aiding them 'as they had in old tymes' (C.A.R.D. I, 183).

A second dispute between the Talbots of Templeogue and the citizens of Dublin in the later Middle Ages illuminates the complexity of municipal riverine rights. Talbot claimed that, as the Dodder was diverted through his estate, he was entitled to payment of 'corn tithe' from the mills which the citizens had allowed to be erected along the course. The citizens claimed in their defence that the water was their right by ancient records and refused to grant these tithes. Talbot responded by damming the water and 'causing great distress in the city through lack of water' (C.A.R.D. II, 307).

The construction of the artificial channels at Patrick Street

The monks of St Thomas's Abbey probably began works soon after their foundation in 1177. The grant of the land of Donore in 1178 originally included 'mills and meadows' as well as other appurtenances. The early mills may have been located on the original course of the Poddle, before the river was diverted, associated with the 'fishponds' marked on the Earl of Meath's estate map (Fig. 4).

The Poddle, little more than a stream, did not contain the quantity of water required by the abbey to run several mills. An increased input was necessary and the site at Balrothery was chosen. Presumably, they entered into some form of agreement with the landholder. The diversion must have increased the water volume considerably, and the construction of the channels in Patrick St may have been as a direct result of this. This infers that the monks may have been responsible for the works in Patrick St. They were engaged in the construction of artificial channels in the area at an early date and were responsible for the increased volume of water in the Poddle river. It is unlikely that the increased volume of water, on leaving the abbey lands, would have been permitted to spill out into the low-lying area at the south end of Patrick St, where it would undoubtedly have caused flooding. The monks may have entered into an agreement with the archbishop by which they continued to channel the water as far as Nicholas Gate and into the city fosse.

The archbishop of Dublin was also engaged in major works in the area at this date. The removal of the archiepiscopal residence from beside Christ Church to Kevin St resulted in a concentration of building activity on the east side of Patrick St. The granting of the cathedral precinct in 1191 increased this activity. The meandering of the Poddle across the valley may have been deemed unsuitable for the development that Archbishop Comyn and his successors intended for the area. The Poddle most probably had to be contained to prevent flooding, and a new channel completely rerouting it was decided upon.

What is clear is that the Poddle, on reaching Nicholas Gate, was utilised in a deliberate overall strategy to defend the south and south-east walls of the city. The Anglo-Normans, on taking Dublin in 1170, were anxious to secure their position within the city, and they began almost immediately to develop and strengthen the existing fortifications. On the south-east, the Poddle was fed into a new city fosse, creating a water-filled moat. The documentary sources may record this work. A confirmation of the possessions of the Priory of the Holy Trinity, dated 1186, mentions 'a garden near the bridge, the garden near St Patrick's and the garden near the new ditch' (McNeill 1950, 15). In 1202, in a second confirmation grant, the same lands are included except for the garden near the new ditch (ibid., 29). Instead, land between St Patrick's Church and the city wall is mentioned. The implication is that the new ditch may have been the new city fosse, located north of St Patrick's and in existence by 1186. The Poddle was then diverted up the new channels.

The incorporation of the river Poddle in these fortifications suggests, perhaps, a municipal impetus for the artificial channels in Patrick St. The charter granted to the Dublin citizens in 1192, which included giving legal recognition to the Guild Merchant, has been cited as being one of the earliest indications of a developing municipal body (Dudley Edwards 1990, 146). However, the early dates for the reorganisation of defences suggest that a responsible body capable of handling such works was in existence considerably earlier than 1192, a reasonable assumption given that the invasion had taken place over twenty years previously.

What is curious about the rechannelling of the Poddle is the fact that two watercourses were constructed on either side of the street. This doubling of the river bed may have been influenced by purely topographical features. The stream coming west along the Coombe valley and the Poddle joined at Cross Poddle. The western channel may have been a continuation of the Coombe stream, and the east channel a continuation of the Poddle. The channels may also have been delineating boundaries between St Patrick's and St Sepulchre's, in much the same way that the Abbey stream was used to provide a permanent boundary on the west side of the lands of Donore. In addition, the increased flow may have necessitated two channels and, because Patrick St was the boundary, the river was divided in two, watering both sides of the street. The archbishop was probably anxious to have a watercourse on his property, an important asset in medieval Dublin. The channel on the east side would have drained the lands around the cathedral to some extent, although the area between St Patrick's and Bride St remained unprofitable to the prebendaries due to the wet and marshy conditions (Ronan 1927, 45).

At a later date, sometime in the early 13th century, both channels were utilised as millraces. The eastern watercourse was the millrace of the Pole Mills, situated downstream of the Pole Gate, one of the mural gates into the city. This mill belonged to the Priory of the Holy Trinity (McNeill 1950, 256). A grant of land outside Patrick's Gate, dated 1390, refers to land on the east side of the street, and the watercourse of the Mill de la Pole is mentioned as a topographical landmark (D.K.R. 20th rep., no. 255, 84). On the western side of Patrick St, the channel was the millrace for a second mill, Shyreclappe Mill, which also belonged to the archbishop of Dublin.

The mill at Patrick Street

The rerouting of water could, as was the case with St Thomas's Abbey, have the real purpose of driving watermills. The mill was a very important and profitable asset of any property. The lord not only ground his own corn there, but his tenants were obliged to do so also on payment of a tithe (Cal. Just. Rolls 1305-07, 401): thus, in the granting of lands, mills and their tithes were often included. There were a number of documented mills operating within the city limits in the medieval period. The Priory of the Holy Trinity and the archbishop held Woodenmill, the Pole Mills (D.K.R 23, 104), a mill at Bridge Street (C.A.R.D. I, 103) and Shyreclappe Mill, in Patrick St. In the Liberty of Donore, St Thomas's Abbey held at least three other mills, while the Hospital of St John the Baptist held Mullinahack close by. St Mary's Abbey, on the north side of the river, held the Doubleday Mills near Dublin Castle, close to the King's Mills, which lay to the north (C. of St M. 1, 233). Further north lay the mills of St Mary del Dame. There were constant disputes over the location of mills and the granting of tithes. St Mary's Abbey acquired the Doubleday Mills from John de Feipo in the 13th century (ibid.). They stood close to Dublin Castle, but in 1266 there was a serious clash of interest when the justiciar, John fitzGeoffrey, erected mills in the vicinity for the king. The abbey complained of an annual loss and in response to this Henry III assigned land as compensation (ibid.). St Thomas's Abbey and St Patrick's were also in dispute at a similar date, over tithes of mills granted in the parish of St Patrick. This was finally resolved, probably in favour of St Thomas's Abbey (Gilbert 1889, 295).

What was just as important as the mill itself was access to the waterway or millrace, since water was easily impeded or obstructed. When St Mary's Abbey received the grant of the mill by the castle, it included the course of the water (C. of St M. 1, 223). At a later date William Walsh received a mill in Swords with 'the watercourse running to the mill and ingress and egress through the mill green' (Cal. Close R. Hen. VIII, 147). The mill excavated at Patrick St was first built in the 13th century and was reconstructed in the later 14th century. The channel, although not originally constructed specifically to power the mill, was later utilised for this purpose.

The owners of the mill

The mill at Patrick St was originally built by the de Wavills, who had a long association with St Patrick's Cathedral. There is some confusion over the dating of the mill, however, since the de Wavills held two mills, one at Patrick St and one on the Dodder, near Rathfarnham. Between 1181 and 1212, William de Wavill is recorded as building a mill on the land at St Patrick's, but the exact location is not given (McNeill 1950, 33). In 1241, however, Elena de Wavill, widow of William, and her son Helias granted lands on the south-east side of the cathedral to the canons of St Patrick (ibid., 70). Included in the grant was a mill on the Dodder at Rathfarnham which was the original mill, built by William before 1212. William had been paying the canons 2½ marks a year, and Elena is recorded as 'restoring the mill to them'. However, the de Wavills had a second mill, not mentioned in the grant of 1245. In *c.* 1230, Elena and her son granted land in the parish of St Patrick to the Hospital of St John the Baptist. The plot is described as lying between the mill of Elsius de Wavill and the land of Thomas de Ultonia (Brooks 1936, 101).

The mill, obviously not the mill on the Dodder since it is in the parish of St Patrick, must have been located either along the Coombe waterway or the Patrick St waterway. The location of the mill is further pinpointed by a later reference in 1286. Thomas de Cheddesworth, dean of the cathedral, granted a messuage and a mill to the vicars of St Patrick's. The mill is recorded as situated in Patrick St and 'was held by him by gift and enfeoffment from John le Hache Junior and were once Robert de Wavill's' (McNeill 1950, 151). Robert, probably son of Elsius, held other properties in Patrick St, before 1255 (ibid., 81). At some stage, the mill had evidently passed to John le Hache.

In 1308 the mill was in the hands of Nicholas de Synterby, who held other properties in Patrick St, as well as New St and Colonia. There was a bakery attached to the mill by this date. De Synterby appeared to be in financial difficulty, being £40 in debt, and the sheriff was given leave to levy the amount on his properties, including his 'watermill in Patrick's St, Dublin' (Cal. Just. Rolls. 1308-14, 38).

Nothing further is known about the mill until 1326 when an extent or account of the Manor of St Sepulchre was taken before the sheriff. Alexander de Bicknor, then treasurer of Ireland (1308-14), was under investigation for irregularities connected with revenue of the see. All the possessions reverted back to the Crown, and financial accounts of all the archbishop's manors were taken (Mills 1889, 119). Fortunately these are preserved in *Archbishop Alen's Register* (McNeill 1950, 171). The accounts list all the possessions of the Manor of St Sepulchre, as well as naming some of the tenants. The accounts list two watermills, Schyteclappe and Woodenmill, both belonging to the archbishop. As Woodenmill had been identified as being located in the Liberty of Donore, Schyteclappe must be the mill at Patrick St. This is confirmed by the fact that Nicholas de Snyterby [*sic*] is recorded as holding the Schyteclappe Mill, paying 70s. a year.

More information is contained in a detailed account or indenture of the mill, dated 1371 (ibid., 220), in which it appears to have fallen into decline. The account records the granting of the mill by Archbishop Thomas to John Passavant. Passavant received 'Shyreclap in St Patrick St now altogether thrown down and void, to rebuild a mill there at his own expense as he thinks best; to have and to hold the said site and mill when rebuilt, with the ancient mill-course and current, ingress and egress (for all going to the mill and willing to grind there) by a certain bridge over the watercourse beside the mill on the south.... Lest the watercourse should be impeded the Archbishop grants John the custody of the pond, stone bridge and "flodrates" during the term' (ibid., 220). The pond mentioned may have been in New St where a mill pond is recorded in Speed's map of 1610 (Fig. 5). The 'flodrates' probably refer to mill gate or sluices, constructed to control the water flow to the mill.

The mill was evidently rebuilt after this date. In a rental list of the Manor of St Sepulchre, dated 1382, John Passavant is recorded as being in possession of the mill and the bakery called Shitclap, for which he was paying five marks a year (Mills 1889, 119).

The mill continues to be mentioned in the documentary sources in the late medieval period. In 1518 Robert Talbot and Nicholas Fitzsimmon paid an annual rent of 5m. 3s. 4d. to the archbishop of Dublin. There were stipulations attached to the rental of the mill. If for any reason the rent was unpaid, the archbishop had leave to 'enter the mill in Patrick St called Shutteclappe Mill' and to seize goods (McNeill 1950, 264). During a Riding of the Franchise, some time before 1533, the mill was used as a topographical landmark (ibid., 233), while by 1551 it was in the hands of Thomas Barby, a Dublin merchant (D.K.R. 24, no. 1231, 146). In 1590 the inhabitants of Patrick St were inconvenienced by water gushing and bursting forth from 'Forde's Mill' in Patrick's St (C.A.R.D. II, 36), and, at a later date, it was in the hands of Andrew de Spersolte (D.K.R. 36, no. 8, 60).

A dispute between St Thomas's Abbey and the archbishop of Dublin

An interesting dispute is recorded concerning relations between the Abbey of St Thomas and the holder of the mill in Patrick St, dated 1306 (Cal. Just. Rolls, 1305-07, 256). Alan the Baker complained that the abbot (of St Thomas's Abbey) and his men had unjustly assaulted him and thrown him into prison on the land of St Thomas's Abbey. On further investigation it was revealed that Alan was assaulted because he had, on many occasions, 'opened the sluices of the Abbot's mill to make the water come to the mill of Thomas, his master'. The abbot's men, obviously aware of the identity of the perpetrator, laid in wait for him and succeeded in capturing him. The 'Thomas' referred to is Thomas de Synterby, canon of St Patrick's. Alan the Baker was most probably the tenant holding the mill from de Synterby at this date, the name suggesting there was a bakery attached by this time. The dispute demonstrates the vulnerability of a watercourse which passed through other lands and was constantly being dammed and ponded.

Dispute between the archbishop of Dublin and the citizens of Dublin

A word should be said here about the continuing dispute between the archbishop of Dublin and the mayor and commonalty, concerning fraudulent bakers and the difficulties encountered when dealing with crimes committed in different liberties. For example, if fraudulent bakers resided on the archbishop's land in the Manor of St Sepulchre, but sold their produce in the city, the question arose over whether the mayor or the archbishop had jurisdiction over them. The penalties were stiff in the 14th century, and any miller convicted of stealing corn or meal was liable to be hanged from the beam of his mill by the mayor and his bailiff (C.A.R.D. I, 230).

Shyreclappe, situated beyond the city walls, was the responsibility of the archbishop. However, the municipal right took precedence. In 1225, an agreement was made between Archbishop Henry and the city by which any miller convicted of selling false bread in the city market was subject to citizen jurisdiction, but the archbishop's bailiff had to be there to see him fairly treated (McNeill 1950, 46).

St Nicholas's Gate

St Nicholas's Gate, one of the main access points into the city, dominated the northern end of Patrick St. One of the six gates along the city wall, it commanded the route from the south. The exact date of the wall or of the erection of the gate is unknown, but the city is known to have been walled when the Anglo-Normans arrived at Dublin, in 1170. Excavations at Wood Quay, towards the river, have produced a date of *c.* 1100 for the earliest Viking wall (Wallace 1988, 130), with a second stretch of this wall excavated at Ross Rd, to the south-east of the city (Hayden and Walsh, forthcoming). References to 'Hasculf Gate' at this side of the town, called after the last Viking king at Dublin, Asculf Mac Turcaill, may suggest that the gate formed part of the original Viking mural circuit (McNeill 1950, 50).

Archaeological excavation has revealed evidence for activity in the vicinity of St Nicholas's Gate from an early stage in the Anglo-Norman colonisation of the town. The rechannelling of the Poddle in the late 12th century to further fortify the defences and the digging of a ditch in 1186 are indications of the works in progress. By 1200 a new gate was built at the west side of the city (Barry 1987, 122). In 1205 the king directed the citizens to re-fortify the city (C.D.I. I, 35) and in 1234 the customs and tolls of St Thomas's Abbey were also used for this purpose (ibid., 317).

In 1585 the city walls were surveyed by order of the lord deputy, Sir John Perrot. From it we learn that 'St Nicholas Gate have towe rounde towres without and square within and the said gate placed bewixte bothe the towres, every towre three heights whereof towre loftes and fowre lowrs in every towre. The wall 5 foote thicke, 39 foote in lengthe one way and 18 foote brod the other waye and the towre 45 foot hie with a perculles for the same gate' (C.A.R.D. II, 551-57). In the 16th century the apartments over the tower were rented out to private individuals. In 1535 William Queytroh of the Dublin Merchant Guild held the tower over St Nicholas's Gate. A year later, the king requested six cannons to be supplied, one for each of the gates, in an effort to defend the city walls (Healy 1990, 23).

Speed's map of 1610 shows little that corresponds to Perrot's earlier survey. The gate is depicted as having a high arch, with two windows. However, the other city gates are represented in a similar simplistic fashion. The gate was probably demolished when the street was widened in the late 18th century (Martin 1969, 8).

St Patrick's Gate

St Patrick's Gate, straddling Patrick St and attached to the west end of the cathedral, was one of several suburban gateways in the area. It was erected at an early date, since in the 13th century Reimund of Poitou was granted 'the entire gate of St Patrick's with cellars and appurtenances, casements underneath and on each side with custody of the gate' (C.A.R.D. I, 90). The gate was situated within the Liberty of the Archbishops (McNeill 1950, 272) and in 1228 was mentioned as a topographical landmark in a grant on Patrick St (C.D.I. I, 246). Similar gates stood in Francis St, the Coombe and Kevin St (Fig. 5), but in Patrick St it was the inhabitants, not the archbishop, who 'had in the building and erection of a gate at the west end of the street' (C.A.R.D. II, 123).

Although the inhabitants reputedly built the gate, by the 14th century it was under the direct control of the mayor and commonalty. In 1342 Richard, son of Richard Exeter, tried to recover the gate which he claimed his ancestor possessed at the time of Edward II (1307-27). However, the mayor and commonalty produced 'a writing', dated 10th January 1341-42, by which the plaintiff had acquitted the claim to 'the tower of St Patrick, Gate of the city of Dublin'. The jury decided the writing was genuine and Richard was arrested (C.A.R.D. I, 174).

It is interesting that the gate is termed 'Gate of the city of Dublin', although it was not part of the circuit of the city wall. The gate stood in Patrick St until the 19th century, and the Malton print of the cathedral, dated 1793 (Drew 1899, 2), depicts what may have been the last remnants of this large structure. Enclosed within the precinct wall, only a hunk of masonry survived. In 1824 the Wide Street Commission, carrying out demolition work in the area, removed it.

The medieval topography of Patrick Street

The Kendrick Survey of 1749 and the survival of medieval buildings into the 19th century makes for a plausible reconstruction of the cathedral and its surrounds in the medieval period. However, little of the original topography was recorded on the western side of Patrick St. Small details are preserved in land-grants, but information on the exact location of such lands is sparse. This is further compounded by a tendency, when giving locations of tenement plots, to identify this property in relation to surrounding tenants (in some cases former tenants) and existing local land-marks of the day.

Despite this, several observations can be made. The construction of a large gate, St Patrick's Gate, at the southern end of the street in the 13th century suggests that the street was extensively built up, with buildings fronting on to the road. The gate was primarily a toll-gate, and so access must have been restricted, probably by houses, to either side.

The availability of water at Patrick St and direct access to it, coupled with the favourable location outside the city jurisdiction, made it an attractive location for local industry. The excavations and documentary sources reveal that in *c.* 1230 there was one mill operating along the watercourse, on the western side of the street, with a probable tanning pit located further south. The latter, dated to the 14th century, was probably part of a tanning complex along the banks of the Poddle. A documentary reference records an incident in the 14th century, in which a certain William Le Deyer was involved in a dispute concerning the buying of 'woad and other articles necessary for dyeing'.

30

He is recorded as residing in Patrick St (Cal. Just. Rolls 1308, 65), and may well have carried out his trade by the banks of the Poddle.

Several references, dated to *c.* 1230, make it possible to attempt to reconstruct the layout of the plots being held at that date. The mill, held by Elsius de Wavill, and located by excavation, was sited north of the modern Hanover Lane. A stone bridge lay immediately south of the mill. A plot or tenement, measuring 22ft x 32ft, and which belonged to the Hospital of St John the Baptist, lay to the south of the mill, with Thomas de Ultonia holding a plot immediately south again (Brooks 1936, 101). This must have come relatively close to the plot of land containing a house and a garden, property of the Prebendary of Clonmethan (Monck-Mason 1818, 13).

The documentary sources for the archbishop's Manor of St Sepulchre provide an insight into what was happening in Patrick St in the 14th century. A series of extents or accounts of all the archbishop's manors, dated to 1326, give an overall view of the problems besetting the Anglo-Norman colony at this date (McNeill 1950, 170-79). The picture is one of overall decline, with some manors towards Wicklow completely deserted due to the rebellious activities of the O'Byrnes and O'Tooles in Glenmalure. However, the Manor of St Sepulchre fared better than the other manors, mainly because of its close proximity to the city (ibid., 170).

The extent reveals a reduction in the income of the manor. In Patrick St, the burgesses who used to pay 45s. 2d. rent only paid 36s. 2d. in 1326. The reduced rent is attributed to the tenements and houses of the manor lying waste. In New St, the rent is almost halved for the same reason. However, the mill, Schyteclappe, was still in operation, rendering 70s. a year. Similarly the 'Wodenmylle' in Donore was also paying four marks a year (ibid., 170). Only two burgesses are recorded by name, Thomas Hattyngleye and Hugh Silvestre, both holding lands at Le Paas but residing in Patrick St. In addition, the buildings at the manor were in a poor state. The stone hall was badly roofed, with a chamber, a kitchen and a chapel in a similar condition. The prison was 'now broken and thrown down' (ibid., 170).

The Edward Bruce invasion, of the early 14th century, has been cited as being a contributory factor in the poor condition of the buildings at the Manor of St Sepulchre. Bruce's brother Robert, the Scottish king, was encamped at Castleknock in February 1317, and was dangerously close to the taking of the city (Otway-Ruthven 1980, 23). The mayor and commonalty, determined to prevent this, burned the suburb 'within 3 leagues of the City' (C.A.R.D. I, 49). This included Patrick St, since St Patrick's Cathedral was damaged to some degree, although the burning was mostly confined to the area around St Thomas's Abbey (Jackson 1975, 83). The cathedral was later partially damaged in an accidental fire caused by negligence on the part of John Sexton in 1362 (Lydon 1988, 34). The neglected state of the Palace of St Sepulchre was also probably due to the continual absences of the archbishop. Due to the archbishop's spending much of his time in England and France, the archiepiscopal palace appears not to have been maintained in his absence (Mills 1889, 32).

The extent records the degree of devastation caused by continual conflict. In outlying parts of the Manor of St Sepulchre, at Milltown and Cullenswood for example, the land lay 'waste and untilled through lack of tenants and want of beasts'. 'Near evil doers', in the form of O'Byrnes, O'Tooles, Walshes, Archbolds and Harolds, maintained a constant state of war which resulted in lands of no value. This depopulation and constant harassment took its toll, especially in the manors of Rathcoole and Shankill.

A second important source for the Manor of St Sepulchre in the 14th century survives in the form of a rental list of the manor (Mills 1889, 33). The document is not an original but a copy made for Archbishop Alen in 1531. It contains the names of tenants and rents paid in Patrick St, New St and Kevin St, as well as other parts of the manor. Various ecclesiastical bodies held lands in Patrick St at this date, for example, the Friary of St Augustine, the Hospital of St John the Baptist and St Patrick's Cathedral, but the bulk of the property was in the hands of the tenants of the archbishop, mostly prominent men of the city. Nicholas de Synterby, canon of St Patrick's and former owner of the mill, had considerable interests in the street, with four properties in his name. John Passavant, mayor of Dublin, 1369-71, who also held the mill, had two other houses in Patrick St. The rental makes no reference to the burgesses mentioned in the extent of 1326, but a particularly bad epidemic of plague swept through Dublin in 1348, causing a considerable reduction in population (Barry 1987, 174).

The dissolution of religious houses in the 16th century had a major impact on property holdings around the Patrick St area. In 1539 St Thomas's Abbey was surrendered by the abbot, Henry Duffe, and the vast holdings passed into the hands of William Brabazon, then treasurer of Ireland (Cal. Close R. Hen. VIII, 145). In 1547 the dean of St Patrick's, Edward Bassnet, surrendered St Patrick's (ibid., 132) and the ten houses they held in Patrick St (Monck-Mason 1818, 97). The site and precinct of the house of the vicars choral was then granted as a grammar school (ibid., 145). The king directed that the possessions of St Patrick should be surveyed, and the properties were subsequently regranted to the new tenants.

Post-medieval Patrick Street

Patrick St was a favourable location for local industry in the 16th and 17th centuries. In 1596 it is recorded that 'divers of the city receive hindrance by the continuance of artisans working in Patrick St, pretending they work upon the liberty of the Lord Archbishop' (C.A.R.D. II, 513). Speed's map of Dublin, dated 1610, depicts thirteen houses on the west side of the street, with only ten houses on the east. The depictions of these houses are suspiciously uniform, and the average house width is an unlikely 50ft to 60ft. The map also shows a marked tendency to widen the streets and is therefore probably not very accurate. A total of thirty-nine houses for the west side and thirty houses for the east side is a more reasonable estimate (Andrews 1983, 218).

In the 1660s the population of Dublin was steadily increasing. The town walls were in disrepair, and cramped and squalid conditions resulted in a diffusion of population into the suburbs. This population was further augmented in 1665 by the arrival of refugee Huguenots and Quakers. The Liberties, as the area became known, outside the city jurisdiction was a suitable location for a population skilled in the textile trade. They quickly established their textile factories on the banks of the Poddle, creating a boom in the trade.

This boom period did not last, however, and by the 1770s the silk trade was at a standstill due to over-production. Conditions did not improve, and by 1792, 5000 weavers in the area were unemployed (Whitelaw et al. 1818, 982). In response to the deteriorating conditions, the Wide Street Commission was set up to improve the communications network. By 1800 their best work was completed and a large number of areas were opened up, most notably in the vicinity of Christ Church Cathedral. It was not until the 1820s–40s that the development around the Patrick St area began.

In February 1824 the lord mayor suggested an improvement to Patrick St by the removal of the projecting sheds on the east side of the street (W.S.C. 1823-24, 175). In March of that year, a project to improve the avenue, from New St through Patrick St as far as the Four Courts, was under review (ibid., 192). Tenants were compensated for land taken from them. By 1824 houses were being demolished in Patrick's Close and along the street. The area around the cathedral was repaved and the railings replaced (ibid., 196). Richard Griffith was appointed in 1841, by an Act of Parliament, to supervise relief work in the squalid tenements. Griffith's Valuation, which fixed the value of land throughout Ireland, detailed the number of houses and tenants in Patrick St at that date. In all there were eighty-three holdings, with some tenants holding more than one holding. The greatest proportion were houses with a small yard. There were two exceptions, however, one of which was No. 49, which was a bakery (Griffith Val., 219).

Under the direction of Sir Charles Cameron, Dublin's chief sanitary officer, slum clearance got underway in Dublin. In 1899 Lord Ardilaun and Lord Iveagh proposed the establishment of an open park or city garden to the north of the St Patrick's Cathedral. This was duly carried out. The west side of Patrick St had forty-nine dwellings, including several pubs, a pawnbroker shop, and a bakery, called Kennedy's Bakery. In advance of the present road widening scheme, the remaining standing buildings were demolished in recent years.

The Poddle river

The Poddle river caused many problems to the mayor and commonalty of Dublin throughout the late medieval and post-medieval period. It is evident from the numerous references concerning the watercourse that it was a constant battle to keep it open and relatively clean. The citizens had, from time to time, carried out repairs along the watercourse, building up the bank to prevent flooding, but there were constant maintenance problems (C.A.R.D. V, 344). The problems included the illegal draining off of water, contamination by the casting in of refuse and the water being rendered undrinkable by its passage through bleach yards (ibid., IX, 65). Eventually, in the 18th century, the watercourse was partly culverted in an attempt to keep the water clean (ibid., VIII, 321).

The Woodenmill in the Liberty of Donore (Fig. 4) was still in operation at Warrenmount at the turn of the century, and the millrace could still be seen in the grounds of the school up until the 1960s. The bakery in Patrick St outlived the Shyreclap Mill, in a surprising continuity from the 13th century through to the 20th. In Griffith's Valuation, No. 49 Patrick St is listed as containing a bakery although there is no mention of a mill. The Poddle watercourse continued to serve many industries, and in 1840 the culvert enclosing the Poddle collapsed, causing the river to flood. At Pimlico, the millers of the area 'requested permission to clean the river at their own expense' (P.S.C. 30 Sept. 1840, 14). Without a free passage of water, the distillers, breweries, mills and many other manufacturers would not have been able to function.

The Poddle river continued to flow in culverted channels up the street. In the 1840s, responsibility for the maintenance of the river passed from the dean of St Patrick's to the Paving Board Committee of Dublin Corporation. One of the first specifications called for 'the river to be cleaned and deepened to the original level and the stuff excavated and removed' (P.R.M., 10). Thankfully this was not carried out, partly because of the 'antiquity of the Poddle River' (ibid.). The Poddle continued to flood the area. The problem was further compounded by the brick arch of the culvert falling in at Pimlico, which resulted in water 'flowing down the street' (ibid., 14). By October 1840, repairs for replacing the culvert were underway.

In the early 20th century the Poddle was again diverted, this time by pipe, running across St Patrick's Park. This returned the Poddle to its original bed, nearly 750 years after it was first diverted.

The Excavations: Site A

During machine removal of soft riverine deposits at the New St/Dean St junction for the construction of the widened roadway, timbers were noted in the black gravel deposits. Machine removal of the overlying deposits was continued under archaeological supervision, and rapid investigation and recording of the remaining *in situ* timbers was undertaken on 24th and 25th October, 1992.

The excavation (Fig. 6)

An area measuring over 10m. north/south x 12m. east/west had been cleared almost to subsoil by mechanical excavator. Subsoil, consisting of a compact, coarse gravel, occurred at a depth of 10.66m. O.D. at the west side of the cleared area. Little remained of the black river silts (3048) which had overlain the gravel, but the recorded maximum depth of these gravels at a short distance further north was *c*. 1.20m.

The best surviving timbers were located *c*. 7m. west of the culverted river Poddle. The entire area from the line of the Poddle culvert westwards to the timbers (and for some distance further west) was covered in black riverine gravel. Animal bones and sherds of medieval pottery (both locally manufactured and imported) were recovered from the gravels.

The earliest feature in this area was a length of post and wattle fencing (3047). This measured 2.40m. in length and stood to a height of 0.25m. It was of single post, but with the posts generally occurring in groups of two. The fence swung to the west outside the limits of machine clearance. At its south end, it had been removed by machine.

Overlying the line of the post and wattle fence was a *c*. 9m. long alignment of timber revetments (3046). These had sustained considerable disturbance from machine clearance- the centrally placed timber (3046b) – was recovered in fragments from the spoil, and its position is reconstructed in the site plan.

Four timbers were recovered. All were of oak, and the northernmost (3046c) still held two of the planks which had formed shuttering to the west side of retaining posts. Details of the timbers are recorded in Table 3.

Timber 3046a had the uppermost element of a through splayed scarf joint, which had one wooden dowel to hold the joint. Timber 3046b was considerably damaged by machine: it too had the upper element of a scarf joint at its northern end, which would have been pegged to its neighbour by a wooden dowel. Timber 3046c had an upright and part of the tenon of a second in position in the mortises. The upright had a barefaced tenon, and both had been dowelled into position. Badly decayed, radially split oak

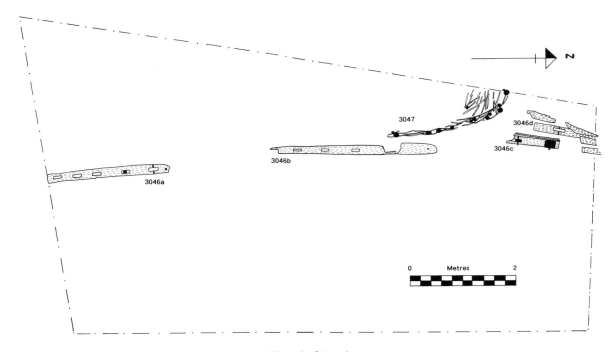

Fig. 6. Site A

34

planking survived to a height of 0.24m. to the west of the upright. Timber 3046c was butt-trimmed at its northern end.

Fragments of further planking lay in the overburden in the immediate vicinity.

A further timber (3046d) was set just 0.12m. to the west of 3046c. This had a butt-trimmed south end which may have originally stood end to end with timber 3046c.

A parallel line of timbers, comprising baseplates and plank shuttering, was recorded during monitoring of the reconstruction of the Poddle culvert. These timbers were located approximately 5m. east of the line of 3046. The alignment had been largely cut away by the construction, in recent times, of the culvert for the river Poddle. None of the timbers from Site A were submitted for dendrochronological dating.

The only find of note from the gravels was a fly-wheel (E543:3048:1) of probable English Millstone Grit.

Evidence of later activity of some interest in the area was a large rectangular-profiled pit (3049), which was lined with red brick. This occurred at quite a high level in the western edge of the cleared area. The pit measured 1.40m. in width and 2m. in depth. The fill was a uniform soft brown silt with abundant finely comminuted oak bark and wood chip throughout. It is possible that this is the northern end of the 'Blackpitts' tannery complex, some of whose vats and tanks were visible into recent times (Murtagh 1973, 48).

Site A: discussion

The presence of river gravels over a wide area at Site A indicate the former presence of a pool in this area. This is historically documented (see Chapter 1). The occurrence of a post and wattle fence at the west side of the area at Site A is paralleled by the fences at Site B. The ground to the west at Site A does not, however, rise to any degree, and there was no surviving evidence of any attempt to contain the Poddle water in an artificial cut. The fencing may have been an attempt to contain the tailrace from the Double Mills at Warrenmount, a short distance upstream, and the later revetments represent either a continuation of this, or perhaps more deliberately part of the structure of the mill pond for the mill at Site E. The placing of timber shuttered revetments in a secondary position to the fencing is a pattern which occurred at sites D and F.

| Context | Intact | Conversion | Max. Dimensions | | | Reused | Mortice |
			Long (m.)	Wide (mm.)	Thick (mm.)		Spacing (cm.)
3046a	No	RSC	>2.30	200	80	No	36
3046b	No	RSC	>3.20	200	70	No	38
3046c	No	RSC	>1.10	190	80	Yes	38
3046d	No	RSC	>1.20	180	80	?	—

Table 3. Timber dimensions, Site A

THE EXCAVATIONS: SITE B

Site B measured 10.20m. east/west x 4.60m. north/south. The upper 1m. consisted of modern rubble, and up to 0.30m. of disturbed medieval material was also removed by mechanical excavator. Disturbance to the archaeological layers continued almost to sub-soil at the eastern end of the site, where the 18th century culvert wall cut through the underlying strata, and only *c.* 0.10m. of river silts dating to the 14th century remained in the area.

Level 1

At the west end of the site, the natural gravels had been cut through to a depth of 0.50m. (Fig. 11). From the base of this cut (57) the gravels sloped eastwards and levelled out to form the bed of the river. Historical sources imply that a pool existed in this area, resulting from the confluence of two of the streams of the river Poddle, and it is likely that the cut may have been part of an attempt to deepen and contain the river. A compacted inorganic grey silt (54, 58) formed on the surface of the gravels. This silt probably resulted from sediments settling in slow-moving water. A similar silt encrustation was observed over the bed of the river Liffey at Arran Quay (Hayden, forthcoming a).

Over this surface, water-borne silts (56) and fine gravels (55) were deposited. Interleaved throughout these were lenses of black/dark grey muds with organic inclusions and a high silt content. Finds from these layers including Dublin wares, Ham Green ware, leather objects, a bracteate, a human mandible and some animal bone. The organic silts and fine sand lenses resulted from natural water deposition, interleaved with debris cast into the area of the river.

The deliberate lowering of the bed of the river (cut 57) was evident only at the lowest level of excavation. The presence of flood-borne silts at a distance of over 8m. from the centre of the river was not encountered elsewhere in the excavated areas on Patrick St, and indicates the presence of a pool or dam close by.

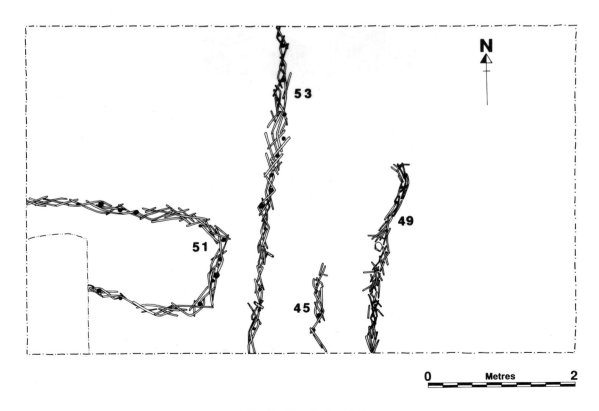

Fig. 7. Site B, level 2

Level 2 (Fig. 7)

A post and wattle fence (53) which extended north/south across the site, was driven into the underlying silts. The fence survived to a maximum height of 0.50m. The posts measured between 0.40m.–0.80m. in diameter. To the east of fence 53, a deposit of river silts (29) 0.55m. in depth extended across the bed of the river Poddle. The silts were interleaved with lenses of matted vegetation and compacted bark/wood chips. Leather, pottery and animal bone were recovered from the organic silts. Contained within it were two rows of post and wattle fencing (45, 49). Both extended northwards into the site for *c.* 2.5m. and were roughly parallel to each other, maintaining the orientation of fence 53. Fence 59 was quite flimsy in construction, with posts averaging 0.04m. in diameter and with up to thirteen rows of very fine wattle surviving. Up to ten rows of fragmentary wattle remained in fence 45.

To the west of fence 53 was a layer of brown peaty silt (48), which contained gravel lenses in its lower levels, but consisted of compacted organic material with a high proportion of wood chips in the upper level. The layer was 0.45m. in maximum depth. Two decorated leather scabbards, a bronze incised club-headed pin and a human skull were among the finds recovered from the silts. These silts appeared to have been rapidly deposited and consisted largely of human refuse.

A small post and wattle enclosure (51) was constructed on top of layer 48. The enclosure measured 2.40m. long, 1.20m. wide, and up to eight rows of wattle survived. No entrance was apparent, but the west side was cut away by later disturbance. The enclosure may have functioned as an animal pen (see also Building CP 96/1, in Murray 1983, 162, which was circular in plan and interpreted as a possible hen house).

The fences represent an attempt to consolidate the soft silts by dumping material behind a successive series of screens, a method still used in land reclamation to this day. The fences are unlikely to have stood to any great height.

Level 3 (Fig. 8)

The wattle fences and pen were overlain by dumps of silty clays and gravels (46, 47) and an organic deposit (44). The clays (47), which were redeposited riverine muds, were tipped over the enclosure (51) and up against the western side of fence 53. A layer of wet gritty gravel (46) was dumped on top of the silts, forming a compacted level surface which was 0.20m. thick. The gravel extended for 2.9m. east to the line of fence 53, and for 3.6m. to the north.

A small post and wattle structure (41), measuring over 3.20m. east/west x 3.20m. north/south, was built on the gravel. The north-east corner of the structure and a pos-

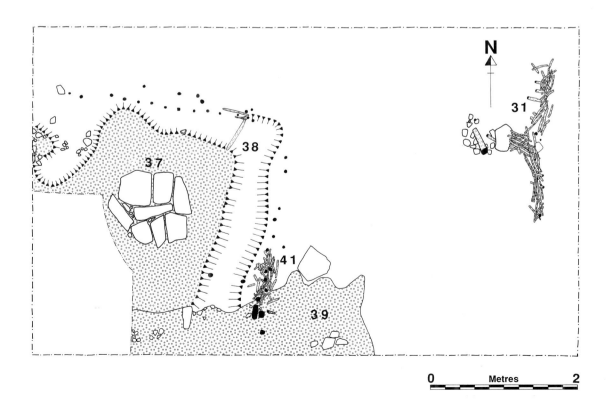

Fig. 8. Site B, level 3

sible entrance on the east side survived. The east wall consisted of a single row of posts spaced at 0.20m. intervals, and the wattle panelling survived to a height of over 0.20m. A decayed rectangular upright, possibly serving as a door jamb, measuring 0.16m. x 0.06m., was set at the southern end of the line of posts, and a second squared post, 0.08m. x 0.08m, was beside it. Four small wooden dowels (E543:41:1) were found at the base of the wall in this area, and were probably discarded by the builders of the structure.

Fragmentary wattle survived along the north wall around the thirteen surviving posts. A rough line of four posts occurred parallel to the wall and 0.20m. north of it. It was unclear whether these represented the remains of a double wall as no wattle survived around them.

The floor of the structure was of well-compacted yellow/brown coarse gravel (37), which was 0.44m. in depth. A hearth of heat-cracked flags, measuring 1.10m. x 1.12m., was set into the gravel at a distance of 1.20m. from the east wall. A layer of charcoal and dark brown silt (37a) overlay the stones, and a thin lens of similar black silt covered the floor area (see 'Plant Remains'). A shallow trench (38) which measured 0.60m. in width and 0.16m. in depth, was dug through the floor along the east wall. The trench did not extend along the north wall, but the floor was scarped in this area, and did not extend up to the wall. The trench may have functioned as a drain, but would have logged water around the walls and contributed to their decay.

A layer of grey black gritty soil (43) to the north of the structure contained small stones, forming a roughly cobbled surface. The cobbled layer was 0.12m. in depth towards the west of the site, deepening to 0.32m. to the east, where it was contained by a line of post and wattle (31). The fence extended north/south for a distance of 2.50m. The posts of the fence had collapsed towards the

east. Three posts at the southern extent of the cobbles may have provided markers for a pathway.

To the east of the structure, layers of grey sticky clay (26, 42) accumulated. These contained lenses of ash, pottery and animal bone, which were probably cast out from the small structure. The entrance area of the structure was refloored with a layer of hard packed beaten yellow/brown clay (39) which was 0.13m. thick. Several large flags were set into the clay, which extended across the entrance and continued for almost 2m. beyond the structure on the east side.

When the structure went out of use, the entire area was covered by a layer of dark grey silt (25), up to 0.10m. in depth, which appeared to have been deposited by floodwaters.

Level 3: discussion

The wattle structure (31) was not a substantial construction, consisting of walls of single wattle which were reinforced in places by additional outposts. A single large post – a probably door jamb – was the only sizeable upright, and no evidence for internal roof supports was recovered. If the roof supports had rested on pads (either stone or wood) these could have been removed, but no pits for the pads were uncovered. The structure may not have been much larger than the area uncovered during excavation, as the hearth, usually centrally located in such structures, is close to the walls. The entrance was placed in the east wall, on the riverside.

The structure is similar to Murray's (1983, 15) buildings of sub-rectangular plan without four-post roof supports, where the entrances were generally off centre. Several of these structures have been interpreted as workshops or byres. Analysis of a sample of the hearth deposit found

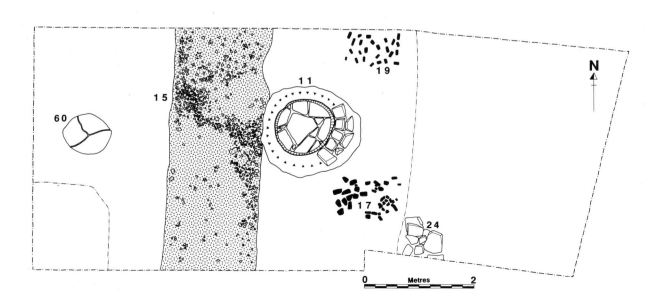

Fig. 9. Site B, level 4

charred grains of wheat and oat, hazelnut shells and blackberry seeds.

The building cannot have been occupied for any great length of time and had only one partial reflooring. It was constructed on soft silts, which had probably accumulated through successive flooding of this area, and was sealed by similar material. It is likely to have been abandoned as a result of flooding.

Level 4 (Fig. 9)

A series of layers of clay and stone were deliberately dumped on the site, apparently to reclaim and consolidate the soft ground. These layers were distinct from each other only through variance in the colour and texture of the clays.

A layer of compacted grey mottled clay and small stones (33), up to 0.18m. in depth, was deposited over the entire site, but thinned out towards the east side of the site, indicating perhaps the edge of the river Poddle. Overlying this was a layer of grey clay and stones (14) and a spread of yellow clay (22). These two layers totalled 0.45m. in depth. A small quantity of pottery, with some animal bone, was recovered from these layers. Both layers tailed off towards the east of the site, and were replaced in this area by grey/brown clays (22, 23). Overlying the clays was a laid pathway of angular cobbles (15) which extended north/south across the site and measured 1.6m. in width. Further clay deposits (5, 7), which varied from 0.32m.-0.80m. in depth, occurred over the site. The clays produced a small number of sherds of Dublin Fabric 003 ware, indicating a depositional date in the later part of the 13th century.

A stone-flagged, stave-lined pit (11) was cut through the clay layer (5). The pit was constructed by digging a circular pit 1.60m. in diameter at the top, which narrowed to 1.20m. at the base. This was 0.70m. in depth. The pit was lined with compacted yellow clay silt and floored with limestone flags. A wooden bucket (13), which consisted of forty-seven oak staves, was placed in the pit. The staves of the bucket were held together by three hoops of ash on the outside. Twelve of the forty-seven staves were attached by small dowels and nails to the hoops, while one stave had eight dowel holes, all unrelated to the position of the hoops. The staves, which were in poor condition, had an average length of 0.47m. and were 0.01m.-0.02m. in thickness.

The upper 0.15m. of the pit was stepped to give a clay-lined lip which was faced with limestones. These only survived on the south-east side of the pit, but are likely to have ringed the entire upper area of the pit.

The fill of pit 11 (Fig. 10) consisted of mottled green clay with inclusions of hard packed pale yellow clay or possibly lime in the upper 0.55m. and soft black and grey organic lenses at its base. A hard mineralised accretion occurred about 0.20m. from the flagged floor and formed a complete horizon which ran through a number of the lenses. Eight cattle horn cores were recovered from the fill, as well as pottery, both local and imported wares.

The pit had been partly overlain by the wooden base of a large barrel (8) (not illustrated), which was oval in shape and measured 1.25m. x 1.05m. A few staves survived to a height of 0.065m. – these were 0.16m. in width and 0.016m. maximum thickness. All the staves had a rebate 14mm. deep cut into them to take a baseplate which was now gone. The bottom part of each stave was also bevelled. The hoop of oak was doubled over for more than a third of its length and fastened in place with ten wooden pegs. The barrel was overlain by a spread of soft grey/green clay silt (9).

Scant remnants of a stone wall along the west bank of the river are evidenced by a length of roughly-faced masonry (24), which extended for 0.60m. north/south, but was largely cut away by the later culvert wall. The masonry, consisting of small limestone blocks, was bonded with yellow/grey clay, and stood to a maximum height of 0.95m. The wall is likely to be the remains of a 14th century river wall, uncovered further north along the river at Sites E and F, where it survived more extensively. Two water deposited layers (32, 52) of dark grey/black silts abutted the east face of the wall. The pottery sherds recovered from the silts indicate a date in the 14th century for their deposition.

Features of a probably medieval date are described below. Two areas of wooden piles (17, 19), were driven into the underlying clays and silts on the west bank of the river. All the squared posts were oak and ranged in length from 0.85m.-1.05m., while the rounded posts, which were all set at the river edge, were a mixture of ash or birch/alder.

An isolated stone column or pier base (60) was dug through the underlying clay. The associated levels of this feature did not survive, but the presence of a late medieval or post-medieval structure is suggested by the column base.

Level 4: discussion

The pit (11) at Site B was probably utilised for some industrial activity. Analysis of the soil behind the oak staves of the pit did not, however, yield any useful information as to what process was carried out in the pit (see 'The Plant Remains'). Superficially, the pit resembles several of the smaller structures in a tanning complex

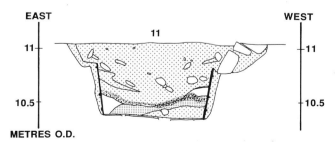

Fig. 10. Site B, section across pit 11

1. Possible tanning pit, Site B

excavated at Northampton (Williams 1979, 98-103; Shaw 1984, 241) and could have been used for soaking small skins. Daire O'Rourke (this vol.) has suggested that the pit would have been suitable for soaking small hides in preparation for vellum. At Northampton, several pits of similar dimensions had oak linings. At Dundas Wharf, Bristol, two barrels which contained lime residues at the base could have functioned in the initial dehairing of the hides (Jones 1991, 26), and lenses of lime occurred in the fill of pit 11. Barrel 3001 at Site G, Patrick St, although of considerably later date, also had a calcite residue in the base (Appendix 3). The pit at Patrick St would have constituted part of a larger complex, and the siting of the pit, adjacent to the river, is a suitable location for tanning.

Cattle horn cores are recognised as debris from tanning activities (Serjeantson 1989, 136), although they are also considered to be evidence for horn-working. It is likely that tanners and horn-workers would have worked in close proximity. Tanners would often have received the hides with the horns and possibly feet bones attached (ibid., 139). The horns could then be passed on to the horn-worker, who would soak them in pits for some weeks before removal of the sheath (MacGregor 1989, 117). An alternative

function of pit 11 could have been in the horn processing industry: a similar pit, excavated in York in 1957-58, was shallow and lined with clay and timber. The fill contained some 200 horn cores, evidence for its function as a soaking pit for horn-working. Steeping the horns loosens the sheaths from the cores, and also makes them more malleable, although over time, if merely left in the open air, when they begin to decompose, the sheath and core begin to separate.

Further support of the possible function of the pit in the tanning process came from an adjacent area. During archaeological monitoring of construction clearance of deposits to the north of Site B in 1991, a further five wood-lined barrels or buckets of medieval date, sunk into the underlying clays, were recorded. These all occurred in very close proximity, and the similarity of construction and in the fills of the barrels indicate that they form components of the same complex. Details of the barrels are given in Table 4. They are all quite small: Sergeantson (1989, 135) suggests a length of 1.2m. for skins (small animals), while pits for soaking hides must be up to 1.8m. or larger. Both round and rectangular wood-lined pits have been uncovered in excavated tanning complexes

Fig. 11. Site B, section

(Shaw 1984, 241: see also discussion of Site G, level 6). A sample from the fill of bucket 3050e, submitted for analysis by Brenda Collins, contained only wood chips and bark (see 'The Plant Remains'). The absence of any weed seeds in the fill suggested that the bucket must have been covered, and that the fill was the original content of the bucket. It is therefore very likely that the fill of bark and wood chips is a residue from the actual tanning process, in which hides are soaked in vegetable tanning agents, namely oak bark (the process is described in detail in O'Rourke, this vol.). As stated above, it is likely that only the smaller hides could have been soaked in this complex.

Level 5: post-medieval

At the south-west corner of the site an unlined cesspit (4), containing finds of post-medieval date, cut through the underlying layers to a depth of 0.90m. A wooden drain (6) led from the pit towards the Poddle. The drain must have functioned as an overflow from a domestic cesspit into the river. A similar cesspit was noted on the west bank of the Poddle during clearance of Site D. A pit or trench (18) adjacent to the west wall of the culvert and probably pre-dating it, produced finds of medieval and post-medieval date from its fill of dark brown stony loam.

The stone culvert wall, of probably 18th century date (Fig. 11), had cut through the underlying medieval levels, and the silts filling the river channel proper had been largely removed by its construction.

Context	Diameter	Fill	Finds	Construction
3050a	1.10m.	Wood chips	Horn cores	Bucket/external hoops
3050b	1.10m.	Wood chips	Horn cores	No timber lining survived
3050c	0.95m.	Wood chips	None	Stave-built bucket, external hoops
3050d	0.90m.	Wood chips	Horn cores	No timber lining survived
3050e	0.95m.	Wood chips (sampled)	None	Stave-built bucket, external hoops

Table 4. The tanning buckets

41

THE EXCAVATIONS: SITE C

Site C measured 4.70m. in width (east/west) and was 11.10m. in length, extending north/south parallel to the line of Patrick St (Fig. 12). A depth of 2.50m.-2.75m. of overburden was removed by mechanical excavator during site clearance. This was made up of 1.65m. of rubble, 0.70m. of brown clay and 0.40m. of grey clay (106) on the east side of the cutting, and the mid-18th century culvert on the west side (Fig. 13). The culvert floor of stone setts which extended for 3m-4m. from the south end of the site was also removed by machine, revealing water-logged medieval deposits immediately beneath this. The maximum depth of archaeological material excavated was 1.10m. but generally the depth of medieval deposits was *c.* 0.80m. The east bank of the river, delimited by a post and wattle fence, lay within the excavated area, while deposits filling the river channel extended beyond the area of excavation on the west.

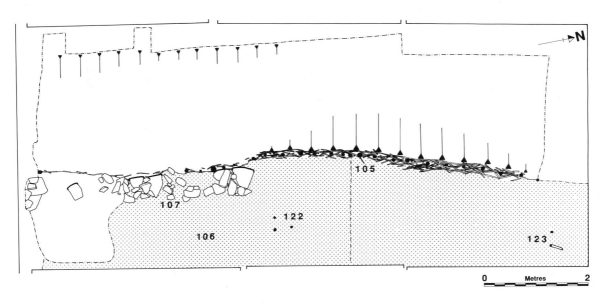

Fig. 12. Site C, levels 1, 2, 3

Level 1

A coarse gravel, containing in places large stones (up to 0.25m. in size), formed the natural base of the site. In the south-west corner of the excavated area, an iron pan had formed on the gravel surface.

A brown water-deposited silt (117), which was 0.06m.-0.10m. thick, overlay the gravel but did not extend to the north-west area of the site. The deposit resembled a grey/brown sticky mud on the west side of the site, but appeared as a dry brown gritty silt with small twigs, grass and a fragment of cockle shell on the east side. No finds other than a piece of cut antler were recovered from the silt, but a bracteate (E543:117:1) was found on the surface of the silt at the interface with the overlying layer. Bracteates date from the early to mid-12th century. The silt may be an indicator of the early, wider rivercourse,

and its absence from the north-west area of the site may reflect the original course where it flowed north-eastwards across the valley now occupied by St Patrick's Park (Fig. 5). The constraints of excavating within a narrow cutting do, however, make this interpretation somewhat tenuous, and the absence of the silt from the north-west corner of the site may be simply a factor of survival and later disturbance in this area.

A substantial post and wattle fence (105) extended north/south for the full length of the site. Due to the insertion of a wall (107) at a later date, there was a gap of *c.* 2.50m. in the line of the fence. For a length of 5.60m. the fence stood in good condition to a height of 0.60m. The main posts were 0.60m.-0.90m. in diameter and they were spaced 0.25m.-0.39m. apart (average of 0.32m.). In a cross-section through the fence, thirty-four strands of wattle were counted, with an average diameter of 0.20m.

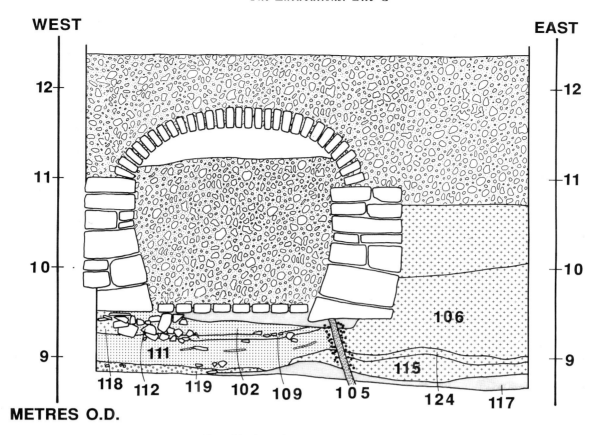

Fig. 13. Site C, section across site

Subsequent pressure had caused the fence to lean west-wards across the stream bed.

The post and wattle fence appears to have been built freestanding on the surface of the silt (117). A deposit of grey/white sandy clay (115), 0.20m. thick, accumulated on both sides of the fence (Fig. 13). This contained pockets of pure whitish silt and a small number of bones and appears to have been naturally deposited. On the west or stream side of the fence, the silt was eroded to a 0.40m.-wide bank against the wattles. Above the level of the silt (125) there was no correspondence between the layers on both sides of the fence. A small cutting was taken through the deposits on the east side of the fence, where the layers (124, 106) appeared to be revetted by it.

Overlying the pale silt (115), a layer of brown silty clay with small pebbles (<10 mm. size) (124) was dumped. This had a very homogeneous texture throughout, with a low organic content. Silts 117 and 124 produced seeds of waste and disturbed ground, along with some of grassy and damp environments. A stony grey clay (106) was dumped behind the post and wattle fence to form a bank with a minimum height of 0.80m. This dump formed the bulk of material on the east side of the post and wattle fence. Due to its sterile nature, a limited area was hand excavated. Excavation of the 1m. wide cutting and digging of a drain and sump produced only a small number of bones and a fragment of leather from 106, with no dating evidence forthcoming from the layers revetted by the

fence. Two isolated groups of wooden posts driven into the silty clay (106) cannot be positively dated to this level.

Deposits filling the river channel (Fig. 13)

In the river bed area along the west side of the excavation, all the deposits were made up of a combination of urban domestic refuse and material laid down by the river Poddle. A maximum of 0.80m. in depth survived. At the base of the watercourse was a layer of fine grey gravel (119), up to 0.12m. thick, which lay on the silt (117). Filling much of the channel over the northern two thirds of the site was an accumulation of peaty clay (111, 113) with many sand lenses, stray wattle fragments, animal bones and 13th century pottery. This layer, up to 0.50m. thick, abutted the fence to the east and extended west-wards beyond the limits of the site.

A layer of mixed brown gravel and yellow clay (103, 109) was spread thinly across the channel. A relatively large amount of pottery and bone came from this layer, and evidently the watercourse was being used as a dumping ground for household refuse.

The uppermost layer of medieval river deposit was a dark grey/black fine peaty silt (102) up to 0.45m. in depth, which contained animal bone, leather, pottery, twigs, grasses and shells. Six small posts, 0.04m.-0.08m. in diameter and 0.14m.-0.62m. long, were driven into the silt.

2. Wattle revetment of River Poddle, Site C

A tumble of limestone blocks (112), some with mortar adhering, lay on and in 102 midway along the west side of the site. They evidently represent building rubble, possibly from a destroyed revetting wall.

The range of pottery from the river deposits was fairly repetitive, consisting of Ham Green, Saintonge, 'Leinster cooking ware' and Dublin wares. The absence of Ham Green from the upper level (102) and the presence of some 'temper-free' sherds suggests that the date of the deposits extended into the 14th century.

Level 2: stone revetting wall

For a length of 4.40m. at the south end of the cutting, the post and wattle fence was cut through by the base of a stone wall (107). The wall measured 0.60m. wide and was faced only on the west or river side. A height of 0.52m. was recorded. It was constructed in a trench cut through

the grey silt (106), which was infilled with a mottled grey/brown clay. A small remnant of stone walling of similar dimensions (120) was built over the 13th century deposits in the river bed, and both walls lay directly beneath the foundations of the 18th century (level 3) culvert. No deposits in the river channel contemporary with level 2 stone walling survived.

Level 3

This phase saw the construction of the post-medieval culvert wall, both sides of which cut through the excavated area. Thick clay and stone rubble deposits on the east side of the trench (106) were probably associated with the construction of the culvert. Few finds of post-medieval date were recovered, indicating, as elsewhere, that the river bed had been cleaned during the later period.

THE EXCAVATIONS: SITE D

An area measuring *c.* 5.6m. east/west x 8.5m. north/south was opened by mechanical excavator. An additional 6m. on the western side of the site was mechanically cleared to subsoil, determining that no deposits of archaeological significance survived beyond the immediate area of the river Poddle. A depth of 1.10m. of modern redbrick rubble and debris was mechanically removed, and on the east side of the site, the 18th century culvert cut through the medieval river channel to a depth of almost 2.5m.

Level 1: the river channel

The earliest feature on the site was the artificial channel for the river Poddle. The alteration in the nature of the underlying surface geology was evident: at Site B this consisted entirely of riverine gravels, whereas at Site D the subsoil was a stiff capping of yellow/brown boulder clay. No sod covering overlay the subsoil to the west of the channel (see also Site F), and this was probably deliberately stripped from the surrounding area for various uses within the town (Bradley 1988, 52). The upcast resulting from the digging of the channel was piled on the west side of the river, artificially raising the gound level while deepening the river bed. This deposited material (205) (Fig. 16) was a compacted clay silt with small stones and flecks of charcoal throughout, thereby distinguishable from the subsoil from which it was derived and which it overlay. No finds were recovered from this material.

The river channel (208) was flat based, with sides steeply sloping at an angle of *c.* 45 degrees. The east side of the river channel was exposed in one machine cutting, where it lay to the east of (behind) the post-medieval culvert wall (Fig. 16). The channel measured 5.8m.-6m. in width, and *c.* 1.6m. in depth.

At the southern end of the site, erosion of the sides of the river channel had occurred, and lenses of organic silt (219) with a total depth of 0.40m. accumulated in the base of the river channel. Surprisingly little weathering of the channel was apparent, and the sides maintained a reasonably regular profile, with only one area of distortion. This occurred in the vicinity of a semi-circular post and wattle enclosure (226) (Fig. 14).

Level 2

The posts of the enclosure (226), spaced at intervals of 0.20m.-0.30m. were driven both into the sides and the base of the river channel. The fence enclosed an area of the river measuring 1.7m. north/south x 1.3m. east/west, and was set in *c.* 0.20m. from the edge of the river. All the posts and the strands of wattle between the posts had collapsed considerably to the east.

A random scattering of posts (234) was driven into the bed of the river to the north of 226. Considerable disturbance of the stakes had occurred, and fragments of wattle strands and twigs, including a forked prop, were dispersed throughout the brown peaty silt which overlay them. This silt (216) produced fragments of leather, pottery and bone objects, and occurred both within and outside the small wattle enclosure.

Revetment 220 (Fig. 14)

The enclosure appears to have been contemporary with the construction of a timber revetment (220). This was constructed on the west side of the river channel, located 1.4m. in from the west side of the river's edge. No corresponding structure on the east side of the river survived.

The revetment was exposed for a 4.6m. length at the south end of the site, where it continued beyond the excavated area (Fig. 16). A central segment had been removed or destroyed in the vicinity of the wattle feature (226).

The underlying silts had been scarped or levelled to provide a firm compacted surface, while the northern part of the revetment rested upon a raft of timbers (Fig. 14).

The timber raft was composed of a pair of parallel runners (232.06, 323.07) overlain by cross pieces (232.04, 232.02, 232.05), upon which baseplate (232.01) of the revetment rested. 232.07 was an unworked ash timber, 232.04 and 232.05 were lengths of squared oak and 232.06 was a reused upright with a stepped and pegged tenon at its northern end. Several large limestones were wedged beneath the runners. Dimensions of the individual timbers are given in Table 5.

The raft may have been a rudimentary crossing place on the stream. Too little remains of the structure to determine its type, but due to the lack of jointing between the members, it is unlikely to have supported a superstructure, and cannot be therefore called a bridge. It may have been a simple 'duck-boarded' pathway (Rigold 1975, 60) across the shallow stream.

At the south end of the site, two baseplates remained, connected to each other by a through splayed scarf joint, with three face pegs holding the joint in position. This portion of the revetment had been laid from south to north, with the small baseplate laid on top of the southern baseplate. The smaller baseplate would have simply butted on to its neighbour on its northern end. A similar displaced

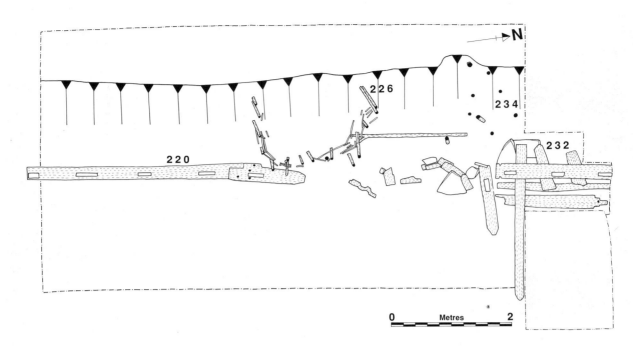

Fig. 14. Site D, levels 1 and 2

timber (232.3), would also have butted on to its neighbours at both ends.

The northern section of the revetment excavated incorporated at least three reused timbers. There were no posts or other means of securing the lower framework of the revetment, and there was no surviving evidence for any bracing mechanism of the uprights.

At the southern end of the excavated area, the revetment stood to a height of almost 0.80m. When the baseplates were lowered into position, vertical uprights with tenoned ends were placed in the mortices of the baseplates. Only three of these survived.

Plank shuttering (220) was placed against the uprights on the landward side, and deposits of organic material and clay were backfilled against it to hold the timbers in place. Dumps of brown peaty organic silts (216) were immediately backfilled against the lower planks of the revetment, holding them in position. These were sparingly secured with iron nails which pinned plank to plank, and did not connect with the uprights. Above the silts, a deposit of pale grey clay/marl (218) was banked in against the baseplate. A further deposit of pale brown clay levelled the ground behind the shuttering. Fifteen oak planks survived from the shuttering of the revetment. The planks were radially split, rectangular in section and averaged 0.10m. in thickness, with widths varying from 0.15m. to 0.28m. The longest plank measured 2.72m. The total length of shuttering excavated was 4.2m. and the maximum height was 0.74m. above the baseplate. The planks overlapped both vertically and horizontally, and several had warped and buckled forwards from their original position. A sample of the planks, which retained sapwood, gave a date of 1202 for their felling.

To the north of the shuttering, a 3m. length of the revetment had been removed, causing the backfill to collapse. This collapse consisted of the distinctive grey marl (218) and organic brown silts (216), containing strands of wattle mixed with fragments of the plank shuttering from the revetment.

Deposits of fine gravel, sand and silt (223, 224) built up against the east face of the revetment. The upper levels of the deposit, which had a maximum depth of 0.40m., were quite heavily contaminated with late 18th – early 19th century pottery, clay pipes and glass fragments. Evidently much of the silts and gravels had been water-deposited, and these were augmented with many fragments of leather, animal bone and sherds of medieval pottery. The continuous coursing of the water through the river channel had resulted in tiny lenses of gravel occurring in the general mass of silts and coarse sands, and also in the contamination of the earlier deposits with modern material.

Level 3: revetment 203 (Fig. 15)

Some fifty years after the construction of revetment 220, when part of the structure had collapsed or been removed, a second, similar revetment (203) was constructed on accumulated river silts slightly to the east of revetment 220. The replacement structure, dated to the mid-13th century, was contemporary with the construction of the mill downstream at Site E. After the excavation was completed, a 1m. length of the revetment on the eastern side of the river channel was exposed. The channel by this time had narrowed from 6m. to a width of 3.25m.

Only the baseplate of revetment 203 survived, the superstructure having been removed prior to the construction

46

3. Baseplates of early 13th-century revetment, Site D

of the modern culvert wall. No other features contemporary with the structure survived in this area.

The timbers uncovered are described briefly below, from south to north, the direction in which, like the earlier revetment in this area, they were laid. Their dimensions are given in Table 5.

203.4 was exposed after the excavation was complete. The northern end formed the lower part of a through-splayed scarf joint with 203.3.

203.3 was a rectangular-sectioned oak timber, whose south end formed the upper element of a through-splayed scarf joint with no pegs or nails holding it in position, while the north end was simply squared off.

203.2, a rectangular-sectioned oak timber, was not jointed on to 203.3 to its south end, but was scarfed on to the adjacent timber at its north end. This timber had two rectangular mortice holes cut into the upper face, and the southernmost mortice held the butt of a tenon for a vertical timber. The northernmost element of the baseplate was a large oak timber (203.1), rectangular in section. Five square mortices were cut into the upper face at regular intervals. The north end of the timber was broken, while the southern end of the timber formed the

upper part of a through-splayed scarf joint. No pegs held this joint in position, although two iron nails in the upper face of the other timber forming the joint (203.2) indicate that it was held lightly together by the nails.

Three vertical squared posts (213) were driven in to the river silts to a depth of over 0.50m. on the east or riverward side of the baseplate, securing it in place.

No bracing apart from posts 213 was found, possibly due to later disturbance. One timber extended east/west underneath and to the west of 203.4. However, the timber was slight and is more likely to have been a prop.

Only a 1m. length of the baseplate (233) on the east side of the river was exposed. A decayed tenon remained in the southernmost mortice. A small squared post 0.06m. to the west of the baseplate may have been driven in to hold the timber in position.

Several further posts (213), were driven deeply into the centre of the channel. Some of the posts were trimmed and squared, while others were crude, with the bark adhering. Gravelly silts (209) accumulated to the east of the revetment. While sherds of 18th-19th century pottery and clay pipe bowls were retrieved from the silts, most of the pottery and other artefacts date to the medieval period.

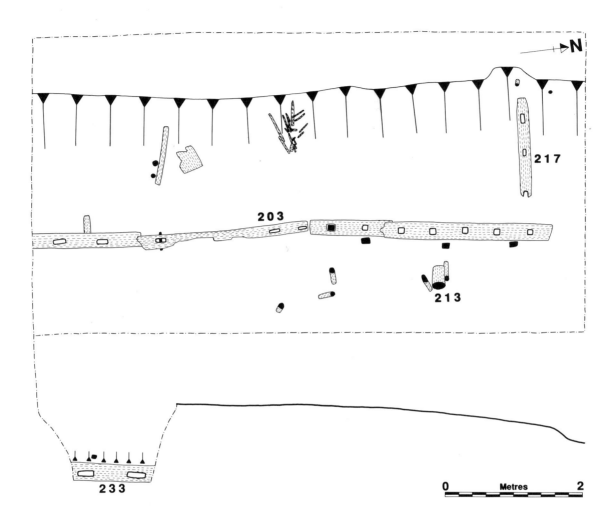

Fig. 15. Site D, level 3

Level 4: post medieval

The modern culvert wall was built directly on the baseplate of revetment 203. The wall was built in sections, 1.8m-2.5m. in length, roughly corresponding with the lengths of the underlying baseplates (Fig. 16).

It is apparent that the builders of the stone channel had excavated down through the underlying medieval deposits, removing most of the later medieval material, and finding a firm base on which to build, had utilised the mid-13th century revetment as a raft foundation. There was no evidence for the 14th century stone channelling of the river, which was found at Sites B, C, E and F.

Context	Intact	Conversion	Max. dimensions			Reused	Mortice Spacing
			Long (m.)	Wide (mm.)	Thick (mm.)		(cm.)
203.01	Yes	?	2.5	240	90	No	37
203.02	Yes	?	1.21	230	90	No	38
203.03	Yes	?	2.5	200	70	Yes	36
203.04	Yes	RSC	1.58	220	50	No	45
203.05	No	RSC	1	190	90	No	–
220.17	Yes	RSC	1.8	250	100	No	–
220.18	Yes	TC	5.54	250	110	No	66
220.2	No	RSC	2.18	270	140	Yes	58
233	No	?	1.2	260	80	No	48

Table 5. Timber dimensions, Site D

48

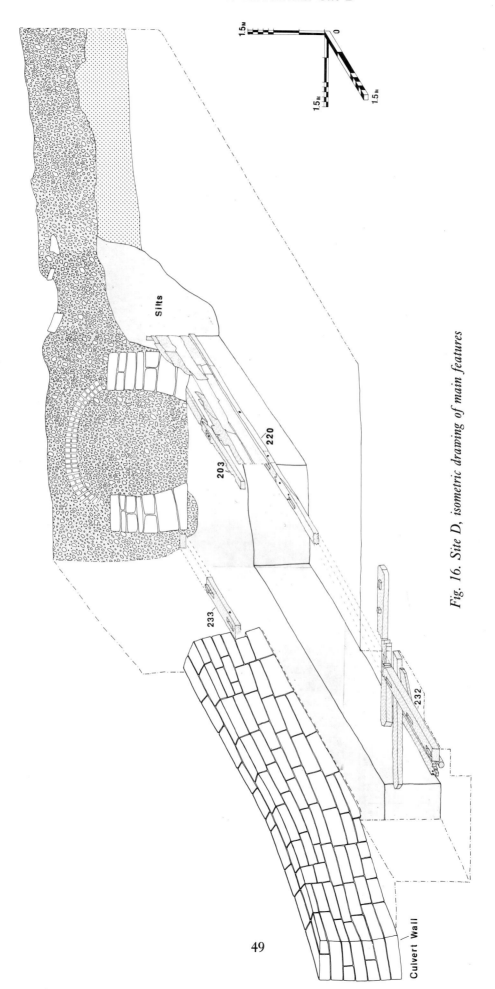

1.5ᴍ   0
1.5ᴍ
1.5ᴍ

Silts

203

220

233

232

Culvert Wall

Fig. 16. Site D, isometric drawing of main features

The Excavations: Site E, The Mill

The site of a timber-framed mill was located during machine trenching, in a previously uninvestigated stretch of the line between Hanover Lane and Dillon Place (Fig. 2). Excavation of the area immediately to the west of the manhole and installed pipe began sometime later and continued for four weeks.

An area measuring 4m. east/west by 7m. north/south was initially opened by mechanical excavator. The area was subsequently extended for a further 7m. to the north. A depth of *c.* 2.5m. of redbrick rubble and concrete was removed by machine clearance. The sides of the excavated area could not be shored, and the rubble overburden was ramped on three sides for safety purposes. The east side of the excavation trench was formed by the installed pipe. Archaeological excavation began at *c.* 10.30m. O.D., and continued to a depth of 8.55m. O.D., which was the lowest point of the bed of the river Poddle at the site.

Level 1 (Fig. 17)

The western side of the river channel (1152) at this site had been heavily truncated by later activity, but the edge of the cut at the lowest level of the river was clearly defined at the southern end of the excavation. Here the channel was cut through fine yellow gravel, and achieved a maximum recorded depth of 1.60m.

A deposit of stratified greenish/grey gritty clays (1110) with a depth of 0.95m. overlay the natural gravels at the west side of the river. This material is likely to have been deposited during the initial construction of the mill, raising the height of the river bank and providing access to the working floor of the mill at ground level.

No evidence survived of the construction method of the mill. The river had been channelled through Patrick St at least fifty years before the construction of the mill,

and at Site D upstream of the mill, at least 1m. of silts had accumulated in the period before 1202, so it is probable that the floor of the channel at Site E had been cleaned prior to the construction of the mill. There is no evidence for shoring, albeit temporary, of the sides of the river while the timbers were being laid in position. A dam must have been constructed further upstream – perhaps at Dean St – to divert or contain the flow of water while the mill was built. Lucas (1955, 32) commented that the normal practice appeared to place the mill not on the stream itself, but on a race drawn off the stream or pool, while the tidal mills uncovered at Little Island, Co. Cork (Rynne 1989a, 111) would have been constructed at low tide on the foreshore of the island in Lough Mahon. The mill at Patrick St could feasibly have been erected during the dry summer months, when mills upstream would not have been in use and the water level was low.

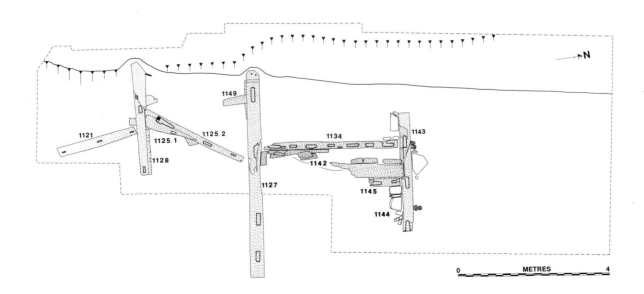

Fig. 17. Site E, level 1

50

4. Level 1 mill: inlet

The mill: inlet or dam

Two parallel beams (1128, 1127), set 2.60m. apart, were laid east/west across the base of the river channel (Fig. 17). The basal silts (1148) consisted of an organic black deposit with a limited spread, overlying the natural gravel base of the river channel to a depth of 0.13m.

The eastern end of neither timber survived *in situ*, but the broken end of timber 1127, retrieved during construction trenching, could be matched, and the entire length of 5.6m. recorded. This seems likely to have spanned the width of the river, which was 6m. maximum at Site D. At the western end of the beams, the natural gravel forming the original edge of the river channel had subsided in the region of the two timbers, so effectively two pockets in the gravel, filled with organic silt, accommodated the beams. These undercutting pockets extended for *c.* 0.30m. into the bank of the river.

The northernmost beam (1127) rested on two timber props which raised the west end of the timber by a maximum of 0.10m. Several stones were also employed in this manner, while slight decayed planks occurred also beneath the southern timber. Beam 1128, located to the south, survived to a length of 3.10m., with a width of 0.35m. and a thickness of 0.26m. The timber was tangentially squared from a large oak and smoothly adze trimmed. The surviving west end was bluntly trimmed. At this end, a large

dowel 0.035m. in diameter was driven obliquely into the north face of the beam to a depth of 0.15m and protruded 0.12m. out from it. The dowel is most likely to have connected a beam or board between the two parallel sleepers, which would have revetted the west bank of the river. No trace of this survived, but the exposed end of the dowel was complete, and this is unlikely to have remained undamaged had it not been protected by another timber. The west end of timber 1127 was scarfed with one face peg, which would have held the north end of the timber. The beam had evidently been crudely jointed at its southern end, with two faces probably merely butted and doweled together. The timber must have been deliberately removed.

Two stopped mortices spaced 1.5m. apart were cut into the upper face of beam 1128. These measured 0.18m.-0.20m. in length, 0.08m.-0.10m. in width, and 0.16m. deep. These are likely to have held the tenons of vertical uprights which would have supported the working floor of the mill. A smaller mortice of uncertain function was cut into the face of the beam off-centre to the two larger cuts.

A regular straight-edged rebate was cut into the timber on its northern face. This measured 0.045m. in depth, 0.10m. in width, and survived for a total length of 1.79m. Six dowel holes, in which two dowels survived, occurred in the upper face of the groove. The dowels were irregularly spaced, with two groups occurring at less than 0.10m.

intervals, and a span of *c*. 0.30m. between the central dowel holes. The dowels would have secured the plank flooring of the dam (see below). Parallel with timber 1128 was 1127, which measured 5.60m. in total length, 0.36m. in width and was 0.30m. thick. The west end of the timber was scarfed with two dowel holes cut into the upper face over the scarf. A groove or slot, measuring 0.07m. in width and 0.035m. in depth, lay immediately to the east of the dowels. A length of decayed wood lay in the groove, sitting flush with the upper surface of the beam. The purpose of the groove is unclear. It extended the full width of the timber, but is evidently too shallow to have held a tenoned upright. The east end of the timber was butt trimmed.

Four stopped mortices were cut into the upper face of the beam. Two of these paired with the surviving mortices of beam 1128, and would have held tie beams supporting the upper floor. The three westernmost mortices were regularly spaced. The mortices measured from 0.30m.-0.38m. in length, 0.10m.-0.11m. in width, and 0.13m.-0.14m. in depth. A shallow rectangular recess occurred in the south face of the beam, while some damage had occurred to the timber on its northern face.

A diagonally set beam (1125:2) was lapped into the rebate along the north face of beam 1128. The north end of this beam lay just 0.12m. from 1127, but the two were not jointed. The beam (1125:2) measured 2.90m. in length, 0.19m. in width and 0.15m. in thickness. Its lapped south end fitted into the housing of 1128, with the upper face of the timbers flush. The joint was secured by two dowels, *c*. 0.025m. in diameter. The beam was evidently in its original position.

A regular edged rebate, with a depth varying from 0.02m.-0.035m., extended the full length of the beam.

A single plank (1125:1) was lapped on to the groove at the south end of 1125:2, fitting flush along this join, and where 1125:2 was lapped on to the southern sleeper (1128). The plank measured 1.38m. long and 0.06m. thick, tapering from a width of 0.32m. at its southern end to 0.08m. at its northern end. Three dowels secured it to the underlying beam (1125:2). The plank is the only surviving part of the floor of the dam. Further dowel holes along the length of the rebate in 1125:2 would have secured the north ends of plank flooring, with their south ends doweled on to the rebate along beam 1128. Two centrally placed mortices were cut into the upper face of beam 1125:2. The northern mortice, with auger holes apparent in each corner, measured 0.25m., with a depth of 0.03m. The larger mortice (a) at the south end of the beam measured 0.43m. in length, with a width of 0.11m. and a depth of 0.115m. The east side of the mortice had an irregular step.

The west side of plank 1125:1 was cut to accommodate mortice (a) in the underlying beam. When excavated, a small rectangular block of wood was found wedged into the south-west corner of the mortice. This suggests that both the upright in the mortice and part of the plank flooring of the dam had been replaced on at least one occasion. A smaller rectangular mortice (b), measuring 0.12m. in length x 0.06m. in width, was cut through the timber. To the north of mortice (b), a notch measuring 0.04m. x 0.03m., with a depth of 0.01m., was cut into the timber.

Two lap notches, occurring at the base of the beam, were cut into the west face of timber 1125:2 . Notch (a) measured 0.16m. in length, 0.12m. in width, and was 0.05m. deep. A large dowel hole was centrally placed in the notch. Notch (b) measured 0.12m. x 0.12m., with a depth of 0.05m. The north end of the beam was trimmed and tapered upwards to an angle of 18 degrees.

When the structure fell into disuse, compacted organic silts and clays (1136), containing lenses of grey gravel (1129), accumulated between the timbers of the wheel house/dam. These layers produced sherds of locally made pottery and imported wares from Bristol and France. A further deposit of mid-brown silt (1115) accumulated over beam 1125. The silt contained pockets of gravel, with lenses of straw/grasses, and produced several sherds of locally manufactured pottery. The blocky, compacted silt appeared to have been deposited by very slow-moving water.

No headrace survived, and the only structural element to the south of the dam was beam 1121, which extended diagonally towards sleeper 1128. Beam 1121 measured 2.14m. in length, 0.24m. in width, and was 0.08m. in thickness. Three rectangular stopped mortices, measuring 0.10m.-0.11m. in length, 0.05m. in width, and 0.07m. in depth, were cut into the upper face of the timber at regular intervals. Two of the mortices had dowels *in situ*, which penetrated the width of the timber. Laminated lenses of waterborne silts and gravels, interleaved with spreads of dark turfy organic material (1137) accumulated around beam 1121. Sherds of locally made pottery and glazed Ham Green pot fragments were recovered from this deposit.

The wheelpit

This timber construction extended northwards for 4m. at the downstream end of the wheel house. Two parallel beams (1134, 1145), set 0.90m. apart and extending north/south, formed the sides of the wheelpit. Both timbers had mortices cut into their upper faces, which would have held tenoned uprights to brace plank shuttering behind the uprights. No uprights or shuttering survived.

Baseplate 1134 measured 3.52m. in length, 0.18m. in width, and was 0.21m. thick. At least two series of mortices had been cut into the face of the timber. In its final position, the timber was not jointed into its neighbour, but appears to have been wedged in place by stones packed in behind it. A wooden wedge was placed in a large mortice which was cut through by a small mortice, showing that the smaller mortices are likely to have been used in the final refurbishment of the wheelpit.

The parallel baseplate (1145) measured only 0.95m. in

length (it was broken at its southern end), and was 0.18m. in width and 0.17m. thick. Two mortices were cut into the upper face. A horizontal mortice was cut into its west face. The timber was not jointed into position, but was held in place by large flat slabs on its eastern side. These stones also held a composite beam (1143) in position. The beam was secured on its north face by further stones and two groups of stakes, which were driven into the underlying river gravels. Several of the stakes leaned sharply to the north. Those in the western group were all squarely trimmed and pointed at their bases, while the posts at the east end were rounded. The beam consisted of two large oak baulks (1143:1, 1143:2), which were laid horizontally on their broad side and joined end to end by a splayed pegged 'tongued and grooved' joint. Timber 1143:1 (the western element) measured 1.48m. in length with a width of 0.27m., and was 0.21m. thick. The west end was roughly squared. The timber was split and was damaged at its east end. The east timber (1143:2) measured 2.06m. in length, and was 0.29m. wide with a thickness of 0.20m. The eastern end was damaged and truncated.

The joint connecting the two measured 0.76m. in length. The east timber had the male element, a double stepped angled tenon, 0.065m. thick and up to 0.10m. wide. This tenon sat in a centrally placed groove, 0.07m. in width, located in the west end of timber 1143:1. Two dowels secured the joint. An angled notch-lap joint housing with a central dowel *in situ* was cut into the western timber, and was cut through by one of three rectangular stopped mortices. These had measurements varying from 0.27m.-0.34m. in length, by 0.08m.-0.10m. in width and 0.10m. deep, cut into the upper face of the composite beam. The mortices were regularly spaced, and the two on the west, positioned at the northern end of the baseplates (1134, 1142), may have held the uprights to brace a sluice mechanism.

The easternmost mortice was packed with slag, which sealed a cache of small bronze objects and a small silver object and nineteen fragmentary carpentry nails. The objects had evidently been deliberately concealed in the mortice, and as the compacted slaggy deposit was almost level with the upper surface of beam 1143, the mortice could not have held an upright. The objects were probably secreted when the mill was dismantled. The pieces would have had little value in the medieval period, so it is likely that they were placed in the mortice for superstitious reasons. The timber is likely to have been reused from the roof of a large building, the scarf joint and the notch-lap joint functioning in the primary use (see carpentry and woodworking).

A rebate 0.09m. long and 0.06m. deep was cut into the upper southern corner of the timbers and spanned the joint between them. The oak planking forming the floor of the wheelpit was decayed and fragmentary, but one plank (1142) survived in good condition at the north end, where it was dowelled into the rebate in the south face of beam 1143. This plank measured 0.40m. wide, 0.06m. thick, and survived to a length of 2m. Slight adze marks were visible

on the plank. Its north end was squarely trimmed and fitted flush with the rebate in timber 1143. Two dowels held the plank in position and penetrated the lower beam to a depth of over 0.05m. Fragments of a second plank also survived. A single iron nail survived in the west end of the rebate, indicating that the decayed plank had been nailed in place.

The planking was laid edge to edge, and simply abutted the parallel baseplates (1134, 1142). At the south end, it appeared to project beneath the main sleeper (1127) of the dam. There was a slight fall (*c*. 0.10m.) from the south to the north of the wheelpit.

The plank flooring was overlain by a thin sheet of fine grey silt (also 1142), from which several sherds of locally made pottery were retrieved. Some fine organic silts (1147) accumulated around baseplate 1134, while to the north of the wheelpit river gravels and water deposited silts (1146), overlying the base of the river channel, yielded several sherds of locally made and English pottery.

No evidence survived of the gear pit or fixings to the west of the wheelpit; these had been removed by the insertion of a stone gear pit when the mill was rebuilt over one hundred years later. Likewise, no traces remained of the axle support for the wheel on the eastern side of the wheelpit, but the presence of large slabs (1144) suggests that this may have been at least partially constructed of stone.

Level 2

That the mill had fallen into disuse is evident from the entry in Archbishop Alen's *Register* for 1371 when 'the Archbishop, with consent of both chapters, demises in form to John (Pasvannd) the site of the mill heretofore called Shyreclap in St Patrick's St, Dublin, now altogether thrown down and void, to rebuild a mill there at his own expense as he thinks best...'

The total excavated length of the later mill is in excess of 11.5m. Less remained of the timbers that projected across the river than in the earlier structure, due to considerable later disturbance.

Main structural features

The headrace or inlet (Fig. 18) was formed by a dry-stone built wall (1105), which was exposed for a length of 5.5m. This extended northwards along the west bank of the river, set in approximately 1.5m. from the original edge of the river channel. At its northern extent, wall 1103 extended for 3m. westwards. Both walls (1103, 1105) were constructed as a unit, and both were set in the same construction trench (1119), which was filled with compact yellow/brown clay and gravel and packed with small stones.

Wall 1105 stood to a maximum height of 0.90m. (three courses), and was built of roughly dressed large limestone blocks, which varied in size from 0.30m.-0.60m. in length,

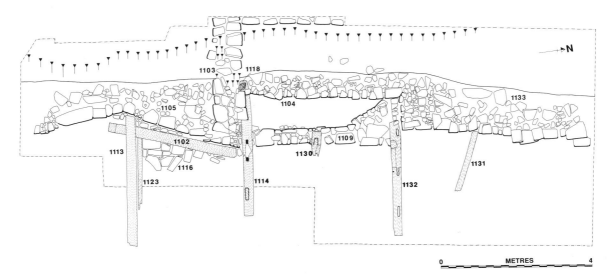

Fig. 18. Site E, level 2a

and were irregularly coursed. The wall was faced on the river ward side only, and utilised the underlying beams (1121,1125, level 1) as a footing.

Wall 1103 stood to a maximum height of 2.10m. at its western end, while elsewhere only the footings survived. The wall was unfaced at its basal level, where a large oak beam (1114) was incorporated into the stonework.

The inlet proper was composed of two parallel oak sleepers, 2.80m. apart, which extended east/west and lay directly over the large parallel sleepers of the earlier structure.

This was constructed as follows:

A paved surface of flat limestone flags (1116) was laid down over the soft silts that had accumulated during the abandonment of the earlier structure. The paving survived in an area measuring maximum 2.30m. north/south x 1.30m. east/west, and was badly truncated on the east side. Delimiting the paving on the southern side was a slender beam (1123), which was laid flush with the paving. This measured 2.40m. in length (it was damaged at the east end), 0.13m. in width and was 0.10m. thick. Two angled lap housings and a series of regularly spaced dowels on the underside of the beam indicate that the timber was reused in this position. This timber abutted but was not jointed to an oak beam (1102), which extended for 3.42m. along the face of wall 1105. The timber measured 0.25m. in width, and was 0.17m. thick. Its northern end was unjointed, while two lap housings spaced 0.30m. apart were cut into its southern end. The southernmost housing, which measured 0.17m. in width with a depth of 0.10m., was empty, while the second lap housing, measuring 0.26m. wide and 0.12m. deep, accommodated an oak beam (1113).

Timber 1113 measured 3.5m. in length (it was damaged at its eastern end), 0.25m. in width and was 0.14m. thick. Apart from its halved west end, where it fitted into the housing on timber 1102, there were no joints or fixings.

The timber was rounded on its upper side and did not lie flush with timber 1102. Samples of both timbers sent for dendrochronological dating gave a date in the latter half of the 14th century for their felling (see report in carpentry and woodworking).

Parallel with timber 1113, beam 1114 measured 3.75m. in length, 0.23m. in width and was 0.23m. thick. Despite its size, too few rings remained to date the felling year. The timber had been broken at its central mortice, but it was possible to match the removed piece, and the full length of the beam was recorded. The timber was squarely trimmed at the east end, while the west end projected beneath wall 1103.

Three stopped mortices were cut into the upper face of the timber. These were regularly spaced and of irregular size. The westernmost mortice held the stump of an upright (1118), which had a two-shouldered tenon and was dowelled into place. The upright survived to a height of only 0.37m. above the base timber, and was in an advanced state of decay. It measured 0.22m. x 0.18m.

The central mortice, which had been damaged by machine action, measured 0.07m. in width, 0.1m. in depth and was over 0.50m. in length. Two rectangular blocks or wedges remained *in situ* at either end of the mortice, reducing its length to *c.* 0.32m. A broken dowel hole would have held the tenon of the upright in position. A damaged side mortice occurred on the north face of the timber. This measured 0.16m. long, 0.07m. wide, and was 0.13m. deep. This would have accommodated the (decayed) west side of the wheelpit.

A third mortice at the east end of the timber measured 0.39m. in length, with a width of 0.09m. and a depth of 0.11m. Auger holes were present in the base of the mortice. Two rectangular blocking wedges (one incomplete) reduced the size of the mortice to 0.14m. in length. This timber had an off-centre horizontal dowel hole which was blocked by one of the wedges. Evidently this component

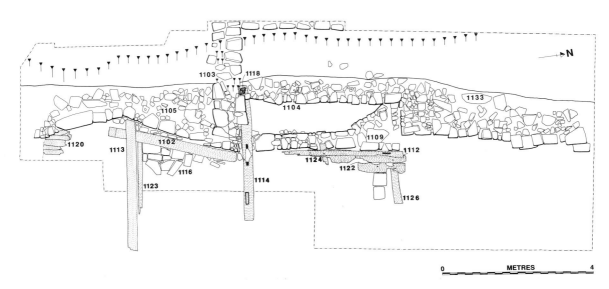

Fig. 19. Site E, level 2b

of the mill had continued in use for some time, with the replacement of the original uprights on at least one occasion. Several overlapping radially split oak planks (1120) extended for only 0.70m. into the southern end of the excavated area. The planks measured on overage 0.14m. in width and were 0.10m.-0.015m. in thickness. They were fragmented and disturbed on their northern limit, but were generally aligned north/south. Several of the planks had nails driven through them. The planks appear to have formed part of the headrace inlet of the level 2 mill, presumably to prevent water from escaping beneath the inlet.

Lucas (1955, 112) describes as characteristic of the Irish mill a wooden floor laid in the pond immediately in front of the dam, in which the planking ran in the direction of the stream, and also mentions the occurrence of wooden floors in Irish mill ponds.

The mill building (Figs 18, 19)

The stone footings of a small building which supported the working floor of the mill were uncovered. Wall 1103 (described above) formed the south wall, standing to a maximum height of 2.10m. and built into a steeply sloping deposit of embanked, sterile clays. At the western limit of the site, the inner face of a stone wall (1103a) was exposed in the site section. This abutted the north face of wall

5. Level 2 mill, Site E

6. Details of timbers 1128 and 1125, level 1 mill

1103 and extended northwards for *c.* 2.5m. The masonry consisted of large (average 0.25m. diameter) unbonded, rough blocks of limestone standing to a maximum of two courses (0.40m. in height). There was scant evidence for a return wall at the north end of wall 1103a, with one or two random stones pressed into the underlying clays.

The gear pit

At a distance of 2m. east from the inner face of wall 1103a, a small stone chamber was constructed up against wall 1103 and beam 1114 in the river bed. This was formed by three stone walls in the following manner:

Wall 1104 was dug into the side of the river bank, and was faced only on the riverward side. The wall consisted of very roughly coursed limestone blocks, standing to a height of 0.65m. (four courses). The basal course projected outwards, forming a plinth (Fig. 20). The wall was unbonded, but traces of a decayed yellow sandy mortar adhered to the outer face. There was a possible ope or putlog at the north end of the wall. This was square, measuring 0.30m., with a depth of 0.30m., and was filled with small stones and soft silt veined with ironpan.

At its northern end, wall 1104 angled to the east for 0.90m. and continued northwards (wall 1133) for a further 5m. This stood to five courses in height, and was constructed of unbonded, randomly coursed limestone blocks, which were poorly faced, some of which were up to 0.55m. in diameter. Traces of yellow sandy mortar occurred in the fill of the construction cut. Wall 1133 formed the tailrace of the mill, and continued northwards beyond the limits of the excavation.

Butted in against the angle of the two walls was wall 1109, which curved in against the right angle caused by the two walls (above). This was well-mortared and was composed of roughly coursed limestone blocks, standing to three courses or 0.85m. in height. The wall was of regular thickness, except at the north end, where it splayed inwards and the construction was markedly rubbly. The inner face was uneven (Fig. 20) and at its base was distanced only 0.35m. from wall 1104. The chamber formed by these walls was irregular, measuring 3.40m. north/south x 0.65m. east/west. It was filled with a series of alternate lenses of grey gritty silt, yellow/brown sand and gravel (1108). The deposit was noticeably more organic nearer the base of the walls, where it included mottles of grey clay. A lens of loose stone and mortar which occurred at the level of the top of the plinth of wall 1104 may indicate the actual level of the chamber while in use. Rubble slabs and small stones occurred particularly towards the upper level of the chamber. Several sherds of locally manufactured and French pottery were recovered from the fill of the chamber.

Wheelpit or penstock: level 2a (Figs 18, 20)

This lay immediately to the east of the stone gear pit described above, and overlay the wheelpit of the earlier mill. The wheelpit appears to have been rebuilt on at least one occasion during the period of usage of the later mill. The remains of the first wheelpit are scant, and consisted of two parallel beams, extending east/west from wall 1109 and set 1.80m. apart. The central beam of the structure (1130) was set at the same distance from beam 1114.

Timber 1130 was set into the lower course of wall 1109, and survived to a height of 0.81m. The west end was squarely trimmed. The beam was 0.23m. wide and 0.21m. thick. Part of a rectangular mortice and a diagonal rebate 0.06m. deep appeared to have been non-functional (the mortice extended into the socket in the wall), and the

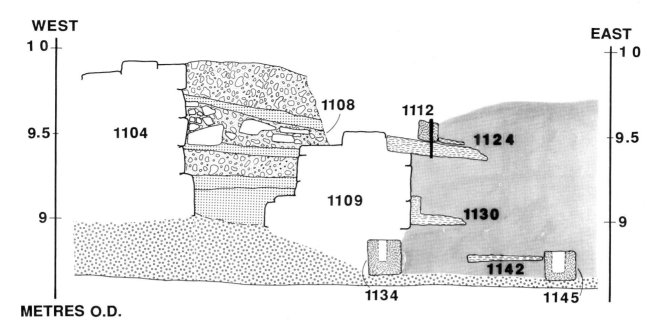

Fig. 20. Site E, section through wheelpit and gearhouse

timber may have been taken from the earlier mill on the site, having been reused on at least two previous occasions (see carpentry and woodworking). Three dowels and a split dowel hole also occurred at the west end of the timber. The timber was probably used as a joist, and two corroded nail shanks driven into the upper surface of the beam may have secured the (removed) plank flooring.

Beam 1132, located at the junction of walls 1109 and 1133, extended for 3.11m. east/west and measured 0.21m. wide and 0.23m. thick. The full length of the timber was recovered. The west end of the timber was sealed beneath the stones of wall 1109. The timber was rounded on its upper plane at the west end. Located 0.50m. from the west end of the timber, a rebate or saddle, 0.12m. deep and 1.10m. long, was cut into the upper face of the timber at the southern side. The rebate sloped gradually for a distance of *c.* 0.13m., then was cut vertically to a depth of 0.04m. The flat surface of the rebate, which would have held the plank flooring of the wheelpit, measured 0.11m. in width. Two iron nail or rivet shanks, driven into the surface of the rebate, confirm this usage. An oak dowel of uncertain function was driven into the south face of the saddle ridge.

Three stopped mortices spaced at intervals of 0.85m. were cut into the upper face of the timber. These measured 0.19m.-0.23m. in length, 0.06m.-0.08m. in width, and 0.04m.-0.10m. in depth. The upright held in the westernmost mortice would probably have stood through the stones of wall 1109. A broken dowel hole indicates that the upright was pegged into position.

The mortice at the east end of the timber held a horizontal dowel in position, and also a rectangular blocking wedge, which reduced the length of the mortice to less than 0.15m. When the timber was removed from the site

for detailed examination and cleaning, a deposit of compacted slag was removed from the east mortice. Sealed beneath the slag in a black gritty deposit was a cache of objects – several copper alloy twists or cloth fasteners (E543:1132:3a-3d), three shroud pins (E543:1132:3e-3g), along with forty-eight fragments of small carpentry nails and a piece of window leading. These objects appear to have been inserted into the mortice when the structure went out of use, and mirror the small cache of objects recovered from the mortice of underlying beam 1143 in the earlier structure.

At the extreme east end of the beam was a shallow curving housing 0.13m. in depth. The lack of dowels and a secure fixing plane suggests that this is unlikely to have held a beam. Although sapwood survived in the west end of the beam, insufficient rings remained to date this beam.

Located 0.80m. to the north of beam 1132, a possible putlog hole occurred in the base of wall 1133. This measured 0.25m. in width, 0.18m. in height and 0.36m. in depth, and was filled with very soft silt with veins of mineral iron. The hole is likely to have held a beam projecting eastwards across the river, suggesting that the tailrace of the mill was also plank floored for some distance.

About 2m. north of beam 1132, beam 1131 extended diagonally for 1.74m. across the river. The timber measured 0.15m. in width and was 0.06m. thick. The west end was notched and slightly tapered where it slotted into wall 1133, while the east end was broken by machine action. Three irregularly spaced dowels driven through the plank protruded up to 0.07m. through its underside. These may have secured additional planking flooring downstream of the mill.

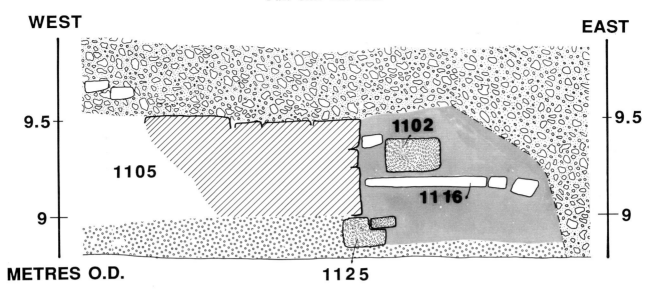

Fig. 21. Site E, section through inlet

Wheelpit: level 2b (Fig. 19)

No dating evidence survived to indicate when the wheelpit was rebuilt. The timbers were too slight for dating, and the few sherds of pottery from securely stratified layers do not indicate any significant time scale between the builds. It is likely that the uprights placed in the mortices of beam 1114 were replaced at this time also.

The structure was similar to the earlier structure (above) consisting of two parallel beams (1124, 1126) which extended eastwards from wall 1109 and had the remnants of decayed planking nailed or dowelled on to them.

Beam 1124 measured 0.94m. in length and was 0.13m. wide and 0.08m. thick. The beam is likely to have been reused from an earlier structure, as a groove extended along its underside and a mortice partially sealed by planking was cut through it. The beam is incorporated into wall 1109, which was truncated to this level. The overlying

planking (1112) was secured by a dowel to the beam.

Beam 1126 directly overlay 1132 and measured 1.66m. in length, 0.17m. in width, and was 0.04m. thick. The west end of the timber was trimmed to accommodate the stones of wall 1109, with a central ridge measuring 0.03m. in width and 0.035m. in maximum height remaining along the centre. Stones were seated in the hollows on either side of the ridge. The timber was broken at its eastern end, but a fragment of timber 1138 of similar dimensions which measured 0.38m. in length, removed during machine clearance of the site, may be part of timber 1126. The fragment was trimmed at its east end, which gives a minimum length of *c*. 2.05m. for beam 1126. The flooring and the west side of the wheelpit was formed of planks (1122) and a morticed beam (1112). The two planks were of ash, laid side by side, and nailed on to beam 1126. Each was 0.02m. thick, and measured *c*. 0.38m. in width. Both planks were trimmed at the northern end.

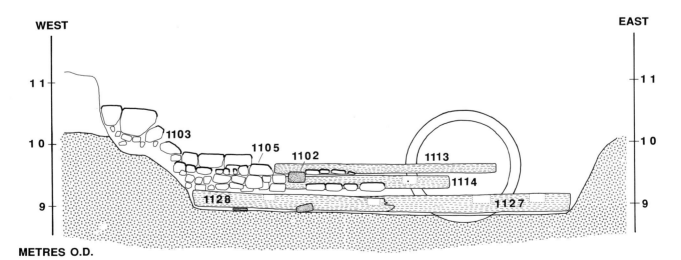

Fig. 22. Site E, section through mill and river

A decayed and damaged beam (1112) was laid over the planks, closely abutting wall 1109. The beam measured 3m. in length, 0.11m. in width, and was 0.09m. thick. One complete mortice and part of a second one were cut into the upper face of the beam. A central groove, 0.055m. at its widest point with a depth varying 0.02m.–0.04m., was incised along the centre of the plank. This could have held plank shuttering, whose ends would have slotted into grooves in the sides of the uprights. Part of a displaced upright from the southern mortice was recovered. The beam was laid on planks 1122 and dowelled to the under-lying joists.

Two large, square, flat limestone slabs wedged the planks into position on their east side. There was no trace of a corresponding timber revetting on this side of the wheelpit. The black gritty sands and silts (1101) which accumulated at the southern end of the inlet yielded both native and imported wares, as well as several floor tiles and an ivory and iron decorated parchment pricker. Post-medieval contaminants were also recovered from the deposits.

Level 3: post-medieval activity

Although the mill appears to have continued in use into the 17th century, no stratified deposits of this period survived on the site. The late culvert wall was constructed using wall 1133 as a footing, and continued across part of the inlet and paving (1116). Closely packed small stones overlay the paving. This was relatively modern in date, and sealed beneath the stones was a 'miraculous medal' bearing an inscription in French which reads 'O Mary, conceived without sin, pray for those who have recourse to thee.'

THE EXCAVATIONS: SITE F

An area measuring 6.15m. north/south and between 3.94m.-4.14m. east/west was opened by mechanical excavator. A further 28.60m. was excavated in stages, on completion of the site, to the south of Site F (Figs 2, 28). A depth of *c*. 1.60m. of overburden was removed from the southern 2.50m. of the trench, while over the remaining area a depth of *c*. 2.35m. was removed. The overall depth of archaeological deposits varied from *c*. 2.25m. at the south end of the trench to 1.50m.- 1.65m. in the remaining area.

Site F was located *c*. 27m. south of the town wall (Fig. 37), whose location had been determined by a machine-excavated trench some months previously. The town fosse, to the south of the wall, was located in archaeological test pits in a development site to the west of the site (Hayden 1992, 13; Hurley 1993, 25), and a section of the north side of the fosse was excavated by the writer (Site G). Site F was sited *c*. 5m. to the south of the outer edge of the town fosse.

Level 1 (Fig. 23)

A series of different types of redeposited subsoil were laid over the area of Site F (Fig. 24), and are likely to derive from upcast resulting from the construction of the town fosse, which formed a low mound on the outer edge of the fosse. The depth of the fosse is *c*. 5m., and in the vicinity of Site F partly exposed the underlying limestone.

A mound of redeposited boulder clays (394) measuring between 2.20m.-3.60m. north/south, was located at the very north end of the site. The clays measured a maximum of 1.20m. in depth and tapered off towards the south of the site. The bank was composed mainly of dense, sterile sticky yellow clays with small stones and flecks of charcoal throughout. No artefacts were recovered from the clays, but animal bone was present. A limekiln (332) was constructed in a pit cut through the clays. The maximum depth of the pit was 1.55m. The sides of the upper 0.87m. of the kiln sloped steeply, while the lower 0.68m. of the pit was vertical and faced here with vitrified

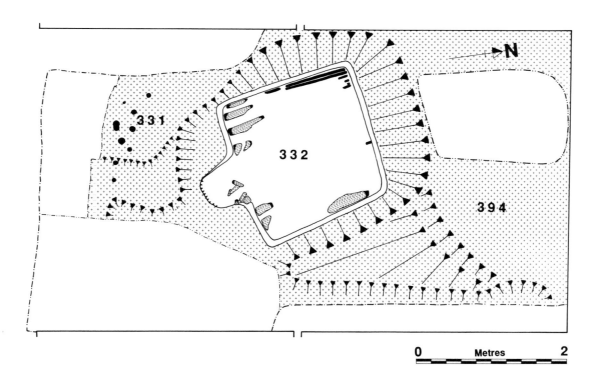

Fig. 23. Site F, the limekiln

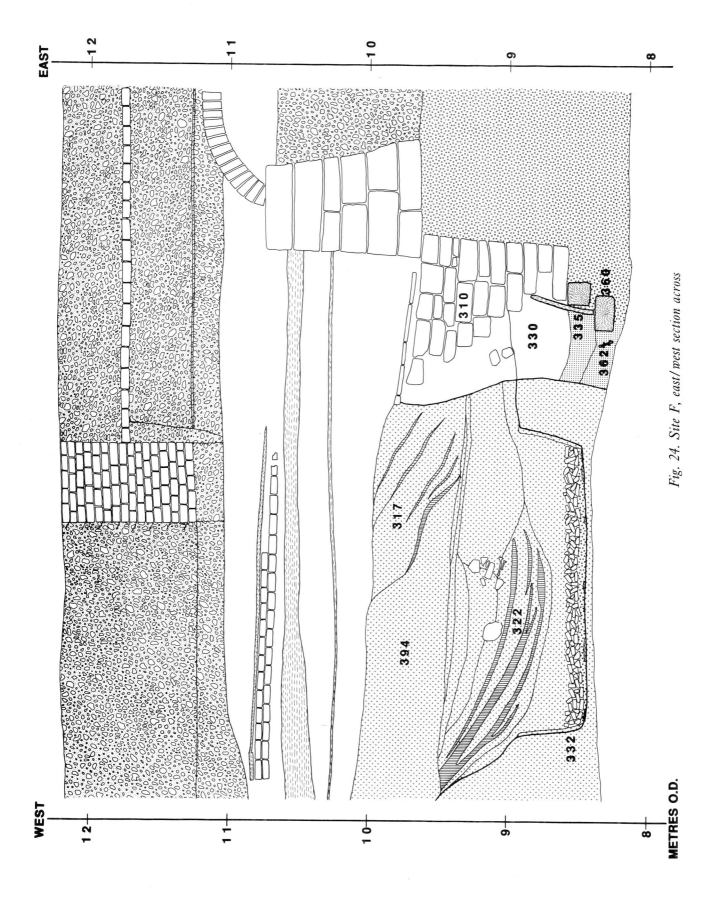

Fig. 24. Site F, east/west section across

clay and small stones. The average width of the facing was 0.04m.-0.07m. The kiln measured 1.80m. north/south x 1.88m. east/west internally.

It was regular in plan, but on its south side a small pit, 0.60m. long, sloped gently upwards and narrowed to a width of *c.* 0.44m. This may have been a stoke hole or 'eye' (Davey 1961, 97).

The base of the kiln was compacted, oxidised boulder clay. Sporadic deposits of pure soft white lime (346) interspersed with patches of brown peaty organic material and lumps of burnt orange clay overlay the floor. Rows of burnt timber rods and charred timbers occurred in these deposits, particularly in the corners of the structure, with quite a density being exposed in the small pit off the south wall. The best preserved timbers were in the south-west corner and consisted of *c.* 5-6 rounded rods, a number of which measured up to 0.80m. in length and *c.* 0.03m.-0.04m. in width. This was the only area within the kiln where burnt rods were identified, as opposed to fragments of burnt or charred timbers. A thin layer, *c.* 0.02m.-0.04m. thick of light grey fine gravel and lime (347), overlay the charred timbers and lime. The lime deposit was covered with a 0.10m.-0.15m. depth of fire-cracked stones. No evidence for a superstructure was recovered.

When the lime kiln fell into disuse, it was backfilled with a number of varying deposits (322) (Fig. 24), consisting mainly of compacted gravels with lenses of fine charcoal and soft red/orange ash. The latter may have constituted earlier rakeout from the kiln.

The partial remains of a female skeleton (340) was cast into the kiln. The skull, vertebrae, pelvis and right arm were articulated, while a small number of bones from the lower body were retrieved.

With the exception of a handful of *c.* 13th century pottery sherds, no other finds of any consequence were recovered.

The lime kiln: discussion

The limekiln is likely to have been of the Periodic or 'Flare' type, where the lime is not placed in contact with the fuel, but with the heat and flames (Davey 1961, 98). The lime produced is evenly burnt and uncontaminated. While no superstructure survived at Patrick St, this is likely to have been constructed of clay and wicker, with an open top somewhat resembling a chimney (Fig. 25, after Davey 1961). Little of this superstructure material survived, with mere lenses of oxidised clay and ash occurring in the backfill of the structure. The process of converting the stone to lime takes three to four days (ibid., 98).

A small cruciform limekiln of late 13th century date was probably used in the construction of the town wall of Drogheda (Campbell 1987, 54). Only the basic ground plan of the kiln survived, with no evidence of a superstructure, although a thick deposit of heavily oxidised clay which overlay the floor of the kiln probably represents

the levelled remains of the domed superstructure (K. Campbell, pers. comm.).

The source of the limestone is likely to have been immediately close by, and the kiln may have converted rock from the digging of the ditch to lime.

Level 2: the channelling of the Poddle (Fig. 26)

Some time after the limekiln was backfilled, the channel for the river Poddle was excavated. Only a small part of the channel was encountered at Site F, where it extended for 3.8m north-east/south-west across the south-east corner of the site. The sides of the channel had been largely truncated by later activity, and it survived to a depth of *c.* 0.85m. The original edges of the channel sloped steeply, with little evidence of erosion of the boulder clays through which it was originally cut.

A wood-lined drain or sewer (341) fed in to the river channel at the south of the site. The drain extended for 2.5m. east/west, extending westwards beyond the area of excavation. Prior to the insertion of the wooden lining, a deposit of richly organic silt (345) accumulated in the base of the drain. This deposit was rich in fruit seeds and may represent faecal matter (see 'The Plant Remains'). The drain may have led from a structure upslope from the west side of the river bank.

Only 1.90m. of the drain remained intact: this sloped steeply with a 1:4 gradient. The drain had a maximum width of 0.70m. with a depth of 0.48m. The base of the drain was composed of three oak planks. No timber lining survived on the south side of the drain, while the north side was delimited by one of the base planks which had been turned upwards and held in place midway along its length by a rectangular post which measured 0.22m x 0.10m. Two

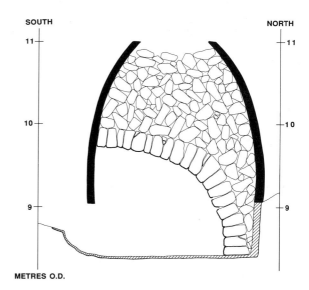

Fig. 25. Site F, schematic drawing of limekiln, after Davey

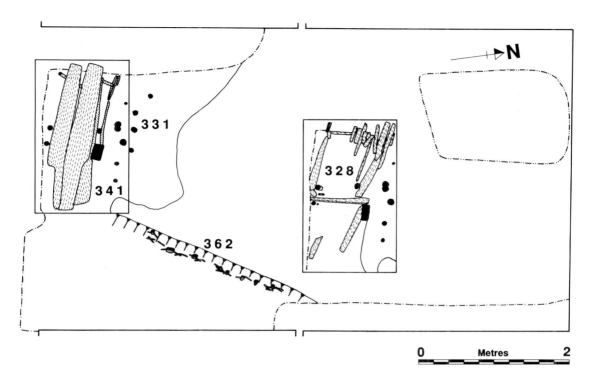

Fig. 26. Site F, river channel and drain

small round posts positioned further to the west also held an east/west plank in place behind the upturned plank: this was probably the original side of the drain.

A thin layer of black organic silt 0.03m. in depth and a thick deposit of mottled grey silt/marl (329) was dumped over the base of the drain. A small circular silver plaque was recovered from the marl. The dumping was probably necessitated by rising water levels in the river.

The wooden lining of the drain was refurbished at this level. A number of planks (of oak, birch, ash and hazel) formed the base of the drain, while to either side, a plank retained by circular posts delimited its width. Midway along the excavated length of drain 328, an upright plank was laid on edge across the drain, held in place on both sides by posts. The plank appears to have functioned as a sluice, allowing effluent to drain into the river, while preventing Poddle water from backing up the drain when the river was high. A single horizontally placed timber, 0.70m. in length, delimited the north-eastern side of the drain. Elsewhere the grey marl (329) formed the base of the drain. A scatter of postholes (331) occurred to the north of the drain at this level, but their purpose is unclear.

The river channel was partially infilled with a deposit of sterile grey marl and highly organic silt. Remnants of a decayed and fragmentary post and wattle fence (362) survived in this deposit. The fence posts were rounded, with diameters from 0.0m.5-0.08m., with butts trimmed to points in every case. It was constructed to retain the riverbank in this area (see also Site D, level 1). The fence and drain are likely to be contemporary.

The fence continued for a distance of 9.5m. to the south of Site F, but generally survived very poorly. It continued beyond the area of excavation to the west of the site, and the edge of the river channel was not exposed in this area.

Level 3: timber revetment (360)

In the early 13th century, probably contemporary with the construction of revetment 220 at Site D, the post and wattle fence was replaced by a substantial timber revetment (360). By this time the water channel had narrowed to 2.8m. While the full width of the river in this area is not known, further upstream at Site D the river measured almost 6m. in width when first channelled up Patrick St. A total of twelve baseplates, laid along the west bank of the river and extending for over 31m., was recorded. At the southern limit of the excavated area, two baseplates at the east side of the river (1011.1, 1011.2), were exposed, while two baseplates were located further north in the centre of the channel. These centrally placed baseplates were replaced by a longer alignment of beams (387), which incorporated two parallel sleepers, lying across the river at right angles to the revetment on the west bank. The dimensions of the main timbers are given in Table 6.

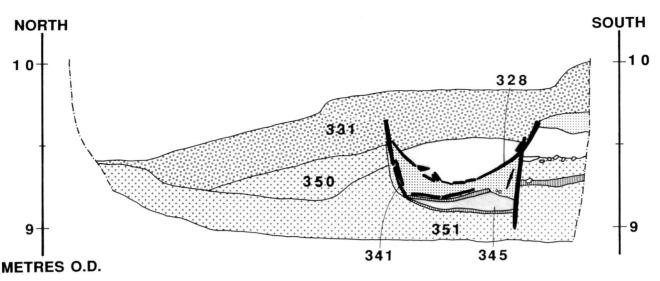

Fig. 27. Site F, section across drain 328

The northernmost baseplate had been split in antiquity along its north/south axis. Three mortices were evident along its length, two of which had been destroyed by the split. No uprights or parts thereof remained *in situ*, and it is possible that the baseplate was split to prise out the uprights.

The third mortice, located at the south end of the baseplate, held an upright post which was wedged in place by a number of small pieces of timber. The upright did not survive past the upper surface of the baseplate. Both subsidiary baseplates were pegged and tenoned at right angles into the principal baseplate. The southern subsidiary baseplate (360.2) extended eastwards from the principal for *c.* 1.52m. Two rough indentations *c.* 0.20m. long x 0.03m. deep were made on either side, between which a chase mortice was cut. Its base sloped from west to east for a depth of 0.08m. and was made to accommodate a 'raking' or supporting brace. The easternmost mortice

had a slanted post driven through it into the river silts to hold the baseplate in position.

A squared dowel hole with peg secured the northern subsidiary baseplate (360.3) in position. This was a squared oak timber, which was decayed at its eastern end. There were no surviving mortices, indentations or other markings on this subsidiary, and there was no corresponding mortice in the principal baseplate. It is likely that the northern subsidiary was inserted solely to secure the principal baseplate in position, as it would appear not to have had any function in bracing the verticals.

No shuttering associated with revetment 360 survived. The type of construction of this part of the revetment is typical of the 13th century wooden waterfront revetments excavated at Wood Quay (Wallace 1981, 109f: 1982, 281) and provides the only surviving evidence for a true front-braced revetment amongst the excavated examples at Patrick St. This method of bracing may have been em-

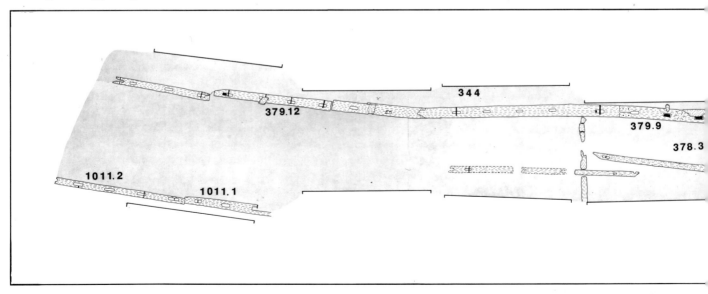

Fig. 28. Site F, level 3,

64

ployed at this particular point on the river Poddle to counter the added pressure to the structure as it followed the curve of the channel to feed into the town moat at St Nicholas's Gate.

The timbers immediately to the south of baseplate 360 were in a poor state of preservation, but do not appear to have been jointed into the northern baseplate. Timber 370 had slight evidence of shuttering, with badly fitted circular uprights crudely slotted into the rectangular through mortices. A third round post was driven through the shuttering on the west side of the baseplate. These uprights are unlikely to reflect the primary use of the structure, and more likely relate to the later refurbishment of this section of the structure (level 4).

Several timbers along the length of the structure were not jointed to the adjacent baseplates. Notable among these was timber 379.12, whose southern end was diagonally trimmed. The timbers to either end of this also had squarely trimmed unjointed butts. Where joints existed, these were simple through-splayed scarves, and had been laid from south to north. The jointed timbers 370.1 south to 379.3 were propped on stones or smaller timbers, and even the lid of a small barrel was employed for this purpose. These smaller timbers generally extended east/west beneath the baseplates, but short lengths of baseplates were aligned with and underneath the main structure. No timbers that could be interpreted as either front or rear braces were recovered, and certainly no mortices existed in the baseplates to indicate their original presence. Several of the timbers had evidently slipped from their original positions, but given the crudeness of the workmanship and the lack of joints and braces, it is astonishing that the structure could have stood for any significant length of time.

The stumps of only six uprights survived in this stretch of the revetment, although several of the mortices had tenons remaining in them.

The east side of the channel (Fig. 28)

Two baseplates with a total length of 5.80m. extended into the southern limit of excavation. Timber 1011.1 to the north had a diagonally trimmed south butt (similar to that of the timber directly opposite it at the west side of the river (379.12), which was oversailed by the scarfed north end of timber 1011.2. The timbers were not otherwise connected. The base of the river in this area shelved steeply downwards to the west, indicating that the edge of the channel lay just outside the excavated area. Soft brown organic silts (344) occurred behind the timber revetments, while the deposits (313) in the centre of the channel consisted of loose inorganic coarse gravels and sands with water-rolled pebbles. Mineral salts had coloured the entire deposit orange/brown. The finds from the channel were not stratified, and the deposit was remarkably uniform throughout. Pottery sherds, recovered in quantity, were often abraded.

The presence of two similar timbers with distinctive non-functional diagonally trimmed butts (379.12, 1011.1) directly opposite one another suggests that the revetments on both sides of the river channel were constructed simultaneously. Both timbers had no further evidence for their original usage and were not submitted for dendrochronological dating.

Timbers in the centre of the channel (Fig. 28)

Two connected baseplates, located 33.5m. to the south of revetment 360 and *c.* 2.5m. in from the edge of the river channel, occurred at a low level in the river gravels, and predate or are contemporary with the revetment on the west side of the channel.

The baseplates were connected by a well-formed through-splayed scarf joint with two face pegs. The south end of timber 382.2 was squared, while the north end of timber 382.1 was trimmed to take a scarf. Three through

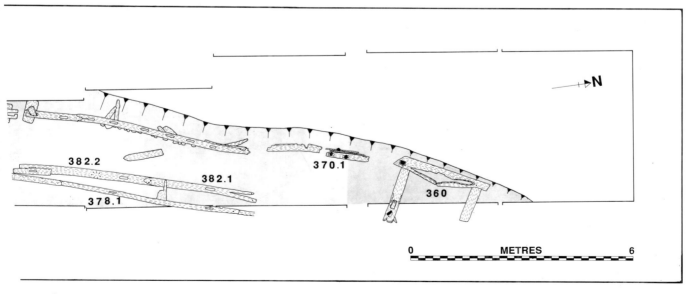

the extensions

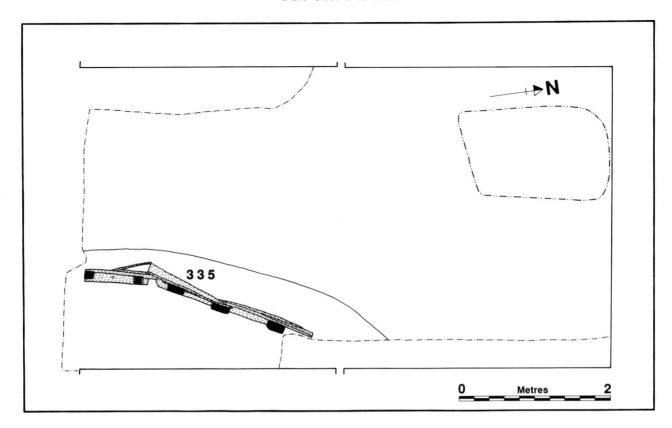

Fig. 29. Site F, level 4

Context	Intact	Conversion	Max. dimensions			Reused	Mortice
			Long (m.)	Wide (mm.)	Thick (mm.)		Spacing (cm.)
335.13	No	RSC	1.85	140	130	Yes	43
335.14	No	TC	0.92	180	120	Yes	52
360.01	No	RSC	2.7	230	145	No	79
370.02	No	?	1.39	190	DMG	No	60
370.03	No	RSC	2.99	160	140	Yes	73
370.04	Yes	?	1.16	180	100	No	25
372.00	Yes	?	3.6	120	130	No	60
375.00	No	?	1.08	200	100	No	–
378.01	Yes	RSC	4.42	120	120	Yes	238
378.02	Yes	TC	6.26	130	120	Yes	229
378.05	No	RSC	1.7	100	90	Yes	–
379.01	No	RSC	4.93	160	110	No	48
379.02	No	RSC	1.53	180	130	No	58
379.03	No	RSC	1.24	300	120	No	58
379.09	No	RSC	2.3	290	145	No	73
379.10	Yes	TC	5.23	315	130	No	75
379.11	Yes	RSC	0.95	250	65	No	–
379.12	Yes	TC	3.86	240	90	No	58
379.14	No	TC	2.54	190	70	No	40
382.01	Yes	TC	2.97	180	85	No	–
382.02	Yes	TC	3.62	210	90	No	229
386.00	Yes	RSC	1.01	170	150	No	–

Table 6. Timber dimensions, Site F

mortices were cut into the surface of the baseplates, with no uprights surviving.

The function of 382 remains an enigma, but it does not represent the east side of the river. If the baseplate held uprights, the structure would effectively divide the channel into two flows. This may have been related to some activity associated with the outfall into the town ditch to the north, or perhaps even a race for a mill further downstream. It seems likely that much of the structure had been 'robbed' in antiquity, probably when the timber alignment (378) was constructed.

Baseplate 378, composed of five scarfed and butted timbers, occurred 0.65m. higher in the river gravels than timbers 382. This extended for almost 16m. north/south, parallel with and 1.60m. east of the revetment on the west side of the river.

Timber 378.1 to the north was scarfed at both ends, and this section of the revetment had been laid from north to south. The north scarf was held by one face peg, while its southern scarf was not pegged into its neighbour. Both timbers 378.1 and 378.2 had been reused in this position. The mortices cut into the upper face of the baseplate were widely spaced, at intervals of *c.* 2.60m. The southern end of the baseplate was very fragmented, and it too had evidence of previous usage.

Three fragmentary and decayed timbers, which spanned the channel, appear to have formed an integral part of the parallel structure (378). All three timbers were very decayed (the middle timber (378.3) was identified as alder), and none showed any evidence of jointing or carpentry. The end of 378.3, where it overlay the western baseplate, appeared to have been cut straight. The beams underlay baseplate 378 in the centre of the channel. The function of the crossbeams is not apparent, and the lack of jointing and other fixtures, and the slenderness of the timbers, belies their usage as subsidiary baseplates or supports for a superstructure either projecting into or spanning the river channel. Were the timbers to have supported transverse boards, as has been suggested for beams spanning the river at Site D, this would have formed a crossing point measuring *c.* 3.5m. in width, and this seems quite unlikely. There was no silting apparent on the down-stream side of the timbers to indicate any significant obstruction of the flow.

The purpose of the parallel baseplate is similarly obscure. The structure is undoubtedly contemporary with the western revetment. In revetment G3 at Trig Lane, London (Milne and Milne 1978, 88), which dates to the late 13th or early 14th century, a continuous subsidiary baseplate, anchored by driven piles, was positioned 2m. from the principal baseplate. The shores or braces were connected by chased tenons to the verticals, and their ends into the subsidiary by bird's mouth abutments. This type of construction is evidently unsuitable for use in a narrow water channel, where a frontage clear of all obstructive front braces is desirable.

Level 4: revetment 335 (Fig. 29)

Some fifty years after revetment 360 was constructed, part of the structure at the north end of the excavation was rebuilt. The refurbished section measured 3.20m. in length, extending beyond the excavated area to the north. There is no evidence that the structure immediately to the south was refurbished at this stage, although it is likely that the upper revetment at Site D was constructed at the same time. The northernmost baseplate (335.13) accommodated three upright tenons, held in place by single rounded dowels hammered in from the river side. The three uprights survived to a height of between 0.18m.-0.30m. above the level of the baseplates.

A gap of 0.09m. separated the northern baseplate from baseplate 335.14 to the south, and neither was jointed in any way. The southern baseplate accommodated one upright post and one single-shouldered tenon. The post had for its most part rotted away at the centre but had been replaced by a slender upright post which did not penetrate the upper surface of the baseplate but was merely wedged into the centre of the post which it replaced, indicating a make-shift repair job. The two uprights survived to a height of between 0.23m.-0.30m. above the level of the baseplate (Fig. 30).

Both the north and the south baseplates showed signs

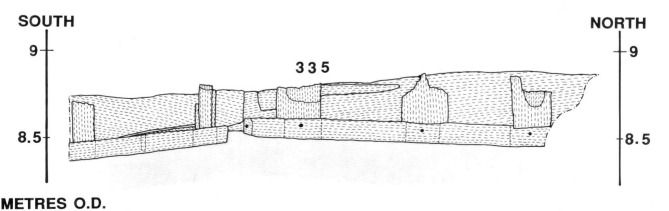

Fig. 30. Site F, elevation of revetment 335

of reuse. A non-functional dowel hole with peg was set into the sawn-off south end of the northern baseplate. The southern baseplate (335.14) showed signs of reuse by the presence of a non-functional dowel hole.

Five planks abutted the landward side of the baseplate (335.14), of which only two remained in good condition. When the shuttering was laid edge to edge in position, a deposit of brown organic silt and coarse gravel (344), containing fragmented cockle shell and hazelnuts, was banked in behind the planks. The planks were not nailed or dowelled together, and one of them had a non-functional dowel hole.

Level 5: stone revetting wall of the river Poddle (Fig. 31)

Several dumps of coarse gravel and clay (325, 323), containing large boulders, were deposited on the river bank, raising the ground level. These partially overlay the fill of the river channel. From the eastern extent of the boulders, the ground surface sloped gently towards the river and was covered by organic silt (321), and a thick deposit up to 0.50m. deep of mottled yellow clay, stones and silt (317).

In the south-east corner of the site, the construction trench for a stone retaining wall (310) cut through the eastern extent of the yellow clay (317). The wall was exposed for a maximum length of 2.40m., and was aligned on the underlying revetment (335). Its width varied be-

tween 0.60m.-0.80m. and it survived to a maximum height of 1.12m. (Fig. 24). Wall 310 was mortar-bonded and extremely well-faced on the river side, while its landward side was rough and showed no evidence for a regular edge. Groups of wooden piles (316) were driven into the clays on the river bank behind the wall.

Two parallel stone drains led downslope and fed into the river. Drain 306 to the south extended out from the west section face for *c.* 2.40m. The sides were intact, while only one capstone remained. It measured 0.16m.-0.20m. internally, and was filled with dark grey/green silt with a maximum depth of 0.09m. Several sherds of 14th century pottery (mostly Dublin wares) were recovered from the fill. The west to east gradient was 0.09m.

The east end of the drain had been disturbed by later activity. Two large stones blocked the channel of the drain, which stopped *c.* 0.20m. short of the river wall (310). There is no doubt, however, that the river wall predates the drain, as the construction trench for the wall was apparent only on removal of the drain.

The western extent of drain 312 had been truncated, and this stone-flagged gully survived only to a length of 1.10m. The drain was set into the river wall and had a slope of 0.09m. along its base. Several sherds of medieval Dublin ware were recovered from the silty fill of the drain.

The north end of a shallow charcoal-filled pit (309), which had a depth of only 0.09m., was located at the extreme south of the site. The pit measured 1.18m. east/

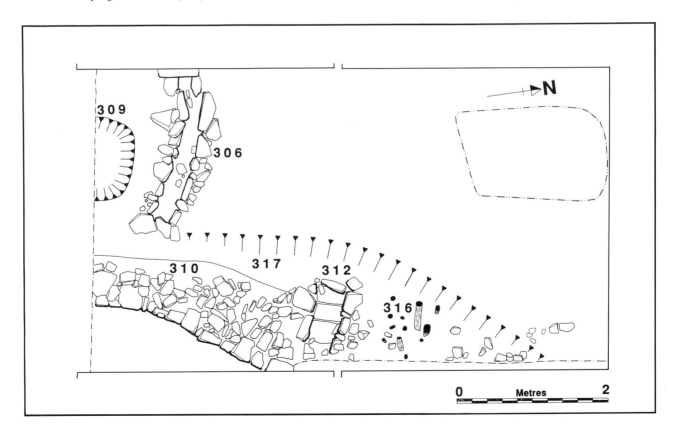

Fig. 31. Site F, stone wall of river

west x 0.48m. north/south, and is likely to have been cut from a higher level.

A later drain (303) (not illustrated), of probable late 14th or 15th century date, overlay part of 306. Oriented east/west, it extended for a length of 2.10m. and was located slightly further to the north than the underlying 306. Its northern side was truncated by later activity.

The pottery assemblage recovered from deposits overlying this level was a mixture of 14th century (or later) Dublin local wares and post-medieval (17th century or later) black wares.

The stone river wall (310) is likely to be contemporary with the stone wall (1133) at Site E (the mill) further upstream, which is dated to the later part of the 14th century. Traces of stone river wall of uncertain medieval date were uncovered at Sites B and C, while at Site D, where the opportunity was available more fully to investigate the standing culvert wall and its predecessors, there was no trace whatsoever of a stone medieval structure. It is possible that the securing of the banks of the river in

this manner was the sole responsibility of the riverside occupants, and the proximity of Site F to the town defences is also a factor which may have influenced the maintenance of the riverbanks.

Level 6: 18th century culvert wall

Located in the very south-east corner of the trench and extending into the eastern section face, a 3m. length of the mortar-bonded stone wall was exposed during machine clearance of the site. The wall partially overlay the 14th century constructions and was distinguishable from the earlier structure by its differing mortar and the many small stones which were used in its construction (Fig. 24).

Located *c.* 0.50m.–0.60m. to the east of the earlier wall, the culvert wall was built further into the medieval river channel, indicating the continual narrowing of the river channel since medieval times.

THE EXCAVATIONS: SITE G

A limited excavation through part of the city fosse was undertaken over a four week period in October/November 1991. The moat at Nicholas St measures *c*. 20m. in width. Due to pressure of time, an area measuring only 5.5m. north/south x 4.5m. east/west was made available for excavation. The intervening area to the south, towards Site F (excavated in 1990), which consisted largely of moat fill, was monitored during machine removal of deposits.

The excavated area became the relocated 'tunnel reception shaft'. Shoring suitable for deep excavation and tunnelling was installed before excavation began. This consisted of interlocking steel sheeting, retained behind a rigid timber frame. As the excavation progressed, the sheeting was mechanically driven deeper, and a continuous site section was maintained. A maximum depth of 6.7m. below the existing ground level was achieved.

The foundations and cellar fill of buildings of red-brick construction (Phase 7, below) were removed by mechanical excavator. Archaeological excavation began at a depth of 9.84m. O.D., and subsoil, which was deepest in the south-east corner of the excavation trench, was reached here at 5.74 m. O.D.

Level 1: cutting of the fosse (3038)

No deposits pre-dating the excavation of the town moat survived in this cutting. The site was located *c*. 4m south of the town wall (Fig. 2), the location of which was determined in two trial trenches carried out in March 1989 and February 1990.

The site contained part of the berm outside the town wall and the northern edge of the fosse. The northernmost part of the trench sloped gently southwards for 2.50m. at the west and for 0.50m. at the eastern side of the trench. Beyond this, the edge of the ditch shelved steeply southwards and at the eastern limit of the site plunged downwards both southwards and eastwards. Subsoil, consisting of a coarse, grey-stained gravel/till mix, was reached within the limits of excavation at a depth of

7.23m. O.D. at the west side (Fig. 32) and 5.74m. O.D. at the east side (Fig. 33).

Further south, where construction trenching was monitored, the ditch was flat based and had a maximum width of 20m.

The depth of deposits overlying subsoil at the northern part of the trench was 4.80m. below present ground level. The top of the town wall was reached at a depth of *c*. 3.30m below ground level in earlier test trenches, where it was seen that its southern face was badly damaged. The wall in this area, therefore, stands to a maximum height of 1.50m., and has a berm measuring 4.50m. in width.

The northwards curve of the berm of the ditch at the east side of the trench and the deepening of the ditch in this direction suggests that the berm is narrowing towards the town gate, sited beneath Nicholas St. Clarke's (1978)

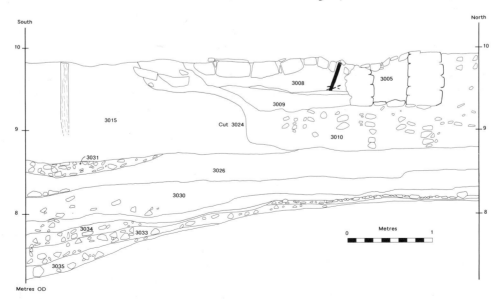

Fig. 32. Site G, west section

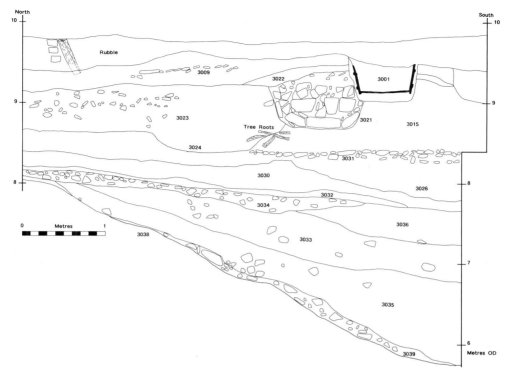

Fig. 33. Site G, east section

map of the walls of Dublin, based on Speed's map of 1610, shows the wall curving towards the north-east, so alternatively, the berm may simply be following the line of the wall. The ditch may be deepening here to receive the river Poddle, which flowed northwards along both sides of Patrick St and emptied into the moat in front of the gate.

Level 2: deposits filling the ditch (Figs 32 and 33)

Some erosion of the sides of the ditch was evident. The steeply sloping subsoil at the side of the ditch was overlain by a 0.12m. thick layer of grey/pink silty clay (3039) mixed with dark brown organic silt. This layer contained many angular stones and also patches of soft grey/white mortar. It is possible that the stones were spalls or chippings from the construction of the town wall. This slight evidence would emphasise the suggestion that the town wall and ditch were constructed in unison, with a new ditch at Patrick St by 1186 (McNeill 1950, 15) and a gate at the west of the city completed by 1200 (Barry 1987, 122).

A thick uniform deposit of dark brown peaty silt (3035), which measured a maximum of 0.95m. in thickness, accumulated over the stony fill (3039). Tip lines, consisting of tiny lenses of black silt striated the thick deposits, and all consistently fell from north to south.

This layer is stratigraphically equivalent to the bulk of organic silt fill (3037) encountered during construction trenching. Few finds, consisting of floor tiles, a fragment of copper and some leather, were recovered from this layer. The pottery comprised mainly local wares, cooking pots and glazed jugs, including a small, knobbed money box. Cliona Papazian (this vol.) suggests a 15th century date for the deposition of the pottery of level 2. This suggests that the fosse here was deliberately kept clean, indicating the strategic importance of the defences here. A block of grey/brown sand and gravel (3033), measuring a maximum of 0.55m. in depth in the excavated area, over-lay silts (3035). The sand and gravel is likely to have been water deposited, possibly from water flowing eastwards in the moat itself, or from water backing up in the moat, where the Poddle river fed in immediately to the east.

Possibly resulting from the wet conditions, a layer of grey/pink clay/marl (3034), with angular and rounded stones set into its upper surface, was thrown down over the accumulated fill, to form a wide path or roadway (Fig. 34). At the same time, a fairly thick accumulation of grey silty clay, lensed with dark organic silt, was thrown down across the sands/gravels (3033). The clays measured a maximum of 0.40m. in thickness, while the road or pathway measured up to 0.25m. in depth. The cobbles ex-tended southwards into the trench for 4m. at the east side of the trench. They too sloped sharply to the south and east, where the underlying silts had compacted. The stones used were primarily of slate and limestone, al-though rounded pebbles also occurred. Diameters varied from 0.06m-0.40m. Fragments of fairly robust grey/white mortar were also used as metalling – this occurred notice-ably on the eastern side of the trench.

A thin layer of firm brown silt, with many stones (3032), accumulated over the roadway. This layer was up to 0.10m. in depth and produced quantities of pottery

71

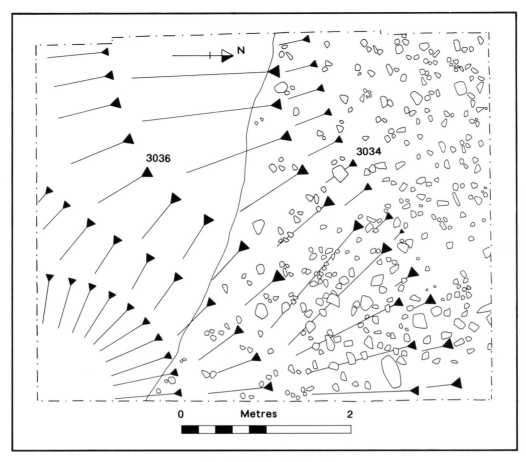

Fig. 34. Site G, level 2

(mainly local wares) and a large iron key. Building debris, including fragments of mortar, and roof and floor tiles, also came from this layer.

Discussion

By the 15th century, the ditch had been infilled to the level from which it had been cut. Much of the fill appears to have resulted from water deposition, and the area outside the ditch must have been flooded for some of the time and marshy for much of the rest. It is likely that the moat carried water from the west of the city eastwards, as suggested by Jackson (1950, 21). This water was an overflow from the mills of the Hospital of St John the Baptist without the New Gate, and flowed both northwards to the Liffey at Ushers Quay, and south-east to Patrick St. It no longer flowed in the ditch after the construction of James' Basin in 1721 (ibid., 22). It is shown on the 1673 (de Gomme) map of Dublin. The date of inception of this artificial watercourse is unclear, but Jackson points out that a lease of 1458 to the Hospital of St John's (C.A.R.D. I, 274) is a renewal of a previous lease.

Monitoring of construction trenching to the south of the excavation revealed that a thick deposit of grey marl *c.* 1.60m. thick overlay the lower, more organic fill of the ditch, which had a depth of *c.* 1.50m. This would occur,

more or less on the same level as marl/clay 3036, suggesting perhaps that what was encountered in the excavated trench is the tail end of a bank.

The purpose of this bank could be to raise the sides of the watercourse in an area prone to flooding. Subsequently, a road or pathway was constructed on the townward side of the bank.

The confluence of two watercourses at St Nicholas's Gate can certainly account for the archaeological evidence which indicates that the ditch deposits were primarily waterborne. At Cornmarket, excavated in 1992 by Alan Hayden, the town fosse was re-cut in the 15th century: this cut was faced with mortared stones walls and acted as a watercourse. Excavation of the town fosse at Bridge St Upper, also in 1992, showed that the town fosse in this area had acted as a watercourse since its construction (A. Hayden, pers. comm.).

Level 3

Thick deposits of organic silt accumulated over the roadway (3034) and covered the entire site. The underlying level (3030) measured 0.40m. in maximum thickness and contained a high quantity of stones. The silt was quite compact and did not contain visible moss, ferns and the usual urban detritus. Instead, tiny non-continuous lenses

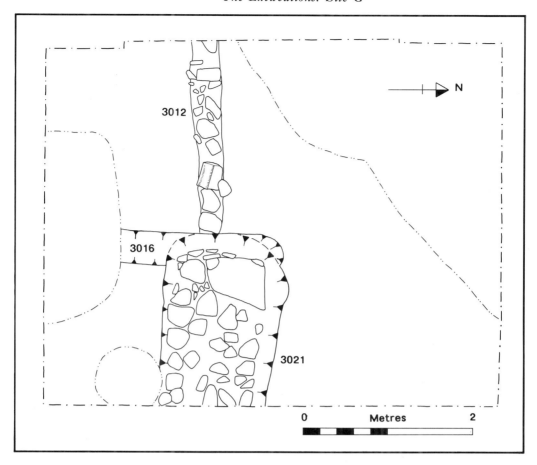

Fig. 35. Site G, level 5

of fine gravel and sand occurred throughout, and 'settling' lenses of black silt were visible. This layer was evidently water deposited. Pottery, almost exclusively of local origin, was present in abundance.

A thick layer of more organic dark brown silt (3026) (see 'Plant Remains'), with a maximum depth of 0.50m., was deposited over the entire site. Fragments of wood, insect carapaces and occasional pockets of moss were visible throughout the silt. Lenses of pure silt and fine gravel had washed through the deposit, which had a highly sulphurous smell. On the western side of the excavation trench, a dump of leather fragments and garments – waste from a cobbler's workshop – had been cast into the ditch fill.

Pottery from this layer was numerous, again consisting almost entirely of local wares. Two of the sherds had been shaped to form counters probably for gaming purposes. Two floor tiles (two-colour type) which had also been shaped into round counters, were recovered from this layer. Other finds were roof and floor tiles and a copper and bronze 'Jew's Harp' buckle.

At the southern end of the excavation trench, a layer of cobbles (3031) was set down into silt (3026). The stones used included angular chippings of limestone and granite, but consisted mainly of slate and incorporated several roof slates. The maximum north/south extent of the cobbles was 2.50m.: this feature was not discernible during monitoring of construction trenching. The cobbles formed a roughly level surface and were evidently part of a path or roadway extending east/west over the infilled ditch.

Level 4

A thick deposit of grey/brown compacted clay silt (3015) with a maximum depth of 0.90m. was thrown down over the pathway (3031). The clay was relatively stone free and inorganic, producing few finds, including many fragments of floor tiles. All the pottery sherds from this layer were small and comprised mainly local wares.

The clay silt represents a rapid, deliberate deposition of soil, the purpose of which was probably to raise the level of the banks of the watercourse. The soil did not survive over the northern part of the trench: whether this is because later features cut into the clay silt, or because it was deposited as a bank, and simply tailed off along this line, is uncertain. The northern edge of the clay/silt deposit was heavily rooted – indeed the stump of an alder tree (3025) was present, and its roots spread along the sides of the deposit of clay (3031).

The dump of clay (3015) constitutes the division between the underlying medieval layers and overlying post-medieval deposits. This section of the infilled ditch was evidently scrubby, open ground: unfortunately a ring

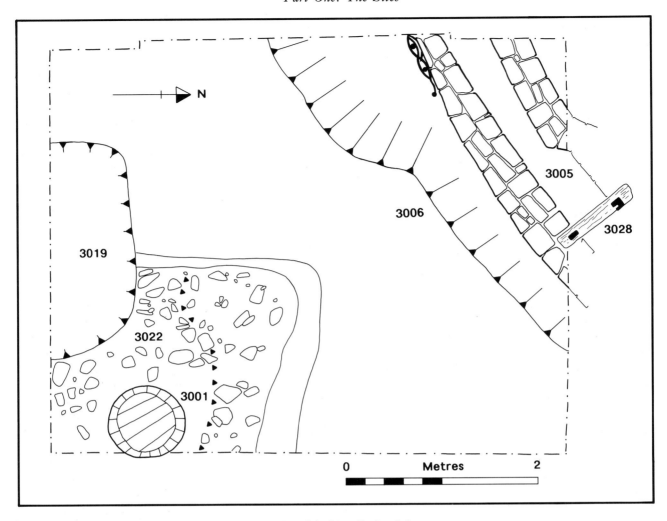

Fig. 36. Site G, level 6

count of the tree stump was not possible, as the growth was diffuse porous. Pottery from the overlying levels, however, indicate that dumping and other activities began over clays (3015) by the end of the 16th century (Rosanne Meenan, this vol.).

Level 5: late 16th–mid-17th centuries (Fig. 35)

The area to the north of clay silts 3015 was infilled with a series of tips of ashy dumps, organic waste and general domestic debris (3023, 3010). This material accumulated to a depth of 0.75m. The pottery assemblage comprised sgraffito, Spanish, black wares, stonewares and glazed earthenwares, with many sherds of residual local wares also present. Other finds include a copper alloy spoon of late medieval type (E543:3010:62), leather shoes and a Nuremberg jeton in mint condition, produced between 1586 and 1635 (E543:3010:59). Small handmade, red bricks were also recovered from this dumped material.

The rear of a building (3020), or annex to a main structure which probably fronted on to Nicholas St,

extended into the eastern side of the excavation trench. Only the north and south walls were exposed. Both walls had been largely robbed or levelled and only the foundation trenches remained. The wall (3021) to the north was quite substantial, measuring 1.30m. in width, and 2.00m. in length, with a depth of 0.55m. The stones (all limestone) were heavily bonded with hard white mortar. The footing consisted of large flat-topped stones, varying in size from 0.10m. in diameter to 0.70m.

The wall stood to a maximum of 0.35m. above the footing, which projected for a distance of 0.30m. on its northern side and was flush on the south side. The west wall (3016) was represented by a trench up to 0.40m. in depth, which extended for 1.95m. north/south. It was cut through at its southern end by a later pit. The trench measured 0.60m. in width and had an uneven base. It was filled with fragments of hard white lime up to 0.15m. in diameter, slates, limestones and yellow sandy mortar in a matrix of brown organic silt.

An alignment of limestone blocks (3012) extended westwards from trench 3016. The stones, up to 0.30m. in diameter, were firmly set into underlying clay silt. A carved stone (E543:3012:1) was reused in the alignment.

The stones may have been the footing for a property wall extending westwards from the rear of the building.

A thick spread of white mortar and slate (3022), up to 0.10m. in thickness, was deposited over the area enclosed by trench 3016 and wall footing 3021. This sealed the construction cut of wall 3021. Some of the mortar may have originally formed the floor of the building, but was spread over the area, and sealed wall trench 3016.

No finds were recovered from any of the features described above.

Level 6 (Fig. 36)

When the small building of level 5 had gone out of use, the area was utilised for a different purpose. Grey/brown silt (3009) with a high organic content accumulated over the mortar floor (3022) and occurred also to the north of the trench. The silt had a maximum depth of 0.16m. Fragments of handmade red brick and 17th century pottery – Bellarmine stonewares, earthenwares and slipwares – were recovered from this layer.

A wooden stave-built bucket (3001) was set into a pit dug through the silt (3009). The pit for the bucket measured 0.82m. in width and 0.50m. in depth. The bucket was a complete straight-sided vessel, wider at its upper end. (0.73m. inner diameter, 0.76m. outer diameter), constructed of eighteen staves (3004), which had a maximum height from the groove to the rim of 0.43m. The base was 0.66m. in diameter and was composed of five pieces.

The groove in the base of the staves was cut with a white cooper's croze to accommodate the base (Frank Ryan, pers. comm.) The staves and base were of oak, radially cut, while the two outer binding hoops were of ash (wood identification by Sarah Cross).

The lower fill of the barrel was a soft white paste (3003), which adhered to the staves and base of the bucket and filled it to a depth of 0.16m. Analysis of a sample (Appendix 3) showed that the material consisted almost entirely of calcite, $CaCO_3$. Over time, lime (CaO) will absorb carbon dioxide to form calcite. Animal bone recovered from the white fill was soft and bleached. One of the uses of lime was in tawing, or dehairing hides, which was fundamental to the tanning process.

A group of wooden buckets and a trough were recorded during test trenching at a development site immediately to the west of the excavation site in 1991 (A. Hayden, pers. comm.). They were sunk into the fill of the ditch and were of post-medieval date. The three buckets and rectangular trough had similar fills of soft brown organic silt with c. 50 per cent wood chip and bark content. A thin skim of a white concreted substance – possibly lime – was evident on the basal stones of each of the wooden buckets and the trough.

This group lay approximately 15m. to the west of the recent excavation. It is likely that bucket 3001 is part of a larger group located further to the east. The upper fill of the bucket consisted of soft brown organic silt (3002)

which contained fragments of red brick. A sherd of 17th century stoneware was recovered from this fill.

Possibly contemporary with the barrel, a stone-built drain (3005) was constructed, which cut obliquely across the northern part of the excavation area. The drain was set in a wide trench (3006), the fills of which (3007, 3008) produced large quantities of 17th–18th century pottery and leather shoes. The drain had cut away a length of upstanding wattle fencing (3013), which survived for a distance of only 0.80m. at the west side of the site. The wattle stood to a height of less than 0.35m. Only three posts and a few strands survived. The stone drain led from the north east to the south west. It was stone flagged, with a channel measuring 0.40m. in width, and walls which stood to a height of 0.56m. above the floor. There were no capstones.

When the shoring was adjusted during excavation, a timber sluice gate (3028), which had stood at the eastern end of the drain, beyond the area of excavation, was revealed. This consisted of three worked pieces of oak, the largest of which (3028:1) was placed lengthways across the drain floor. Two mortices were cut into its upper surface, and shouldered uprights were dowelled into these housings. The uprights were sited to lie flush with the walls of the drain, which had widened at this juncture. One of the timbers had a groove or rebate cut along its length to hold the gate of the sluice. The other timber was decayed along this side. The uprights stood to a maximum height of 0.48m. above the baseplate. All the timbers had slight lime staining on them. The drain was infilled with a mineralised, orange/brown gravel, which produced large quantities of 18th century pottery.

The presence of the sluice mechanism in the drain is surprising, as it would seem to have been unlikely that water in the moat would have risen this high. The drain does not appear to have been related to any industrial function: rather, it may have lead from a building adjacent to St Nicholas's Gate, which by the mid-18th century (1763) was rented by the Corporation to Robert Rochford for £4 a year (Healy 1990, 187).

Also dating to this level was a large, vertically sided, ovoid pit (3019) which partially extended into the southern side of the excavation site. The pit measured 2.46m. in width, narrowing slightly towards the base, and 0.54m. in depth. The lower fill of the pit (3018) was a 0.28m. thick deposit of grey clay silt, lensed with dark brown organic matter. Sulphurous, grassy material resembling stabling muck (3017) formed a 0.30m. thick dump over the clay. A sherd of glazed earthenware was recovered from this material, which was sampled (see 'The Plant Remains'). Capping the pit was a levelling dump of pale grey clay marl (3011) with a depth of 0.18m.

The pit does not appear to be related to the wooden bucket (3001) described above. The clay fill at the base did not continue up the sides, and the main body of fill may have derived from stabling waste.

Level 7

This relates to the construction of red-brick cellar buildings along the present alignment of Nicholas St/Patrick St, probably sometime in the 19th century. This area came under the scrutiny of the Wide Street Commissioners in 1824, which probably dates the demolition of both St Patrick's and St Nicholas's Gates. Monitoring of construction trenches along the length of the present roadway has shown the presence of demolished buildings beneath the present road surface.

Cellar and demolition rubble measured 2.5m.–2.7m. below present ground level. The south wall of the cellar, which overlay the excavation site, was constructed on a series of oak piles (3029). These varied from 0.90m.–1.60m., and were all squared or rectangular in section, with pointed bases. Two of the piles had dowel holes, indicating the reuse of earlier timbers. The eastern or streetwards wall of the cellar was constructed on an oak beam (over 3.30m. in length) in a decayed condition, which was a structural timber reused from an earlier building.

PATRICK STREET:
SUMMARY AND CONCLUSIONS

The reappraisal of the surviving historical records in the light of recent archaeological evidence has resulted in a clearer picture of the Patrick St area in the medieval period. A date in the mid-13th century has formerly been accepted for the rerouting of the Poddle, but it is apparent from the excavations and from a review of the historical sources that these works were carried out at a considerably earlier period, and a date *c*. 1185 can now be taken with certainty. The scale of the new engineering works initiated by the Anglo-Normans is better understood when considering the events of the later 12th century in terms of differing interests: the town defences; the maintenance of a water source, particularly for the powering of mills and the expansion of the Cathedral of St Patrick. The extensive historical evidence and background to the area is detailed earlier, 'Historical Background to the Patrick Street Excavations' (pages 17-33).

Town defences

The northern limit of the excavations approached within an estimated 5m. of the town wall at the south side of the town. The position of the town wall in this area was determined in a machine trial trench (Fig. 37) which was undertaken in advance of the excavation programme, the purpose of which was solely to record the depth of modern debris overlying medieval deposits. The position of the town wall and the outer limit of the town fosse in this area are depicted in Fig. 37. The fosse in this location measures *c*. 20m. in width. The limekiln at Site F, constructed through a *c*. 1m. depth of redeposited boulder clay, may have been associated with the refurbishment of the town defences, which action predates the channelling of the river in this area. Further excavation of the town defences at the south side of the town were undertaken by F. Hurley in 1992 in the adjacent development site, and by the writer and A. Hayden at a development site at Ross Rd.

Although scant evidence for dwellings or other medieval activity along the banks of the river Poddle survived, it could be inferred that a sizeable population existed outside, solely from the sheer quantity of refuse cast into the river channel along the length of Patrick St. The wood-lined drain or sewer at Site F (level 3), dating to the late 12th century, must have led from a dwelling a short distance upslope of the river. Much of the rubbish which accumulated in the river was probably brought out of the town by the inhabitants and tipped (illegally) into the stream (Keene 1982, 28). This character of the river is perhaps reflected in two of the medieval names for the watercourse: the Salogh, from the Irish 'salach' meaning dirty, and its anglicised form, the Puddle or Poddle (Carroll 1954, 156). The defensive fosse, in contrast to the watercourse, appears to have been deliberately kept clean, possibly into the 15th century, reflecting the strategic importance of the defences at this location.

Medieval Nicholas Street

During construction trenching across Nicholas St, east of Site F (Fig. 37), a paved level, occurring approximately 2m. below present ground level (10.23m. O.D.), was briefly exposed. The paving covered an area measuring *c*. 1.30m. north/south x 1m. east/west. A reasonably level surface was formed by limestone flags measuring up to 0.40m. in diameter, which were bedded in a *c*. 0.30m. thick deposit of gravel. Smaller stones filled the interstices between the flags.

The paving had a distinct edge along the west side where the ground level sloped steeply away, indicating that the roadway had been built up like a causeway. The paving overlay a thick layer of dark, organic silt up to 3m. in depth, which overlay bedrock. No finds were recovered. It was overlain by modern rubble and hardcore.

At the west of the trench, the timbers at the east side of the river continued into the section, while the post-medieval west wall of the culvert curved across the trench. It seems likely that the organic deposits encountered in the machine cutting were filling the southern lip of the town fosse. The paved level obviously dates to a later stage, as it overlay the ditch fill. The causeway across the fosse to St Nicholas's Gate was probably much narrower than the street.

St Patrick's Cathedral

No evidence of activity connected with the early settlement of 'St Patrick's *in Insula*' was recovered, and few artefacts significantly pre-dating the Anglo-Norman colonisation were recovered. Three bracteates of early to mid-12th century date came from the lower deposits at the south end of Patrick St. These coins or tokens are not attributable to any known authority, but did not continue in circulation into the Anglo-Norman period (M. Kenny, pers. comm.). The assemblage of pottery from the associated deposits at

Site A includes Dublin types more usually dated to the late 12th or 13th centuries. The nature of the river silts has been previously discussed, and no secure stratification of river-rolled material can be expected.

Elsewhere, finds such as the parchment pricker (E543: 1101:68) and floor tiles, more usually associated with religious establishments, occurred amongst the general domestic refuse that accumulated in the river. These are all of 13th century or later date.

During monitoring of construction works along the west side of Patrick St, the granite pier of a small bridge was noted on the east side of the stream, in the area directly opposite the west doorway of St Patrick's Cathedral. The bridge is not shown on Kendrick's survey of this plot, dated 1757, although a bridge across the east stream leading to the north close of the cathedral is depicted. It presumably is not later, as the stream was partly culverted at this point, and could therefore date to the medieval period. This area was known as 'Cross Poddle'.

The river channel

The river was diverted from its original course, to run northwards instead of east across the plain in the area immediately west of St Patrick's Cathedral. The river was coursed in two artificial channels on either side of Patrick St in the late 12th century. The reasons for the rerouting are discussed in detail in Chapter 1. The conclusions are that the works arose from the diversion of the Dodder water into the Poddle, resulting in a huge increase in the volume of water carried in the small stream bed, which would effectively have flooded the entire plain on which St Patrick's Cathedral now stands. The added usage of the increased volume of water as a defence mechanism is

parallelled at a later date by the diversion of the City Watercourse overflow, the Glib stream, into the town fosse at Newgate (Jackson 1950, 21). The original stream course is likely to have deposited large banks of silt over the plain, a particular problem with small or intermittent streams (Keene 1982, 26), carving over time several channels across the level plain. Prior to its rerouting, the Poddle meandered between widely spaced contours (Simms 1990, 43) with two branches forming an island in the plain on which St Patrick's Cathedral is sited.

While Ronan (1927, 42) has observed that the re-routed upper reaches of the Poddle, as it flowed on a *c.* 3-mile diversion through the lands of St Thomas' Abbey, appear to have been deliberately chosen to create falls for the various mills along its route, the channel along the west side of Patrick St was actually sited along a slightly higher contour than its natural course had taken (Clarke 1990a, 66). The fall in the base of the river channel from Dean St (Site B) to the mill at Site E is less than 1m., and it does not seem that the channel was created deliberately for the purposes of powering a mill. The excavation results have shown that utilisation of the watercourse for this purpose occurred at least forty years after the channel had been rerouted, with the construction of the mill at Site E sometime after 1235.

We have speculated that the western extent of the original river course or flood plain was delimited within the excavated area of Site C (level 1). North of Site C, the river channel was dug through the underlying boulder clays in what was evidently a man-made channel. Surprisingly little erosion of the sides of the watercourse had occurred (Site D, level 1; Site F, level 1). At Site D, the full width of the river was recorded at 6m.

Little survived of the earthen bank which would have been piled on either side of the river channel – this had been largely cut away at Site D by the construction of the

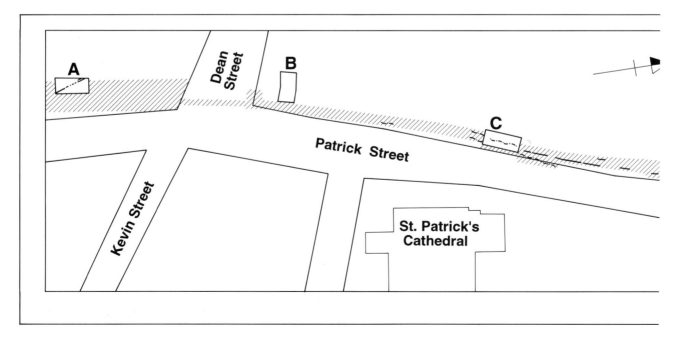

post-medieval river wall (Fig. 16). At Site E (level 1) the embankment had a minimum height of 1m., while at Site F, successive deposits of boulder clays had raised the original ground level on the west side of the river by at least 0.90m. (Fig. 24).

The post and wattle fence at Site C was built freestanding along the western limit of the floodwaters of the original course of the Poddle, and clays and silts were embanked on the east side of the fence. A corresponding post and wattle fence was observed during construction on the west side of the river in this area (Fig. 37). The line of the west fence was continued, at a later date, by the lower revetment at Site D of baseplate and plank construction, northwards to Nicholas St, where the river curved eastwards to spill into the town moat. Almost 122m. of adjoining revetments were uncovered, with the line of the timbers along the west side of the river broken only where the mill was constructed some forty years later.

The revetments

The construction of the early revetment is simple, with only the through-splayed-and-pegged scarf joint used to extend the baseplate. In several cases, particularly where the structure nears the town moat, no jointing is used, with the timbers merely butted against one another. The instance of reuse of timbers is also significantly higher further north. Front bracing, in a similar technique to that employed in revetment 1 at Wood Quay (Wallace 1982, 275), was evident only at the northern end of the excavated area, where the curving placement of the timbers is likely to have increased the lateral pressure on the structure. Revetment 1 at Wood Quay, dated by dendrochronology to 1210, stood to a height of at least 1.75m. and was consolidated to the rear by 'tons of gravel, estuarine mud,

and redeposited urban refuse' (Wallace 1984, 120). The original height of the structure of Patrick St is unknown, but it is unlikely to have stood much higher than 1.20m. and would not have had significant lateral pressure brought upon it. The common system of front bracing employed throughout Europe in the 13th century (Milne and Hobley 1981) would have significantly impeded water flow in a narrow water channel, but it is apparent that the structure must have been braced in some form. Where plank shuttering survived, this was kept vertical only by the pressure of accumulated silts to the front and rear of the structure.

The poor survival of structural uprights, coupled with the severe truncation of the embanked material to the landward side of the revetments, means that a plausible reconstruction of the bracing system is pure hypothetical.

Back-braced revetments or palisades are recorded from the Wood Quay excavations from the 10th through to the 13th centuries, using variations on a simple method (Wallace 1981, 116; 1982, 273). The later 13th century revetment (Wallace 1981, 116) was anchored on its landward side by a horizontal tieback threaded through the upright posts. This was secured at the outside by a wedging post, and on the landward side a post was driven through the tieback into the ground. As neither the uprights nor the ground level contemporary with the revetments at Patrick St survive, this reconstruction of the bracing method is speculative (Fig. 38). The lower level of revetments at Patrick St were constructed in piecemeal fashion, probably by the individual owners of the properties along the west bank of the stream. The properties are likely to have varied considerably in width: the entry in Archbishop Alen's *Register* for the year 1336 records a grant of land on the east side of Patrick St to Walter le Gret, clock maker, which was 55ft wide in front, and 66ft wide at the rear (MacNeill 1950, 203). There is

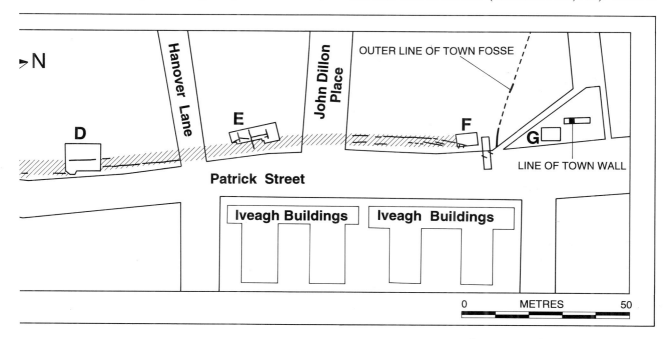

Fig. 37. Patrick Street: the revetments

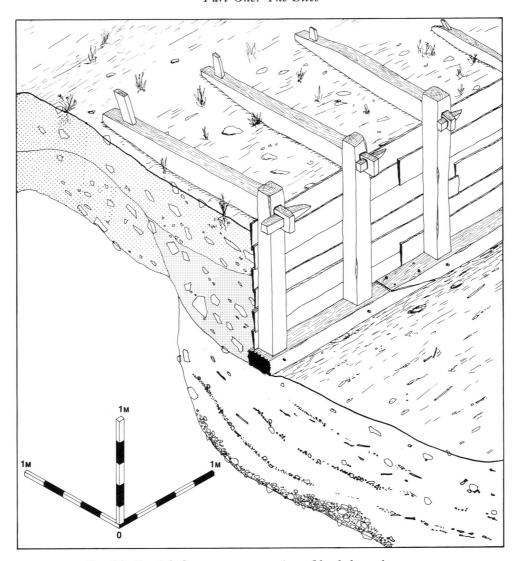

Fig. 38. Patrick Street: reconstruction of back-braced revetment

little archaeological evidence for this division of properties, and no documentary references to revetments on the
river at Patrick St survive from the medieval period.
Nonetheless, construction of the revetments is likely to
have been instigated as a response to flooding of the
street. Coleman's brook, an overflow stream for the City
Watercourse within the city walls and under the city's
jurisdiction, is better documented. Here, levies for cleans-
ing the stream are mentioned in the later 16th century,
and those who lived about the stream were bound to build
up as much of the river walls as extended to their lands
(Berry 1891, 565).

The second level of revetments is more likely to have
been built by the owner of the mill and is perhaps directly
attributable to it. A new series of revetments was constructed upstream of the mill (Site D, level 3), while the
archaeological evidence shows that downstream of the
mill, less importantly for the workings of the mill, the
timber revetments here were only partly refurbished (Site
F, level 4). Later still, in the 14th century, the riverbanks
were partly walled in stone.

Little evidence for the mill pond, depicted on Speed's
map at the north end of New St/Dean St, was forthcoming from the excavations, although it is suggested that the
timbers recovered from Site A may represent the west
side of such a pond. The main part of the mill pond would,
therefore, lie beneath the present roadway intersection.
The considerable archaeological evidence for flooding at
Site B appears initially to pre-date the construction of the
mill in the mid-13th century, and probably resulted more
from the confluence of the Coombe stream with the
Poddle proper at this low-lying place. By the 14th century
at least, the ground at this point was raised by successive
dumps of clay, and a cobbled pathway extended along the
west bank. Some evidence for industrial activity, perhaps
tanning, is indicated by the presence of a small oak-lined,
flag-bottomed vat by the river's edge. A further group of
sunken barrels along the west side of the riverbank
between Sites B and C also appear to have been used for
this purpose. The ground at Site B may have been somewhat drained by the presence, at a short distance to the
south, of the pond for the mill.

THE PATRICK STREET WATERMILLS

Their technological context and a note on the reconstruction

Colin Rynne

The vertical undershot waterwheel, as has recently been established, was already in use in Ireland as early as the 7th century AD (Rynne 1989), but up until the excavation of the Patrick St site (and despite the existence of comprehensive documentary evidence for the Anglo-Norman lordship for vertical-wheeled feudal mills), it has not featured in the archaeological record for the Anglo-Norman period. Both horizontal and vertical-wheeled mills were quite common in Ireland throughout the medieval period (Rynne 1988), and while the archaeological evidence for water-powered mills in the early medieval period (particularly for horizontal-wheeled mills) is impressive, the sites involved thus far have been exclusively associated with rural environments. With the evolution and growth of population centres based on Viking trading ports, however, came the necessity of establishing watermills within reach of urban areas and with it the need to adapt to different hydrological conditions. In both medieval Dublin and Cork, for example, which were both established on tidal rivers, water-powered mills tended to avoid their tidal reaches and were established on tributaries which traversed higher ground overlooking the towns before discharging into the river. By the later medieval period, these natural water channels became extensively regularised, with construction of hydro-power dams, the formation of mill ponds, and ultimately became canalised, as the Patrick St mill site clearly demonstrates.

As will be seen below, the Patrick St mill site provides us with valuable insights into the type of watermill likely to have been established near medieval Irish towns like Cork and Dublin. In such conditions the preferred option may often have been to position the millwheel directly over the stream bed where suitable falls were available, thus obviating the need to build weirs to raise the water level. Indeed the construction of mill weirs on spate rivers like the Poddle may also have increased the dangers of flooding, where in any case the available flow may have been sufficient to power a succession of undershot mills established along its course.

The level 1 mill

The headrace

Beam 1121 (Fig. 17), which appears to have been in its original position, defined the western end of the headrace or inlet channel, which directed incoming water into the feeder trough (see below). It was not contiguous with the western soleplate of the feeder trough, and this would suggest that the inlet channel was angled backwards upon itself upstream. This hypothesis is largely confirmed by the stone headrace wall of the level 2 mill, which also angled outwards from the later feeder trough.

The feeder trough

The operational head of the level 1 mill was retained in what appears to have been a plank-lined trough, which would originally have formed an apex with a similarly placed beam at the east. Incoming water would have been retained here under pressure before being admitted into the wheel casing or plank-lined trough positioned underneath the waterwheel. Traditionally, undershot waterwheels operate with high water velocities, typically around 1.5m./sec. (Reynolds 1983, 11), with an increased fall being provided for the inlet channel in the area immediately beneath the waterwheel. The transverse soleplate (1127) is likely to have positioned a sluice gate, but the fall from this to the wheel casing would have been slight, as indeed was the angle at which the wheel casing was inclined from the horizontal. We must assume, therefore, that either the build-up of water pressure in the feeder trough was sufficient to compensate for this, or that the millwright was unaware of the benefits of doing so.

The waterwheel casing

The area enclosed by the parallel beams (1134, 1145), which would have originally been entirely floored with planks laid along the long axis of the channel, suggests that this feature was the lower casing or trough for a vertical undershot waterwheel. The casing was over 3.6m. long, and *c.* 0.90m. wide, which would suggest a wheel diameter of between 2.5m.-3m., slightly less than 0.90m. wide, depending of course on the closeness of the fit of the rim of the waterwheel and the inner faces of the casing, and whether or not the floats on the periphery of the waterwheel were shrouded (see below).

Two of the mortices on the beam defining the northern extremity of the casing (1143) are likely to have functioned as a sluice outlet. In normal circumstances the desired effect would be to allow the water to escape from beneath the wheel as quickly as possible so as not to impede its rotation. The likely existence of such a feature raises the question of whether provision for a bypass was originally present. Such a provision seems likely, either in the mill pond or in the vicinity of the feeder trough, both to direct water around the millworks when the mill was not in use and to prevent flooding (see below). But if flooding in the tailrace was a constant problem, water 'backing up' it may have periodically damaged the waterwheel, unless steps were taken to protect the channel directly beneath the waterwheel. The excavator noted that the waterwheel casing was provided with a fall of only 0.10m. from the south to the north, which probably reduced the outfall velocity of water passing beneath the waterwheel. Furthermore, the profile of the outfall for the mill suggests that the stream bed to the north of the wheel casing had not been sufficiently modified to facilitate a rapid runoff of water exiting from the waterwheel. In the 13th century the gradient of the outfall of the mill beyond the area of excavation may well have been sufficient to ensure that water leaving the wheel casing did so in such a way that it did not impede the rotation of the waterwheel. Yet if flooding was a problem (particularly during winter months), the bypass channel and the outfall may not have been able to prevent water backing up the tailrace channel, and in such conditions the provision of an outlet sluice for the level 1 mill may well have been necessary.

The mill building

The arrangement of the basal plates in the level 1 mill suggests that the gear pit was to the west of the wheel casing. The gear pit served two purposes. Its western wall is likely to have supported one of the gudgeons or axle bearings of the waterwheel, whilst the area enclosed by it would have allowed sufficient clearance for the pit wheel, the gear wheel positioned on the waterwheel's axle and set immediately beneath the lantern pinion. The latter component would have engaged the pit wheel at right angles (Fig. 39), and its drive shaft would have been tied to the spindle, an iron power-take-off device. A T-shaped bar attached to the upper end of the spindle would have been slotted into the lower face of the upper millstone, through which the motion of the vertical drive shaft would have been communicated to the upper or runner stone (see below).

The absence of the gear pit in the level 1 mill, as the excavator has suggested, is likely to have resulted from the construction of the level 2 mill, whose foundations were built with stone. The foundations of the level 1 mill, however, may well have been set on soleplates, or indeed, earthfast. In either case some provision would have to have been made to retain the redeposited material used to build up the bank of the stream. The transverse soleplates (1128, 1127), are likely to have extended into the banks of the stream to provide extra lateral support for the penstock and for the foundation of the mill house, a practice found at nearly all of the contemporary mill sites recorded elsewhere (see below). The composite beam (1143), by way of contrast, appears not to have been subject to the same stresses as the other transverse beams, and needed only to be held in place by driven posts.

The level 2 mill

The complete rebuilding of the mill in the second half of the 14th century copied some of the principal features of the 13th century mill, but this stage in the evolution of the site was accompanied by substantial stone revetment walls for the inlet and outlet channels. The latter provide some important clues as to the relationship of the mill to the original stream bed. As was indicated above, the position of the western soleplate (1121) of the headrace was followed with the construction of the later headrace revetment wall (1105), although the angle in this instance was slightly more acute. There can be little doubt that the mill building itself was built on the western bank of the stream in each of the main phases of its use. The waterwheel in each phase was suspended over a modified section of the stream bed, and as has been seen above, a large transverse soleplate in level 1 (1127) seems likely to have extended into the eastern bank of the stream. What, then, became of the eastern section of the original stream bed? If, as seems likely, the mill was built on one side of an existing watercourse, with its inlet and outfall channels constructed parallel to it, then the eastern section of the channel could be deliberately narrowed by the construction of further revetments, or left narrowed by the construction of further revetments, or left open. The results of the excavation suggest that there is no evidence that the eastern section of the stream bed beyond the feeder trough and wheel casing, in either phase, was deliberately narrowed. However, the construction of casings in each of the main phases must surely have interrupted the water flow across the entire width of the stream. And if this were the case, the eastern part of the stream bed may have been put to use as a bypass channel, which directed water away from the mill when it was not in use.

A further refinement of the level 2 mill (and one which may never have been present in the 13th century mill) is the lining of the bed of the headrace with boards, a practice investigated at a number of contemporary English sites. But the most remarkable survival of the level 2 mill

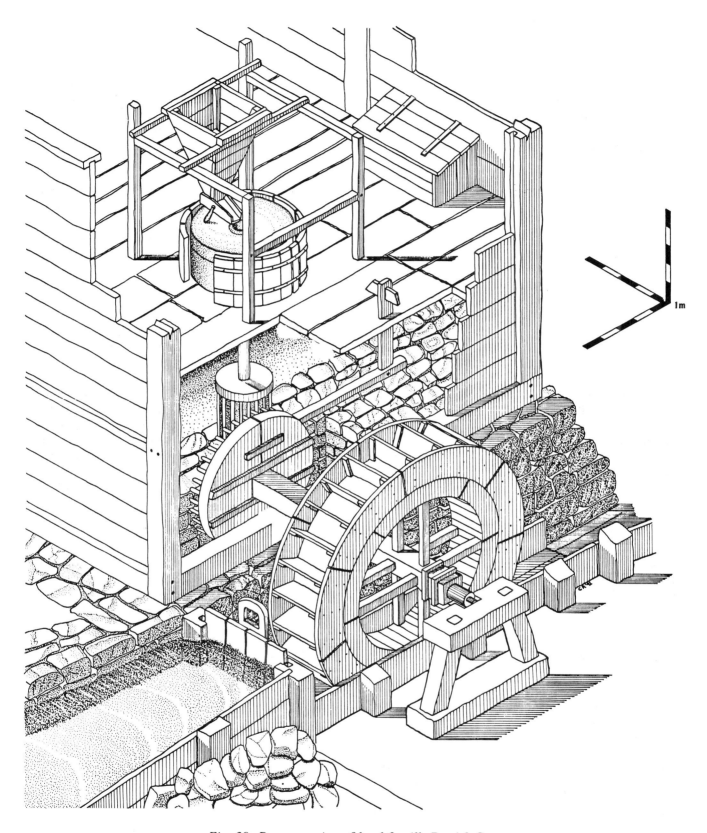

Fig. 39. Reconstruction of level 2 mill, Patrick Street

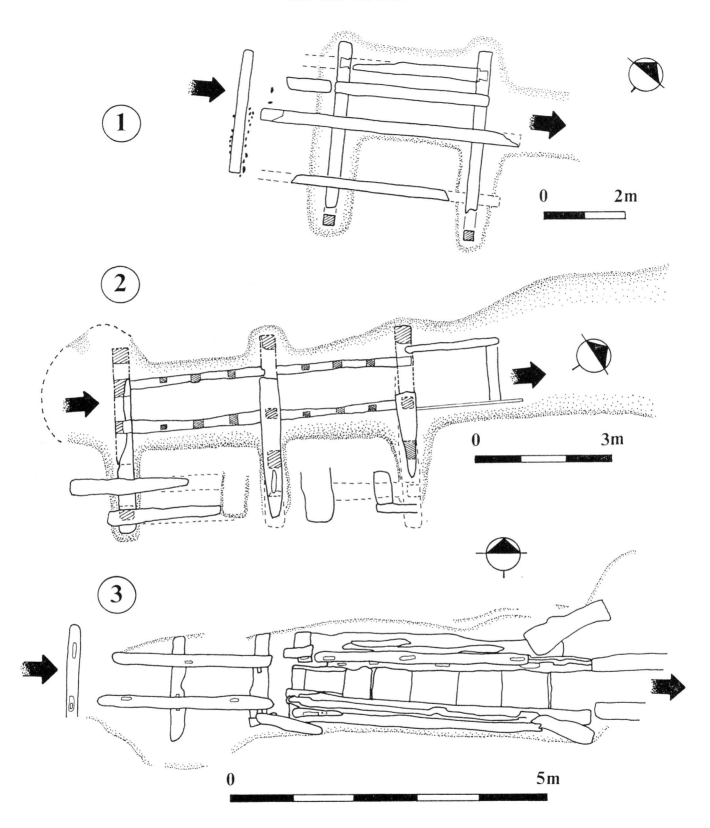

Fig. 40. English medieval mills: 1. Batsford (after Bedwin 1980a);
2. Chingley (after Crossley 1975a); 3. Bordesley Abbey (Med. Arch. 1985)

is the stone-walled gear pit, examples of which in the existing corpus of medieval vertical-wheeled watermill sites are quite rare. The skew end wall at its northern extremity is reminiscent of more recent examples of gunpowder incorporating mills at Ballincollig, Co. Cork, although its overall length does not necessarily imply that a large pit wheel was involved. For the large area enclosed by the gear pit may also have been intended to facilitate maintenance works such as greasing the bearing at the western end of the waterwheel's axle, and the replacement and greasing of the cogs on the pit wheel. Tallow was the main lubricant used in medieval watermills, and its use, along with the practice of greasing the cogs, is referred to in both contemporary Irish and English sources (Cole 1955, 172; Lydon 1981, 259). Indeed the putlog investigated on the western wall of the gear pit may well have positioned a cross piece to facilitate such works.

The gear pit was not equipped with a drainage outlet, which could be an indication that the amount of water dripping from the axle of the waterwheel or splashing from its floats was quite small owing to the manner in which it was constructed (see below). On the other hand, it is equally possible that excess water was bailed out manually when the mill was not in use or, indeed, that the underlying strata allow this to drain off naturally.

Discussion

The inlet and outlet channels for Roman and medieval undershot vertical-wheeled mills, as the rapidly growing corpus of sites clearly indicates, were lined with either boards or stone, or with a combination of the two. The earlier of the two Roman undershot mills at Ickham in Kent (*c.* 150-280 AD) for example, seems likely to have had its leats lined with boards (Spain 1984a); whilst the sides of the channel of the 4th century mill were both lined and floored with boards, to form a leat 1.4m. wide and *c.* 28m. long (Young 1982, 33-34; Spain 1984b, 170). Similar practices have been recorded at two early medieval Irish undershot mills at Little Island, Co. Cork (*c.* 630 AD) and Morett, Co. Laois (*c.* 710 AD), both of which exhibit what can now be considered to be the characteristic 'funnelled in' and 'funnelled out' arrangement of the inlet and outlet channels of medieval undershot mills (Rynne 1989b, Fig. 2). The races of the successive phases of the Patrick St mill also follow this arrangement, as does the inlet channel of the medieval undershot mill at Ahrensfeld near Hamburg (Thun 1963), the outfall channel of the main phases of the Bordesley Abbey mill, near Redditch (Fig. 40; Astill 1989, 285) and the inlet channel of the late 17th century 'double' mill at Caldecotte, Buckinghamshire (Petchey and Giggins 1983). The leats of medieval overshot mills were also commonly lined with planks, as was evidenced at 14th century and later mills at Chingley, Kent (Fig. 40; *c.* 1300-1750; Crossley 1975a), the 14th century mill at Batsford, Sussex (Fig. 40; Bedwin 1980a) and possibly

also at a late 11th century (breast-shot?) mill at Castle Donnington, Leicestershire (Clay, 1986).

The development of stone-lined channels for vertical-wheeled mills can also be traced to the Roman period, examples which have been investigated at Nettleton, Wiltshire (early 3rd century AD; Wedlake 1982) and the Gallo-Roman mill at Martres-de-Veyre, Puy-de-Dome (Romeuf 1978). For the late medieval period, however, the Patrick St channel revetment walls are clearly the best preserved examples investigated to date. Combined wood and stone-lined channels, in so far as the archaeological record is concerned, are normally associated with the post-medieval period, such as the 17th century hydraulic blast-furnace at Pippingford, Sussex (Crossley, 1975b) and the 18th century fulling mill at Ardingley, Sussex (Bedwin 1976). Nonetheless, the techniques employed at Patrick St to prevent the erosion of the banks of the channel are likely to have been employed all over medieval Europe. The same techniques indeed are known to have been used in Europe up until quite recent times.

The practice of lining the bed of the headrace channel is not so well documented archaeologically where later mills are concerned, although the tailrace of the undershot mill at Bordesley Abbey was floored with large planks (Fig. 40), as were those of the early medieval examples at Little Island and Morett (Rynne 1989b, Fig. 2), the 16th century hydraulic blast furnace at Batsford, Sussex (Bedwin 1980b) and possibly also at Ardingley fulling mill (Bedwin 1976). However, on the evidence available from medieval undershot mill sites, it seems likely that the lining of the channels (at least in the areas immediately in front of the pit wheel and on the tailrace side of the wheel casing or trough) may have been a priority, given that inlet and outlet velocities greater than those associated with breast-shot and overshot wheels are likely to have been involved.

The apex formed by the sides of the headrace channel and the western wall of the penstock in the main phases of the Patrick St mill has a close analogue at the 7th century Little Island undershot mill. As at the Patrick St site, it was not possible to investigate the other arm of the inlet channel at Little Island. Nonetheless, almost 10m. of the northern arm of the Little Island headrace continued to angle inwards into the headrace (Rynne 1989, Fig. 2), which suggests that this feature (as at Patrick St) was intentional. The most likely explanation for this feature is that a large cistern was formed immediately in front of the penstock, and that the angling in of the sides of the channel enabled a sluice gate to control the flow of water into the cistern. In view of this, it is quite possible that a similar feature was also in place at Patrick St.

The remains of the wheel casings of the levels 1 and 2 mills at Patrick St are a valuable addition to our knowledge of the operation of medieval undershot watermills. In early medieval Ireland these took the form of elaborate troughs carved out of large oaken baulks, in either single or composite constructions. At Little Island (the earliest known Irish example) the trough was a two-piece construction,

3.11m. long, 1.30m. wide at the rear and 0.80m. wide at the fore end, and as investigated 0.28m. deep (Rynne 1989b, 26). The early 8th century Morett trough was 4.22m. long, 0.61m. wide and 0.29m. deep (ibid., 24). The remains of plank-lined wheel-casings have, in addition, been recorded at a 3rd century undershot mill at Haltwhistle Burn Head on Hadrian's Wall (Spain 1984b), whilst the existence of a similar feature is implied by the remains of the medieval undershot mill at Ahrensfeld (Thun 1963, ab. 2). I have discussed the medieval iconographic evidence for the existence of these troughs elsewhere (Rynne 1989b, 28-29, 31, n. 35), along with the evidence from recent examples of undershot mills from Europe and America (ibid., 29), and concluded that both the archaeological record and the documentary record concur in this respect.

To date, the Ahrensfeld undershot waterwheel is the only medieval example to have been investigated in Europe. This latter was over 4m. in diameter, 0.50m. wide, and was equipped with up to twelve compass arms (the radial struts which tied the outer rim of the wheel to the axle) (Thun 1963, ab. 2). However, the complete dimensions of at least one undershot wheel of the Roman period have been extrapolated from lava impressions at Venafro in Italy. The Venafro waterwheel was 1.85m. in diameter and *c.* 0.30m. wide (Jacono 1938; Reindl 1939). For the other examples of both Roman and medieval undershot wheels, however, we are wholly reliant on measurements derived from the dimensions of their wheel casings. The dimensions of the undershot wheel for the Roman mill at Great Chesters are estimated at 3m.-3.6m. in diameter and *c.* 0.61m.-0.91m. wide, and that at Haltwhistle Burn Head at 3.6m. in diameter and *c.* 0.35m. wide (Spain 1984b, 105-06). The corresponding dimensions for the Little Island waterwheel would be *c.* 2.8m.-3m., *c.* 0.75m.-0.80m. and for Morett *c.* 3.5m.-4m. and *c.* 0.50m.-0.58m., whilst the relative completeness of their troughs will also allow us to posit a length of at least 0.30m. for their floats.

The waterwheel in the level 1 Patrick St mill was perhaps 2.5m.-3m. in diameter and less than 0.80m. wide, and that of the level 2 mill perhaps similar in overall diameter but *c.* 0.60m. wide. These figures are comparable not only with those for Little Island (see above), but also with those for excavated examples of medieval overshot wheels. At Batsford, Kent, where almost half of the waterwheel was recovered, the rim diameter was calculated at 2.60m., whilst the surviving buckets were 0.30m. wide (Bedwin 1980a, 191). The remains of the Chingley forge Period 1 waterwheel (also recovered *in situ*) would have originally been 8 ft. 3 in. (2.47m.) in diameter and c. 0.30m. wide (Crossley 1975a, 10). Figures for the performance of Roman and medieval waterwheels (both undershot and overshot), especially in cases where the waterwheel has not survived, are somewhat contentious. The theoretical power output for the undershot Haltwhistle Burn Head waterwheel has been estimated at 1-2hp. by Terry S. Reynolds (1983, 41) and at *c.* 1.1hp. at the driven gear (based on a theoretical impact velocity of

4-5m/sec.) by R.J. Spain (1984b, 107). These figures compare favourably with those calculated for the overshot wheels recovered from Chingley: Chingley forge (*c.* 1300-50), 1.5hp. (1.12kw.); Chingley furnace (*c.* 1558-80), 1.2hp (0.09kw.) and Chingley forge: chafery (*c.* 1670-1780), 1.5hp (1.12kw) (Crossley 1975a, 42); but are they realistic? Can we really believe that a Roman undershot waterwheel of similar diameter to a 16th century overshot waterwheel (which would be at least 30 per cent more efficient) could theoretically generate the same amount of power?

The theoretical velocity of the water striking the floats of the Patrick St level 1 mill would be in the region of 2.2-2.5m/sec., but as we have no idea as to how many paddles the original waterwheel had, it is impossible to calculate either the wheel's speed of rotation or the linear velocity of a paddle at the point where the water impacts against it. Nor can it be safely inferred that the linear velocity of any given paddle would be approximately one third to one half that of the water striking it, as in more recent mills. Thus if we do not have the means with which to produce a realistic reconstruction of the original waterwheel, any calculations based on the dimensions of the feeder channels will at best be approximate or at worst erroneous. The type of waterwheel likely to have been used at the Patrick St site is discussed below in connection with the conjectural reconstruction.

To date no gear pit for a medieval undershot mill has been recorded elsewhere, but the length of the Patrick St example is similar to that recorded at a medieval overshot 'double' mill at the Benedictine Abbey of Abbotsbury, Dorset (Graham 1986). A further Irish watermill site of unknown date, at Ballyine, Co. Limerick, which seems to have been powered by a breast-shot wheel, had a stone-lined gear pit 2.90m. x 1.25m. in extent (Walsh 1965). The Ballyine excavation is also notable for the discovery of what are likely to be the pegs of a lantern pinion, and for a series of stone bearing blocks, upon which the pintle of the vertical drive shaft's footstep bearing would have rotated. Similar 'pivot stones' were found at the 8th century Morett site (Lucas 1953) and at the undershot Bordesley Abbey mill (Young et al 1985, 186), though this need not imply that the Ballyine site was medieval; for similar stone bearings have been used up to recent times in both horizontal and vertical-wheeled mills (Rynne 1988, 1, 77).

In each of the main phases of the Patrick St mill the larger soleplates laid at right angles to the channel appear to have been built into at least one side of the channel. Similar practices have been recorded at other medieval vertical-wheeled mill sites such as Batsford (Fig. 40; Bedwin 1980a) and Chingley (Fig. 40; Crossley 1975a), where in each case the sockets for the outer ends of the transverse soleplates extended beyond the cut made to position the base frame of the wheelpit. A similar procedure indeed was also recorded at the 17th century Caldecotte 'double' undershot mills (Petchey and Giggins 1983; Fig. 3), where the larger transverse soleplates also extended into the sides of the channel.

The construction and maintenance of dams, mill ponds and mill leats, in both the early and later medieval periods, required considerable resources and, once established, mill sites were often continually reused. The excavation of the Chingley ironworks, for example, demonstrated that the site was in use (for various processes) between *c.* 1300 and *c.* 1780 (Crossley 1975a). The various rebuilding phases of the Patrick St mill suggest that for its different owners the site itself was a valuable asset whose continued use, when both the will and the resources were available, is likely to have justified the resources expended upon it. In the records of the Anglo-Norman lordship of Ireland and in the yearly accounts of contemporary English reeves, the considerable outlay involved in the construction of new and the refurbishment of existing mills is often carefully detailed (e.g. Lydon 1981, le Patourel 1956). The initial work involved in the rebuilding of the Patrick St mill in the 14th century is echoed in a late 14th century bailiff's account for the Manor of Kingsland, Herefordshire, which lists 6s. 3d. as the wages of twenty-five men employed for a day in 'clearing away the old timber of the said mill and clearing away the foundations of rubbish for the new works....' (Cole 1955, 172). The wheelpit of the Chingley forge was rebuilt at various stages in the evolution of the site (Crossley 1975a), whilst between the early 13th and late 14th centuries at least three later mills were built over the original 12th century mill at Bordesley Abbey (Astill 1989, 285). Furthermore, timbers from the earlier mill at Bordesley Abbey were also reused in a later building phase (Young et al 1985, 185), as at Patrick St and at the 7th century undershot mill at Little Island (Rynne 1988, II).

The reconstruction (Fig. 39)

The conjectural reconstruction of the mill as shown in Fig. 39 is based on the level 2 excavated structure, in which the gear pit was clearly defined. The presence of the latter clearly implies that right-angled gearing was involved, which suggests that the mill powered millstones for either flour, meal or malt.

The waterwheel

The first question that needed to be addressed in preparing a 'paper' reconstruction of any of the successive Patrick St mills was the likely form of a 13th-14th century Irish undershot watermill, a question which applies to all undershot mills of the later medieval period, by which time we might expect that different varieties had already evolved throughout Europe. Indeed, by the late Roman period in Europe there is evidence from Hagendorn in Switzerland (2nd-3rd centuries AD; Gahwiler 1984) to suggest that kinetic energy wheels of types that do not fit into the traditional categories of undershot, breast-shot, etc., were already in existence. The Hagendorn wheels

are similar in certain respects to the 1st century AD undershot example discovered at Venafro. The floats of the Venafro waterwheel (Reynolds 1983, 38) had annular rims (shrouds) affixed to the extremities of the paddles (as did wheels I and III from Hagendorn; see Gahwiler 1984); whilst a 5th century Byzantine mosaic depicts what is, to all intents and purposes, a similar undershot wheel with shrouded floats (Brett 1939). With the sole exception of the Ahrensfeld example (see above) there are no excavated examples of medieval undershot wheels and this, as has already been seen, was also shrouded. What, then, would have been the main types of undershot waterwheel used in medieval Europe?

Medieval iconography, on the one hand, is of little direct assistance in this regard, even though the majority of mills illustrated in medieval manuscripts show undershot wheels (Reynolds 1983, 47). Apart from being highly schematised, these are hardly representative of the main types of vertical waterwheel found throughout medieval Europe. All of the latter depict undershot waterwheels with floats, which has led Reynolds (ibid., 98-99) to suggest that the shrouding of the wheel may no longer have been necessary because of improvements in waterwheel design. However, the earliest medieval depictions of waterwheels which would imply an overshot delivery, as Reynolds points out (ibid., 100), do not show clearly defined buckets; which led Reynolds (who is clearly unaware of the Batsford and Chingley overshot waterwheels) to suggest that these may have been 'overshot-impact wheels'. Reynolds also suggests that the surviving medieval illustrations 'give some indication of the wheel type which was preferred late in the medieval period' (ibid., 97), and goes on to claim that Abbott Payson Usher's curious assertion that the undershot waterwheel was commoner than the overshot variety (1954, 170) was supported by Dembrinska's work on medieval Polish mills (1973, 264). In the first instance, it is entirely specious to suggest that the handful of surviving medieval illustrations are in any way representative of the types of watermill commonly used in medieval Europe. There are more examples of vertical overshot mills from the Roman period, for example, than there are late medieval illustrations of the same type of watermill (Wikander 1985); whilst there are no reasonable grounds to suggest that this variety of waterwheel was in any way a rarity in the immediate post-Roman period. Moreover, if we apply Usher's criterion that the number of surviving illustrations of a particular type of waterwheel is a useful index of the frequency with which it was used in the later medieval period, then the horizontal-wheeled mill (which we know from other sources to have been quite common throughout both Europe and Asia in the same period, see Rynne 1988) must surely have been non-existent. The earliest European illustration of a horizontal-wheeled mill, to be sure, is to be found in a 15th century treatise on engineering (Rynne 1988, II, 206). Furthermore, Maria Dembrinska's conclusion that undershot waterwheels were much more frequent than any other variety likely to have been used in medieval Poland (1973, 264) cannot be taken as an indication that similar preferences were expressed elsewhere.

Nonetheless, all of the surviving medieval illustrations of undershot waterwheels have unshrouded floats;[1] but can these be considered to be in any way more representative of the types of undershot waterwheel used in the later medieval period than those of the surviving illustrations of early overshot waterwheels? It is worthy of note that in the 15th century treatises on machines, which in many ways provide us with the first accurate illustrations of machines known to have been common in the medieval period, that both shrouded and unshrouded undershot waterwheels feature with almost equal prominence. Further, non-schematic details of features associated with undershot waterwheels recovered at medieval sites also serve to highlight the accuracy of the images depicted in these treatises. The Sienese engineer Mariano Jacobus ('il Taccola') in his treatise *De Machinis*, completed in 1439, provides the earliest known three-dimensional view of an undershot waterwheel suspended over a trough (Berthelot 1891, Fig. 91; Rynne 1988 II, 218), an arrangement recorded at the Little Island and Morett sites in Ireland. The waterwheel in Mariano's illustration is clearly shrouded, but elsewhere he also illustrates unshrouded waterwheels (Prager and Scaglia 1972, 387); as also does Francesco di Giorgio Martini in his *Trattati* (*c.* 1480-90), who again illustrates these with lower troughs similar to those from early medieval Ireland, along with a number of shrouded waterwheels (fol. 34, tav. 63; fol. 38v, tav. 67; Maltese 1967).

On the basis of a survey of all the printed books on water power which appeared between *c.* 1500-1750, Terry S. Reynolds (1983, 164-165) concluded that 'shrouding and soling were optional on undershot waterwheels'. Yet while a large proportion of these had sole boards (which formed a drum linking the lower edges of the shroud), the majority of the wheels illustrated did not have shrouded rims (ibid., 165). The surviving distribution of traditional undershot waterwheels in Europe, however, is not so conclusive. Although in northern and central Europe unshrouded waterwheels are almost universal, in certain regions of southern Europe such as Portugal (Galhano 1978) and Romania (Lungescu and Godea 1978), shrouded undershot waterwheels were quite common up to recent times. The extent to which the existing distributions relate to medieval practices cannot be accurately gauged.

In view of the foregoing, therefore, it is impossible to postulate the frequency with which certain types of vertical undershot waterwheel occurred in medieval Europe. The waterwheels of the Patrick St mills could thus be 'open' (i.e. without shrouds), shrouded, or soled and shrouded. The floats of the level 1 millwheel are likely to have been up to 0.80m. wide, and while this is not large by contemporary standards, it still raises the question (one which is partly posed by the Ahrensfeld waterwheel) of whether shrouding would have been necessary to stabilise the wheel. In *moulins de ponts* or bridge mills of the medieval and post-medieval periods, and in the floating mills (mills mounted on barges) of the same period (and which survived in many parts of Europe up until recent times), this tended not to be a priority. Both of the latter were normally set directly on main rivers whose currents were used to actuate undershot waterwheels with large floats (Nice Boyer 1982). In *moulins de ponts*, however, the waterwheel could actually be lifted out of the river to suit varying stream conditions, whilst a floating or ship's mill could also be hauled to a more suitable location when the necessity arose. A 13th century undershot mill at Ptakowic in Poland, whose building elevated on piles straddled a river, appears to have operated as a bridge mill, where the two undershot waterwheels believed to have powered its mechanism could presumably have been raised or lowered in accordance with the level of the river (Bagniewski and Kubow 1977). But would the conditions in which stationary undershot waterwheels operated in the medieval period oblige the millwright to provide extra support for the floats positioned on the periphery of the waterwheel? R.J. Spain has argued that as the undershot waterwheel of the Roman mill at Ickham (see above) did not appear to have been equipped with a tight fitting trough, it was likely to have had shrouded floats, both to stabilise the wheel and to prevent water from rising over the top of the floats (1984a, 176). The evidence for the development of such waterwheels, ancient and modern, however, would suggest that it had (Rynne 1989b). Nonetheless, the suggestion that it was shrouded is entirely plausible, and this, along with evidence from Ahrensfeld (whose waterwheel was also equipped with a lower casing) and the likelihood that the Patrick St waterwheels would have required similar support, had led to the reconstruction of the wheel of the level 2 mill shown in Fig. 39. The addition of sole boards is, of course, entirely speculative, there being an equal likelihood that the original waterwheel was not equipped with them. Their primary advantage is that they aid the guidance of water on to the floats of the waterwheel and reduce the degree of splashing after impact, although they did have the disadvantage of slowing down the exit of water from the wheel after impact (Reynolds 1983, 164-65). The compass arm construction of the waterwheel is based on the 14th century Batsford waterwheel (Bedwin 1980a, 194).

The gudgeon sockets at each end of the waterwheel's axle are likely to have been bound with iron hoops, whilst the gudgeons themselves are likely to have been of either iron or steel. The accounts for the King's Mills in Dublin for 1314, for example, refer to 25s. 6½d. expended on 'iron and steel bought for shafts and other large and small apparatus' (Lydon 1981, 260), which probably included the thrust bearing for the base of the auxiliary shaft for the stones. The gear pit for the level 2 mill would suggest a relatively large pit wheel or cogged trundle wheel (but need not imply that this gear wheel occupied most of the area enclosed by it; see above) which would have meshed with a lantern pinion positioned at right angles to it. A fragment of pit wheel whose estimated diameter was 48in. (*c.* 1.20m.) was recovered from the Period 1 (c. 1300-50) phase mill at Chingley (Crossley 1975a, 15), which led Owen Bedwin to suggest that this was originally associated with a grain mill (1980a, 191). In all likelihood, each of the successive Patrick St mills were geared up, with gear ratios in the region of 4:1-6:1.

The lower base of the lantern pinion is likely to have been positioned on an adjustable beam (Fig. 39, the bridge tree), which would have allowed the distance between the millstones to be adjusted to allow shelling and grinding. The earliest archaeological evidence for the existence of such beams in Europe is to be found in early medieval Irish horizontal-wheeled mills (Rynne 1990, 27), although their existence is also implied in medieval illustrations of undershot watermills.[2]

The mill spindle, the metal rod affixed to the top of the vertical drive shaft, and the rynd tied to the top of the spindle are also likely to have been of iron. The spindle, indeed, as many English accounts indicate, would often have been in need of regular repairs (Holt 1988, 124). The documents of the medieval lordship indicate that millstones were imported into Ireland through Dublin, principally from Wales (Lydon 1981, 260) but also from France (O'Neill 1987, 92), a circumstance which brings with it the possibility that the Patrick St site may have been equipped with imported millstones. However, we have virtually no information on the size and dressing of the type of millstone used in late medieval Irish vertical waterwheels, and no satisfactory comparanda from either Britain or Europe. The large runner stone recovered from Rathmullan, Co. Down, which is considered to be part of a vertical-wheeled mill on account of its size (Lynn 1982), could easily have been turned by a horizontal waterwheel. A hopper, suspended over the upper millstone, would have fed grain automatically into the opening or eye of the upper millstone by means of an oscillator attached either to the hopper's supporting frame or to the shoe, a hinged chute positioned at the base of the hopper (Fig. 39). The oscillator or clapper would have been allowed to come in contact with the rotating upper millstone, and the joggling motion created by this would then be communicated to the shoe to ensure a steady trickle of grain from the hopper, via the shoe, into the eye of the upper millstone. The earliest European illustration of a clapper is to be found in the *Hortus deliciarum* (see above, Rynne 1989, Fig. 4).

The mill building could have been built with weather boards or wattle. Contemporary Irish accounts refer to the purchase of large numbers of boards, as at the King's Mills in Dublin in 1314 (Lydon 1981, 260), some of which are likely to have been used to repair defects in the mill buildings themselves; or, as was the case at the King's Mills at Ardee, Co. Louth, in 1304, with wattles (ibid.). Needless to say, the same practices were current in medieval England (Holt 1988, 129-31). The roofing material, as in the contemporary English practice, is likely to have involved thatch; although the roof of one of the Ardee mills, which was valued in 1305 at 20s., is likely to have involved something more elaborate such as tiles or slate. By way of comparison, the ceramic tiles purchased for a malt mill at Standon, Herefordshire, in 1337 cost 16s. 7d. (ibid., 129).

Notes

[1] The 12th century *L'Image du Monde* by Gautier of Metz (British Library Harl. MS. 334, 71b; Bennett and Elton, II, 73; Reynolds 1983, 97); the *Hortus deliciarum* (*c.* 1202 AD, MS. Strasbourg, Bibliothèque publique f. 112a); the *Veil Rentier* (*c.* 1275 AD, Verriest 1950; fol. s 13r, 24v, 47v, 98v and 116v; Reynolds 1983, 98); a 13th century (French?) bestiary, MS. Bodleian Library, Oxford, reproduced in King (1966, 249) and in an illustration in a 13th century Spanish reliquary, reproduced in Singer et al. (1956, Fig. 591) Reynolds (1983, Fig. 2-36). Each of these illustrations provide few technical details, and so a proper investigation of the morphology of the medieval undershot waterwheel must, of necessity, await further archaeological discoveries.

[2] See *Hortus deliciarum* (Rynne 1989b, Fig. 4) and Reynolds (1983, Fig. 2-36); where in each case the bearing at the base of the lantern pinion is set into a horizontal beam.

WINETAVERN STREET EXCAVATIONS

The nature of the archaeological deposits at Winetavern St was anticipated from the extensive excavations that had been carried out by the National Museum of Ireland at Wood Quay (Fig. 50). At that site a significant section of the Hiberno-Norse earthen defences, succeeded by the construction of a stone wall *c.* 1100, were uncovered. A succession of reclamation structures of the Anglo-Norman period, mainly timber revetments, was uncovered along the Liffey Quays. The present sites at Winetavern St were located along the route where features uncovered at the earlier excavations would be projected, specifically the Hiberno-Norse town wall and the Anglo-Norman riverside revetment 1, constructed *c.* 1210.

The results of the 'keyhole' excavations at Winetavern St confirmed some of the expectations of this area. The town wall was uncovered at Site I, but revetment 1 did not extend to Winetavern St, Site J. Subsequent excavations at Wood Quay, carried out by Andrew Halpin for Dublin Corporation in 1993, indicated that this structure, in fact, may have turned southwards some distance east of Winetavern St (Halpin 1994, 29-31).

THE EXCAVATIONS: SITE H

A trench measuring 6m. x 6m. was opened by mechanical excavator in an area immediately north of Christ Church Cathedral (Fig. 3, location; features not illustrated). The site was designated as the excavation shaft for the proposed tunnel linking the Winetavern St sewer line with Patrick St. This site was thought to be that of the Guildhall, which was the public court of the citizens of Dublin from the 12th to 14th centuries (Gilbert 1859, 153; Clarke 1978a)

Three metres of modern demolition rubble was removed to a depth of 8.00m. O.D. at which depth boulder clay was encountered. In the southern section of the trench, a well-faced limestone wall with red-brick infill was found, indicating that the whole area had been deeply cellared in the late 17th or 18th century.

A 3m. x 3m. trench was then opened to the immediate south of this cellar wall. Limited archaeological strata, consisting of two inorganic layers (409) containing locally manufactured and imported French wares of the 13th century, survived between the cellar wall and a modern service trench in an area measuring 2m. x 0.5m. The layers are likely to represent the base of a refuse pit, cutting into the subsoil, and no other medieval features survived.

The Excavations: Site I

An area measuring 7m. north/south x 2.5m. east/west was opened by mechanical excavator (Fig. 3). Some weeks after completion of the excavation, features which extended beyond the site were observed during open-cast trenching. These features were rapidly recorded and are included on the site plan. The site was located to expose the town wall, constructed *c.* 1100 (Wallace 1981, 109). The wall was founded on subsoil, bisecting the site, so that layers occurring to the north of the wall could not be linked with those occurring to the south.

Level 1: the earthen banks (Figs 41, 42)

The earliest feature on the site was a bank of redeposited sterile clays (511), which sloped from south to north with the natural contour, where they directly overlay subsoil. The clays were observed during trenching to the south of the excavation trench, where they continued for a further 5m. and survived to a maximum height of .55m. Above this, late 17th–early 18th century cellars and a Victorian red-brick sewer had truncated all medieval deposits. The clay was not a uniform deposit, and several lenses or differentiations were apparent during excavation. Dark grey/green clay, gravel, mudstone fragments, pale brown gravelly clay, all with occasional charcoal flecking, were distinguishable. Three very decayed posts (525) were bedded in the clays. The posts, 0.05m. in diameter, were exposed directly under the cellar fill and may relate to later activity.

In the 2.5m. wide pipe trench to the south of the excavation, it was observed that the bank of redeposited clays appeared to extend from the north-east to the south-west, that is, following the contour of the gravel ridge of St Michael's Hill, rather than extending in true parallel alignment with the river Liffey. To the north of the trench, a deposit of fine grey charcoal-flecked silt (520) overlay the subsoil. The silt had a maximum depth of 0.50m., and its occurrence suggests that at one stage the river extended as far south as the bank. The ground level to the south rose steeply, and only the extreme base of the possible bank(s) was revealed. No finds were retrieved from the dumped earth.

At the southern end of the site, a shallow pit (509) cut through the redeposited bank material. The pit measured more than 2.4m. east/west by over 1m. north/south, extending beyond the area of excavation. The north side sloped quite steeply, and the maximum depth was 0.40m. Several distinct fills were present: grey silt (513), ash (512), brown humic silt (509). No finds were recovered from this material, and it is possible that the pit is significantly later than the redeposited clay.

The redeposited clays are likely to constitute part of the early earthen defences of the town. At Wood Quay (Wallace 1981, 1990; Mitchell 1987, 7-14), and at Ross Rd on the south side of the town (Hayden and Walsh, forthcoming) a succession of earthen banks dating from the early 10th century to the later 11th century constituted the earliest town defences. The first embankments recorded at Wood Quay were less than 1m. high and were to function primarily as flood banks (Wallace 1992, 44).

Level 2 : the town wall (Figs 41, 42)

The town wall (500) was constructed at the northern or tail end of the redeposited clay (511), and extended east/west across the centre of the site. To the south of the wall, a narrow trench (510) was cut into the underlying clays. On the eastern side of the site, the cut was almost 0.70m. in width and had a sloping southern edge, which narrowed on the western side of the site to 0.60m. where it was v-shaped in section. The base of the cut was filled with iron-stained silt (518) and yellow/grey charcoal-flecked clay (517), which contained a human skull. Lenses of ash, charcoal and silt overlay this. The trench is likely to have resulted from the scarping of the slope to accommodate the town wall (500), which was built in against the slope. No finds, apart from the skull, were recovered from the trench.

The wall was exposed for a length of 2.5m. and excavated to its base. The stones were not dismantled. It stood to a maximum height of 1m. and had a width of 1.6m. The upper part of the wall was overlain by 17th century fill, and a surface of stones contemporary with later construction was laid on its butt.

The wall was faced on both sides with large, roughly rectangular limestone blocks, which averaged 0.30m. x 0.20m. in diameter. The core was infilled with rough flags and rubble. The southern face was rougher than the northern. The base of the wall rested directly on subsoil, and there was no projecting footing on its north face. Some traces of grey/white mortar remained on its north face, indicating that it may have originally been rendered, but the structure itself was not bonded with mortar.

To the north of the town wall, a wide, shallow ditch-like feature (521) cut through the underlying river silt (506). The pit or ditch extended east/west across the site 1.7m. to the north of the wall and parallel with it. The southern part of the cut was excavated, while the northern

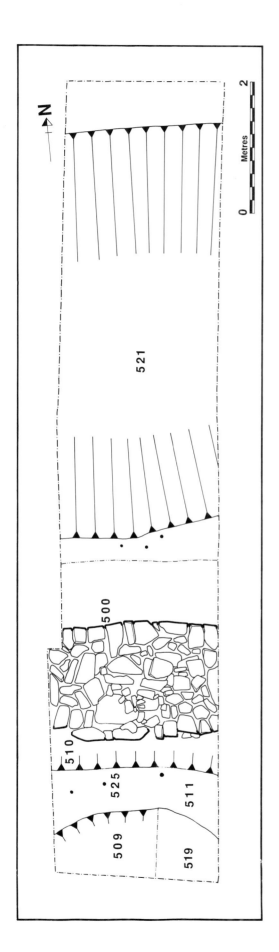

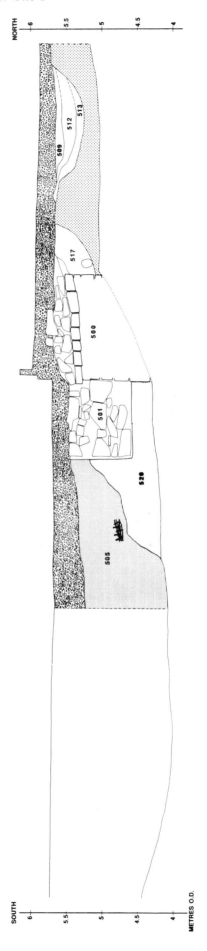

Figs 41 & 42. Site I, plan and section across site

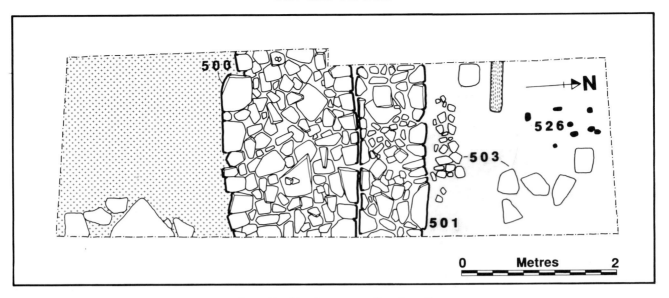

Fig. 43. Site I, post-medieval wall

part of the feature was recorded during construction trenching. The feature measured almost 6m. in width. The southern edge sloped quite steeply to a flattish base, while the northern edge had a very gentle slope southwards. The maximum depth recorded was 0.95m. in the excavated area.

Several discreet layers of organic silt had been cast into the cut. 505 was the basal layer (see 'Plant Remains'). An antler comb, a wooden bowl, fragments of leather and two human skulls were recovered from this dump. Layers of less organic, pale brown clay (522, 523) had slipped from the south side downslope, sealing the lower fill. Brushwood and loose wattles had been cast into the fill. Above this, further layers of gritty black silt (504, 524) had been dumped. Lenses of fine sand occurred throughout the deposit. Two sherds of glazed Ham Green ware were recovered from the upper level, indicating a date later than the mid-12th century for these layers.

The ditch is unlikely to have been dug for defensive purposes, and the absence of a significant deposit of river silts in its base indicates that the Liffey at that stage did not extend this far south.

Level 3: post-medieval cellar construction (Fig. 43)

A wall foundation (501) was dug through the organic silts down to subsoil on the north side of the town wall (500). The wall was built of large rough stones and was not faced on either side. The narrow construction cut (502) was visible on the western side of the site, but was not easily distinguished in the eastern section face. The town wall had been levelled by the time wall 501 was built, as several slabs resting on the butt of the earlier wall were incorporated into the later wall. The date of the later wall is uncertain, but a sherd of stoneware (late 16th–early 17th century) was recovered from the upper stones of the wall during site clearance. Several flat slabs (503) represent the base of the cellar floor foundation. These rested directly on top of the organic silt (504) of level 2.

A group of piles (526) was driven down deeply into the medieval silts to the north of the site, and part of a decayed timber, possibly a baseplate or floor joist, directly underlay cellar fill (507, 508).

94

The Excavations: Site J

An area measuring 10.8m. north/south x 2.4m. east/west was opened by mechanical excavator (Fig. 3). Up to 3m. of deposits, consisting of road surfacing materials and brick rubble, were removed by machine. The maximum depth of the archaeological deposits excavated by hand was 2.30m.

Level 1 (Figs 44, 45)

Natural river bed gravel (630) was encountered at both ends of the site, sloping evenly from 2.80m. O.D. in the south to 2.54m. O.D. in the north. A trench 1m. x 0.70m. was dug through the gravel at the south end of the site to expose the weathered surface of bedrock at a depth of 2.35m. O.D. The compacted gravel (630) contained some animal bone and strands of wattle but no pottery or other datable finds. All these inclusions had been naturally deposited or washed in by flood.

Deposits of brown organic silt (626, 629) occurred on the surface of the river gravel. Covering an area 2m. x 2m. in the south-east corner of the site, 629 was 0.20m. thick and contained a small quantity of pottery (Ham Green glazed and Saintonge ware), bone, shell and loose wattle in its upper surface. Overlying 629, a thin wash less than 0.10m. thick of black-stained sand and gravel (628) contained wood fragments and French and English pottery. This layer filled hollows in the underlying silt and extended out over the surface of the river gravel. To the north the organic silt (626) covered a 2.50m. length of the cutting and was up to 0.30m. thick. Both 626 and 629 contained reeds and probably largely resulted from natural deposition at the waterside. A thick deposit of grey clay silt (618) covered most of the area of excavation up to a depth of 1.60m. and comprised the bulk of hand-excavated material on the site. Bands of flattened reed-like vegetable matter occurred throughout the silt, which was otherwise sterile. It represents a build-up of riverside mud over a period of time and is equivalent to the 'estuarine mud' in G.F. Mitchell's report on the section from the city wall to the river in Winetavern St (Mitchell 1987, 12, Fig. 14).

During the later stages of the accumulation of the grey silt (618), dumping of urban domestic refuse took place, and some light wooden structures were erected on the mud.

The domestic refuse appeared within and on the grey clay as thin brown organic lenses (622, 606, 617, 619) which contained pottery, animal bones, cockles, moss, twigs, hazelnuts, etc. At the north end of the site, towards the river, the estuarine mud (618) and the underlying brown silt (626) had been subject to erosion and on excavation resented an irregular north-east facing slope, shelving quite steeply down towards the river Liffey. A series of tips of organic refuse interleaved with lenses of sand and gravel filled in the hollow (Fig. 45). Overlying the silt was a mantle of interleaved sand, clay and organic lenses (625), which produced pottery, ridge tile fragments and animal bones. A layer of river gravel (624), possibly a flood deposit, lay up to 0.24m. thick on the slope over the sand. A thick dump of organic debris (619) was tipped over the slope of the largely naturally deposited layers (625, 624), levelling the ground in this area. This organic deposit measured up to 1.45m. thick and contained layers of clean sand and clay within it, particularly in the lower levels towards the east side of the site. The dump (619) was roughly contemporary with and possibly a continuation of the organic layer (606), which spread over the south end of the site and which also contained many lenses of sand.

The presence of late 12th century pottery below the mud and the occurrence in it of a wooden structure dated also to the late 12th century (see below) indicates that the deposit accumulated rapidly and is best explained as a mud bank.

The jetty or boardwalk (Fig. 44)

While the estuarine clay continued to accumulate, two wooden structures (616, 621) were constructed. Each consisted of a long horizontal timber held in place by vertical posts driven into the mud. Small boards placed through horizontal mortices in the main beam were designed to prevent the structure from sinking into the mud (Fig. 46).

The principal timbers (616.1, 621.1), 2.20m. apart, were aligned east/west and were approximately parallel. They may be explained as sleepers to support a walkway or jetty running south to north towards the water across the soft mud, the connecting rails having been removed.

The dimensions of all the timbers are given in Table 7. In 621, the main horizontal beam (621.1) was held by four verticals arranged in pairs. Five small flat boards sat horizontally in the west mortice and two in the east. Although three of the four uprights had evidence for reuse, two were submitted for dendrochronological dating. One of the dated timbers had a three-shouldered chopped tenon at its base. The two uprights at the south end of 621 were from the same tree, and both had complete sapwood. The date of felling (Q8164, Q8165) was between the autumn of 1188 and the spring of 1189. Both uprights may have been split from the same piece of timber, one piece only displaying evidence of its original purpose. Alternatively, the upright with the superfluous working at its base may have been a

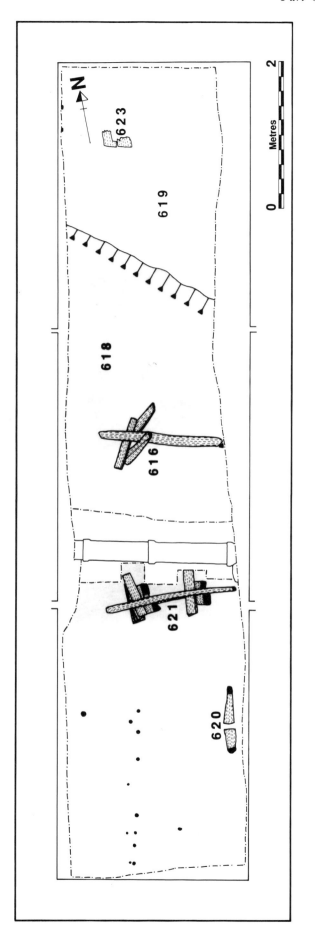

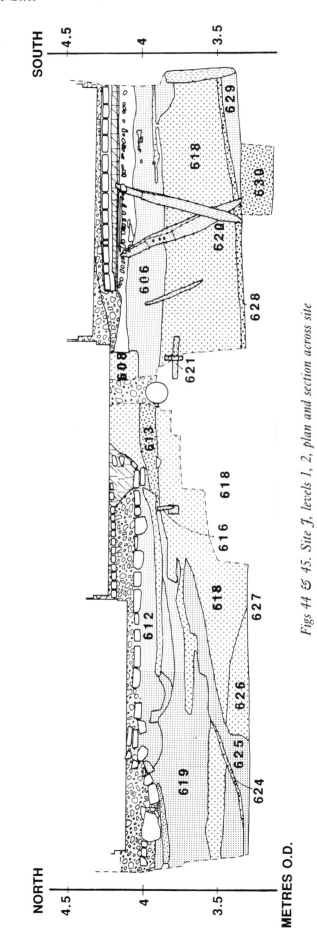

Figs 44 & 45. Site J, levels 1, 2, plan and section across site

7. Late 12th-century jetty or boardwalk, Site J

piece that 'failed' in its original design and was immediately incorporated into the rather mediocre structure under discussion. Whatever its origin, the timber cannot have been in use for a significantly long period before its use in this structure, because of the presence of complete sapwood (Conor McDermott, pers. comm.).

Timber complex 616 to the north was less elaborate than 621, and consisted of a main beam (616.1) which was held in place by two uprights at the west end and supported by one timber (616.4) placed through the single mortice. The uprights of both groups listed eastwards.

Two further timber features may also have been part of the supposed jetty. Situated 2m. to the south of uprights 621, 620 consisted of two stout oak uprights, both reused. Timber 620.1 leaned to the north while timber 620.2 leaned to the south, but both probably originally stood vertical. A single post (631) which was located 1.90m. south of 620 was embedded in the east section face of the site. Since both 620 and 631 were positioned approximately in line with the vertical supports on the east end of 621, and as there was a broad similarity in the spacing of the timber groups 616, 621, 620 and 631, it is possible that all four features represent parts of a dismantled jetty.

The structure is rough carpentry, incorporating mainly reused timbers, with incomplete trimming and dressing of the wood (beam 621.1). Horizontal 616.1, which had a split evident in the inner wood, is a poor quality timber from the upper reaches of the tree. The mortices on both main horizontals were too large for the shorter wedging planks. Axe or adze marks were apparent on all timbers, while the short, radially split wedging planks in complex 621 all had sawn ends. Many of these planks were crushed or warped from downward pressure.

The construction of the feature is quite unlike that of the timber revetments encountered by the N.M.I. excavations. The use of the sleeve mortice with through timbers to prevent the structure from sinking into the mud was employed in timber complex B at Bakers Lane, Kings Lynn (Clarke and Carter 1977, 80). At this late 13th century level, a series of parallel horizontal logs which extended for *c.* 3.5m. along the bank of the Purfleet river had been laid in shallow water and evidently functioned as a boardwalk.

Level 2

A pair of vertical oak posts (623.1, 623.2) occurred in the upper level of the dumped organic debris (619). (Fig. 44). These posts are stratigraphically later than the wooden structures (616, 621) noted above and are unlikely to be associated with them.

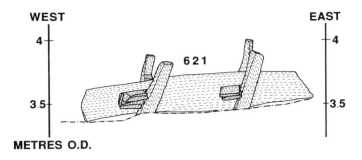

WEST   EAST

METRES O.D.

Fig. 46. Site J, timber structure 621

Random small round posts with trimmed points were noted (Fig. 44). Seven posts averaging 0.04m.-0.06m. in diameter (615) extended in a north/south line for a distance of 2.10m. in the ashy surface of organic layer 617. This represents the base of a post and wattle fence. Four additional smaller posts, 0.02m.-0.05m. in diameter, were positioned along the west side of the line at short, irregular distances. The ground level contemporary with the fence had been truncated by the insertion of post-medieval cellars.

Level 3: post-medieval cellar construction

Cellars were constructed along the street sometime in the late 17th century. Portions of two adjacent cellars were present in the area covered by Site J. A cellar wall formed the southern limit of the excavation. Running east/west across the site, a wall (608, Fig. 45) *c.* 0.40m. wide divided the two cellars. The cellar to the north was built at a slightly lower level (*c.* 0.20m. lower), reflecting the stepping down of the buildings along the street.

The original cellar floors were of cobbles (604) and stone flags (611). The cobbled floor was edged with bricks at the south end. Soil (612), with bones, slate, shell and pottery, was dumped preparatory to the laying of the stone floors. Pottery recovered included north Devon sgraffito and gravel-tempered wares. At a date probably in the early 18th century, both stone floors were replaced by brick floors (602, 609), at least three consecutive mortar surfaces (603) having already covered the cobbles (604).

A deposit (601) of black greasy soil, 0.050m. thick, lay on the brick floor and produced pottery of late 18th century date. The backfill of the destroyed cellars consisted of loose brick rubble which was excavated to a depth of 2.30m. below the road surface.

Context	Part	Max. dimensions			Reused
		Long (m.)	Wide (mm.)	Thick (mm.)	
616.01	Main Horizontal	1.65	120	180	No
616.02	Small Horizontal	0.77	90	100	No
616.03	Upright		180	70	No
616.04	Upright		170	60	No
620.01	Upright	1.73	170	170	Yes
620.02	Upright	1.76	150	140	No
621.01	Main Horizontal	1.75	300	60	No
621.02	Upright	1.04	160	90	No
621.03	Upright	1.02	90	80	Yes
621.04	Upright	1.01	160	90	Yes
621.05	Upright	1.01	140	80	Yes
621.06	Horizontal Wedge	0.575	130	30	No
621.07	Horizontal Wedge	0.59	150	30	No
621.08	Horizontal Wedge	0.57	130	40	No
621.09	Horizontal Wedge	0.53	150	30	No
621.01	Horizontal Wedge	0.57	100	30	No
621.11	Horizontal Wedge	0.61	140	40	No
621.12	Horizontal Wedge	0.59	140	50	No
623.01	Upright	1.05	150	130	Yes
623.02	Upright	0.89	130	80	No
631.00	Upright	0.86	140	100	No

Table 7. Timber dimensions, Site J

The Excavations: Site K

An area measuring 10.5m. north/south x 2.5m. east/west was cleared by mechanical excavator to a depth of 2.6m. below present ground level (Fig. 3). Deposits were then excavated by hand for a depth of 1.5m. to the formation level of the proposed pipe. A small area towards the south end of the trench was fully excavated to natural gravels which occurred at 2.14m. O.D. Construction trenching to the north and south of the site was monitored for archaeological purposes, and features uncovered in these sections were rapidly planned, photographed and recorded. Finds and structural timbers were also recovered.

Level 1: the wooden revetment (Fig. 47)

A trench 0.60m. deep was dug through river gravel. No finds were recovered. Overlying the natural gravels was a layer of grey organic silt up to 0.07m. in depth (726, 730) (Fig. 49, section A-B), which contained wood chips, leather and a small number of pottery sherds. The silt was thickest on the west side of the trench and dipped quite steeply to the east.

A dry-stone wall (721), extending north/south along the east side of the site, was constructed in a shallow trench dug through the silt and resting on the river gravel. The wall was uncovered for a total length of 21.5m. At its southern extent, it ended and turned to the east. To the north, the top of the wall had been disturbed by a later construction. It varied in width from 0.90m.-1.10m. and had a maximum height of 0.80m. (Fig. 49, section A-B). It was faced on both sides with large sub-rectangular limestone blocks (0.60m. maximum diameter) which were laid in rough courses and set back to back. In places where the backs of the stones did not meet, smaller stones were packed into the gaps. No mortar was used in the construction, but the stones were carefully chosen and set tightly together. The western face of the wall tended to contain the largest stones and to be the better build. The top of the wall was levelled by smaller, thin flag-like stones. In places, part of the upper portion of the wall had slipped slightly to the east.

Several large upright squared oak posts (720A, C, D and E, Table 8) were incorporated into the wall. Each was held tightly in place by the stones of the wall, which must have been built up around the posts. Two oak baseplates (719A and B) with a total length of 17m. were joined by a scarf joint and set on the eastern side of the wall. The timbers were laid from south to north. The scarf joint had no face pegs, but was originally held by two uprights set in mortices that cut through both timbers in the area of the joint.

A total of twenty-two mortices were cut through the joined baseplates. These were generally regularly spaced, at intervals of c. 0.40m. apart, with one irregularity in timber 719A indicating a possible replacement of the upright. The mortices averaged 0.25m. in length, and varied from 0.07m.-0.12m. in width.

Traces of uprights, consisting only of the partly rotted tenon, survived in three of the mortices. All but four of the mortices had dowel holes driven horizontally through the baseplate to hold the uprights in position. These did not occur in the vicinity of the single scarf joint which held the baseplates.

On the east side of the wall, a 0.30m. thick deposit of soft very fine, light brown silt, fine gravels and sand (729, 724) evidently deposited by water, occurred. Inclusions of any type were absent from all but the upper levels of the deposit, where small quantities of organic material and wood chips were present. This deposit partly overlapped the top of wall 721 and abutted the east side of baseplate 719. In places stones that had slipped eastwards off the wall were mixed into the top of the sand.

On the west side of the wall, a thick layer of light grey organic silt (718) and refuse (714) was dumped to raise the ground level. The surviving height of the organic deposits suggests that the revetment had originally stood to a height of at least 1.1m. (Fig. 49, section A-B, E-F). Presumably when the uprights were pulled out, the dumped deposits to the west of the revetment collapsed to the east, partly to overlie the baseplates.

The structure of the revetment is similar in most respects to those uncovered along the Poddle river in Patrick St. It lacks any apparent form of front or rear bracing apart from the vertical timbers (720). However a number of timbers that occurred in the dumped deposits to the west side of the revetment may have anchored it.

The three horizontal timbers (713, 734, 737; Fig. 47) lay east/west on the west side of the trench. All were of rectangular section and laid on their narrower sides. These timbers may have been linked into the uprights that originally stood in the baseplates and may have been anchored by uprights at their west ends, bracing the structure from the rear. Alternatively they may have been sleepers for a walkway behind the revetment.

Towards the north of the site, two groups of three timbers (727, 728) occurred at the west side of the site (Fig. 49, section C-D). Each group consisted of two vertical posts (727A, B; 728A, B) which held an east/west horizontal (727C, 728C). These timber constructions are similar to the groups that occurred in Site J (level 1) and may possibly have been part of a walkway along the side of the dock/jetty.

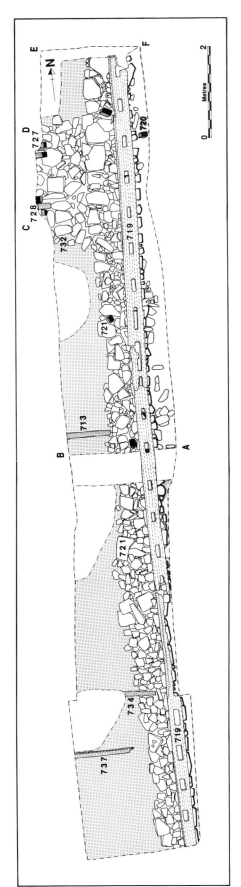

Fig. 47. Site K, level 1

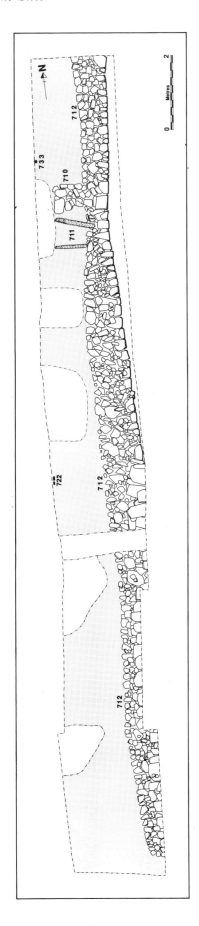

Fig. 48. Site K, levels 2, 3

8. Base of early 13th-century pier, Site K

Context	Part	Conversion	Max. Dimensions			Reused
			Long (m.)	Wide (mm.)	Thick (mm.)	
719A	Baseplate	TC	7.35	320	130	No
719B	Baseplate	TC	10.60	290	135	No
711A	Horizontal	RSC	1.18+	110	185	No
711B	Horizontal	RSC	1.19+	65	170	No
713	Horizontal	RSC	1.90+	200	140	No
720A	Upright	RSC	0.32+	90	150	No
720B	Upright	RSC	0.35+	80	150	No
720C	Upright	RSC	1.32	140	250	Yes
720D	Upright	RSC	0.86	90	130	No
720E	Upright	RSC	0.74	160	100	No
722A	Upright	?	0.80	100	100	No
722B	Upright	?	0.80	100	100	No
727A	Upright	?	1.20	90	80	No
727B	Upright	?	1.30	108	70	No
727C	Horizontal	?	N.Exc.	70	120	No
728A	Upright	?	1.05	105	95	No
728B	Upright	?	0.85	95	52	No
728C	Horizontal	?	N.Exc.	190	140	No

Table 8. Timber dimensions, Site K

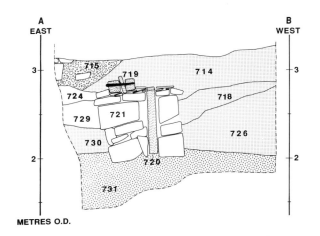

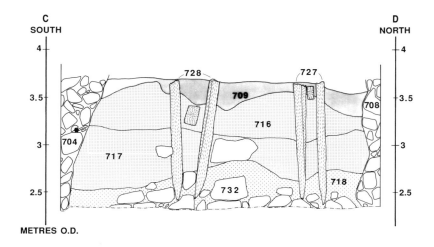

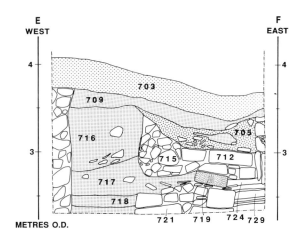

Fig. 49. Site K, sections

Discussion

A date in the early 13th century is indicated from the dendrochronological report. From the early 12th to the beginning of the 14th century, the inhabitants of the town encroached upon the riverside. The most intense period of reclamation appears to have been in the early 13th century (Wallace 1981, 114), and in the N.M.I. excavations at Wood Quay, the remains of three successive timber revetments were uncovered. The most substantial of these was a front braced, *c*. 75m. long structure, dated to *c*. 1210 by dendrochronology (ibid., 115). The closeness of the dates for this structure and the revetment uncovered at Site K suggests that both are in fact part of the same integral unit. Revetment 1 (1210) lies some 20m. further to the south than the structure at Winetavern St (Fig. 50), and the turn of the revetment (and a later structure: level 2) to the east suggests that the Site K revetment may have delimited a projecting jetty or pier. High tide in the Liffey at this period was likely to have been the same as today (de Courcy 1984, 164), ranging from 3.3m. O.D. (neaps) to 4.70m. O.D. (springs) under normal conditions. It is evident that the pier or jetty would have provided only shallow anchorage for vessels.

Level 2 (Fig. 48)

This phase of activity on the site saw the replacement of the wooden revetment by a stone wall (712, 715). The wall extended north/south over the earlier revetment, and turned to the east at its south end in the same place its predecessor had turned. It also extended northwards beyond the limit of excavation.

The wall was built in a foundation trench cut into the underlying deposits. For most of its length, the base of the trench lay just above the timber baseplate (719), but to the north of the site the wall had cut through the timbers.

The wall varied in width from 0.7m.-1.05m. and stood to a maximum height of 0.8m. It consisted of an east face of roughly-coursed sub-rectangular limestone blocks (up to 0.6 x 0.4m. maximum), revetting smaller blocks and water-rolled stones in a matrix of yellow sandy mortar. A similar mortar was used to bond the stones of the east face. The wall had been partly robbed at a later stage, as evidenced by a trench along its line which was backfilled with a mixture of mortar from the wall and small stones and organic material.

To the north end of the excavated area, the wall had an extension (710), 0.80m. in length, to the west. This was *c.* 0.80m. wide and seems to have been a buttress.

On the east side of the wall, a coarse sand and fine gravel continued to accumulate (Fig. 49, section E-F). However limestone slabs (723) had been inserted vertically and had removed almost all the sand in this area. These stones stood to a greater height than the wall, which was subsequently robbed. The rubble/shale slabs were deposited to block up the west side of the pier or jetty at some later stage. The robber trench was sealed by a series of refuse deposits (709, 703), up to 0.06m. in depth. Both deposits contained medieval pottery, indicating a relatively early date for the abandonment of the structure.

Two groups of timbers (711A, B; 722A, B) occurred on the west side of the wall. 711 consisted of two east/west oak beams set on their narrow sides, which ran roughly parallel to each other and were 0.70m. apart. Their west ends were truncated by a later feature, but their east ends were squared off. 722 consisted of two

pointed upright posts set side by side and driven into the underlying organic silts. Their tops were truncated, but they occurred higher, i.e. later, than the earlier group. It is possible that the 711 timbers may have been part of a structure similar to that formed by the level 1 groups 727 and 728, being part of a timber jetty or walkway in soft ground.

Level 3

Between the last surviving medieval deposits and the overlying cellars, a group of four features (704, 706, 707, 708, 735) occurred. These were deep (at least 1m.) sub-rectangular cuts, filled with large stones and yellow sand. They all occurred at the west side of the site, and extended for a maximum of 1m. into the excavated area. They were regularly spaced *c.* 3m. apart and measured from 1.5m.-2.1m. across (north/south). None was excavated to its base, and the tops of the four stone-filled pits were truncated by later cellars. Their function is unclear but they may be no more than the foundations of buttresses against the front of large post-medieval buildings that pre-dated the cellars. No finds were recovered.

Level 4

In the late 17th century, large stone and red-brick buildings with deep cellars were built along the street front. Several cellars were uncovered, and they were of uneven width, varying from 5m.- *c.* 9m. in width.

The cellars were on average some 2.7m. deeper than the present ground surface. The front walls of the buildings to which they belonged extended north/south immediately outside the east side of the trench. These were of stone, while the dividing walls between individual buildings were of red brick set on stone footings.

Beneath the south-western corner of the northernmost cellar was a red-brick 'manhole' (702), which was 0.88m. square internally. This yielded an assemblage of late 17th to early 18th century pottery. Two red-brick drains fed into it from the north and west. A wooden pump stick was laid against the south side of the manhole. The pump stick consisted of four planks measuring 0.02m. x 0.02m. nailed together to form a square-shaped hollow tube 0.60m. long. Two hoops of lead, held in place by iron wire, reinforced the object. In the top of the interior, two c-shaped pieces of iron served to narrow the mouth of the pump stick.

The floor of the cellar covered the top of the manhole except for a small hole over the pump stick. The function of the structure is unclear, but it would appear to have been for drawing off water that reached the manhole through the red-brick drains. Whether this was for use in the household or merely a way of keeping the cellar dry is unclear.

103

WINETAVERN STREET: SUMMARY AND CONCLUSIONS

The recent excavations at Winetavern St have provided us with scant evidence for the early development of the waterfront, but new and significant information for the later medieval period was recovered from Site K.

The series of earthen embankments uncovered in the National Museum of Ireland excavations are barely represented in the profile of the street revealed in the present excavations (Fig. 50). The redeposited silts (Site I, level 1) which overlay the boulder clay at the south end of that site may be the levelled remnants of the earthen embankments which formed the earliest riverside defences at the north side of St Michael's Hill (Wallace 1981, 110; 1992, 44). No independent dating evidence was forthcoming from the limited excavation of Winetavern St, but the material in question evidently pre-dated the construction of the town wall, which was dated by Wallace to the later 11th or early 12th century. The direction that the banks were taking was inconclusive from the N.M.I. excavations. Wallace states that bank 2 appeared to follow higher ground towards the west of the site, where it appeared to turn south-westwards, while Simms (1990, 45) has projected the banks westwards, to cross Winetavern St well south of the town wall. Construction trenching in the area to the south of Site I did not reach boulder clay, and in most of the trenching, modern service trenches had displaced the medieval strata. In summary, the banks do not appear to extend as far north as the present excavation line. Thus it cannot be said conclusively if the clays encountered in Site I (and for some distance to the south) relate to the previously excavated embankments or to a further unconnected, though doubtless contemporaneous, series of earthworks further west along the ridge.

The absence of the ditch, contemporary with Wallace's bank 2, and dated to the mid-10th century, further supports the theory that the embankments hugged the high contour line on which Christ Church Cathedral now stands. The wide shallow cut located c. 1.70m. to the north of the town wall in Site I (level 2) bears no resemblance to that described by Wallace, which was 1.60m. in depth and c. 2m. in width.

The material filling the cut to the north of the town wall at Site I was organic refuse, and thin lenses of fine gravels occurred throughout the material. Mitchell's (1987, 12) analysis of samples from outside the town wall at Winetavern St has indicated that periodically – at spring high tides – the tide would have reached the foot of the wall. This is also evidenced from the present excavations by the presence throughout the organic refuse of water-rolled stones and abraded animal bone.

Little corroborative evidence for the dating of the town wall is forthcoming: dateable objects from the dump which accumulated outside the wall are a class F2 comb (E543: 505: 2) which Dunlevy (1988, 365) dates from the late 9th to the early part of the 12th centuries, and several class 3a leather shoes. No pottery was recovered. The same deposit yielded two skulls, which the pathologist has suggested may have hung for some time after decapitation. Mitchell (1987, 14) observes that the name of the gate in the town wall at Winetavern St – the King's Gate – suggests that it might have been thought to be the appropriate place to impale the heads of traitors, as was likely the case with the skulls recovered. The gate was renamed the King's Gate in honour of Richard I (the Lion-Heart) in 1195 (Walsh 1984, 107), but it seems likely, if our dating of the deposits is correct, that the practice of displaying the heads of traitors here had commenced some time earlier.

North of the town wall, the ground level sloped steeply from Sites I to J. Construction trenching in this area showed that c. 0.30m. of dark, sulphurous, naturally deposited gravel overlay bedrock. A deep deposit of blocky grey/brown river-deposited silt occurred over the gravel. Most of the overlying deposits had been removed by the insertion of cellars in the late 17th century, but in places, thin skims of organic refuse had been dumped on top of the mud. Attempts at reclamation of the swampy marsh are evidenced here by randomly laid brushwood masses and occasional groups of stakes driven into the mud. As expected, where the pipeline crossed the junction of Cook St, there were no cellars, but there was no indication of an early street surface in this area.

North of Cook St, a post and wattle fence extended east/west across the construction trench. The fence was strongly built, with posts averaging 0.10m. in diameter. While this fence is c. 15m. further north than the post and wattle breakwaters encountered in the N.M.I. excavations (Mitchell 1987, 12; Wallace 1981, 114) and evidently not continuous with it, the fence is likely to have

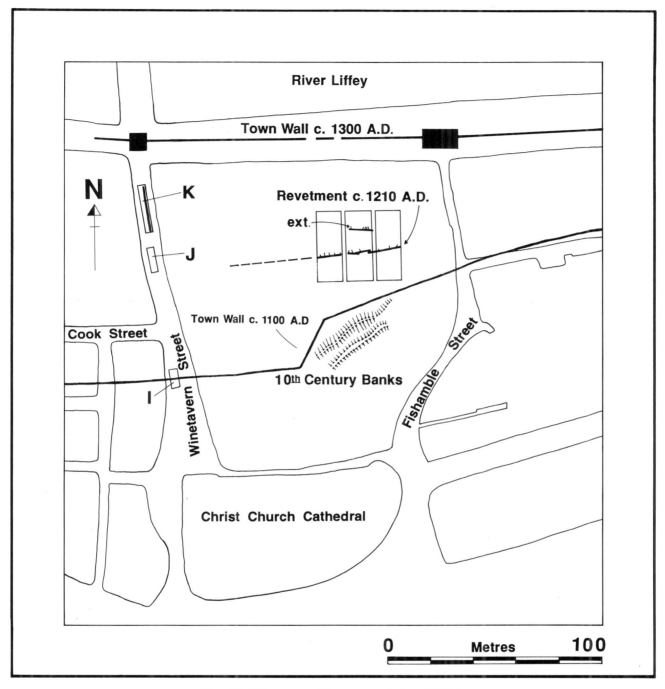

Fig. 50. Winetavern Street area (after N.M.I.)

functioned in a similar fashion, serving both to consolidate the dumped refuse on its landward side (ibid., 15) and possibly to increase the draught of water for shipping.

The thick accumulation of grey silts encountered at Site J (level 1) are parallelled in Mitchell's (1987, 15) description of estuarine mud in this area. Beyond the jetty or boardwalk supports, dating to *c.* 1189, the estuarine mud sloped steeply down towards the river. This slope was the likely result of water tidal action, and the mud resulted from tidal-deposited silts. The ground was later levelled by the deposition of organic refuse, laid in shallow water and interleaved with more gradually accumulated riverine silts and gravels. Sherds of late 12th century pottery throughout the deposit indicate that the mud continued to accumulate until the construction of revetment 1 (Wallace 1981, 115) and the contemporary pier or jetty at Winetavern St (Site K, level 1).

It was remarkable chance that the narrow cutting at Site K exposed for its entire length a timber revetment which is contemporary with, and perpendicular to, the *c.* 80m. long front-braced revetment uncovered in the adjacent site at Wood Quay (Fig. 50). The structure at Site K was constructed on a stone footing, and organic refuse was piled in on its west face, thus forming a tongue of reclaimed land which projected out into the river. The structure at Site K is distanced a good 20m. from the projected line of revetment 1. Unlike that structure, it was built on a stone footing, and does not appear to have been of the front-braced type. The vertical timbers of the Site K revetment are likely to have been reinforced by a series of tiebacks, which would allow an uncluttered face towards the water, which is essential for drawing up craft.

We do not know whether a parallel revetment existed on the east side of Winetavern St, although the suggestion is that the wall turned to the east at its south end. The nature of the shoring of the projecting spur on its north and west sides will only be determined through further excavation. As the area west of Winetavern St was called the Strand in the 13th century, it has been suggested that the riverside here lacked a quay wall (Clarke 1979, 37). Limited archaeological trenching at Merchants Quay (Meenan 1990, 25; 1991, 31; D. Murtagh, pers. comm.) uncovered a post and wattle fence within a sizeable dumped deposit of medieval date, but no further evidence of the form of intensive reclamation that was uncovered at Wood Quay. A grant of lands from King John in 1192 allows 'every citizen, for his own advantage [to] build, wherever he wishes, on the bank [of the river] but without damages to the City or Citizens' (C.A.R., I, 2). In a confirmation of lands to Holy Trinity Church in 1202, John King of England grants 'all these with their appurtenances in churches and chapels, in sands and mud banks, with wreke that come to their land, with ports and vills, within the burg and without, and on each side of the watercourse of the Amliffi...' (MacNeill 1950, 29). Both provide ample documentary evidence that lands by the riverside were under reclamation.

The pier was later rebuilt in stone (Site K, level 2), but the date of the rebuild is unknown. The stone quay wall, first referred to in 1260 (Reg. of St John, no. 56, 33; C.R.D., vol. 1, 95), and Prickett's tower on the line of the quay wall lie some distance to the north of the excavated area (Fig. 50). If the stone-built pier was in use when the quay wall was built, then the structure became an inlet or wharf rather than a pier. The inlet or pier was deliberately infilled with stones in the medieval period, and it is likely to have gone out of use by the early 14th century. It is possible that what is represented by this wall and revetment at the foot of Winetavern St is one side of a small harbour or inlet, not dissimilar to the harbour excavated in 1991 at Usher's Quay (Swan 1992, 15). The stone quay wall at this site pre-dates the construction of a front-braced timber revetment dating to 1192 (L. Swan, pers. comm.).

The presence of a pier at the foot of what must, at this stage, have been a street is not surprising. The King's Gate in the town wall at Winetavern St was dedicated in 1195 (Walsh 1984, 107), and a grant to the canons of the Holy Trinity in 1234 allows them to close up the street to the west of their church to expand the nave, 'provided that they carry a road along the neighbouring land of the priors and canons extending to the old street on the other side of that land' (Drew 1990, 177).

The existence of a slipway – the 'fyssche slypp' at Fishamble St – from an early date is suggested from the archaeological evidence (Wallace 1981, 116). That the pier at the foot of Winetavern St is not a feature of the later medieval records may be because it went out of use prior to, or at the same time as, the construction of the stone quay wall. At Winetavern St, this may have been in the early 14th century. The location of the 'crane' at the west side of Winetavern St (Clarke 1979, 38), which is well documented in the later medieval records, may have been chosen partly because it was a recognised landing stage in the earlier period. Because of navigational difficulties caused by silting at the mouth of the Liffey, by the 14th century large sea-going vessels unloaded heavy cargo at Dalkey before continuing to Dublin (MacNeill 1987, 52).

The street was known as the Taverners Street since at least 1311 (*Liber Albus*, 109). The King's Gate (later called the Winetavern Gate) appears to have been a feature of the street until the late 17th century. William Kennedy appeared as a claimant in 1701 of a house called the 'Winetavern Gate-house' (Gilbert 1859, 154). The use of the town wall as a plinth for later cellar construction is parallelled at Lower Bridge St (Hayden, forthcoming c). The wall was levelled to a uniform height at Winetavern St and along the east side of Cook St (McMahon 1990, 21), and in the late 17th or early 18th century, cellared houses were built along the street. These were terraced downslope and cut through the medieval deposits. Many of the buildings lay derelict for some time while the Wide Street Commissioners acquired the premises, further to widening the thoroughfare to its present width in the early 1830s (W.S.C. 157, 203). The tenements later constructed along the street in the 19th century are now almost entirely vanished in the face of new development on the west side of the street, while the Dublin Corporation Civic Offices now occupy the entire east side of the street north of Christ Church Cathedral.

PART TWO
THE FINDS AND
ENVIRONMENTAL EVIDENCE

MEDIEVAL POTTERY

Audrey Gahan and Claire Walsh

The pottery from the Winetavern St and Patrick St excavations (with the exception of Site G) was examined, and fabric types identified. Post-medieval pottery was present in small amounts. A minimum number of vessels (MNV) for each pottery type was calculated from the percentages of rims and bases present, and number of sherds of spouts and handles present. The results are given in tables 9 and 10. The number of sherds of medieval types, divided by country of origin, are expressed as percentages of the total sherd count. 5045 sherds of medieval pottery, representing a minimum of 213 vessels, were recovered. The assemblage is divided into three groups: English imports, pottery imported from France and Spain, and vessels of Irish manufacture.

English imports (Figs 51, 52)

English imports represent 6.30 per cent of the total number of sherds from Patrick St. At Winetavern St, 29.85 per cent of the total sherd count consisted of English wares.

A small range of types were present, the majority of which originated in Ham Green. All of the English pottery present comes from the western and south-western regions of England, particularly Bristol, which is in agreement with the known general pattern of English imports (Hurst 1988, 237; Barton 1988, 279).

Ham Green wares (Figs 51, 52)
Both glazed and cooking wares are present. All glazed forms in the assemblage are jugs. With the exception of a few sherds of Ham Green 'A' ware, all the glazed Ham Green sherds from Patrick St and Winetavern St belong to the 'B' fabric group, dating from the later 12th to the mid-13th century. Ham Green 'A' wares are now thought to date from *c.* 1140 (Ponsford 1991, 95). By *c.* 1250, Ham Green wares appear to have been superseded by wheel-thrown wares produced in Redcliffe. One tubular spout occurred (Fig. 51, 5). Decoration is normally concentrated on the vessel body, handle and base. The body usually combines several decorative types, the most common being rows of horizontal shallow grooving over which applied strips (often roller stamped) are attached (Fig. 51, 2, 3, 4, 9). Frequently, the motif is anthropomorphic (Fig. 51, 6). Incised decoration was also used. Handle decoration usually takes the form of stabbing and slashing (Fig. 51, 1, 7, 9). This would also have ensured an even firing. Bases are usually thumbed or frilled: this also helped stabilise a vessel with a convex base (Fig. 51, 8).

Ham Green cooking ware also ranges in date from the 12th century to the mid-13th century. Decoration when present consists of combed straight or wavy lines with occasional applied thumbed strips and frilling along the rim edge (Fig. 52, 6).

Minety-type wares (not illustrated)
One vessel, a tripod pitcher, is represented in the assemblage. Vince (1988, 266-67) has suggested that Minety wares from Dublin sites range in date from the 12th to the early 13th centuries.

Wiltshire wares (Fig. 52, 3)
The sherds present in the assemblage are too small to allow identification of vessel type although jugs and tripod pitchers were forms produced. These wares were imported into Dublin during the later 12th century (Hurst 1985, 140).

Chester wares (Fig. 52, 4, 5)
A small group of sherds were identified as having originated in the Chester region. Jugs were the most common form produced, often having highly decorated bodies. The examples present contain multiple applied rouletted or notched strips (Fig. 52, 5). Strap handles are plain (Fig. 52, 4). These wares are dated from the 13th to the mid-14th century (Sweetman 1984, 183-84).

Redcliffe wares (Fig. 52, 1, 2).
A small group of Redcliffe sherds, all from jugs, were recovered. Decoration is in the form of applied curvilinear strips to the body which already contains horizontal shallow grooving. Redcliffe ware is found on Dublin sites from the early 13th to early 14th centuries (Papazian, forthcoming b).

French imports (Figs 53, 54)

The majority of the French imports are from the Saintonge region of south-west France, although fabrics from both northern and southern France were present. These range in date from the 12th to the 16th centuries. They comprise 8.13 per cent of the total sherd count for Patrick St, and 25 per cent of the total sherd count for Winetavern St, representing a minimum of 27 and 11

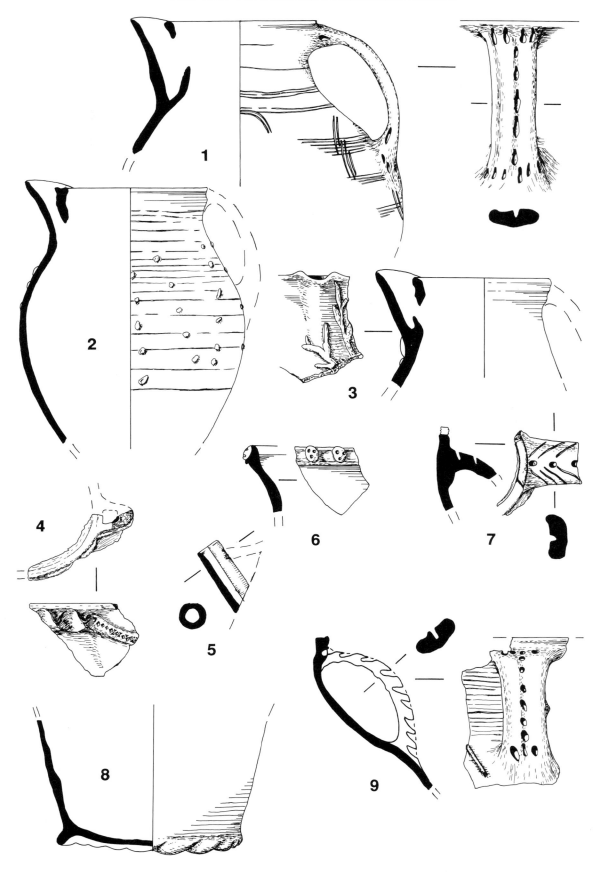

Fig. 51. Pottery: Ham Green glazed (scale 1:3)

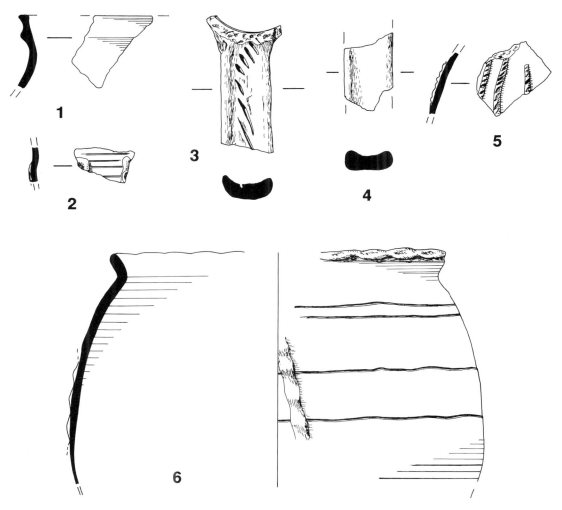

Fig. 52. Miscellaneous English (1-5) and Ham Green cooking ware (6) (scale 1:3)

vessels respectively. A small quantity of sherds of northern French origin were recovered: their importation appears to have declined during the 13th century and they are generally absent in the 14th century. This was due at least in part to the loss of this region by the English in 1205, resulting in an increase in the wine trade with south-west France. Trade with the latter area dropped during the 15th century (McNeill 1987, 45), with a corresponding decline in the importation of these regional wares (Hurst 1988, 238).

Normandy ware
One probable storage vessel of Normandy ware was recovered from Winetavern St (Fig. 54, 1). The rim has the angular form common to this region. A band of roller-stamped lattice design is present on the upper body. These wares date to the 12th century: this sherd is residual.

Saintonge wares
Wares from the Saintonge are found extensively on excavated sites in the southern port cities of both England and Ireland, most particularly in Waterford and Cork, where they dominate the assemblages (Gahan and McCutcheon

1997). Mottled green glazed jugs are the most dominant form, with small quantities of polychrome, sgraffito, all-over-green, and unglazed wares present in the assemblage. A date in the mid-13th century is accepted for the intensification in the importation of Saintonge pottery into this country, but sherds have been recorded on some Irish sites dating from the early 13th century. The Saintonge vessels present in this assemblage date from the early 13th century at Winetavern St to the later 14th century at Patrick St.

The most common form present are jugs (Fig. 53, 6, 8, 9). One of the bases recovered (Fig. 53, 9) retained a maker's mark. Sherds of two mortars were also recovered from Winetavern St. Mortars may be decorated, usually in the same manner as the jugs (Fig. 53, 4). One example (Fig. 53, 3) was decorated with a moulded applied face. A similar example was found in Wood Quay (Wallace 1983, 228) and Peter St, Waterford (Gahan and McCutcheon 1997).

Polychrome, sgraffito and all-over-green decorated jugs are generally smaller in size than the mottled green glazed examples (Fig. 53, 10, 11). The sherds present in the assemblage are too small to make motif identification possible. Importation can be more precisely dated, from

Type	Patrick Street	Winetavern Street
Dublin fabric 004	36 (25 Jugs, 8 Skillets, 2 Dripping dishes, 1 Grain measure)	4 (Jugs)
Dublin fabric 002	47 (35 Jugs, 6 Skillets, 2 Bowls, 5 Small vessels, 1 Dripping dish)	1 (Jug)
Dublin fabric 003	8 (7 Jugs, 1 Skillet)	1 (Jug)
Dublin cooking ware	25 (Cooking pots)	1 (Cooking pot)
Leinster cooking ware	16 (Cooking pots)	3 (Cooking pots)
Ham Green glazed	13 (Jugs)	3 (Jugs)
Ham Green cooking ware	3 (Cooking pots)	1 (Cooking pot)
Minety type	1 (Tripod pitcher)	1 (Tripod pitcher)
Wiltshire	2 (Pitchers)	1 (Pitcher)
Redcliffe	1 (Jug)	1 (Jug)
Chester	1 (Jug)	1 (Jug)
Saintonge mottled green	7 (Jugs)	3 (1 Jug, 2 Mortars)
Saintonge unglazed	1 (Pégau pitcher/jug)	1 (Jug)
Saintonge all over green	1 (Jug)	–
Saintonge sgraffito	1 (Jug)	–
Saintonge polychrome	1 (Jug)	–
South-west French	6 (5 Jugs, 1 Costrel)	1 (Jug)
Rouen green	–	1 (Jug)
Rouen polychrome	1 (Jug)	1 (Jug)
Orléans type	1 (Jug)	1 (Jug)
Beauvais	1 (Jug)	–
Normandy	–	1 (Cooking/Storage pot)
Misc. French	7 (Jugs)	2 (Jugs)
Spanish amphora	1 (Olive jar)	1 (Olive jar)
Merida type	1 (Storage pot?)	–
Low Countries	1 (Storage pot)	–

Table 9. Medieval pottery: minimum number of vessels

the later 13th–early 14th century (Dunning 1968, 45).

Of the unglazed wares, most common are large *pégaux*, pitchers, which characteristically have three strap handles and a large bridge spout (Fig. 53, 7, 8). This example had a maker's mark on the handle (Fig. 53, 5). These vessel types date from the late 13th century (Allan 1984, 23), with examples in Cork city dated to the early to mid-14th century (Hurley 1989, 37).

South-west French wares
These wares, while having fabric consistent with a south-west French origin, cannot be assigned a specific kiln production site. Apart from a single costrel spout (Fig. 53, 2) jugs are the only vessel form present. One example (Fig. 53, 1) has some hatching around the spout. They would appear to date to the late 13th-14th century.

Rouen wares
Rouen in northern France produced two forms of jug for export, those with a monochrome green glaze and those with dichrome decoration. A monochrome rod handle with two incipient ears at the rim/handle junction (Fig. 54, 5) is represented, while two dichrome jugs are present in the assemblage (Fig. 54, 8, 9).

Evidence from Dublin sites indicate that Rouen wares were imported in the late 12th century (Papazian, forthcoming a, b). The examples from Winetavern St and Patrick St all appear to date from the 13th century.

Orléans-type ware
A few sherds of this ware, exhibiting characteristic diagonal grooving (Fig. 54, 6). are present in the assemblage. Their importation appears to start in the early 13th century, and does not continue after *c.* 1300 (Allan 1984, 21). Orléans-type jugs have been identified from other excavations in Dublin (Wallace 1983, 228; Papazian, forthcoming b) as well as the Waterford and Cork assemblages (Gahan and McCutcheon 1997).

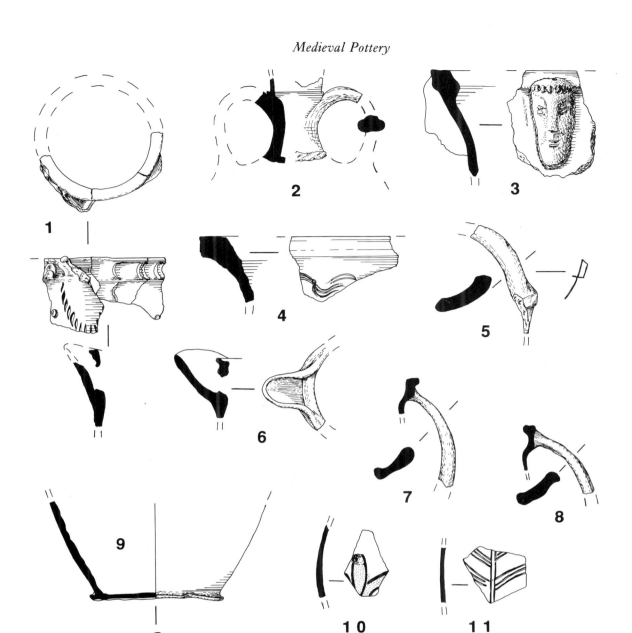

Fig. 53. Pottery: Saintonge and south-west French wares (scale 1:3)

French green glazed wares

Several body sherds and part of a strap handle, from jugs, are unprovenanced within France. One sherd is decorated with an applied moulded plaque which depicts a man on horseback and other standing figures (Fig. 54, 4). They were recovered from levels dated to the 13th-14th centuries.

Beauvais ware

Pottery production in Beauvais in northern France began in the 7th or 8th century and continued until the 19th century, although the majority of wares present on Irish sites date to the 15th-17th centuries. Plates and dishes as well as jugs were common forms produced. A stamp applied mask on a small jug or drinking vessel (Fig. 54, 3) is 16th century or later in date.

Low Countries ware

Only one example of possible Low Countries imported ware, a sherd from the rim of an unglazed jar, was present (Fig. 54, 2). It was recovered from a later 13th century context.

Spanish wares (not illustrated)

Sherds from two types of Spanish wares were recovered. These were Seville coarsewares (olive jars) and Merida-type ware. Coarsewares occur frequently on Irish sites (Meenan 1992, 186). The date range of these vessels extends from the Roman period to the 19th century. Two sherds were recovered from secure 13th century contexts,

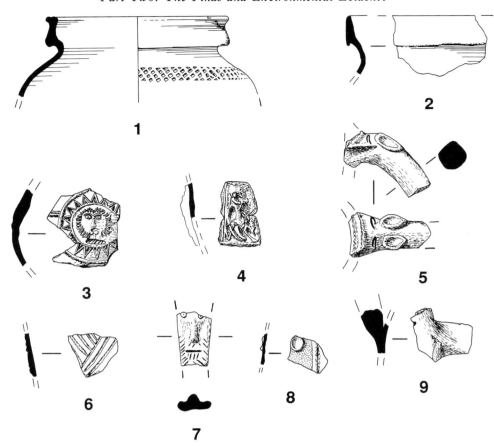

Fig. 54. Pottery: miscellaneous French wares and Low Countries (scale 1:3)

at Winetavern St and at Patrick St. A single vessel of Merida-type ware is represented in the Patrick St assemblage. These were imported into Ireland from the late 13th century onwards (ibid., 188).

Locally produced wares

Irish manufactured wares were dominant in the assemblage, comprising 85.57 per cent of the total sherd count from Patrick St (minimum of 132 vessels) and 41.5 per cent of the sherd count from Winetavern St, representing a minimum of ten vessels. This dominance of local wares follows a pattern established from other Anglo-Norman sites in Dublin, at Dublin Castle (Papazian 1989) and Christchurch Place (Papazian, forthcoming b), where locally manufactured pottery comprise almost 90 per cent and 72 per cent respectively of the total medieval assemblage.

The frequency of occurrence of the differing fabrics and forms is given in Table 9. The nomenclature follows that established by Papazian (1989).

Although medieval pottery kilns have yet to be located in the Dublin area, literary references to the existence of kilns around the city stem from the later 12th century. In 1190 a reference to 'vicus pottorum' is generally thought to refer to a group of potters working on the western side of the city outside the wall (Wallace 1983, 228). It is likely that some, if not all, of the Dublin-type wares were produced in or around the city.

Fabric 004: hand–built, glazed pots (Figs 55, 56, 57)
For fabric see Papazian (1989, 112, 140-42).
The most prevalent vessel forms present are jugs and/or pitchers (Figs 55, 56) and skillets (Fig. 57, 1-5). Sherds from several curfews (not illustrated) were also present but these were unglazed. Dripping dishes (Fig. 57, 8) and grain measures (Fig. 57, 9) were also recovered.

Jugs with rim diameters of 10cm.-14cm. and base diameters of 12cm.-18cm. are recorded, although some base diameters range in size from 20cm.-24cm. These were possibly from pitchers. Spouts are generally pulled, but several bridge spouts were present, and one tubular example was recovered (Fig. 55, 5). Bases are convex and are thumbed or frilled. This probably served a dual purpose, to steady the pot as well as being decorative. Strap handles are the more usual form but some examples of rod handles were recorded (Fig. 57, 6-7). Decoration is heavily concentrated on the handles and bases with only a moderate amount of body decoration. Only strap handles are decorated. These were usually stabbed and/or slashed and line-incised in the style of Ham Green jugs. Body decoration consists mainly of horizontal shallow grooving, occasionally with the further addition of applied and stabbed strips (Fig. 55, 4; Fig. 56, 6, 8). Rims and bodies were also decorated with rouletted lines of subrectangular indentations (Fig. 55, 3; Fig. 56, 2). Two examples of decorated spouts were uncovered (Fig. 55, 5; Fig. 56, 3).

Skillets, with their distinctive trumpet handles (Fig. 57, 2, 5), were generally undecorated. Bases were also convex but were not frilled. Pouring was by means of a simple pulled spout (Fig. 57, 1).

This fabric ranges in date from the later 12th century through to the 14th century, declining in the early 15th century (Papazian, this vol.).

Fabric 002: Dublin glazed wares (Figs 58, 59, 60)
For fabrics: see Papazian (1989, 68, 138-39).
Forms were almost exclusively jugs or pitchers (Fig. 58, 1, 2, 8-10) although part of an unglazed curfew, some dripping dishes and part of a candlestick (Fig. 59, 15) in this fabric were recovered. Skillets (Fig. 59, 1, 3) were also present.

Jugs with rim diameters between 8cm.-12cm. and base diameters of 10cm.-16cm. were recorded but larger vessels, probably pitchers, with rim diameters of 12cm.-18cm. and base diameters of 18cm.-22cm. were also noted. Jug forms remain consistent with those of fabric 004, with pulled spouts (Fig. 58, 1) and rod handles (Fig. 58, 13) present. Twisted rod handles are also represented (Fig. 58, 7).

Decoration is concentrated on the rim and body areas, with little or no decoration on handles and bases. Rims are decorated with the addition of thumbed or frilled applied strips (Fig. 58, 3) and high relief pellets (Fig. 58, 1). Vessel bodies generally have a combination of two or more decoration types. Usually there is horizontal shallow grooving to which applied strips (which may be rouletted, thumbed, notched or plain) were added and/or stamped applied 'raspberry' roundels and/or pinched pellets (Fig. 59, 5-12). It has been suggested that these decorations forms may have been ceramic skeumorphs of contemporary metalworking and/or basketry (McCarthy and Brooks 1988, 127-28). A white slip was sometimes applied under the glaze to produce a lighter green colouring probably in imitation of Saintonge wares. Where decoration does occur on handles it is generally in the form of single or multiple incised grooves. Those bases which are decorated are thumbed or have a slightly raised footing. One example has a flanged base similar to those found on some Saintonge green glazed jugs (Fig. 59, 14).

Part of an aquamanile in the form of a stag (E543:391:175, Site F, level 3, 13th-14th centuries) was recovered. Only the head and front quarters survive from what would have originally been a complete animal.

The vessel was handmade in Dublin fabric 004, and covered with an amber-coloured lead glaze. It consists of two main pieces. The body is hollow and the head is a separate tube of clay applied at the neck. The body is decorated with vertical rows of applied tongues of clay alternating with rows of rouletting. The head is decorated with rows of impressed dots forming the eyes and snout. The remains of clay antlers survive, applied above the eyes.

More recently, a very similar aquamanile manufactured in a local fabric was recovered from an excavation at Back Lane/ Lamb Alley (T. Coughlan, pers comm). Part of the rim of that vessel is extant. Another fragment of an aquamanile in the form of a ram was found in a 13th century context at Christchurch Place (Hayden and Walsh, forthcoming). That particular vessel is very finely executed and it was imported from the Bristol area. A ram aquamanile, produced in Scarborough and dated to the late 13th century, is illustrated in Alexander and Binski (1987, 439). The aquamanile fragment from Patrick St came from a 13th-14th century deposit in the Poddle river.

Evidence from other Dublin sites (Papazian, forthcoming b, c and d; see also this vol.) suggests that production began in the later 12th century, with significant quantities present by the mid-13th century, and a decline in the 15th century.

Fabric 003: Dublin temper-free wares (Fig. 61)
For fabric description see Papazian (1989, 96-97, 142).
Fabric 003 represents the smallest group of locally produced glazed wares in the assemblage. Jugs appear to be the most common form, but some fragments that are glazed internally may come from bowls.

The vessels range in size with rim diameters of 8cm.-22cm. and base diameters of 12cm.-26cm. Both bridge and simple pulled spouts are present. Handles are generally straps (Fig. 61, 1, 2) but some examples of rod handles (Fig. 61, 4) and a twisted rod handle are also present. Bases may be slightly convex and are either plain (Fig. 60, 3) or thumbed.

Decoration was noted on all jug parts. Rims were decorated by means of frilled applied strips, which were usually partially glazed. Vessel bodies were decorated in several styles. The most common type is notched applied strips which have been glazed brown, contrasting with the green glaze of the rest of the vessel. Applied strips in conjunction with stamped applied raspberry roundels are also common. Pellets, which may be pinched, were sometimes applied to the vessel body, often to a body which has already been shallow grooved. This grooving may also be present on its own.

Evidence from other Dublin sites indicates that fabric 003 is the latest of the local wares, coming into production probably in the early 13th century, and continuing in circulation into the 15th and possibly even the 16th century (Papazian, forthcoming b; see also, this vol.).

Local cooking wares (Fig. 62)
For fabric description of Dublin cooking wares see Papazian (1989, 125, 136-38); for Leinster cooking wares see O'Floinn (1988, 327).
Cooking vessels represent the largest group of locally produced wares in the assemblage. Most vessels are handmade but a small number of sherds present appear to be wheel-thrown.

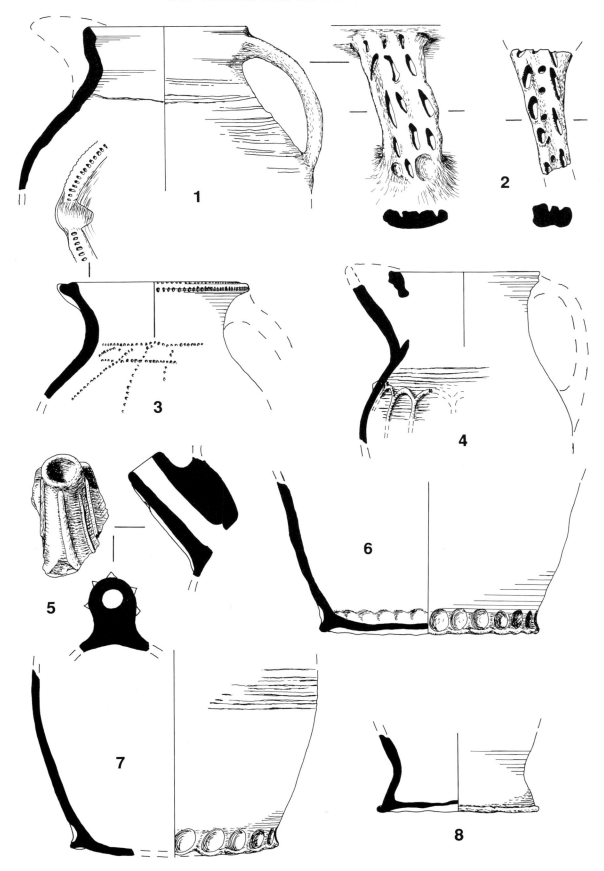

Fig. 55. Pottery: Dublin fabric 004 (scale 1:3)

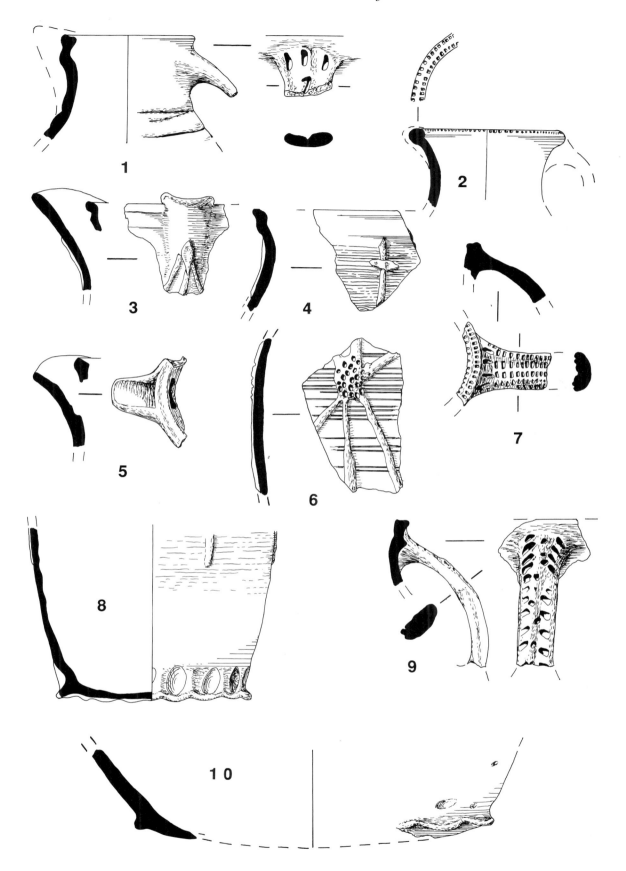

Fig. 56. Pottery: Dublin fabric 004 (scale 1:3)

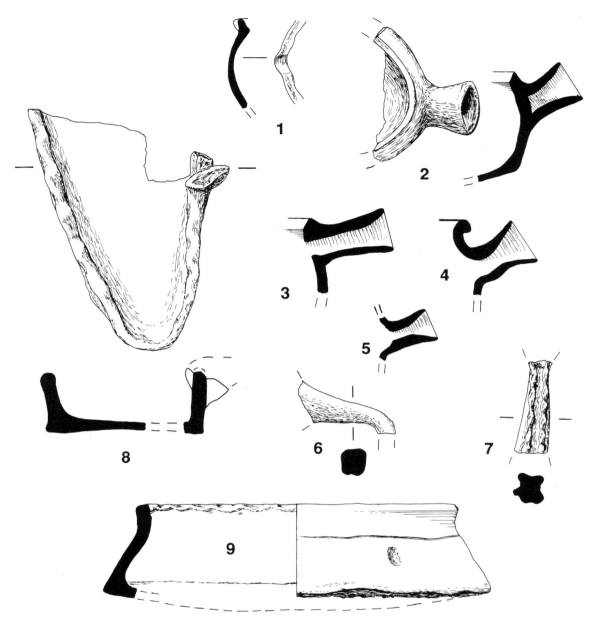

Fig. 57. Pottery: Dublin fabric 004 (scale 1:3)

Vessels in this assemblage range in size with rim diameters of 14cm.-28cm. and base diameters of 12cm.-28cm., although some smaller vessels with rim diameters of 10cm.-12cm. and base diameters of 8cm.-10cm. were noted. Vessels generally have everted rims (Fig. 62, 5, 6) (although a few straight rims were recovered, Fig. 62, 7), large globular bodies and generally have slightly convex bases (Fig. 62, 4). Decoration was noted on only a small percentage of vessels. This took the form of horizontal shallow grooving on the upper body (Fig. 62, 4) and some thumbing along the rim edge. Several rim sherds had similar decoration of shallow oblique stabs.

Vessels of a distinct group of cooking wares, classified as Leinster cooking ware (O'Floinn 1988, 325; Fig. 62, 8-14) were also recovered. These unevenly fired vessels have a very coarse fabric, characteristic sand pitted bases,

and fracture easily. This type is found on most medieval sites throughout Leinster, and is thought to have been produced in crude 'clamp' kilns.

Apart from cooking vessels, some shallow, handled bowls (Fig. 62, 12, 14) in this fabric were rcovered. Eight handles in total occurred, of which six were straps. A rod handle, and a hollow, trumpet handle, from a skillet, were also recovered.

Dating: see Papazian, this vol.

Post-medieval pottery (not illustrated)

Sherds of post-medieval pottery were recovered as surface finds from clearance over both Patrick St and Winetavern St. At Patrick St, 203 sherds of pottery, representing a

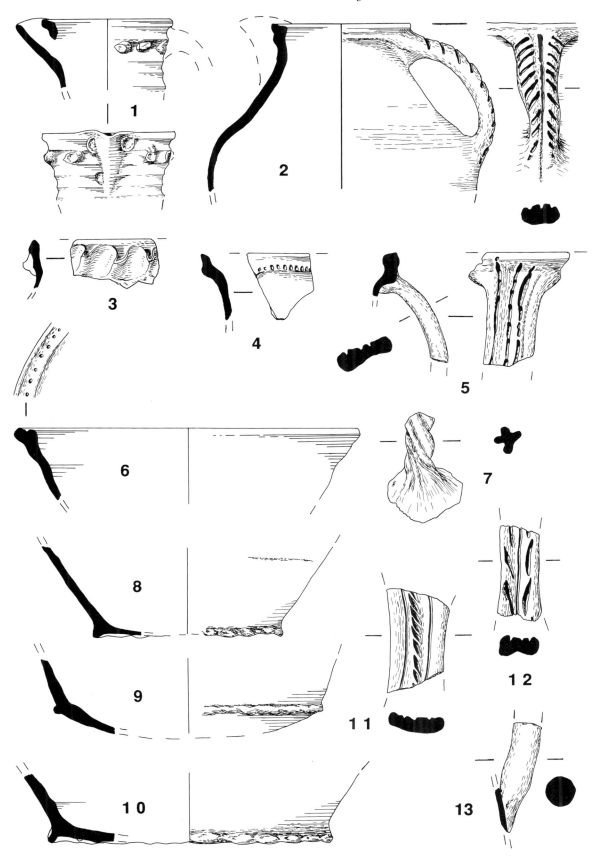

Fig. 58. Pottery: Dublin fabric 002 (scale 1:3)

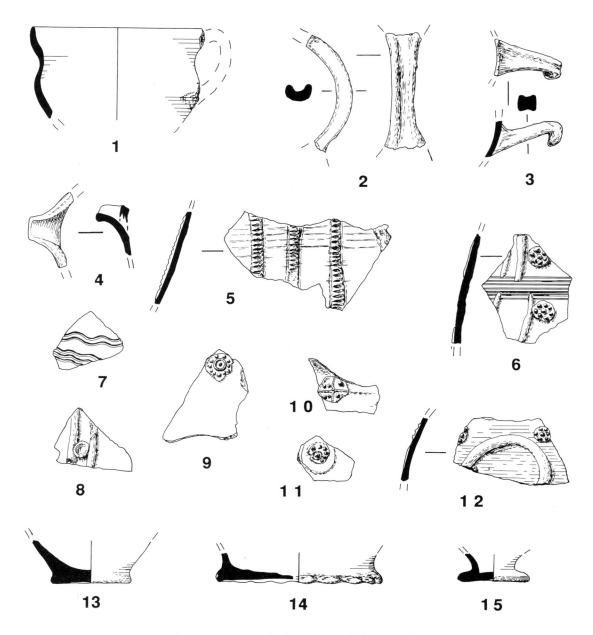

Fig. 59. Pottery: Dublin fabric 002 (scale 1:3)

minimum of 75 vessels, ranging in date from the late 17th – 19th century were recovered as surface finds (Table 10).

Summary and conclusions

The nature of the sites, and in particular the Patrick St deposits, prohibits an attempt at an independent dating of the local wares. The dating of Ham Green wares and French imports into Ireland has been more securely dated from Dublin sites such as Christchurch Place, Dublin (Papazian, forthcoming b) and Waterford (Gahan and McCutcheon 1997).

Several trends can, however, be identified from the assemblage under discussion. Fabrics 004 and 002 are present in small quantities from securely stratified deposits dating to the 13th century at Winetavern St, sites J and K, but do not occur in the lower levels at these sites, where Ham Green wares and northern French pottery is present in small numbers. A single sherd of local cooking ware was recovered from a deposit dating to before *c*. 1204 at Site K. The later levels of dumping on both sites returned sherds of fabrics 004 and 002 in lesser quantities than the imported wares. A single sherd of fabric 003 was recovered from Winetavern St, which confirms that it is the latest in manufacture of the local wares.

At Patrick St, fabric 004 and cooking wares occur in small quantities in the lowest levels at Site B, in association with Ham Green B wares. Fabric 002 is present from the first part of the 13th century. Fabric 003 is present in

120

lesser quantities, and occurs only in the later levels at each site, which reinforces the suggestion that it is later. Here it occurs in association with fabrics 004 and 002, and the cooking wares. Generally the absence of stratified deposits from the later 14th-15th centuries prohibits the establishment of a terminal date for the production of Dublin wares (see Papazian, this vol.). The absence of these later levels from Patrick St is readily explicable by disturbance from the construction of the stone culvert wall in the mid-18th century, and the probable attendant cleaning of the river bed. Late 17th-18th century pottery is also not present in significant quantities, a further testimony to the civic hygiene of the 18th-19th centuries.

While there is no evidence from Patrick St to provide a terminal date for the production of local wares, production is likely to have continued into the 15th century. Vince's (1985, 65) statement that 'the late medieval period from the Black Death to the accession of the Tudor kings is a notoriously difficult period for pottery studies' holds true for the evidence from the Patrick St assemblage.

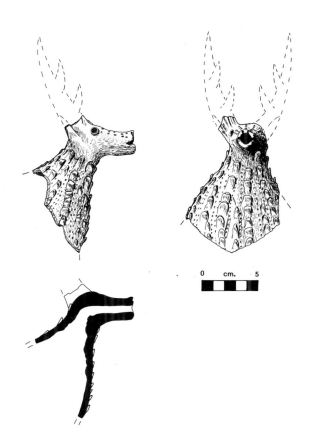

Fig. 60. Aquamanile: Dublin fabric 002

Type	Patrick Street	Winetavern Street
Black ware	7	9
Chinese porcelain	0	1
Cream ware	7	1
Glazed earthenware	8	9
Glazed red slipware	2	1
Metropolitan	1	0
Misc. Delftware	8	3
Misc. French	2	0
Modern stoneware	1	1
N. Devon gravel tempered	8	13
N. Devon sgraffito	2	1
Pearl ware	6	1
Spanish	0	1
Staffordshire slipware	6	2
Staffordshire mottled ware	5	1
Unglazed red earthenware	2	0
Westerwald	0	1

Table 10. Post-medieval pottery: minimum number of vessels

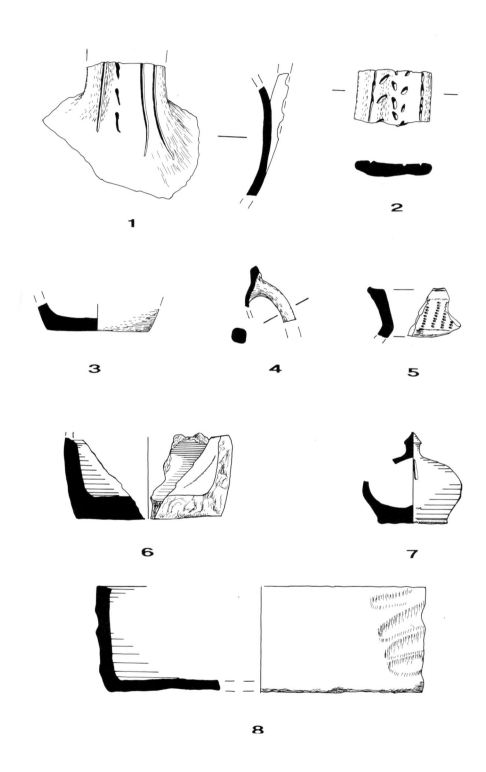

Fig. 61. Pottery: Dublin fabric 003 and Site G (scale 1:3)

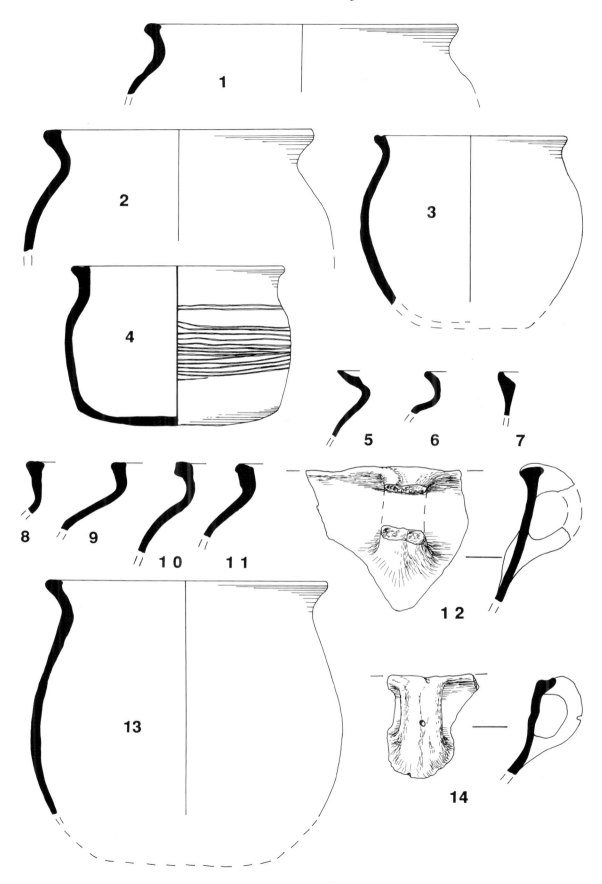

Fig. 62. Pottery: Local cooking wares (scale 1:3)

MEDIEVAL AND LATER POTTERY FROM SITE G

Cliona Papazian

Over 1,200 sherds of medieval pottery were recovered from the Anglo-Norman ditch uncovered at Site G. The construction of this ditch is thought to have commenced *c*.1186 with a completion date *c*. 1200. A few sherds which are probably contemporaneous with the construction of the ditch were recovered from level 1. The ditch seems to have been kept relatively free of dumped material until level 2, dated to the 15th century, when it was gradually infilled with refuse. In the 16th century, levels 3 and 4, the moat was deliberately backfilled with large dumps of material in advance of development over the ditch. The bulk of the medieval pottery comes from this level, but the forms present suggest that the pottery derives from redeposited material. A coin dated 1586-1635 and the associated pottery from level 5 suggests an overall date to 1600 (Meenan, this vol.). Locally made pottery dominates the assemblage (Table 11), while English and Continental imports account for only 5 per cent of the assemblage and mainly occur as residual finds.

	Sherd count	Count %	MNV*	Weight (g)	%
Dublin/ Leinster wares	1,216	95	123	20,649	94.9
English	10	0.7	5	223	1
French	50	3.8	13	902	4
Spanish/ German	2	0.4	2	27	0.1

(*Minimum number of vessels)

Table 11: Assemblage by sherd count, weight and MNV, Nicholas Street

Methodology

The assemblage was examined and sorted into groups, then counted and weighed. The pottery was recorded as follows: a separate sheet for each context/feature, another for each phase/level and thirdly a site summary spreadsheet.

There are disadvantages to using sherd counts as a system of quantification (Vince 1977; Orton and Tyers 1990) and this was offset by weighing the groups and calculating the minimum number of vessels for each group. For simplicity, count values are used when describing the frequency of each group, but the reader is invited to refer back to Table 11 when considering such values.

The appellation for imports is common name; the local Dublin wares are described by fabric codes 001-004 with common names. The individual pottery groups are discussed; because detailed fabric descriptions are available for all of the groups, this information is not duplicated here and the reader is referred to the relevant texts. References are also given to published examples of vessel forms for each group.

The imported groups are discussed in the following order: 1. French, 2. Spanish and German, 3. English, followed by the local wares: within each section the pottery groups are discussed in chronological order.

Apart from approximate dates for the construction of the Norman ditch and the numismatic evidence from level 5, there is otherwise no independent dating evidence for the assemblage. The known dates for each group, based on dating evidence from sites in England and Ireland, are outlined, and these 'master dates' are discussed in the light of the evidence from Site G.

Finally, the ceramic sequence is discussed, albeit in three unequal periods.

The Imported Wares

Approximately 5 per cent of the medieval pottery was imported. The evidence from Christchurch Place (Papazian, forthcoming b) suggests that imports are not commonly found after the 14th century. Given the suggested date range for the Site G asemblage the paucity of imports from this site seems to support the evidence from Christchurch Place of an overall decline in imports after the 14th century.

The majority of the French wares are from the Saintonge (Table 12), although there are sherds from both known and unknown production centres in northern France. Potteries in and around Bristol account for the majority of the English wares recovered.

1. The French wares

Rouen (none illustrated)
Fabric and forms: see Barton (1965) and Vince (1983, 1985).
A single jug is known from the site; a classic dichrome jug with a rod handle decorated with small pads of clay on either side of the handle/rim join.
Dating and frequency: the evidence from 1-3 High St and Christchurch Place (Papazian, forthcoming a, b) indicates that Rouen imports are known from contexts dating to the late 12th century. Allan (1984, 198) suggests a terminal date for Rouen wares in the mid or last quarter of the 13th century. Rouen imports occur in level 2 as residual finds.

Northern French white ware (none illustrated)
Fabric and forms: fabric similar but coarser than northern French monochrome (Vince 1983, 1, 220); fires to a brilliant white colour.

Very similar forms and decoration motifs to both northern French monochrome and Rouen; a production source in northern France seems likely (ibid).
Dating and frequency: at Christchurch Place (Papazian, forthcoming b) an overall date range from the late 12th-early 13th centuries was suggested for this group. A single sherd was recovered from a post-medieval context at Site G, and is therefore residual.

Saintonge green glazed ware (none illustrated)
Fabric and forms: see Barton (1963a); Platt and Coleman-Smith (1975); Vince (1983, 1, 225-28).
Dating and frequency: Barton (1963a, 201-04) and Allan (1983, 199) suggest a wide date range from the end of the 12th century to the end of the medieval period. At Christchurch Place, Dublin, Saintonge green glazed wares were first present in phase 1 (late 12th century) contexts but were most frequent in contexts dated to the early 13th century. Saintonge green glazed wares were recovered from all subsequent levels; however it is uncertain whether they occur as contemporaneous or residual finds in later levels (Papazian, forthcoming b). Given the broad date range for Saintonge green glazed wares, it is difficult therefore to determine whether they occur as contemporaneous or as residual finds at Site G.

Martincamp type 2 (none illustrated)
Fabric and forms: see Hurst et al (1986, 102-04); Meenan (this vol.).
Dating and frequency: dated to the 16th century (Hurst et al (1986, 104). A single sherd was recovered from a level 3 context.

2a: Spanish imports (none illustrated)

Merida-type wares/ Iberian red micaceous
Fabric and forms: see Hurst et al (1986, 69-70); Meenan (1992).
Dating and frequency: one sherd recovered from a 16th century context.

2b: German imports (none illustrated)

Paffrath wares
Fabric and forms: see Dunning (1968, 35-58).

Levels	?13th 1	1400 -1500 2	1500 -1600 3 & 4	Post- medieval 5 & 6	Unstratified	Sherd totals	MNV*
Rouen	0	2	0	0	0	2	1
French white	0	0	0	0	1	1	1
Saintonge green	1	26	17	1	1	46	10
Martin-camp type 2	0	0	1	0	0	1	1

(*minimum number of vessels)

Table 12: Medieval French imports by period, group, sherd count and MNV

	?13th	1400 -1500	1500 -1600	Post- medieval	Unstratified	Sherd totals	MNV*
Levels	1	2	3 & 4	5 & 6			
Merida/ Iberian	0	0	1	0	0	1	1
Paffrath	1	0	0	0	0	1	1

(*minimum number of vessels)

Table 13: Medieval Spanish and German imports by period, group, sherd count and MNV

Dating and frequency: Jennings (1981, 25) suggests a 12th-13th century date range for these wares. A single sherd was recovered from the earliest fill of the ditch and probably dates to the early 13th century.

3. The English Imports

Ham Green 'B' wares (none illustrated)
Fabric and forms: see Barton (1963b, 1988); Ponsford (1991).
Dating and frequency: Ponsford (1991, 98) suggests that 'B' jugs can be dated to 1175-1250, with some forms datable to *c.* 1275. At Christchurch Place (Papazian, forthcoming b) Ham Green 'B' wares were first deposited in the last quarter of the 12th century, but by the mid-13th century, the frequency was in decline. All the sherds from Site G occur as residual finds.

South-east Wiltshire wares (not illustrated)
Fabric and forms: see Vince (1988, 264).
Dating and frequency: at Site G, a single sherd was recovered from a suspected 15th century context, and is therefore residual.

Unidentified English wares (none illustrated)
Fabric and forms: a possible unknown Bristol import, fabric not recognised by the author.

Dating and frequency: a single sherd from level 2. As this ware was thought to date from the late 12th-early 13th century at Christchurch Place (Papazian, forthcoming b), this ware is probably residual.

Chester wares (none illustrated)
Fabric and forms: see Sweetman (1984, 183-84).
A single jug decorated with notched leaded applied strips is present, probably residual.
Dating and frequency: suggested date range from the 13th-mid-14th century (J. Rutter, pers comm). At Christchurch Place the greatest frequency of Chester wares was evident in contexts dated from the early to mid-13th century (Papazian, forthcoming b). The sherds from Site G are probably residual as they occurred in suspected 15th and 16th century contexts.

Redcliffe wares (none illustrated)
Fabric and forms: see Vince (1983, 1, 52; 1988, 260-61).
Dating and frequency: Ponsford (1991, 95) suggests that by the mid-13th century, Redcliffe wares had taken over from Ham Green wares. At Christchurch Place these wares first appeared in contexts suggesting an early 13th century date, although they occurred with greater frequency in mid-13th century contexts (Papazian, forthcoming b). Vince suggests a terminal date of the end of the 15th century for these wares: given the wide date range for Redcliffe wares it is not possible to state with

	?13th	1400 -1500	1500 -1600	Post- medieval	Unstratified	Sherd totals	MNV*
Levels	1	2	3 & 4	5 & 6			
Ham Green 'B'	0	0	1	1	0	2	1
S-E Wilts		1	0	0	0	1	1
Chester	0	1	2	0	0	3	1
Unidentified	0	1	0	0	0	1	1
Redcliffe	0	1	2	0	0	3	1

(*minimum number of vessels)

Table 14: Medieval English imports by period, group, sherd count and MNV

accuracy whether they occur as contemporaneous or residual finds at Site G.

4. The Dublin wares

Fabric 004: Dublin hand-built glazed and cooking pot wares (none illustrated)

Fabric and forms: for macroscopic fabric description see Papazian (1989, 112); for petrological analysis see ibid. (140-42).

For an account of the forms recovered at Dublin Castle see ibid. (116-18; forthcoming c) and for an account of the forms recovered from Back Lane.

Most of the 004 forms are glazed; only a single sherd of cooking wares was recovered – contrast this with Cornmarket (22 per cent glazed, 19 per cent cooking wares; Papazian, forthcoming d) and Back Lane where 42 per cent of the 004 assemblage are cooking wares.

Dating and frequency: at 4-5 High St (Papazian, forthcoming a) fabric 004 wares are known from contexts dated to the late 12th century. The evidence from Christchurch Place indicates that fabric 004 wares are the earliest Dublin wares found at that site, as these were found in late 12th century contexts. Present evidence suggests that the floruit of these wares occurs from the late 12th-mid-13th centuries.

Fabric 004 is present in significant amounts throughout the later 13th-14th centuries, but is absent by the 15th century as fabric 002, Dublin glazed and fabric 003, temper free wares dominate Dublin assemblages. It seems probable that the fabric 004 wares from levels 2-6 are residual.

Fabric 002: Dublin glazed wares

Fabric and forms: for macroscopic fabric description see Papazian (1989, 68): for petrological analysis see ibid. (138-39). See also Papazian (forthcoming d and 1989, 75) for a list of known vessel types; also Gahan and Walsh (this vol.).

The forms in this ware from Site G include jugs, condiment dishes, bowls and jars. Jugs predominate; the rims are moulded or simple with thumbed applied strips. Bridge spouts are common and are sometimes decorated with thumbing on the spout/neck join. Decoration motifs include grooving or combing, applied stamped roundels and notched applied strips. Handles are broad strap handles decorated with slashing: only a single rod handle was found.

3037:1 (Fig. 61, 7). Money box fragment. See Barton (1988, Fig. 15, No. 20) for comparison.

Dating and frequency: dated at Christchurch Place from the late 12th-16th century. By the end of the 16th century it is suggested that this ware is no longer in production or circulation (Papazian, forthcoming b).

Fabric 001: Dublin cooking ware

Fabric and forms: for macroscopic fabric description see Papazian (1989, 125); for petrological analysis see ibid. (126-28). For a gazetteer of known vessel forms see ibid. (128-32).

3030:77 (Fig. 61, 8). Bowl, rim diameter 24 cm., base diameter 26 cm., slightly concave in profile. Undecorated: exterior soot marked.

3036:24 (Fig. 61, 5). Rim fragment, decorated with comb stabbing.

Dating and frequency: at Christchurch Place, these wares are dated from the late 12th-16th centuries; their relative frequency over this long period of production is very similar to fabric 002 in that significant amounts were found in early mid-13th century contexts, but thereafter the amount recovered (and presumably deposited) declined. The amount deposited increased in contexts dated to

	?13th	1400 -1500	1500 -1600	Post- medieval	Unstratified	Sherd totals	MNV*
Levels	1	2	3 & 4	5 & 6			
Fabric 004	0	9	6	1	0	16	2
Fabric 004 cook ware	0	0	0	0	1	1	1
Fabric 002	1	331	162	6	25	525	56
Fabric 001	0	18	100	10	17	145	23
Fabric 003	2	17	462	17	31	529	41

(*minimum number of vessels)

Table 15: Medieval Dublin wares by period, group, sherd count and MNV

15th-16th centuries, although their greatest frequency was in contexts dated to the first part of the 13th century (Papazian, forthcoming b). At Site G, these wares were recovered in greatest frequency from 16th century contexts and this is probably a factor of the volume of material dumped into the moat at this time.

Fabric 003: Dublin temper free wares

Fabric and forms: for macroscopic description see Papazian (1989, 96-97); for petrological analysis see ibid. (142).

A description of forms is given in ibid. (116-18). At Site G, jugs are the most common form; these have rims decorated with thumbed applied strips, pulled spouts, and apart from slight grooving on the body of the pot, are usually undecorated. Where decoration occurs the commonest motif is applied pinched pads of clay, like small rivets in the body of the vessel or applied notched strips. Bases are usually continuously thumbed. Pedestelled or plain bases are rare. Additional forms include bottles, bowls, condiment dishes and (possible) lids. See also Papazian (forthcoming b), for further illustrations of fabric 003 forms; the profile of a condiment dish, glazed internally and externally is illustrated in Fig. 61, 6, 3025:126.

Dating and frequency: fabric 003 wares are dated from the late 12th or beginning of the 13th century to the end of the 16th century at Christchurch Place. The evidence from Site G suggests these wares occur with greatest frequency in 16th century contexts. This differs from the deposition patterns at Christchurch Place where it was noted that the amounts of fabric 003 wares from 15th and 16th century contexts remained the same. Clearly the volume of this ware from levels 3 and 4 at Site G (Table 15) indicates concentrated localised dumping.

The ceramic sequence

The dating evidence for the assemblage from Site G is based on the stratigraphic evidence and the numismatic evidence from the later levels. In addition the dating evidence is buttressed by comparison with the ceramic sequences from other Dublin medieval sites. The sequence discussed below represents a relative, not an absolute sequence and is subject to refinement when more closely datable assemblages are excavated.

Level 1: late 12th-early 13th century

Only a few sherds of pottery were recovered from the earliest layers. These sherds might be contemporary with the construction of the ditch and the primary fills. The limited amount of ceramic finds suggests that initially the moat was kept relatively free of dumped material, otherwise the author would have expected the volume of material which characterises the filling of the moat elsewhere in Dublin during this period (for example, the moat fills at Dublin Castle; Papazian 1989).

Level 2: 14th-15th centuries

Based on the stratigraphic evidence and the recovery of a sherd of Martincamp type 2 from the overlying level, level 3, it seems possible that the pottery from this level could have accumulated over a wide period – perhaps over 200 years. However, the evidence from Christchurch Place (Papazian, forthcoming b), suggests that by the 15th century fabric 004: Dublin hand-built wares had died out, and that fabrics 001-003 dominated ceramic assemblages from the 15th to the end of the 16th century.

Clearly this evidence is tenuous, but in the absence of other assemblages dating to the later medieval period, the author ventures to suggest that at Site G also, fabric 004 wares are virtually absent from the stratigraphically later levels. In this respect the two assemblages are quite similar and it is suggested that the majority of the assemblage from level 2 post-dates the known production period for fabric 004 wares, and can thus be dated to the 15th century.

Fabric 002: Dublin glazed wares dominate the assemblage from level 2. Fabric 001: Dublin cooking wares and Fabric 003: Dublin temper free wares occur in small amounts (Table 15). Imports are rare finds, while it is possible to state that Ham Green 'B', south-east Wiltshire and Chester are residual by the 15th century. The long production periods for Saintonge and Redcliffe make it difficult to state whether they occur at Site G as residual or contemporaneous finds in 15th century contexts.

Levels 3-4: 16th century

The bulk of the medieval pottery assemblage was recovered from the latest dumps into the moat. The quantity of the pottery may have much to do with the fact that the material was being deposited not through the gradual build up of household refuse (as in level 2), but via a concerted effort to infill the ditch in advance of the construction of a road or pathway over the ditch.

The bulk of the pottery is fabric 003: Dublin temper free wares. The ceramic evidence indicates, however, that much of the pottery from levels 3-4 is residual, and that material pre-dating the 16th century was used to backfill the moat at this period.

This evidence warns against drawing conclusions from the evidence of a single site and enforces the need to understand the nature of the ceramic evidence in the context of all Dublin sites rather than on an individual site by site basis.

POST-MEDIEVAL POTTERY FROM SITE G

Rosanne Meenan

This assemblage of pottery has been sorted into find contexts. A detailed catalogue of sherds recovered has been lodged with the archive, and the summary of wares present in each context is given in Table 17. None are illustrated. A date range is suggested for each context.

Context 3000

There is quite a wide range of wares present in this group - the earliest being the late Saintonge wares and a possible medieval pipkin, while the latest are the mid-18th century black wares and the few sherds of industrially produced wares. Context 3000 is a surface clearance context number; in this case it is surprising that there were no cream wares, pearl wares or later wares. The assemblage as examined provides a latest date of the mid-18th century. The brown wares were interesting in that the quality of the vessels was high-grade. The black ware assemblage was also interesting in that there were a lot of 17th century types and the incidence of a Rainford type tyg, represented by a single body sherd, is certainly noteworthy.

Context 3002

Body sherd of mottled ware tankard. C. 1680-*c.* 1760, but it seems probable that these wares did not become popular in Dublin until the early 18th century.

Context 3005

A probable date in the early to mid-18th century is suggested for this group. The Lancashire self-coloured ware tankard can be dated to the late 17th century but may be residual in this context.

Context 3006

This group is difficult to date as there are no Continental imports. It would probably be safest to assign a general 17th century date.

Context 3008

This group is not easily dateable; the Low Countries slipware is the earliest element in the group, but as an exotic it may have survived longer after manufacture than the other wares which were more serviceable. Possible 17th-18th century.

Context 3009

The imported sherds from this layer all date to the late 16th century into the 17th century. The black ware sherds may also be dated to the end of the 16th century so a date *c.* 1590-1630 would appear to be acceptable for this group. Although this group is stratigraphically later than 3010, 3023, this is not reflected in pottery assemblage.

Context 3010, 3023

The same proposition holds for this group of pottery as for that from 3009. The Continental imports would tend to date around 1600 and the other wares would fit into that range. The date provided by the pottery coincides with the date for the Nuremberg jeton (1586-1635) found in 3010. The only problematic piece is the tankard base which is reminiscent of the late 17th or even into the 18th century. However, this is a subjective assessment of the type and with further research this tankard type may prove to be typical of the decades around 1600. Otherwise, the sherds from this context form a typical assemblage of the late 16th-17th century, probably 1590-1630. The absence of the ubiquitous tin-glazed wares, apart from the Italian examples, would tend to confirm the earlier date.

The occurrence of handmade bricks in these features is extremely interesting; a brick was found in a pit in 23-27 Lr Stephen St, Dublin, in association with late 16th century pottery and textile.

Context 3011

A single sherd. Probably Frechen, probably late 16th-early 17th century.

Total number of sherds 94

Ware	No. of sherds	% of total
Black	38	40.42
Beauvais	2	2.127
Martincamp	2	2.127
Late Saintonge	4	4.25
Low Countries	3	3.19
Rhenish stoneware	12	12.76
Iberian	6	6.38
North Devon	7	7.44
Misc. & unidentified	7	7.44
Italian	1	1.06
Werra	2	2.12
Glazed red earthenware	10	10.63

**Table 16. Percentage of wares
by sherd count, Site G**

129

Context	3000	3002	3005	3006	3008	3009	3010/23	3011	3014	3017	3044
Pottery											
Black ware	P		P	P	P	P	P		P	P	P
Local black ware	P										
Lancashire ware			P								
Unidentified	P										
Bris.-Staff. slipware	P								P		
Normandy stoneware	P										
Martincamp stoneware	P						P				
Werra slipware	P						P				
Low Countries	P				P	P	P				
Late Saintonge	P								P		
Beauvais	P					P	P		P		
Seville amphora	P						P		P		
Merida type	P										
Tin-glazed earthenware	P										
N. Devon wares	P			P	P		P		P		
English stonewares	P										
Frechen	P						P	P			
Cologne	P						P				
Raeren	P						P				
German stoneware (unidentified)	P						P				
Mottled wares	P	P	P								
Yellow ware	P										
18th century ware	P										
Brown ware	P		P	P	P	P	P		P		P
Slipware	P										
Imported brown ware	P										
Italian majolica					P	P					

(p = present)

Table 17. Post-medieval wares, Site G

Black ware	38 sherds	panel jug	1
storage vessel	5	drinking mugs/jugs	5
bowl or jar	1	**Iberian**	6 sherds
drinking vessel	3	amphora	2
costrel	2	unidentified Merida-type vessel	2
Cistercian ware drinking vessel	1	oil jug	1
cooking vessel	1	**North Devon**	7 sherds
Beauvais	1 sherds	storage vessel	1
dish	1	spouted bowl	1
Martincamp	2 sherds	bowl	1
flask	2	**Italian maiolica**	1 sherd
Late Saintonge	4 sherds	dish	1
unidentified vessels	2	**Werra**	2 sherds
possible candlestick	1	dish	1
Low Countries	3 sherds	**Brown ware**	10 sherds
cauldron	2	salter	1
Malling jug	1	unidentified vessel	1
Rhenish stoneware	12 sherds	tankard	1

Table 18. Sherd count and MNV in each ware

Context 3014

This is a mixed assemblage; the Beauvais is the earliest sherd (apart from the medieval strap handle which is residual) but the presence of Bristol/Staffordshire material confirms that there was contamination from later levels.

Context 3017

A single black ware body sherd, possibly of cup. Probably 17th century.

Context 3044

The presence of locally made black ware crock suggests an 18th century date for this group.

Discussion

The predominance of the black wares in this assemblage is clear. These comprised both drinking vessels, food processing and storage vessels. Unfortunately this cannot yet be compared with the material from Dublin Castle as the final processing of the data has not yet been completed, but my recollection is that there were not groups which would be so tightly dated. However, it does suggest a definite trade with the Lancashire area which at this time may have been carried out though Chester rather than Liverpool. Continental imports comprise 34.01 per cent of the collection, the biggest element of which were the Rhenish stonewares at 12.76 per cent. These were all drinking vessels – at Exeter stoneware drinking vessels were very popular up to *c.* 1600 but then fell into a sharp decline in the following decades (Allan 1984, 101).

Local brown wares formed 10.63 per cent of the assemblage.

SMALL FINDS

Alan Hayden and Claire Walsh

Coins. With thanks to Michael Kenny.
The date of the context from which each catalogued find was recovered is given

Bracteates (Fig. 63)
Bracteates are coins consisting of thin metal foil struck on one side only. It is unknown who issued them in Ireland, and their exact value and use is unclear. They do not appear to have continued in circulation after the Anglo-Norman colonisation. Several bracteates have been uncovered from the N.M.I. excavations in Dublin. The coins from Patrick St belong to the late series, and are loosely dated to the early mid-12th century (M. Kenny, pers. comm.).

E543:48:1 (Fig. 63, 1). Quatrefoil? in circle.
Much of the centre is missing. Edge is uneven. Copper alloy. 19.4mm. x 20mm. Breadth: 0.2mm.
Site B, level 2, early 13th century river silts.

E543:56:9 (Fig. 63, 2). Quatrefoil in circle, with pellets in the four spandrels. Debased pseudo inscription around edge. Very worn. Copper alloy. Similar to Ulster Museum 399 (Seaby).
18.7mm. x 21mm. Breadth: 0.2mm.
Site B, level 1, later 12th century river silts.

E543:117:1 (Fig. 63, 3). Voided long cross with 'hammers' within circle. Radiating ribs (debased pseudo inscription) outside circle. Copper alloy.
18.5mm. x 17.7mm. Breadth: 0.3mm.
Site C, level 1, later 12th century river gravel.

Late medieval/post-medieval coins (not illustrated)
E543:1100:147. Silver groat. Date range 1483-1550.
Obverse worn, and coated with sulphides. Crowned escutcheon, quadrants. Triple fleur-de-lis and lions.
Diameter: 25.7mm. Breadth: 0.7mm.
Surface find, Site E.

E543:1100:150. Half crown of James II.
'Gunmoney', minted at Dublin and Limerick, was made of brass.
Reverse reads MAG {BR......F} RA.ET.HIB.REX. XI. The month of issue is not decipherable, but is likely to be January. Obverse: the monarch's head is eroded, reads {JACO} B {US}. DEI. G {RATIA}.
Diameter: 23.1mm. Breadth: 1.2mm.
Surface find, Site E.

E543:3010:59. Information from Michael Kenny, N.M.I.
Brass jeton, Nuremberg, by Hans Kravwinckel II, 1586-1635.
Obverse: * HANNS KRAVWINCKEL IN NURNBE:
Reverse: VERBUM DOMINI. MANET IN ETERN.

The Kravwinckel family dominated Nuremberg jeton production for well over half a century until the death of Hans (Hanns) II in 1635. Damianus, his brother Hans I and his sons Equidius and Hans II, between them produced vast numbers of jetons of varied design, weight and metal. Hans II, first noted in 1586, had business links with and used the services of the well-known engravers Valentin and Christian Maler, striking jetons in the French and Spanish as well as the German style (Mitchener 1988, 435-38).

Modern coins (not illustrated)
Eight copper coins, pennies, halfpennies, and two farthings were recovered from clearance layers. These range in date from 1714-1964.

Copper alloy

Spoon
E543:3010:62 (Fig. 64, 1). Intact spoon, of copper alloy or latten, with pear-shaped bowl. Knop consists of flat octagonal plate with collar, which is hammered on to the stem.

1　　　　**2**　　　　**3**

Fig. 63. Bracteates (scale 1:1)

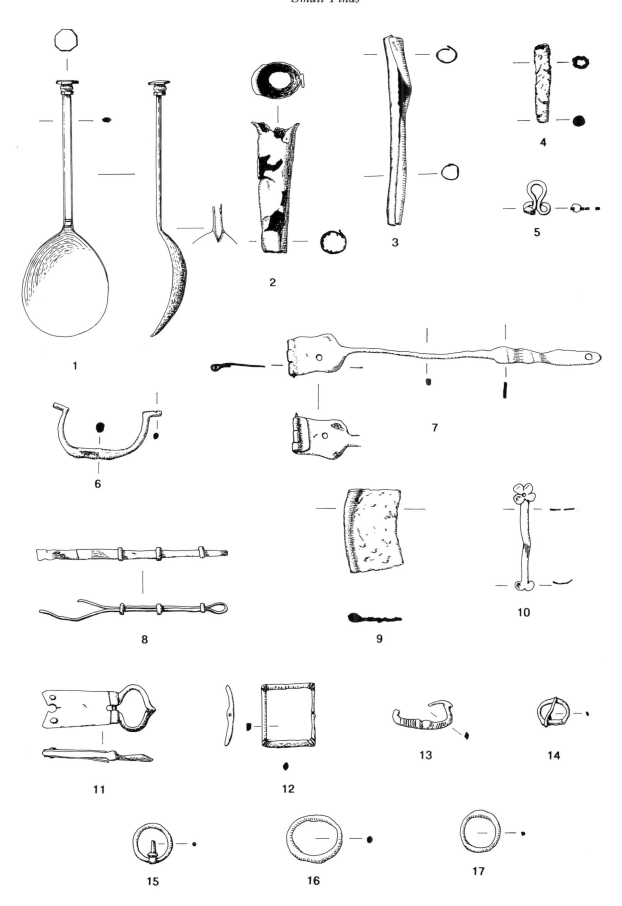

Fig. 64. Copper alloy small finds (scale 1:2)

Two pairs of lightly incised lines occur as decoration at the base of the stem. A similar spoon, in pewter, was recently recovered from a 17th century context at the Bridge St, Dublin, excavations (A. Hayden, pers. comm.), while a similar spoon was recovered from the excavation at Cowlam deserted village (Brewster and Hayfield 1988, Fig. 15, 31). Length: 139.5mm. Width of bowl: 46mm. Depth of bowl: 14mm. Stem: rectangular sectioned; width: 4.5mm., thickness: 2.5mm.
Site G, level 5, late 16th-early 17th century.

Ferrule
E543:313:2 (Fig. 63, 2). Copper alloy sheet 1mm. thick, fashioned into a tapering cylinder. Everted rim at wider end. Traces of wood in interior. Centre corroded.
Length: 69.9mm. Maximum diameter: 23mm.
Site F, surface find.

Tubes
E543:3010:70 (Fig. 63, 3). Formed from a rolled piece of sheet copper alloy. Function unknown.
Length: 102mm. Diameter: 10.5mm.
Site G, level 5, late 16th-early 17th century.

E543:301:154 (Fig. 63, 4). Circular section tube, open and broken at one end closed at other. Heavily corroded.

Length: 43.5mm. Diameter: 4.1mm.
Site F, level 5, 14th century or later.

Eye loop
E543:1106:5 (Fig. 63, 5). Annular loop of rectangular section (1.1mm. diameter). Copper alloy. Terminals bent outwards to form circles. Iron stud/rivet survives in one terminal. Handle.
Length: 17.6mm.
Site E, surface find.

E543:1100:153 (Fig. 63, 6). C-shaped handle of oval section. Terminals project outwards.
Length: 57.6mm. Width: 5.9mm.
Site E, surface find.

Hinge
E543:32:5 (Fig. 63, 7). Silvered copper alloy hinge, probably from book cover or casket. Broad flat end with central perforation and two flanges bent around iron rod. Third flange from second part of hinge (latter missing) also survives. From this end hinge narrows to round section rod before broadening into flat end with perforation close to end.
Length: 165mm. Maximum width: 21.5mm.
Site B, level 4, 14th century.

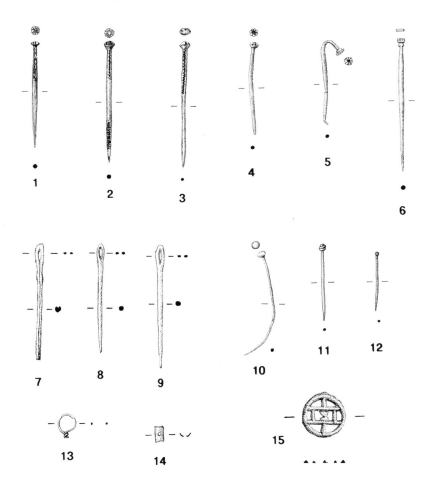

Fig. 65. Copper alloy and silver small finds (scale 1:2)

Tweezers

E543:328:1 (Fig. 64, 8). Fashioned from single piece of copper alloy sheet. Three sliding loops survive. One highly corroded. Ends of both arms broken. Undecorated.
Length: 101.2mm. Maximum width: 6mm.
Site F, level 2, late 12th century.

Vessel rim

E543:1100:145 (Fig. 64, 9). Fragment of broad flat everted rim with thickened and rounded edge. Rim originally *c.* 170mm. diameter.
Length: 30.3mm. Width: 15mm. Thickness: 1.2mm.
Site E, surface find.

Mounts

E543:3010:65 (Fig. 64, 10). Cut from sheet metal, this has one intact and one broken quatrefoil motif, perforated in the centres for attachment.
Length: 55mm. Width: 4mm. Thickness: 1mm.
Site G, level 5, late 16th-early 17th century.

E543:3010:69 (not illustrated). Cut from sheet metal. Rectangular. Plain with rivet hole at one end.
Length: 79mm. Width: 7mm. Thickness: 0.5mm.
Site G, level 5, late 16th-early 17th century.

Buckles and rings

The buckles uncovered include both shoe (E543:378:2:20) and belt (E543:111:11, E543:377:3, E543:3026:28) buckles. The annular buckle/brooches may have been used in a number of ways, on clothing or harness. The two rings are simple undecorated annular loops and were probably not finger rings.

E543:3026:28 (Fig. 64, 11). Oval framed buckle with composite rigid plates. Copper alloy frame, copper plates. Notch for missing pin. Frame is lipped and bevelled. A separate sheet is soldered on to back and front to form a hollow plate. Plate has two copper rivets. Widespread mid-14th-early 15th century form in Britain (Egan and Pritchard 1991, 78).
Length: 55.5mm. Width: 19.5mm. Thickness: 5mm.
Site G, level 3, 14th-16th century .

E543:377:3 (Fig. 64, 12). Rectangular double sided belt buckle. Loop of rectangular to oval section, 2.8mm. diameter maximum. Loop decorated at corners by three incised parallel lines. No pin and pin bar but holes for suspension of pin bar survive.
Length: 34.5mm. Width: 28.6mm.
Site F, surface find.

E543:111:11 (Fig 64, 13). Incomplete D-shaped belt buckle. Pin bar incomplete, no pin. Loop: flat back, convex front, decorated on front by six incised parallel vertical lines on either side of raised and notched pin rest.
Length: 31.5mm. Width: 14mm. Maximum thickness: 3.7mm.
Site B, level 1, 13th century.

E543:378:2:20 (Fig. 64, 14). D-shaped shoe buckle. Loop: flat back, convex front. Rectangular section pin looped

around pin bar. Notch on loop for pin rest.
Length: 17.3mm. Width: 14.8mm. Loop: 2.6mm. wide.
Site F, found in mortice of 13th century revetment, presumably deposited when structure went out of use. 15th century type. (D. O'Rourke, pers. comm.).

E543:1012:1 (Fig. 64, 15). Annular buckle/brooch of circular section, 2.2mm. diameter copper alloy. Seating with stump of plain collared pin survives.
Maximum diameter: 21mm.
Site F, level 2, 13th century.

E543:1004:2 (Fig. 64, 16). Plain oval annular ring of oval section copper alloy, 4.5mm. maximum diameter.
Maximum diameter: 29.5mm.
Site F, level 2, 13th century.

E543:301:155 (Fig. 64, 17). Plain annular ring of 2.8mm. diameter copper alloy wire.
Maximum diameter: 22.5mm.
Site F, level 5, 14th-15th century.

Stick pins

Six copper alloy stick pins were recovered. Pins of these types are commonly recovered from medieval excavations. They appear to have functioned as dress pins, hair pins and shroud pins.

E543:216:5 (Fig. 65, 1). Stud head decorated with incised radiating lines. Shank: circular section tapering to square section point. Upper shank decorated on four sides with incised vertical zig-zag lines.
Length: 58.7mm. Maximum shank diameter: 2.2mm. Width of head: 4.4mm.
Site D, level 2, 13th century.

E543:48.3 (Fig. 65, 2). Club head, decorated with incised radiating lines, narrow collar on underside. Shank: circular section tapering to four-sided point. Upper shank decorated on three sides with incised vertical zig-zag lines. Pointed end also decorated with incised zig-zag lines – the latter form of decoration is quite unusual.
Length: 66.6mm. Maximum shank diameter: 2.5mm. Width of head: 5.5mm.
Site B, level 2, 13th century.

E543:1052:2 (Fig. 65, 3). Oval club head, decorated with five sub radial incised lines. Shank: circular section tapering to sharp point. Upper shank decorated on three sides by incised vertical zig-zag lines.
Length: 69mm. Maximum shank diameter: 2.4mm. Width of head: 5.4mm. x 3.5mm.
Patrick St, surface find.

E543:324:1 (Fig. 65, 4). Club head, top divided into seven lobes by incised lines. Shank: circular section tapering to a point. Point broken. No expansion of shank.
Length: 50.7mm. Maximum shank diameter: 2.1mm. Width of head: 4.7mm.
Site F, level 5, 14th century.

E543:219:1 (Fig. 65, 5). Expanded stud head, flat and

decorated with incised lines radiating from central hollow, hemispherical collar on underside. Shank: circular section tapering to point, bent at point and below head.
Length: 58mm. Maximum shank diameter: 2.2mm. Width of head: 4.6mm.
Site D, level 1, late 12th century.

E543:1101:69 (Fig. 65, 6). Squared spatulate head decorated on long sides with five lightly incised vertical lines, contraction below head, collar with pointed projection at both ends. Shank: circular section with marked expansion tapering to point.
Length: 72.9mm. Maximum shank diameter: 2.4mm. Width of head: 4.4mm.
Site E, level 2, 14th century.

Copper alloy wire (not illustrated)
Lengths of drawn, twisted wire were recovered from the following contexts:
E543:3010:61, E543:3023:1. Both Site G, level 5, late 16th-early 17th century.
E543:3026:297. Site G, level 3, 14th-16th century.

Wire drawn pins
Eighteen pins made of round section drawn copper alloy wire were recovered.
The heads of the pins take three forms:
   Globular – the wire wound around the head was moulded into a rough sphere.
   Coiled – the head was formed of a twist or two of the same wire as used in the shank.
   Spherical – the head is formed of a separate globular piece of copper alloy.
Pins of this type are commonly found in medieval and post-medieval contexts. They are generally thought to have been used in dress-making but were also used for fastening veils and headdresses (Egan and Pritchard 1991, 297). They were also frequently used as shroud pins, occurring for example, with burials in the graveyard of St Peter's Church, Waterford.

Globular headed
E543:203:60 (not illustrated). Incomplete.
Length: 23mm. Shank diameter: 0.8mm. Head diameter: 1.6mm.

E543:203:61 (not illustrated). Incomplete.
Length: 12.7mm. Shank diameter: 0.6mm. Head diameter: 1.4mm.
Both Site D, level 3, 13th century.

E543:1100:154a (Fig. 65, 10).
Length: 31.9mm. Shank diameter: 0.9mm. Head diameter: 2mm.

E543:1100:154b (not illustrated).
Length: 30mm. Shank diameter: 0.6mm. Head diameter: 2.2mm.

E543:1100:154c (not illustrated).
Length: 30mm. Shank diameter: 0.7mm. Head diameter: 1.5mm.

E543:1106:3 (not illustrated).
Length: 25.5mm. Shank diameter: 0.7mm. Head diameter: 1.6mm.
All Site E, surface finds.

E543:1132:3a (not illustrated).
Length: 28.5mm. Shank diameter: 0.9mm. Head diameter: 2mm.

E543:1132:3b (not illustrated).
Length: 28.4mm. Shank diameter: 0.6mm. Head diameter: 1.9mm.
Both Site E, level 2, 14th century.

E543:3010:64a (not illustrated).
Length: 20.5mm. Shank diameter: 0.3mm. Head diameter: 1mm.
Site G, level 5, late 16th-early 17th century.

Coiled headed
E543:737:4 (not illustrated). Incomplete.
Length: 16.5mm. Shank diameter: 1mm. Head diameter: 2.4mm.
Site K, surface find.

E543:1052:1 (not illustrated). Incomplete.
Length: 7.5mm. Shank diameter: 0.7mm. Head diameter: 1.8mm.
Patrick St, surface find.

E543:1100:209 (Fig. 65, 11).
Length: 41.5mm. Shank diameter: 1.1mm. Head diameter: 3.3mm.
Site E, surface find.

Spherical headed
E543:1143:5 (Fig. 65, 12).
Length: 63mm. Shank diameter: 0.8mm. Head diameter: 4.6mm.
Site E, level 1, 14th century.

E543:3026:278 (not illustrated).
Length: 37mm. Shank diameter: 0.5mm. Head diameter: 4mm.
Site G, level 3, 14th-16th century.

Head absent (not illustrated)
E543:1132:3c. Incomplete.
Length: 21.2mm. Shank diameter: 0.4mm.
Site E, level 2, 14th century.

E543:1143:2.
Length: 19.5mm. Shank diameter: 0.5mm.
Site E, level 1, 14th century.

E543:3010:64b.
Length: 37.5mm. Shank diameter: 0.6mm.

E543:3010:64c.
Length: 23mm. Shank diameter: 0.2mm.
Both Site G, level 5, late 16th-early 17th century.

Loops

Objects of uncertain function, consisting of a loop of round section copper alloy wire with the ends twisted together. They are known from domestic contexts, for example, St Peter's St, Northampton (Williams 1979, 260–61), but also appear to have functioned in a secondary context as shroud fasteners as they occurred with several burials in the graveyard of St Peter's Church, Waterford.

E543:1132:3a–d.
a. Diameter: 8.2mm. Breadth: 1mm. Incomplete – only penannular ring survives.
b. Diameter: 10.2mm. Breadth: 0.8mm.
c. (Fig. 65, 13). Diameter: 9.2mm. Breadth: 0.9mm.
d. Diameter: 7.2mm. Breadth: 0.55m.
All Site E, level 2, 14th century or later.

E543:3010:66, a and b.
a. Diameter: 9mm. Breadth: 0.7mm.
b. Diameter: 8.4mm. Breadth: 0.5mm.
Site G, level 5, late 16th–early 17th century.

Lace ends (not illustrated)

These are short lengths of rolled thin copper alloy sheeting, used to bind the ends of laces in clothing.

E543:3010:68, a and b.
a. Length: 28.5mm. Diameter: 2mm.
b. Length: 28.5mm. Diameter: 1.6mm.
Site G, level 5, late 16th–early 17th century.

E543:3015:237.
Length: 24mm. Diameter: 2mm.
Site G, level 4, mid–late 16th century.

Sewing needles

E543:1100:237 (Fig. 65, 7). Shank fashioned from rolled sheet of copper alloy, circular in section, tapering to point, latter broken. Flattened head. Oval eye set in countersunk groove.
Length: 63.5mm. Shank diameter: 3mm. Width of head: 4mm. Length of eye: 7mm.
Site E, surface find.

E543:1100:236 (Fig. 65, 8). Shank: circular cross section, tapering to point, latter broken. Flattened head. Oval eye set in countersunk groove.
Length: 58.7mm. Shank diameter: 1.8mm. Width of head: 3.1mm. Length of eye: 4.5mm.
Site E, surface find.

E543:1110:1 (Fig. 65, 9). Shank: circular section, tapering to point, latter broken. Flattened head, square top. Oval eye set in countersunk groove.
Length: 66.7mm. Shank diameter: 2.7mm. Width of Head: 3.3mm. Length of eye: 5mm.
Site E, surface find.

Sheets/offcuts (not illustrated)

E543:1147:1b. Copper alloy strip with central perforation encased in corroded iron nails (1147:1a).

Length: at least 33mm. Width: 11.5mm. Thickness: 0.5mm.
Site E, level 1, 14th century.

E543:391:1. Rectangular section strip with irregular edges, ends broken, fractured in centre.
Length: 57mm. Width: 4.5mm. Thickness: 0.6mm.
Site F, level 3, early 13th century.

E543:1004:6. Strip.
Length: 50mm. Width: 4.1mm. Thickness: 1.8mm.
Site F, level 2, late 12th–early 13th century.

E543:1100:232. Strip: irregular edges, one end cut.
Length: 92mm. Width: 13mm. Thick: 1.3mm.
Site E, surface find.

E543:1101:72. Subrectangular sheet, three edges cut, one broken.
Length: 34mm. Width: 28mm. Thickness: 0.7mm.
Site E, level 2, 14th century.

E543:1101:70. Strip bent into open hoop, irregular edges, pointed ends.
Length: 30.3mm. Width: 15mm. Thickness: 1.2mm.
Site E, level 2, 14th century.

E543:3010:63. Fragment of sheet metal, folded over several times.
Length: 38mm. Width: 22.5mm. Thickness: 4.5mm.
Site G, level 5, late 16th–early 17th century.

E543:3035:149. Off-cut from sheet copper.
Length: 34.5mm. Width: 27mm. Thickness: 2mm.
Site G, level 1, 13th century.

Silver

Plaque or Badge

E543:329:1 (Fig. 65, 15). Cast circular open-work plaque of D-section pewter or silver. Interior divided into eight open areas by perpendicular lines. Small circular raised boss at centre. Flashing from casting present. Decorative device to be sewn on to clothing.
Diameter: 24.3mm. Thickness: 1mm.
Site F, level 1, late 12th century.

Mount

E543:1143:3 (Fig. 65, 14). Small convex section strip with central perforation. Possibly edge strip of metal object.
Length: 9.5mm. Width: 5.3mm. Thickness: 1.1mm.
Site E, level 1, 14th century.

Gold

Offcut

E543:1143:4 (not illustrated). Offcut from thick sheet, irregular edges, tapering at both ends.
Length: 65.2mm. Width: 3.3mm. Thickness: 0.8mm.
Site E, level 1, 14th century.

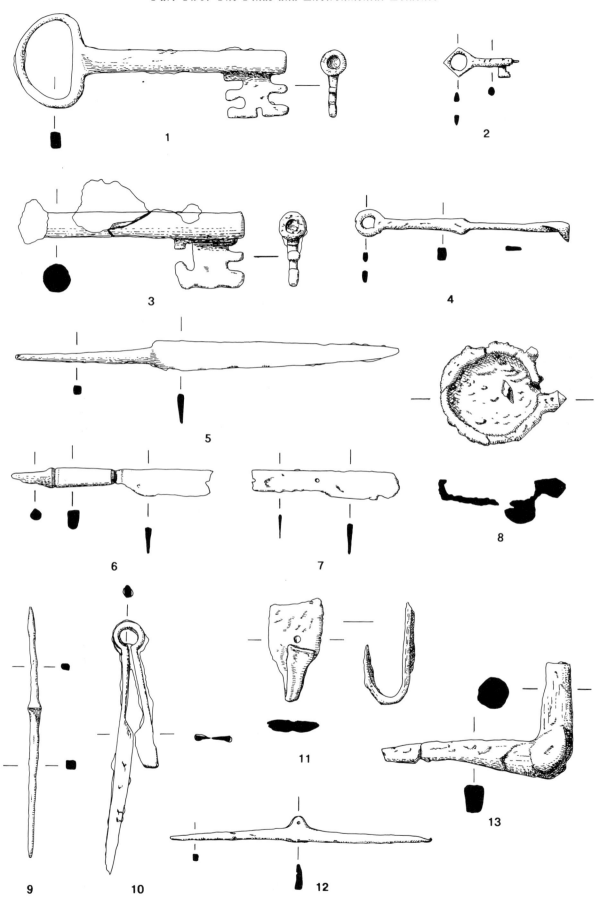

Fig. 66. Iron small finds (scale 1:2)

Iron

Keys

E543:3032:138 (Fig. 66, 1). Door or chest key (London Museum 1940, 136, type 3). D-shaped bow, hollow circular stem. Bit has five ward cuts.
Length: 144mm. Diameter of stem: 11.5mm. Length of bit: 32mm. Width of bit: 24mm.
Site G, level 2, 14th-15th century.

E543:31:1 (Fig. 66, 2). Casket key. Lozenge shaped bow with circular opening. Stem of square section, with pointed end. Stepped bit.
Length: 41.2mm. Width of head: 15.9mm.
Site B, level 3, late 13th century.

E543:3030:113 (Fig. 66, 3). Door or chest key (London Museum 1940, 136, type 3). Bow missing, hollow circular stem. Bit has three ward cuts.
Length: 112mm. Diameter of stem: 13mm. Length of bit: 34.5mm. Width of bit: 25.5mm.
Site G, level 3, 16th century.

E543:201:17 (Fig. 66, 4). Barrel padlock key. Broad rectangular section shank changing to flattened rectangular section mid way along. Bit broken.
Length: 114:5mm. Width: 15.8mm.
Site D, surface find.

Knives and blades

E543:3015:235 (Fig. 66, 5). Knife with triangular blade, tip broken. Blade length: 97mm. Width: 15mm. Thickness: 4mm. Whittle tang, length 73mm., central on blade, straight shoulder, tapering.
Site G, level 4, mid-late 16th century.

E543:3023:94 (Fig. 66, 6). Knife, incomplete. Blade, tip broken, length: 59.5mm. Width: 14mm. Thickness: 2.4mm. Shoulder plate, rectangular section, cast in one with blade, tapers from blade to tang. Length: 32mm. Width: 13mm. Thickness: 7mm. Whittle tang, centrally placed, traces of a wooden handle. Two holes in blade: corrosion? May be part of E543:3015:236: see below.
Site G, level 5, late 16th-early 17th century.

E543:3015:236 (Fig. 66, 7). Part of blade, possibly E543:3023:94 (above). Two small holes in blade, purpose unknown.
Fragment length: 78mm. Width: 14.5mm. (cutting edge eroded). Thickness: 2.2mm.
Site G, level 4, mid-late 16th century.

E543:1132:12 (not illustrated). Curving sub-triangular shaped object. Rounded triangular section. Broken at broader end. Possible tip of curved blade.
Length: 57.1mm. Width: 21.7mm. Thickness: 3.8mm.
Site E, level 2, 14th century or later.

E543:306:24a (not illustrated). Highly corroded sub-triangular object of triangular section. Possibly a fragment of a blade.
Length: 88.2mm. Width: 22mm. Thickness: 14mm.
Side F, surface find.

Shears

E543:3023:1 (Fig. 66, 10). Blade triangular, one complete. Length: 76mm., Width: 8mm. Thickness: 3mm. Handle length: 38mm: Width: 4mm. Thickness: 3.5mm., square section. Bow circular.
Site G, level 5, late 16th-early 17th century.

Glassmaker's pan

E543:201:16 (Fig. 66, 8). Shallow bowl with lateral broken projection from rim (handle). Sheet iron. Heavily corroded, traces of melted deposits on interior.
Length: 68.5mm. Width: 54mm. Thickness: 10mm.
Site D, surface find.

Strap hinge

E543:377:2 (Fig. 66, 11). Incomplete strap hinge with U-shaped hanging eye. Rectangular section, iron bent back on itself. One arm narrow and splaying outwards at end. Other arm broad, with central perforation filled with corroded deposits. Heavily corroded.
Length: 53.6mm. Width: 28.2mm. Thickness: 5.5mm.
Site F, level 3, 13th century.

Awl

E543:25:61 (Fig. 66, 9). Square section shank, 82mm. long, tapering to point, latter broken. Shank expands where it meets tang, which is of round section and is 56.8mm. long. Corroded.
Length: 138.8mm. Maximum diameter: 7.2mm.
Site B, level 3, late 13th century.

Balance beam

E543:715:1 (Fig. 66, 12). Balance beam of weighing scales, rectangular section. Suspension hook survives at one end only. Suspension hole visible but filled with corroded deposits.
Length: 142mm.
Site K, level 2, 13th century.

Hinge pivots

E543:1004:4 (Fig. 66, 13). Rectangular cross-sectioned, tapering shank, circular cross-sectioned pivot. Corroded, stones adhering.
Length: 104.2mm. Width: 65.5mm. Thickness: 16mm.
Site E, level 2, 14th century or later.

E543:3026:272 (not illustrated). Rectangular cross-sectioned tapering shank, circular cross-sectioned pivot. Lime mortar adhering.
Length of shank: 109mm. Width: 12mm. Thickness: 7mm.
Site G, level 3, 14th-16th century.

Vessel rim

E543:1132:15 (not illustrated). Possible fragment of vessel rim. Slightly curved lengthways. One side straight and bevelled, other side broken. Corroded.
Length: 38.5mm. Width: 7.6mm. Thickness: 2.5mm.
Site E, level 2, 14th century.

Mould

E543:223:48 (not illustrated). Possible mould. Heavily corroded iron tapering cylinder with lateral flange at closed end. Stones and corroded deposits adhering.
Length: 85.1mm. Maximum width: 45.9mm. Core diameter: 10.3mm.
Site D, level 2, 13th century.

Chisel

E543:100:172 (not illustrated). Highly corroded square section bar flattened and splaying outwards at one end. Stones and wood adhering.
Length: 108mm.
Site C, surface find.

Staple

E543:369:1 (not illustrated). Heavily corroded U-shaped staple or handle of rectangular section.
Length: 89mm. Width: 92mm. Thickness: 13.5mm.
Site F, level 3, 13th century.

Unidentified object

E543:3026:279 (not illustrated). Flat, rectangular sectioned bar of metal, broken at one end, crudely curving and tapering to a point. Possibly a rough clasp. Found with a thin loop of iron, diameter 24mm.
Length: 108mm. Width: 14mm. Thickness: 5mm.
Site G, level 3, 16th century.

Concreted objects

1147:1A (not illustrated). End of iron horseshoe, and horseshoe nails concreted together with copper alloy strip and fragment of lead. Not taken apart during conservation.
Site E, level 1, 14th century.

Lead (not illustrated)

Bar

E543:377:8. Round section tapering to blunt point at one end, flattened and splayed outwards where cut at other end.
Length: 80.7mm. Maximum width: 6.7mm.

Site F, level 3, 13th century.

Waste piece

E543:3023:84. Cut, curving strip.
Length: 106mm. Width: 12mm. Thickness: 3.2mm.
Site G, level 5, late 16th-early 17th century.

Mount

E543:714:1. Roughly cut rectangular section strip with central perforation, 4.5mm. diameter.
Length: 135mm. Width: 14mm. Thickness: 2.4mm.
Site K, level 1, 13th century.

Window leading

E543:1132:17. X-shaped fragment of window leading, flattened and twisted.
Length: 36.5mm. Width: 22mm.
Site E, level 2, 14th century or later.

E543:1143:7a, b, c. Three fragments of fine window leading, twisted and flattened.
Maximum length: 26mm. Width: 6mm.
Site E, level 1, 14th century.

Iron nails

The typology utilised in this report follows that of Ford and Walsh (1987, 137-39).
Two hundred and ten nails or fragments of nails were uncovered. Of these, 138 were identifiable to type (Chart 19), the remainder being either too corroded or incomplete to allow identification.

Carpentry nails

Types A-H were probably wrought. The majority of identifiable nails are of type 'A' and 'B'. All probably date from the 13th-16th centuries and were used in carpentry.

Type A. Circular, oval or square flat head, with square or rectangular section shank. Seventy-seven examples uncovered (Fig. 67, 1 [E543:1101:36] and Fig. 67, 2 [E543:333.3]).

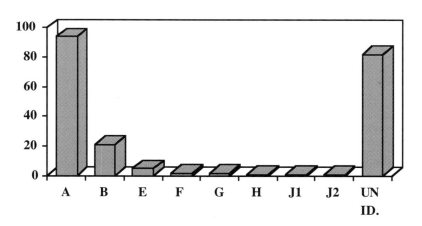

Chart 19. Nail types, Patrick Street/ Winetavern Street

140

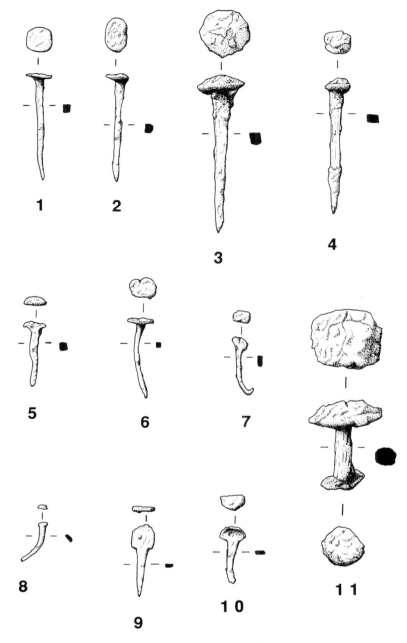

Fig. 67. Iron nails (scale 1:2)

Type B. Circular, oval or sub-rectangular domed head, with square or rectangular section shank. Nineteen examples uncovered (Fig. 67, 3 [E543:1004:3] and Fig. 67, 4 [E543:301:1531]).

Type E. Flat L-shaped head with square or rectangular section shank. Five examples uncovered (Fig. 67, 7 [E543:1146.1b]).

Type F. Flat T-shaped head with square or rectangular section shank. Two examples uncovered (Fig. 67, 5 [E543:1143.1]).

Type G. Flat figure-of-eight-shaped head with square or rectangular section shank. Two examples uncovered (Fig. 67, 6 [E543:357.5]).

Type H. Square or rectangular flat head formed by flaring, rectangular or square section shank. One example uncovered (Fig. 67, 8 [E543:1146:1a]).

Horse shoe or ox shoe nails
Type J1. Fiddle headed nail with a semi-circular flat head, square or rectangular section shank. One example uncovered (Fig. 67, 9 [E543:1136:23a]). Type J1 nails were used with ox and horseshoes with wavy edges and large countersunk nail holes. They are previously recorded from 13th and 14th century contexts.

Type J2. Flat topped and lobed head. Square or rectangular section shank. Two examples uncovered (Fig. 67, 10 [E543:1136:23b]). Type J2 nails were used with horseshoes with a plain outline and rectangular nail holes. They are previously recorded from contexts dating to the 14th and 15th centuries.

Iron rivets
Of a total of five rivets uncovered only one had both heads intact (Fig. 67, 11 [E543:391:72]). The heads of the rivets are either flat or slightly domed and are either round or rectangular in shape. The shanks are of rectangular section.

Bone, antler and ivory

Combs
E543:505:2 (Fig. 68, 2). End of incomplete decorated single sided class F2 composite antler comb (Dunlevy 1988). Four iron rivets survive. Decoration on sideplates consists of incised double outline saltires and incised vertical lines at surviving end. End plate trapezoidal in shape. Six tooth plates survive, teeth rather uneven; 5-6 per cm. Sideplates cracked.
Length: 96mm. Width: 26.5mm. Thickness: 9.5mm.
Site I, level 2, 12th century.

E543:619:1 (Fig. 68, 3). Fragment of sideplate of composite single edged class F2 antler comb (Dunlevy, 1988). D-shaped in section, broken at both ends. Three rivet holes. Decorated with incised triple outline zig-zag. Saw marks on base indicate teeth at 10 per cm.
Length: 33.9mm. Width: 0.3mm. Thickness: 2.3mm.
Site J, level 1, late 12th century.

Roughout for object
E543:3030:111 (Fig. 68, 1). Square sectioned, centrally hollowed and smoothed bone, unfinished object of unknown function. Decoration of horizontal bands crudely executed in relief on one face, saw marking only on other faces. Crude cruciform motif on one face formed by incised lines terminating in drilled holes.
Length: 104mm. Width: 18mm. Thickness: 17.5mm.
Site G, level 3, 14th-16th century.

Roughout for object
E543:3040:2 (Fig. 68, 4). Made from sheep metacarpal. Unfinished object, square in section, saw marks visible on all four sides. One end sawn through: saw ring started on the other. Possibly to have been used as a knife handle, whistle or needle case.
Length: 97mm. Width: 9.5mm. Thickness: 9mm.
Site B-C, unstratified.

Toggle
E543:1:89 (Fig. 68, 6). Pig or sheep metapodial, polished, with central lateral perforation 4.7mm. diameter.
Length: 54.1mm. Diameter: 14.3mm.
Site B, surface find.

Whistle or Flute
E543:1004:1 (Fig. 68, 5). Carved and polished sheep/goat

metatarsal, tool marks visible. Section: hollow square with rounded corners. Ends sawn. Ring of saw marks close to one end. Towards opposite end, oval perforation, 8.2mm. long. 4.7mm. wide.
Length: 58.7mm. Maximum diameter: 11.5mm.
Site F, level 2, late 12th century.

Spindle whorl
E543:3032:132 (Fig. 68, 7). Formed from the unfused epiphysis of a bovine femur. The asymmetric process is trimmed. Central perforation is drilled from both sides, 5mm. maximum diameter, no wear or polish evident.
Diameter: 43mm. Height: 17mm.
Site G, level 2, 14th-15th century.

Hollow bone cylinder
E543:29:1 (not illustrated). Fragment of highly polished hollow bone cylinder made from horse metapodial. Saw marks on ends.
Length: 21.4mm. Width: 24.2mm. Thickness: 7.4mm.
Site J, level 1, late 12th century.

Unidentified object
E543:1012:2 (Fig. 68, 8). Made from animal longbone. U-shaped object, polished on exterior. Top face decorated with nine dot-in-circle motifs arranged in three rows of three. Perforated laterally, wear marks on interior suggest object turned on axle passed through it. Chatter marks from saw on ends and on one edge.
Length: 20.5mm. Width: 19mm. Thickness: 19mm.
Patrick St, unstratified find from Poddle river.

Die
E543:605:1 (Fig. 68, 9). Small bone dice have a long currency stretching from the Roman period to the modern day. Pre-Norman dice, like post-medieval and modern day examples, generally had the faces arranged so opposing ones added up to seven. The uncovered example is post-medieval in date.
Ivory cube, 11mm. x 12.5mm. x 12.5mm.
Site J, level 3, 18th century.

Pen
E543:337:5 (Fig. 68, 10). Polished goose radius. Proximal end pointed from one side, point bevelled and split to form nib. Similar to examples found in 13th and 14th century levels at Barn Road, Norwich and Cambridge (MacGregor 1985, 125). Metal examples are also known, e.g., a copper alloy pen found in the river Thames with 15th century material in 1982 (Alexander and Binski 1987, 384).
Length: 115:3mm. Diameter: 6.4mm.
Site F, level 2, late 12th century.

Stylus or parchment pricker
MacGregor (1985, 124-25) argues for these objects being *punctoria* (parchment prickers) used to make small holes in manuscript pages to aid in laying out the script. More recently, however, Ramsey (in Alexander and Binski 1987,

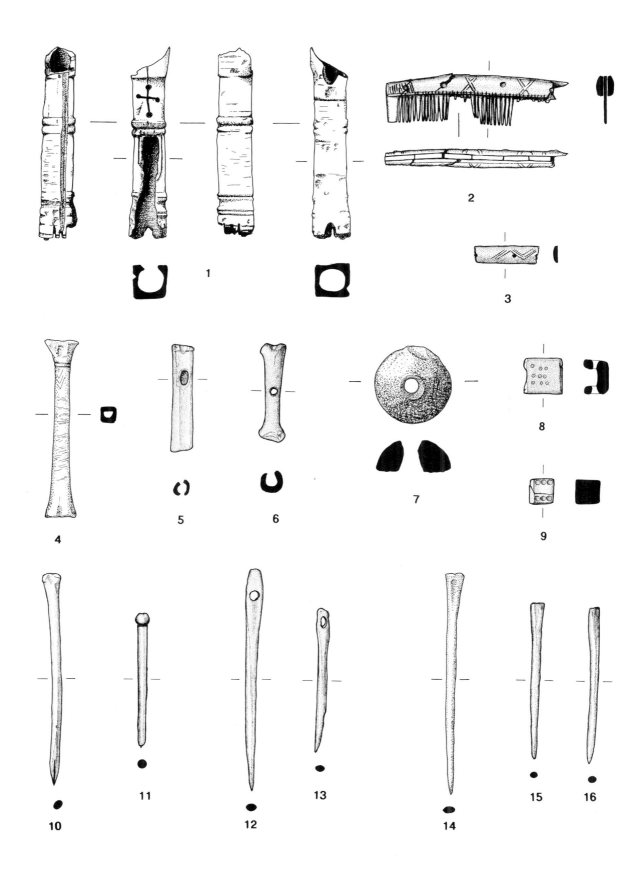

Fig. 68. Bone and antler (scale 1:2)

382-83) has argued that they may in fact be styli.

E543:1101:68 (Fig. 68, 11). Ivory, lathe turned. Shank: round section, rounded end. Iron pin *in situ* in end. Head spherical, 7.4mm. diameter. Narrow rib and hollow collar on underside.
Length: 72.7mm. Shank diameter: 5.1mm.
Site E, level 2, 14th-15th century.

Pins/needles
E543:703:12 (Fig. 68, 12). Pin/needle carved from small animal bone. Shank: oval section tapering to point. Head: broad and flattened, central round perforation, 5mm. diameter. Top of head broken. Tool marks visible, polished.
Length: 120.2mm. Maximum width: 8.8mm. Maximum thickness: 4mm.
Site K, level 2, 13th century.

E543:1100:148 (Fig. 68, 13). Pin/needle carved from small animal/bird bone. D-section shank, tapering to point. Head, flattened and broad, with pointed oval eye, 5.1mm. long, 1.8mm. wide. Tool marks visible, polished.
Length: 77mm. Maximum width: 6.9mm. Maximum thickness: 3.4mm.
Site E, surface find.

E543:3026:276 (Fig. 68, 14). Carved from a bird bone. Highly polished, sub-circular sectioned shank, tapering to a point at one end. Head unworked.
Length: 118.7mm. Head width: 6.5mm. Shank diameter: 4.5mm.
Site G, level 3, 16th century.

E543:506:1 (Fig. 68, 15). Carved from small animal/bird bone. Shank: sub-circular tapering to point at one end. Head: broad and flattened, top broken.
Length: 83.8mm. Maximum width: 7.6mm. Maximum thickness: 3.5mm.
Site I, level 1, early 12th century.

E543:216:4 (Fig. 68, 16). Pin carved from small animal bone. Shank: sub-circular section, tapering to point at one end. Head: flattened and splaying outwards. Tool marks visible, polished.
Length: 84mm. Maximum width: 5.5mm. Thickness: 4.5mm.
Site D, level 2, late 12th century.

Handles (not illustrated)
E543:3:29. Possible ivory knife handle. Oval section, bluntly pointed top end tapers to broken lower end. Socket to receive tang of blade present in latter end. Probably post-medieval in date.
Length: 59mm. Width: 13.7mm. Thickness: 10.5mm.
Site B, surface find.

E543:5:538. Ivory knife handle. Oval section with rounded top end. Tapers to broken lower end which retains stump of iron blade tang. Probably post-medieval in date.
Length: 67.5mm. Width: 22.3mm. Thickness: 17.7mm.
Site B, surface find.

E543:3006:11. Split, highly polished and faceted bone handle. Central perforation for tang turned on an axle. Tapers slightly to a rounded butt.
Site G, level 6, 17th century.

Blank
E543:15:29 (not illustrated). Small bone slip cut on three sides, broken on fourth. Saw marks on underside, upper side polished. Central perforation: 5.7mm. diameter surrounded by 1.5mm. wide groove that almost penetrates thickness of the bone. Probably a blank from which a small bone ring/spacer was to be cut.
Length: 19mm. Width: 14.1mm. Thickness: 1.5mm.
Site B, level 4, 14th century.

Blank for button production
E543: 223:52 (not illustrated). Matrix from which button was cut. Sub-rectangular fragment cut from animal long-bone. Flat underside, convex upper side. Large central circular perforation, 17.88mm. diameter, bored from both sides. Saw marks on underside and ends.
Length: 34.4mm. Width: 28mm. Thickness: 5.5mm.
Site D, level 2, 13th century.

Miscellaneous worked bones (not illustrated)
E543:1:91. Sheep/goat metatarsal, one end unworked except for ring of saw marks, other end sawn off, second ring of saw marks close to latter end.
Length: 76.7mm. Diameter: 12.5mm.
Site B, surface find.

E543:1:90. Sheep/goat metatarsal, one end unworked, other end roughly knife trimmed, blade marks evident. Bone has been trimmed with blade and polished.
Length: 58mm. Diameter: 12.5mm.
Site B, surface find.

Glass (not illustrated)

E543:3045:1. Complete later 17th century wine bottle. Dark green in colour. Globular body, diameter 130mm., short neck length 60mm. Overall height 142mm. Kick-up: diameter 84.5mm., depth 30mm. String ring for holding down cork present.
Dean St, clearance find.

MEDIEVAL FLOOR TILES

Alan Hayden

A total of ninety-six fragments of medieval floor tiles were recovered from the excavations. No tiles were discovered *in situ*. The majority (sixty-four fragments) were recovered from deposits dumped into the Anglo-Norman ditch at Nicholas St (Site G) and from the Poddle river channel, from the 13th-16th centuries.

The tiles are described following Eame's and Fanning's (1988) typology. The initial letter signifies the category of tile (T = two colour, L = line impressed and R = relief) and the following number refers to the decorative motif on the tile.

Two colour mosaic tile

3035:2 (Fig. 69, 1). A previously undiscovered type, which is half of a diamond shaped tile with decoration formed of strips of white clay set in channels up to 3mm. deep.
Site G, level 2, 14th-15 century.

Two coloured tiles

Sixteen fragments were recovered.

Six fragments (1100:30, 3026:19, 3035:148, 3026:264, 3023:128, and 3021:129) were not identifiable to type.

Two fragments are of type T104 (3026:207 and 3026:129), one is of type T123 (3026:265) and one is of type T201 (3026:215).

One complete tile (1101:65) 105mm. x 111mm. was recovered.

Two fragments (313:36 and 5:540) are variants of the T131 type. They may differ from the T131 type in the shape and spacing of the fleur-de-lis; however, they were too worn to clearly discern their full decoration.

Six fragments representing six types of previously unrecorded designs were recovered.

Previously unrecorded type
3023:128 (Fig. 69, 2). Variant of the T63 design with birds either side of a tree.
Site G, level 5, late 16th-mid 17th century.

1101:65 (Fig. 69, 3). An almost complete rectangular tile. The tile is a border tile. Its decoration consists of a curvaceous vegetative scroll. The tile is also bordered on one edge by a line. The details of the endings of the scroll are blurred but appear to have been three-lobed. The pattern is similar to the T26-29 series but differs in detail - it is not gapped like the T26-29 types. The line on one side of the tile also would appear to indicate that the scroll would run in the opposite direction to the T29 type.
Site E, level 2, 14th century or later.

313:44 (Fig. 69, 4). A fragment of the lower left corner of a tile in the style of types T200 and T201. The recovered fragment differs from the T200/T201 type in the arrangement of the leaves (and in their shape - three-lobed rather than two-lobed) between the curving diagonal bands.
Site F, unstratified river find.

1136:22 (Fig. 69, 5). Corner of a tile. The fragment is too small to allow reconstruction of the decoration but it would appear to have partly taken the form of a curving diagonal band enclosing further decoration.
Site E, level 1, 14th century.

3000:192 (Fig. 69, 6). Tiny fragment with curving branches.
Site G, clearance.

3026:238 (Fig. 69, 7). Tiny fragment with curving bands, one with circular opening.
Site G, level 3, 16th century.

Line impressed mosaic tile

1100:141 (Fig. 69, 8). A small fragment which appears to be from a mosaic tile of sharply pointed lozenge shape. It is clearly not a fragment of a tile halved or quartered due to the unusual angle of its sides. Both sides in any case are bevelled and moulded, not cut.

The decoration appears to consist of a double outlined motif following the shape of the tile. In thickness (28mm.) it is greater than the rest of the line impressed tiles (except L38) which vary from 19mm.-25mm. thick.
Site E, surface find.

Line impressed tiles

Thirty-four fragments of line impressed tiles were recovered. Of these, four fragments were not identifiable to type. The remaining fragments represent twenty-three types. Of these sixteen are previously recorded designs and are listed below with the number of fragments uncovered in brackets:

L1(1), L4(1), L8(1), L10(1), L12(1), L14(1), L20(1), L21(1), L23(1), L33(1), L38(1), L47(8), L54(1), L65(1), L72(1), L77(2).

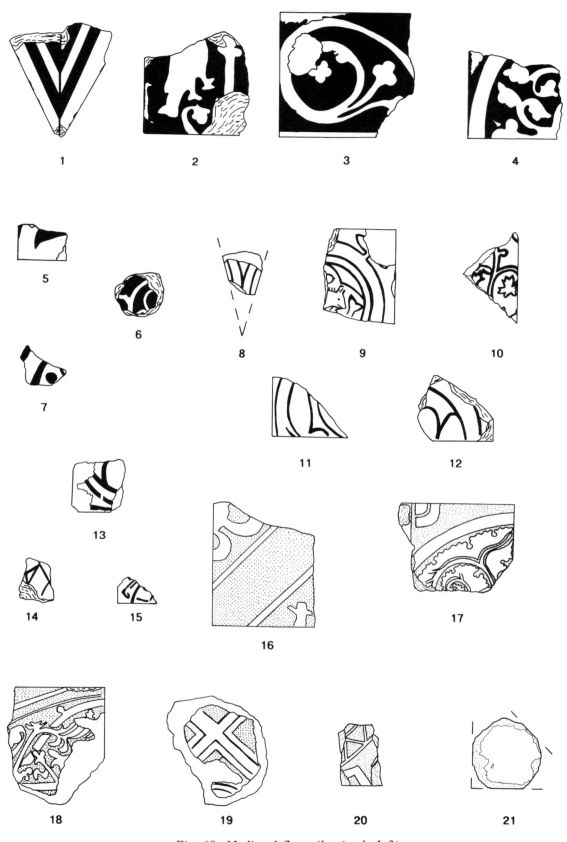

Fig. 69. Medieval floor tiles (scale 1:3)

The fragment of the L38 tile (377:12, unstratified find from Poddle river, Site F) is unusual in that it is much thicker than the other line impressed tiles (*c.* 32mm. thick) and as a result has a hollow in the rear to aid firing. No complete examples were recovered but two tiles, each with one complete edge measuring 123mm. and 115mm., occurred.

Fragments (5:542 and 5:43) which fit together appear to be of L47 type. Their upper surfaces, however, are largely obscured by small fragments of fired clay and large bubbles of glaze and a mortar-like substance. These fragments appear never to have been used and are probably wasters.

Previously unrecorded types
3026:256 (Fig. 69, 9). Boar (like L1 type) in double circular frame with trefoils at corners.
Site G, level 3, 16th century.

1100:176 (Fig. 69, 10). A small fragment from the centre right hand side of a tile. It appears to be a variant of the L20 type, differing in the shape of the small lobes on the foliate stems and also in the thickness and curve of the stems.
Site E, surface find.

3000:213 (Fig. 69, 11). Variant of L20 type. Has extra stroke at lower left corner.
Site G, surface find.

3023:131 (Fig. 69, 12). Double curving band with arched motif inside.
Site G, level 5, late 16th–mid-17th century.

1007:138 (Fig. 69, 13). Corner fragment. The decoration appears to consist of a circular motif with central decoration and small motifs at the corners of the tile. The impressed channels are quite broad (3mm. wide).
Site E, surface find.

3015:37 (Fig. 69, 14). Tiny fragment, line with straight lines branching from it.
Site G, level 4, 16th century.

3015:26 (Fig. 69, 15). Tiny fragment of corner of tile. Curving stem with other unclear motifs.
Site G, level 4, 16th century.

Relief tiles

Ten fragments were uncovered. Two were not identifiable to type due to wear. Five fragments were of five previously unrecorded types.

3000:193 (Fig. 69, 16). Straight diagonal bands with other unclear motifs.
Site G, surface find.

345:5 (Fig. 69, 17). A variant of the R66 type. It differs from the example of the R66 type illustrated by Eames and Fanning (1988, 132) in the details of the foliage and in the interlace in the top left corner.
Site F, level 2, 13th century or later.

3010:60 (Fig. 69, 18). Curving diagonal band enclosing foliage some of which overlies the band.
Site G, level 5, late 16th–mid-17th century.

3023:9 (Fig. 69, 19). Outlined saltire with other motifs in spandrels.
Site G, level 5, late 16th–mid-17th century.

313:39 (Fig. 69, 20). A small fragment of a previously unrecorded type. Decoration consisted partly of a band of alternating triangles and other motifs.
Site D, level 5, 14th–15th century.

Plain tiles

Thirty-six fragments of plain glazed tiles or unidentifiable fragments were recovered, including three complete examples (313:38, 377:144, 3026:258). These measured 104mm. x 105mm., 108mm. square, and 103mm. square respectively. The tiles varied in thickness from 25mm.–40mm. and some had hollows on their undersides to aid firing or adhesion. Three fragments (12:75, Site B, level 4, 14th century onwards; 3023:12, Site G, level 5, late 16th–mid 17th century; 3026:266, Site G, level 3, 16th century; Fig. 69, 21) were rounded and reused as counters. Two fragments of pottery were also similarly rounded and possibly also used as counters (see miscellaneous ceramics).

A number of fragments are obviously wasters as their surface is bubbled and unworn.

Discussion

With the exception of one fragment (plain tile, 400:3) which was uncovered on Site H (adjacent to Christ Church Cathedral) all the other fragments were recovered from sites on Patrick St. It appears likely that the majority of the tiles may have originally formed part of the floor of St Patrick's Cathedral or the nearby parish church of St Nicholas Within. A number of the types uncovered are previously known from St Patrick's Cathedral (types T131, L1, L8, L10, L12, L47 and L79). Two of the previously unrecorded types (the variant of the type T26-29 series and the possible variant of the L20 type) are also variants of, or close in style to, tiles already known from St Patrick's Cathedral.

A number of the remaining types uncovered (L38, L54 and L77) are previously recorded from other Dublin contexts (Dublin Castle, Christ Church Cathedral, St Audeon's, Kilmainham), or are variants of types previously known from Dublin (for example the variants of types T200/201 and R66).

Only one of the previously recorded types uncovered, L23, is not known from Dublin, but is recorded from Drogheda (Eames and Fanning 1988, 88). However, a variant of this type (L24) is known from St Patrick's Cathedral.

All the tiles uncovered appear to be of local manufacture. Their fabric closely resembles that of locally produced pottery, containing large amounts of mica flecks, which is presently dated to the 13th-15th centuries.

The tiles, therefore, fit comfortably into the known series from St Patrick's and from other locations in Dublin. It is unusual that such a variety of types are represented in such a small assemblage - almost as many different types as numbers of fragments uncovered. The types of tile represented range in date from the two colour variety (13th century) (ibid., 29) to the relief type (later 14th to 16th century) (ibid., 44). None were recovered from a primary context. With the exception of the plain tile (400:3) which from its provenance probably derived from Christ Church Cathedral, the tiles no doubt found their way into the river Poddle as a result of the many refurbishments to St Patrick's Cathedral in the medieval period.

ROOF TILES

Joanna Wren

The excavation recovered seventy-seven sherds of ceramic roofing material. These include examples of medieval and post-medieval ridge tiles, curved roof tiles, finials, louvers and pan tiles.

Medieval crested ridge tiles

The assemblage produced forty-seven sherds of medieval crested ridge tile. These tiles were first introduced into Ireland with the Anglo-Norman building campaigns of the 13th century. They usually have a V or U-shaped profile with cresting applied to the ridge. The tiles were made by joining two flat slabs of clay over a frame made of wood or basketry (Wren 1987, 20). Impressions of a wood frame were found on one sherd from this site (E543:3036:23; not illustrated). The cresting was made by applying clay to the ridge and cutting or moulding it into shape.

All of the ridge tiles found were made in micaceous local fabrics. Thin-section analysis of these fabrics suggests that all three clays came from a similar source (see M. McCorry, this vol.). A gradual improvement in the levigation of the clay, from the earlier to the later fabrics, was observed. A visual examination of the sherds revealed grass inclusions in fabrics 2 and 3. Potters sometimes add plant extracts to clay to improve its malleability and cohesiveness (Sheppard 1976, 52).

Four sherds in fabric 2 have diagnostic features. One (E543:3042:1; Fig. 70, 1) has a high hand-moulded cockscomb crest and thumb marks along its vertical edge. Tiles with cockscomb cresting and thumbed, incised or applied strip decoration were common in central and southern Leinster in the 13th century (Wren, forthcoming b). Another sherd (E543:3000:122; Fig. 70, 2) is decorated with a vertical applied strip on its exterior face. This may have come from a similar tile.

A third sherd (E543:3015:14; Fig. 70, 3) has a thumbed strip applied diagonally to its exterior face. This tile is a copy of a type popular in Bristol from the late 13th century onwards. They usually had high cockscomb crests and the strips were applied in imitation of cross-stringing in thatching (Rahtz 1960, 246). Finally, one sherd (E543:3023:16; Fig. 70, 4) has a flat-topped crest. Tiles with this type of crest began to be produced in central and northern Leinster in the 13th century and they continued to be made until the 14th century (Wren 1987, 36). Examples are known to the writer from sites in Dublin, Drogheda (Sweetman 1984, 22; K. Campbell, pers. comm.), Kildare (Manning 1981, 2) and Kilkenny (the late T. Fanning, pers. comm.).

Boxed crested tiles

Two sherds in fabric 3 came from boxed crested ridge tiles.

One tile (E543:301:4; Fig. 70, 5; Site F, level 5, 17th century) had its crest remaining and the other (E543:3026: 259; Fig. 70, 6; Site G, level 3, 16th century) had a double incised curving line on its exterior face. Boxed crested ridge tiles are a modification of the earlier flat-topped crested tiles (Wren 1987, 39). The more elaborate flat-topped crests gave way to more standardised and simpler boxed crests. These crests have a straight back and front and a sub-rectangular profile. The valleys between the crests are usually flat, and when these tiles are viewed from the side it appears that a series of rectangular box shapes have been applied along the ridge. These tiles are usually decorated with double incised lines, curving or vertical, on their exterior faces. The vertical lines are a development of the stab marks in the earlier flat-topped crests. Due to improved firing techniques the marks were no longer functional and were retained as decoration. The curving lines probably developed as a combination of the double vertical lines with curved line motifs found on earlier tiles. Boxed crested ridge tiles usually date to the late 14th-15th centuries (Wren, forthcoming a), and they were common in Dublin at this time. Examples have been found at Wood Quay (P. Wallace, pers. comm.); Winetavern St (B. O'Riordan, pers. comm.); Dublin Castle (Wren, forthcoming c); St Mary's Abbey, (M. McMahon, pers. comm.); High St (D. Murtagh, pers. comm.), and Arran Quay (Wren, forthcoming a). In particular, seven ridge tiles of this type, including one kiln waster, were found with late 14th-15th century floor tiles at the Magdalene St kiln site in Drogheda (Campbell 1985, 48). Their distribution is mostly confined to mid and north Leinster. One example from Cork city is known to the writer (Wren, forthcoming d) but this may be an import.

Finials

Several sherds (E543:3026:148; Fig. 70, 7; Site G, level 3, 16th century) made in fabric 2, come from the stem of a Dunning type 2 'bottle-neck' finial. This type is identified by its open tubular stem above a bulbous central body which narrows again towards the top. The finials were attached to the roof by fitting the stem into a hole or socket. Some finials in this class also functioned as smoke ventilators. There was, however, no evidence for smoke staining on these sherds and the finial was probably decorative. They were made in a fabric dated to the 13th- early 14th century (see Table 20), and examples of this type of

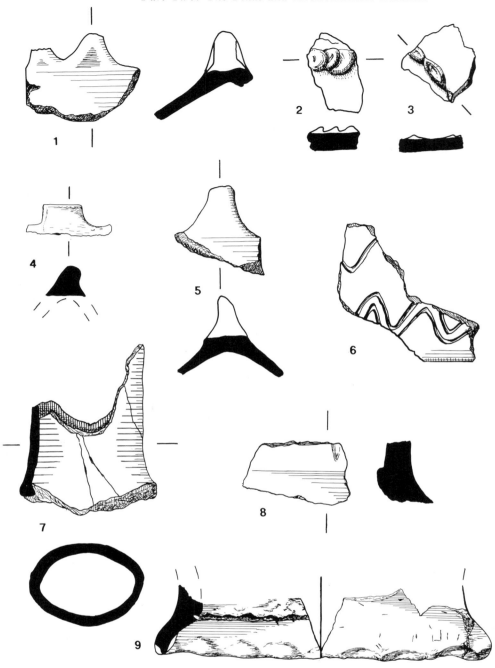

Fig. 70. Medieval roof furniture (scale 1:3)

finial in England date to the 13th-14th centuries (Pearce et al 1985, 48).

Louvers

This assemblage includes two sherds from louvers. These were ventilators placed on roofs to allow the smoke to escape from the open central hearths found in medieval halls. They were often made of wood (Wood 1965, 277) but by the mid-13th century they were being produced by the ceramic industry. The pottery louvers had the advantage of being fireproof. They are rounded objects, usually

wider at the base than the top, with holes cut in their sides. The holes are surrounded by canopies and arranged in a series of tiers divided by decoration. The canopies served to keep the wind travelling across the aperture at sufficient speed to cause a decrease in pressure inside the louver. This then caused the air from the room to rise upwards and outwards through the louver.

Sherd E543:343:43 (Fig. 70, 9; Site F, level 3, 13th century) is from the base of a louver with thumbed decoration along its bottom edge. It is made in fabric 2 (13th-14th century) and covered with an olive green lead glaze. This louver would have been attached over a hole in the roof. The second sherd (E543:3030:90; Fig. 70, 8; Site G, level 3, 16th century) comes from a different type of louver built as one with a ridge tile. This sherd is made in fabric 3 (late 14th-15th century). Dunning identified the type specimen for both types of louver. The first, at Great Easton, Essex, dates to the late 13th century (Dunning 1975, 186) and the second, at Goosegate, Nottingham, dates from the mid 13th-15th century.

Curved roof tiles (not illustrated)

The assemblage produced three sherds of curved roof tile. These tiles can function as ridge tiles but they normally covered the body of the roof. Sometimes they were used with flatter flanged tiles, which were placed on the roof with their flanges facing upwards. The curved tiles were then fitted over them, joining two flanged tiles together. When the curved tiles were used on their own, every second one would be laid upside down to function as a flanged tile.

Curved tiles have been found in Dublin in 11th century contexts (Wren, forthcoming c), and they continue in use to the present day. Two of these tiles came from 13th century contexts (F111, Site C, and F624, Site J).

Post-medieval ridge tiles

This assemblage includes three sherds of gravel-tempered ridge tile imported from north Devon. From the beginning of the 17th century, Ireland was a major market for north Devon pottery, and the trade from this area to Dublin increased later in the century when the city's population expanded (Grant 1983, 102).

Two of the sherds were 16mm. thick, complying with the dimensions for tiles regulated in England in 1477 (Salzmann 1952, 230). No complete tile survived, the longest (E543:1100:32; Fig. 71, 1; Site E, surface find) measuring 70mm. This sherd also retained the low cockscomb cresting characteristic of tiles made in this fabric. Directly below the crest, three stab marks had been

made in the tile's exterior face. Ridge tile crests are often stabbed for the functional purpose of helping to fire the thicker fabric in this area, but the marks could also have had a secondary, decorative role. All three tiles were recovered from unstratified clearance levels. Gravel-tempered ridge tiles from other Irish sites generally date to the late 17th or 18th centuries.

One sherd (E543:100:26; Fig. 71, 2; Site C, clearance) of ridge tile was found with its ridge formed into a series of flat-topped crests, separated by fingered depressions. The body of the tile is decorated with an incised, curving line. Tiles with this type of cresting and decoration were found at Dublin Castle where they appear to date to the 18th century (Wren, forthcoming c). The tile from Patrick St is made in a hard fabric, fired to a brick orange colour, with angular quartzite inclusions. It is covered in a brown lead glaze. The examples from Dublin Castle were made in a wide variety of fabrics and these tiles are likely to be local in origin. Their flat-topped cresting and curved line decoration is reminiscent of the late medieval boxed, crested tiles.

Pantiles (not illustrated)

This assemblage produced twenty-two sherds of pantile. These tiles are sub-rectangular in shape with a nib on their sanded underside and their bottom left hand corner removed. They have a curved or slightly S-shaped profile. Pantiles are seen as a development of the oldest form of clay roofing where clay curved roof tiles or imbrices were used in conjunction with flat flanged tiles or *tegulae* (Davey 1961, 53). The *tegulae* were placed on the roof with their flanges facing upwards, and the curved tiles fitted over them joining two *tegulae* together. In the case of the pantile, the two tiles are combined in one. The pantiles are then secured to the roof with their long edges overlapping.

These pantiles were made in fabrics which had been highly fired to a brick red or orange colour. One sherd (E543:343:12; not illustrated) had black glaze on its exterior

Tile no.	Fabric no.	Contextual information	Suggested date
E543:625:41	1	100% from 13th century contexts	13th century
E543:7:9	2	47% from 13th century contexts 18% from 14th century contexts 35% from post-medieval contexts	13th-14th century
E543:3010:11	3	55% from 14th-16th century contexts 22% from mid-16th-late 17th century contexts 23% from unstratified material	Late 14th-15th century

Table 20. Dating of roof tiles, by fabric

face. Black glazed pantiles are found on sites in Ireland and England (Betts, pers. comm.) and are generally recorded as rare. These tiles had a fairly standard thickness, between 12mm.-15mm. This is close to the thickness of pantiles previously found in Cork (Wren, forthcoming e) and Dublin (ibid., forthcoming c). No complete lengths of pantile were found. The longest surviving sherd measured 135mm.

As no complete pantiles were found, the sherds were weighed as the most accurate way of assessing the relative quantities of tile deposited in different periods. 2647 grammes of pantile were found: 36 per cent (950 grammes) came from 17th-18th century contexts, 36 per cent (947 grammes) came from unstratified material and 28 per cent (750 grammes) came from a lower fill of the Poddle containing 13th century pottery. Pantiles begin to be made in the 17th century and they continue in use to the present day. These tiles are therefore likely to be intrusive in this context.

The assemblage contains no kiln wasters to indicate local manufacture for these pantiles. That pantiles were being made in Dublin at this time is shown by the presence of kiln wasters in the Dublin Castle assemblage (ibid.). Pantiles were also imported into Ireland. There is a record of pantile from Bristol being imported into Galway in 1799 (Ó Cuillean 1958). This assemblage is likely to include a mix of locally made and imported material.

Petrological Report
on the Roof Tiles

Maureen McCorry

Three roof tile fragments were submitted for thin section examination. They are of varying thickness and fabric and are coarse, fine and medium grained respectively. The hand specimen and thin section fabrics are described below.

Sample A, fabric 1, E543:625:41

Edge fragment of a thick-walled roof tile, maximum thickness 20mm. Grey fabric with reddened lower margin. Thick dark green glaze on upper surface and edge, with uneven sanded lower. Coarse grained, mainly white angular quartz up to 3mm. and some calcareous material.

Thin section
Black matrix, poorly sorted, very coarse grained. Size ranges from <0.1mm.-5mm. for background inclusions. The glaze is of very variable thickness, filling gaps and hollows in an uneven ceramic surface. The majority of the larger inclusions are composites, from rock fragments, rather than single grains. Quartz is present in sub-angular or sub-rounded shape. Feldspar is present as large angular grains of alkali, microcline and low extinction angle plagioclase. A few mica needles and laths of white mica are scattered throughout and there are occasional grains which look like very altered calcareous material up to 0.88m. Apart from large granitic rock fragments composed of quartz/feldspar/mica, there are grains of very fine grained flint-like type up to 1.5mm. and a sandstone grain with fine granular texture plus a few black ore-like fragments.

The source rock is granitic with additional rock types which may have been present in the original clay.

Sample B, fabric 2, E543:7:9

Edge fragment of a thin-walled roof tile, maximum thickness 11mm. Grey core with red margins; green glaze upper and lightly and finely sanded lower; scratched edge. Many voids with some calcareous inclusions – these are most likely due to burning out of calcareous material. Other inclusions seen are quartz up to 3mm. in size and white mica flakes.

Thin section
Matrix black, moderately well sorted and medium to coarse grained. The inclusions range in size from <0.1mm.-2mm., but the majority are of the order of 0.4mm. Quartz grains again are in the majority and vary from sub-angular to sub-rounded in shape. Both single clear grains and composite grains are present. Angular to sub-angular grains of feldspar are present, both alkali and plagioclase. The plagioclase would appear to have small extinction angles consistent with those from a granitic source. Long needles of white mica are scattered throughout, up to 1mm. with additional larger chunks. There is also a small number of altered calcareous inclusions up to 0.6mm. in size and two or three small grains of pyroxene. A few of the larger grains are very fine grained flint-type, one containing lozenge shaped, possibly chloritised crystals. These reach 2mm. in size. One red/brown grain, possibly of altered biotite, is seen also.

The suggestion here is that the main source rock used is granitic but that there are also limestone or calcite fragments present, and possibly flint. The calcareous inclusions are altered and since there are so many voids present, it is likely that the temperature of 898C was exceeded and the calcium carbonate decomposed. The few remaining grains are now cryptocrystalline.

Sample C, fabric 3, E543:3010:11

Large fragment of roof tile with one edge present. Maximum thickness 18mm.: partial glaze on upper surface, yellow to dark olive green. Rough, lightly sanded lower surface. Fabric generally red/brown with grey patches, not fully oxidised. Fabric is fine grained although some inclusions are clearly seen; angular quartz grains up to 1.5mm. and small white mica flakes. There are also dark fragments up to 2mm. in size.

Thin section
The matrix is dark brown and very well sorted: very fine grained, as though the inclusions are present naturally in the clay rather than added deliberately. Size of the inclusions ranges from <0.1mm (majority)-1.5mm. The very fine background inclusions are mainly quartz with some mica needles scattered throughout. These are seen to swirl around the many ore-like bodies, mainly dark brown in colour, that are seen throughout the sherd. The larger are also mainly quartz with smaller amounts of feldspar and sandstone. The quartz varies in shape from sub-angular to

sub-rounded. Feldspar is present mainly as intergrowths with quartz and tends to be sub-angular in shape. The feldspar is alkali with a few smaller plagioclase grains present. Ore or iron rich clay bodies are numerous. They are rounded and contain the same tiny inclusions as the matrix. There are also one or two very fine grained inclusions which may be flint.

The suggestion is therefore that the very fine grains are present naturally in the clay and that the larger grains are derived most likely from a granitic source. The quality is similar to that of a well-fired pot.

Conclusions

The three fabrics are of varying quality, 1 being the coarsest, 2 moderately coarse-grained, and 3 being the finest. It seems likely, however, that the potters were using similar source material with somewhat different traditions. No. 1 contains very large freshly broken rock fragments as well as the background inclusions common to all three. Flint-like grains of unknown source are also common to all samples. No. 2 is very well sorted in that the added temper is of a restricted size, while 3 is obviously made from well levigated clay and lacks the calcareous material present in the other samples.

It would be difficult to pinpoint the exact location of the raw materials used in the manufacture of these roof tiles, but an area adjacent to both the Caledonian granite and the Carboniferous limestone is the most obvious.

MISCELLANEOUS CERAMICS

Rosanne Meenan

Tiles

E543:603:8 (Fig. 71, 3). Corner of wall tile. Buff fabric with quartz and haematite inclusions, 8mm. thick. White tin-glaze on the surface. The pattern is worked in manganese (purple) on the upper surface though it is poorly executed. The scene, contained within a double ring, may be Biblical though it is not possible to work out as so little survives. The ox-head on the corner is a variation on the ox-head motif; it is not similar to the typical Dutch ox-head motif nor the barred ox-head common on English tiles. However, the thick, lustrous quality on the glaze on this sherd suggests that it may be of English origin.

Tiles with Biblical scenes were produced in England from about 1680 through to the end of the 18th century, with the bulk of production probably falling in the middle of the century.

Site J, fill of late 17th century cellar.

E543:400:2 (Fig. 71, 4). Corner of 'paving tyle' or tin-glazed floor tile. Buff fabric with quartz and haematite inclusions, 15mm. thick with chamfered edges. White tin-glaze

on the upper surface. The pattern is worked in blue and consists of a fleur-de-lis at the corner of the tile and unclear motifs on the rest of the tile.

Tin-glazed floor tiles were produced in the Low Countries in the 16th-early 17th centuries and in London and Norwich at the same time. However, they were not practical as the tin-glaze was easily damaged through wear. Production in the two centres were very similar, and it is virtually impossible to differentiate between them. The fleur-de-lis pattern is typical of the tiles in production at the time.

Site H, surface find.

Stoneware spheres (not illustrated)

E543:1100:173 and E5433:1100:76 are two stoneware balls, 3.5cm.-4cm. in diameter. The fabric is light grey or buff and the surfaces are lightly glazed or burnished. The function of these objects is not known but it is suggested that they were bowls (D. Skinner, pers. comm.). They probably date to the 18th-19th centuries

E543:1100:76. Almost complete stoneware sphere. Fabric: fine off-white with fine gritty inclusions. Glaze: cream to light brown in colour. Probably English.
Diameter: 35.6mm.
Site E, surface find.

E1100:173. Incomplete stoneware sphere. Fabric: buff, slightly porous with fine gritty inclusions. Glaze: light brown.
Diameter: 39.2mm.
Site E, surface find.

Crucible

E543:109:53 (not illustrated). Rim and body fragment of a crucible.
Site C, level 1, 13th century.

Counters

E543:3026:205 and 267 (not illustrated). Two counters, both 38mm. in diameter, formed from base sherds of Dublin fabric 003 vessels. The counters are crudely formed.
Site G, level 3, 16th century.

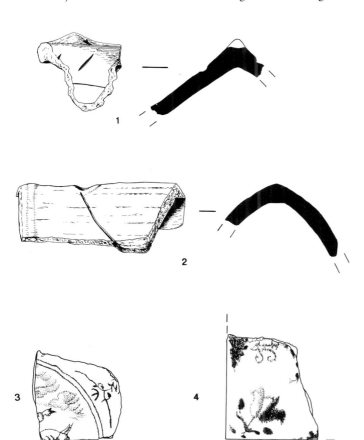

Fig. 71. Roof and Floor Tiles

155

STONE OBJECTS

Alan Hayden

(Geological identifications by Professor J. C. Brindley)

Small Stone Vessels   *Michael Moore*

Lamp

E543:390:1 (Fig. 72, 1). Roughly carved sub-circular stone lamp. Flat base, irregular sides and top. Sub-circular roughly cut central vertical-sided and flat-bottomed hollow, 34mm.–37mm. diameter, 35mm. deep. Chisel marks on interior. Handle vertically axe dressed. Traces of burning on interior of hollow and on outside of lamp.
Irish or English white Carboniferous sandstone.
Length: 102.7mm. Maximum width: 81mm. Height: 51mm.
Site F, surface find.

Vessels

E543:369:1 (Fig. 72, 3). Irregular shaped stone with rounded V-shaped hollow in top. Hollow 49.5mm. in maximum diameter, 26mm. deep. Iron staining on lip. No apparent tool marks. Small vessel cut from larger stone or fragment of spudstone.
Irish or English white Carboniferous sandstone.
Length: 84mm. Width: 74mm. Height: 46.5mm.
Site F, level 3, 13th century.

E543:3030:112 (Fig. 72, 4). Sub-rectangular stone vessel, square in shape with shallow, concave top. Hollow 46.5mm. diameter, 11.5mm. depth. Punch dressed. Iron staining on exterior and part of interior.
Limestone, probably local.
Length: 64mm. Width: 61.5mm. Height: 45mm.
Site G, level 3, 14th-16th century.

E543:377:10 (Fig. 72, 5). Small stone vessel, square with rounded corners. Vertical axe marks on exterior. Base and top irregular. Central steep-sided flat-bottomed hollow 24mm.–26mm. in diameter, 29mm. deep. Chisel marks on interior. Iron staining on interior.
Irish or English white Carboniferous sandstone.
Length: 49mm. Width: 47mm. Height: 48mm.
Site F, surface find.

These stone vessels, E543:369:1, E543:3030:112, E543:377:10 (not illustrated), do not appear to be lamps as they lack handles. E543:377:10 may be a mortar as it has quite a smooth interior. The rough inside of E543:369.1 makes it unlikely to have been a lamp; it may have been part of a spudstone or pivotstone.

E543:390:1 (Fig. 72, 1). A lamp of the handled cup-shaped type. Its closest parallel both in form and size is a lamp from Newtowncrommelin, Co. Antrim (N.M.I. S.A. 1927, 43). Both lamps are about half the size of most of the Irish lamps of this type.

The handle of E543:390:1 is narrower than usual but this may be accounted for by later reworking of the side of the handle - vertical axe marks occur on the side of the handle. Lamps are normally dressed by pecking and then rubbed smooth.

The reservoir is crude and rough with chisel marks visible and may also have been reworked at a later stage.

This type of lamp is found only in Scotland (*c.* 100 examples), where they are generally attributed to the Iron Age, and in Ireland north of a line from Arklow to Limerick (*c.* 35 examples). Some of the Irish lamps have decoration of sub-Roman form and may date well into the 1st millennium AD. The example uncovered in Patrick St probably dates to the early 1st millennium AD, though it appears to have been reworked at a later stage.
Site F, unstratified.

Mortars

E543:231:14 (not illustrated). Stump of handle and part of body of stone mortar. Handle sub-square in section, 32.3mm. x 36.2mm., tapers towards middle. None of the interior surface of vessel survives. Possibly burnt. Cracked and leached from lying in water.
Decalcified white sandy/cherty Carboniferous fossiliferous limestone.
Length: 62.3mm. Width: 73.1mm. Height: 63.3mm.
Site D, surface find.

E543:227:82 (Fig. 72, 2). Fragment of rod handle of stone mortar. Handle five faceted and of oval shape. Tapers from 32.3mm. x 26.7mm. to 27.1mm. x 23.2mm. Turn of handle towards body survives at one end. This is also five faceted, 40.2mm. x 46.8mm.
Carboniferous limestone.
Length: 98.8mm. Width: 40.2mm. Thickness: 42.6mm.
Site D, level 2, 13th century.

Whetstones

E543:3010:71 (Fig. 72, 6). Perforated whetstone. Section: rectangular, thickens towards base, fractured at narrow end. Highly polished on one side, smooth on the other, and worn at base.
Grey mudstone.
Length: 100mm. Width: 28mm. Thickness: 8.8mm.
Site G, level 5, late 16th-early 17th century.

E543:343:1 (Fig. 72, 7). End fragment of whetstone. Section: square with rounded corners. Tapers to bluntly pointed end. Abrasion marks on one face.
Fine red siliceous sandstone, possibly Irish Old Red Sandstone.
Length: 59.6mm. Width: 16.5mm. Thickness: 15.2mm.
Site F, level 3, 13th century.

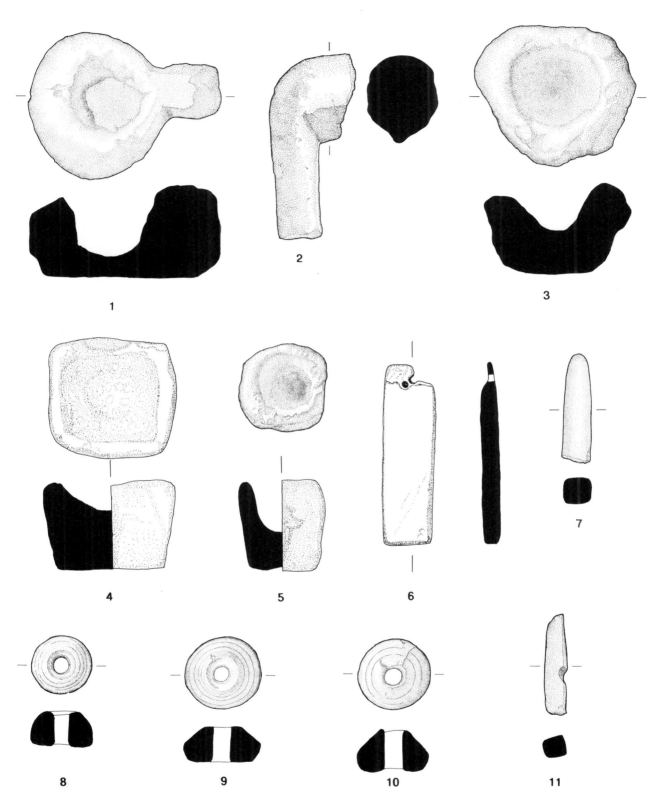

Fig. 72. Stone objects (scale 1:2)

Spindle whorls (all are Irish or English fine grained Carboniferous siliceous sandstone)
E543:202:1 (Fig. 72, 8). Beehive-shaped, with slight raised flat-topped ridge around mouth of central perforation on top. Several lightly incised lines around the body. Central perforation vertical sided, 7.6mm.-8mm. diameter. Small cracks in base.
Diameter: 31.4mm. Height: 18.2mm.
Site D, surface find.

E543:606:3 (Fig. 72, 9). Biconical with flat top and base. Nine lightly incised lines around body. Central perforation widest at base, 8.7mm.-10.6mm. diameter. Small cracks on base, some iron staining.
Diameter: 39.3mm. Height: 19.3mm.
Site J, level 1, 13th century.

E543:29:170 (Fig. 72, 10). Biconical with flat base. Five widely spaced lightly incised lines around body. Central perforation vertical, 10mm. diameter, top cracked and chipped.
Diameter: 38.3mm. Height: 23.3mm.
Site B, level 2, early 13th century.

Peg
E543:1101:71 (Fig. 72, 11). Pointed peg with semicircular notch on one edge. Broader end fractured, pointed end polished.
Fine grained metamorphic quartzite from the margins of the Leinster granite areas or from west Connaught/ Ulster.
Length: 53.8mm. Width: 11.9mm. Thickness: 12.5mm.
Site E, level 2, 14th century.

Projectile
E543:391:94 (not illustrated). Spheroid partly iron-stained ball.
Leinster granite.
Length: 86mm. Width: 78.3mm. Thickness: 69.8mm.
Site F, surface find.

Stone flywheel or grindstone
E543:1100:157 (Fig. 73). Incomplete thick stone disc with square central perforation, 49.5mm. maximum across. Iron staining around rim of perforation. Axe dressing on edge of stone. Function unclear. May possibly have had some function in milling as it was recovered from disturbed

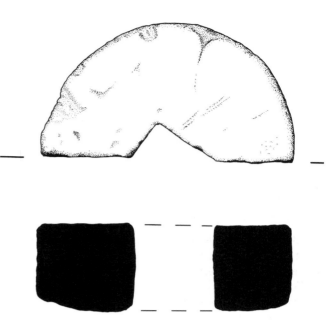

Fig. 73. Stone flywheel/grindstone (scale 1:4)

deposits overlying the mill in Patrick St. Possibly a fly-wheel or the centre of a composite millstone.
Carboniferous white sandstone, most likely English mill-stone grit.
Diameter: 270mm. Thickness: 94.5mm.
Site E, surface find.

Architectural fragment (not illustrated)
E543:3012:1. Oolitic limestone, probably Dundry stone. Rectangular block, 43cm. x 25cm. x 40cm., with rebate. Part of reveal of doorway or window.
Site G, level 5, late 16th-mid-17th century.

Roof slates (not illustrated)
Four roof slates were recovered from Site F, one from a 13th century level, the others as surface finds. All are incomplete, and of east Leinster red slate. The perforations range from 7.3mm.-8.9mm in diameter.

WOODEN OBJECTS

Species and conversion identification by Sarah Cross

Bowls

E543:505:1 (Fig. 74, 1). Almost complete lathe-turned wooden bowl. Simple rounded vertical rim. Slight footring on exterior of base.
Birch.
Rim diameter: 142mm. Height: 56mm. Maximum thickness: 14mm.
Site I, level 2, early 12th century.

E543:111:12 (Fig. 74, 2). Rim and body fragments of a lathe-turned wooden bowl. Two incised lines on exterior of neck. Slightly everted rim.
Willow.
Length: 73mm. Width: 36mm. Maximum body thickness: 8.6mm. Rim: 10.3mm. thick.
Site C, level 1, 13th century.

E543:3009:27 (not illustrated). Fragment of lathe-turned bowl.
Ash.
Length: 100mm. Width: 60mm. Thickness: 7mm.
Site G, level 6, late 16th-mid-17th century.

Toggle

E543:1100:218 (Fig. 74, 3). Circular section with bluntly pointed ends. 0.8mm. long central notch. Cracked and broken at one end.
Birch, trimmed twig.
Length: 63mm. Maximum diameter: 19.2mm.
Site E, surface find.

Tuning Peg

E543:1052:3 (Fig. 74, 4). Sub-rectangular shank, with V-section notch to hold string at lower end, broken at this point. Rectangular head, 9.5mm. long, 8mm. x 7mm. across. Decorated on sides with:
  a) incised concentric lozenges
  b) incised diagonal lines
  c) incised outlined saltire
  d) incised cross hatching.
Top of head may originally have had diamond-shaped cap.
Willow, carved from larger piece.
Length: 59mm.
Patrick St, unstratified find from Poddle river.

Forked Object

E543:1007:1 (Fig. 74, 5). Rectangular section object with expanded pointed terminal. Other end forked and broken. Function unclear.
Oak, radial conversion.
Length: 106.5mm. Thickness: 5.7mm. Maximum width: 17.3mm.
Site F, level 3, 13th century.

Carpenters' pegs

E543:41:1a (Fig. 74, 6). Triangular section shank, 16.2mm. x 17mm. Broken at one end. Rectangular head. 16mm. long, 22.2mm. x 17mm. across.
Oak, squared quarter conversion.
Length: 98mm.
Site B, level 3, 13th century.

E543:41:1b (Fig. 74, 7). Shank crushed, broken at lower end. Head rectangular, half missing, 16mm. long.
Birch, squared quarter conversion.
Length: 94.3mm.
Site B, level 3, 13th century.

E543:41:1c (Fig. 74, 8). Sub-rectangular section shank, 17mm. x 15.5mm., broken at lower end. Rectangular head 19mm. long, 25mm. x 17.5mm. across.
Birch, squared quarter conversion.
Length: 96mm.
Site B, level 3, 13th century.

E543:1108:1 (Fig. 74, 9). Square section shank, 11.8mm. by 14mm. across, broken at lower end. Head square with bevelled edges, 17.3mm. x 16.5mm. Cracked.
Willow, cut from larger piece.
Length: 90.1mm.
Site F, level 2, early 13th century.

Netting needle

E543:3010: 60 (Fig. 74, 10). Incomplete.
Hazel, sub-circular section, with flattened ends.
Length: 170mm. Diameter: 6mm.
Site G, level 5, late 16th-early 17th century.

Trimmed rods and pins

E543:3041:1 (Fig. 74, 11). Worked piece of yew, cut to a blunt point at one end, fashioned to a narrow point at the other. Rectangular cross-section.
Length: 165mm. Width: 9mm. Thickness: 4mm.
Site G, unstratified.

E543:3000:209 (Fig. 74, 12). Trimmed rod, slightly charred on one side. Tapers from sub-square sectioned head to a narrow sub-circular shank.
Yew.
Length: 135mm. Width: 15mm. Diameter: 6.5mm.
Site G, clearance find.

E543:3032: 137 (Fig. 74, 13). Pin: trimmed rod. Circular section.
Yew.
Length: 126mm. Diameter: 5mm.
Site G, level 2, 14th-15th century.

E543:3026:282 (Fig. 74, 14). Roughly trimmed rod with perforation. Worn smooth on one narrow side.
Yew.

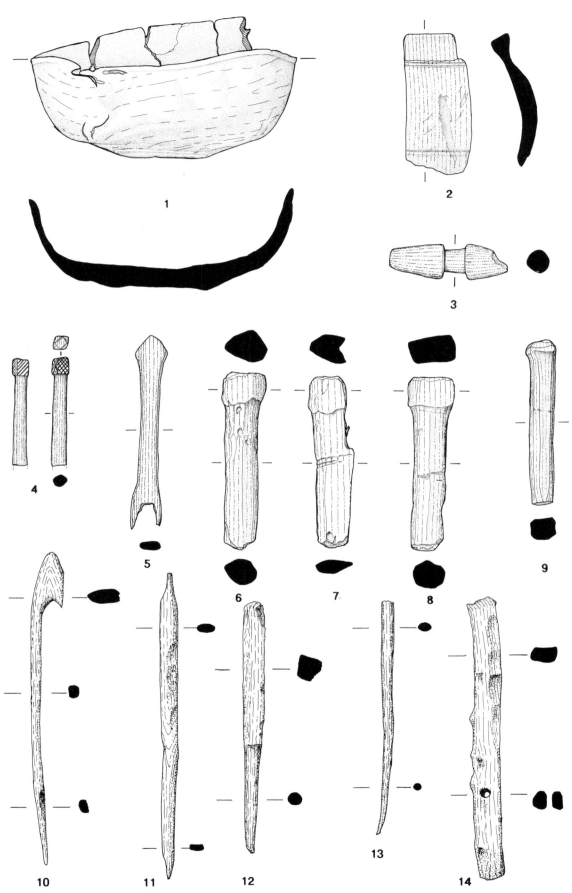

Fig. 74. Wooden objects (scale 1:2)

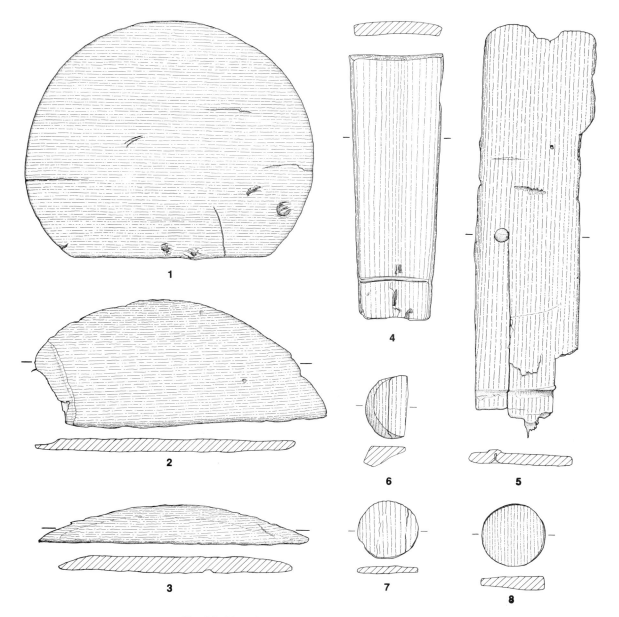

Fig 75. Wooden staves and barrels (scale 1:4)

Length: 148mm. Width: 13mm. Thickness: 7.5mm.
Site G, level 3, 16th century.

Wedge (not illustrated)
E543:3030:117. Square section tapering to wedge shape,
smoothed on all sides.
Slow-growing ash, radially split.
Length: 117mm. Width: 12mm. Thickness: 11.5mm.
Site G, level 3, 16th century.

Stave built vessels
Lids/bases
E543:371:1 (Fig. 75, 1). Incomplete round base/lid. Single
nail hole in edge. Original diameter *c.* 235mm.
Oak, tangential conversion.
Diameter: 230mm. Thickness: 12mm.
Site F, level 3, 13th century.

E543:1052:42 (Fig. 75, 2). Incomplete round base/lid,
original diameter *c.* 350mm. Partly iron stained.
Oak, thin radial conversion.
Length: 230mm. Width: 100mm. Thickness: 13mm.
Patrick St, unstratified find from Poddle river.

E543:377:4 (Fig. 75, 3). Fragment of wooden barrel base/
lid. Original diameter *c.* 450mm.
Oak, radial conversion.
Length: 218mm. Width: 33mm. Thickness: 14mm.
Side F, surface find.

E543:3026:280 (not illustrated). Base of small stave built
vessel, with bevelled edge.
Oak, radially split.
Diameter: 125mm. Thickness: 8mm.
Site G, level 3, 16th century.

Staves

E543:102:42 (Fig. 75, 4). Complete stave. Concave in horizontal section. Rebate to hold base 2mm. wide located 29mm. from lower end of stave. Rim slopes down to interior.
Oak, radial conversion.
Length: 220mm. Maximum width: 73mm. Thickness: 9.5mm.
Site C, level 1, 13th century.

E543:102:43 (not illustrated). Fragment of stave. Rectangular section. Both ends broken. Nail hole at one end.
Oak, radial conversion.
Length: 74.2mm. Width: 65mm. Thickness: 13mm.
Site C, level 1, 13th century.

E543:102:44 (Fig. 75, 5). Incomplete stave. Slightly concave in horizontal section. Rebate to hold base 4mm. wide. Nail, off centre mid way down stave. 34mm. wide, 8mm. deep notch in rim, possibly original.
Oak, radial conversion.
Length: 334mm. Width: 88.5mm. Thickness: 6.8mm.
Site C, level 1, 13th century.

E543:100:3 (not illustrated). Fragment of stave. Possible central nail hole. Both ends broken, cracked across middle. Partly iron stained.
Oak, radial conversion.
Length: 258mm. Width: 62.5mm. Thicknes: 8.5mm.

Site C, surface find.

E543:100:4 (not illustrated). Fragment of stave. Rectangular section. Two semi-circular iron stained notches on one edge, possible nail holes.
Oak, radial conversion.
Length: 143mm. Width: 49.5mm. Thickness: 19.4mm.
Site C, surface find.

E543:3015:239 (not illustrated). Possibly part of a stave of a small vessel.
Oak.
Length: 130 mm. Width: 48mm. Thickness: 5mm.
Site G, level 4, 16th century.

Bungs

E543:100:1 (Fig. 75, 6). Fragment of barrel bung.
Oak, tangential conversion.
Diameter: 53.5mm. Thickness: 19.5mm.
Site C, surface find.

E543:1101:107 (Fig. 75, 7). Round barrel bung. Cracked.
Oak, tangential section.
Diameter: 49mm. Thickness: 6mm.
Site E, level 2, 14th century.

E543:1052:4 (Fig. 75, 8). Round barrel bung.
Oak, radial conversion.
Diameter: 51.8mm. Thickness: 7mm.–12mm.
Patrick St, surface find.

LEATHER FINDS

Daire O'Rourke

There are 353 worked leather pieces from the excavations in Patrick St and Winetavern St, of which twenty-four are post-medieval in date. A further forty-three pieces came from Site G, most of which were post- medieval in date. A number of off-cuts (213 in all), scrap pieces, stitching channels, and rand fragments were also uncovered. Of the 346 medieval leather pieces, only thirteen are from objects other than footwear. Most of the leather was recovered from the dump layers of medieval date which filled the Poddle river channel, with an evident concentration of leather pieces in specific layers.

Medieval footwear technology

Medieval footwear was made in the turnshoe technique. The upper and sole are seamed together while wet and inside out and then turned the right way round. It is unclear whether a last was used in this process. Two illustrations, dated to the 15th century and German in origin, show lasts as part of the shoemaker's tools (Grew and de Neergaard 1988). One turnshoe sole has a small hole in the centre towards the tread/waist area which may have been used for attaching the sole to a last (E543:1052:46; not illustrated; Patrick St, unstratified find). Another sole (E543:255:403; not illustrated; Site D, level 2, early 13th century) has two small holes in the centre of the waist which may have had a similar purpose for attachment to a last.

Occasionally a thin strip of leather - a rand - is stitched along the lasting margin between the upper and sole. This functioned in keeping the shoe watertight and also in strengthening the lasting seam. Although the rand has been used since the 7th century (a shoe from the Anglo-Saxon ship burial of Sutton Hoo was found with a piece of rand *in situ* (East 1983, 788-812), it occurs only in a number of cases in the present assemblage.

The turnshoe, while it was ubiquitous in the medieval period, had its limitations. As the shoe was turned, the thickness of upper and sole had to be similar or else the shoe would have torn along the lasting margin. Thus the shoe was relatively fragile. It was composed of a vamp, vamp wings and quarters and a separate sole, while generally following a wrap-around pattern. Among slightly later medieval styles a quarter insert was included to complete the wrap-around pattern. This was occasionally a triangular or rectangular piece of leather which was stitched between the wing and quarter. Twelve such inserts were uncovered from Patrick St, ranging in date from the 12th-14th centuries. Among side-laced ankle boots, this insert would take on a fastening function (see below).

Support for the heel was also important and often a triangular or semi-circular piece of leather was stitched inside the heel, with the grain side next to the foot. There are six such reinforcers or stiffeners from the excavations. Five date from the 13th century, with one from a 14th century layer.

Historical background

The trade in hides from Ireland is well documented (O'Neill 1987, 77-83). Sufficient hides for export implies an established industry that was undoubtedly related to the meat market. However, whether these hides were exported as raw hides or as tanned hides is unclear. The lack of tanning pits in the excavation record is interesting, if not curious. The possible tanning pit from Site B, level 4, while being the first of its kind from the medieval period in Dublin, is too small to facilitate hides and may have been used for smaller skins like those of calf, goat and sheep. Its proximity to St Patrick's Cathedral may be significant, and could imply some connection with the establishment, i.e., a pit used in the process of vellum making. The skins of smaller animals such as calves, kid or sheep were used as vellum. To provide good quality parchment, it was necessary to let the blood drain completely from the animal, so as to keep the skin clear. Parchment made from kid of about four to six weeks old is the finest form. It was made by soaking the pelts in a solution of water and lime for three to eight days. The pelt was then stretched on a frame and the hair scraped off. It was soaked again in water and left to dry while being stretched. Occasionally small stones were attached to the edges of the pelt to further aid in the stretching process. When dry it was rubbed with egg whites and linseed oil (Reed 1972, 118-73).

Though there may be a dearth of information on tanning, there are good documentary sources to suggest that by the 13th century, Dublin had a thriving leather industry. In 1289, in the reign of Edward I, the tanners of Dublin were granted a charter. In 1226, of 224 people being admitted to the Guild of Merchants, several by association with their name appear to have been leather workers (Webb 1929, 4). Willelmis Filius Johannis Tanur and Eduardus Tannator were undoubtedly tanners. A currier, Simon Le Curier was also included. It was a currier's job to 'finish' the leather. Vegetable tanning (the most common method of tanning in the Middle Ages) produces quite a rough type of leather. On attaining the leather from the tanner, the currier soaked the leather again, and trampled it while wet to make it more supple. Next it had to be scoured, by being stretched out and cleaned. As cow hide is quite thick, it may then have been pared down or shaved on a straight beam. The hide was then placed in tanning liquor again and hung up to dry. While still damp, fats were massaged into the hide. After about a week, the excess fat was scraped away and the leather was then ready for use.

'Walterus Whittawer' refers to the trade of whittawyer which evolved from that of the tanner. These trades dif-

	Boot up.	Upper	Sole	Vamp	Q'ter	Toecap	Patch	Thong	Insert	Stiff.
Cow	0	5	157	1	0	0	5	0	2	0
Calf	3	23	0	7	1	1	0	10	5	1
Cow/calf	3	13	0	7	1	2	0	2	1	1
Sheep	0	4	0	1	0	0	0	0	0	0
Goat	4	4	0	0	0	0	1	0	1	0
Sheep/goat	0	4	0	1	1	0	0	1	3	3
Other	0	2	0	0	3	0	0	0	1	0
Abraded	0	6	0	0	0	0	0	1	0	1
Delam.	0	0	0	0	0	0	3	0	0	0
Clogged	1	0	0	0	0	0	0	0	1	0

Table 21. Medieval footwear

	Sheath	Belt	Bag	Clothing	Binding	Misc.	Offcuts
Cow	0	1	0	0	1	5	102
Calf	4	1	0	2	4	9	29
Cow/calf	0	2	0	0	0	8	59
Sheep	0	0	0	1	0	1	4
Goat	0	0	0	0	1	0	8
Sheep/goat	0	0	0	1	2	3	0
Pig	0	0	0	0	0	0	1
Other	0	0	0	0	2	1	6
Delam.	1	0	0	0	0	2	13
Abraded	0	0	1	0	2	1	0
Clogged	0	0	0	0	0	0	1

Table 22. Medieval worked leather

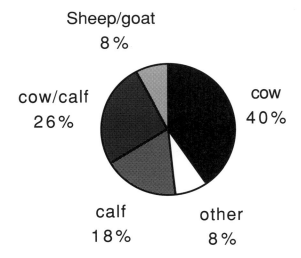

Chart 23. Percentages of differing hides used in medieval footwear

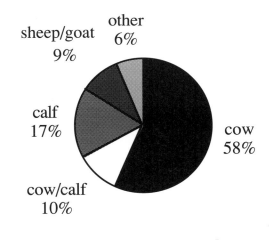

Chart 24. Percentages of hides used in medieval worked leather, excepting footwear

fered in that the tanner treated cow hides with oak bark while the whittawyer treated the skins of other animals with alum and oil. Reginaldus the Letherkersuere and Hobekin the Ledere were undoubtedly involved with leather working, as was Johannes Le Corduaner. A cordwainer was a term used from the 12th century onwards to denote a shoemaker who worked with vegetable tanned goat skin, by a tanning technique which was developed in Cordoba in Spain (Veale 1966, 36-56).

Thus the implication is that by the 13th century, distinct trades were recognised in Dublin. However, the first references in the Civic Records to a company of shoemakers does not appear until 1427, in a charter from Henry VI to the Guild of Shoemakers in Dublin (Webb 1929, 63).

The hides used in leather manufacture

The excavations produced 567 leather pieces in all from the medieval period, including all worked leather objects, scraps and offcuts, but excluding rands and stitching channels. Table 21 shows the relationship between hides used and various parts of footwear. Table 22 deals with the other worked leather pieces from the medieval period and the relationship to hides used.

Charts 23 and 24 show that the predominant leather

used was from cattle. The relatively small amounts of sheep and goat skin used contrasts with the evidence from Christchurch College, Cork. At that site, of a similar period, goat skin was quite popular as an upper leather. Thirty-two per cent of the upper leather from the Christchurch College excavations came from sheep/goat skin as opposed to only 15.15 per cent from cattle. However, in the case of other worked leather 73.7 per cent is made from cattle and only 12.89 per cent is from either sheep or goat skin (O'Rourke, forthcoming b). The leather from the Waterford city excavations shows a similar pattern to Dublin, though not in such overwhelming proportions. Here, 36 per cent of upper leather is made from cattle as opposed to 21.24 per cent which is made from sheep/goat skin (O'Rourke 1997).

Footwear: uppers, class 1 (Fig. 76)

A number of styles of footwear were distinguishable from the uppers recovered. The most popular style was a shoe made in the wrap-around tradition of which there are thirteen complete or fragmentary examples. In this style, the upper is wrapped around the foot and seamed at the side. As none of the pieces are complete it is difficult to say if an insert was stitched between the wing and quarter

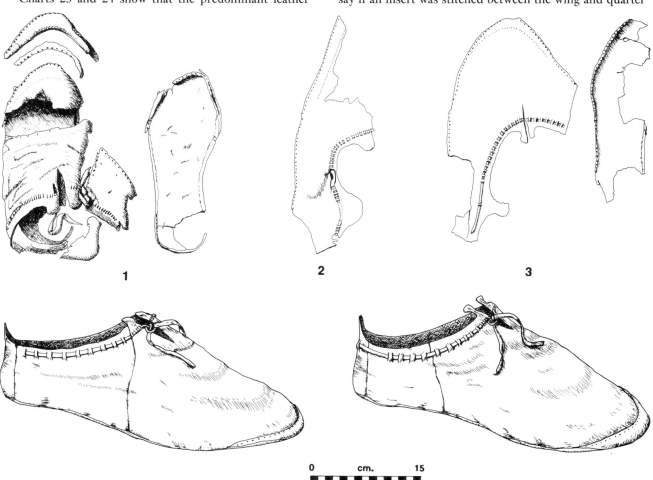

1 2 3

0 cm. 15

Fig. 76. Class 1 footwear (reconstruction not to scale)

165

Fig. 77. Class 2 and 3a footwear (scale 1:4) (reconstruction not to scale)

to complete the upper. They are distinctive as a row of slits run beneath the top edge, where in the majority of cases there is a piece of thong *in situ*. A whip seam runs along the top edge. The instep is invariably slit for a few centimetres towards the toe and the whip seam also runs along the edge of this slit. In this instance, the seam here is possibly to reinforce the leather at the slit and to prevent it tearing further. This slit would have been made by the shoemaker to facilitate the wearer in taking on and off the shoe.

Where the upper is complete enough to tell, the leather on either side of the slit extends upwards and is cut higher than the rest of the instep, so as to extend up the instep. The heel is also cut dramatically higher than the quarters. This upper style is also unique as in all cases there is evidence for a toe cap. This is indicated by a line of stitching just below the toe where in some cases this cap is still *in situ*. The strip on average measures 136mm. x 25mm. It fits neatly over the toe of the vamp and probably acted in protecting the toe from tearing and the leather here from getting scuffed. This ingenious device is unparalleled to the author's knowledge and seems to be unique to this style of footwear.

Illustrated: E543:29:1 (Fig. 76, 1) and 29:146 (Fig. 76, 2), Site B, level 2, early 13th century; E543:109:10 (Fig. 76, 3), Site C, level 1, late 12th century.

In all cases where identification of the leather was possible it was found to be calf or cattle. The use of good quality calf leather is of interest. It is the preferred leather in uppers due to its fineness, coupled with its suppleness and strength. As this fine skin is used in every example of this class and the uppers are quite stylish, perhaps the wearers belonged to a higher strata of society, one where fine calf leather was perhaps affordable.

Upper E543:29:1 (Fig. 76, 1) was found in association with a very thin top band. This is a strip of leather generally folded in two, which would have been stitched along the top edge of the upper. Its function was possibly to increase the height of the quarters, in some instances effectively making the shoe an ankle boot. In this instance the top band is very narrow and would merely have been a thin strip above the top edge, being decorative as opposed to functional. While this top band was not *in situ*, its presence with the upper suggests that such a top band was probably an aspect of this style of footwear.

Class 2 (Fig. 77)

The side-laced ankle boot is the second most popular style of footwear. There is only one complete example of this type of footwear (E543:216:129; Fig. 77, 1; Site D, level 3, mid-13th century). The left hand quarter extends to the right hand side where there are eight thong holes. An insert would have been stitched between the quarter and the wing. The quarters and heel are cut lower than the instep, and they are cut regularly along the top edge; thus it would have been quite a low cut shoe. There is evidence

for a small triangular heel reinforcer being stitched at the heel. This style of shoe was common in the 13th century while a similar one to above was found at King's Lynn and dated to the 14th century (Clarke and Carter 1977, Fig. 164.38). This upper is made from cattle hide. A second upper (E543:3033:43; not illustrated; Site G, level 1, 13th century) is a wrap-around upper with square instep. The leather extends from the left-hand wing, the lasting seam is torn away and a whip seam runs along the top edge. The quarter insert is still extant, although not stitched *in situ*. It is seamed on all sides, with three fastening holes at one side. On the flesh side there is evidence for a lining. This would have strengthened the thong holes. The sole is intact while the upper is made from goat skin.

While there is only one complete shoe upper, there are nine inserts (not illustrated), all of which have thong holes for side fastening and belong to this style. Seven of these belong to ankle boots and two to boots. E543:203:57 (Site D, surface find) consists of a long insert strip, attached to a piece of upper. There are six thong holes along the edge of the insert and these are haphazardly threaded with a leather thong to the upper. The 13th century examples are all dated to the early part of that century and all are made from calf or cattle. One piece (E543:216:146; Site D, level 2, early 13th century) is slightly different from the others. It is triangular in shape, with a slit at one side with a thong hole to either side and two other thong holes placed vertically to the slit. It is quite small, measuring 83mm. x 76mm.

Of the two inserts for a side-laced boot, E543:102:9 (Site C, level 1, late 12th century) is similar to one from London (Grew and de Neergaard 1988, Fig. 97) from a 14th century context. E543:111:39 (Site C, level 1, late 12th century) has seven thong holes along one side. A line of stitch holes to one side of the thong holes indicates that a lining would have been stitched here. The presence of a lining is quite common with the side-laced ankle boot, as it acts as a support and a strengthening mechanism for the upper to prevent it tearing while the leather is being fastened.

Class 3a (Fig 77, 78)

Boots were also popular in the 12th and 13th century. The earliest boot in the assemblage is E543:524:4 (Fig. 77, 2; Site I, level 2, mid-12th century). It is made completely of goat skin and is a wrap-around boot for the left foot. The vamp and the right hand side are torn away. The right hand quarter ends in a butt seam. There are traces of a whipped seam along the top edge. The lasting seam is torn away, though there are traces of secondary stitch holes along the left hand quarter, where a patch, or perhaps a new sole, was stitched. A curious decorative element consists of two vertical lines on the left hand quarter which has almost torn the leather in two. These seams do not appear to be functional, though their presence has weakened the leather and almost torn it apart. A somewhat similar

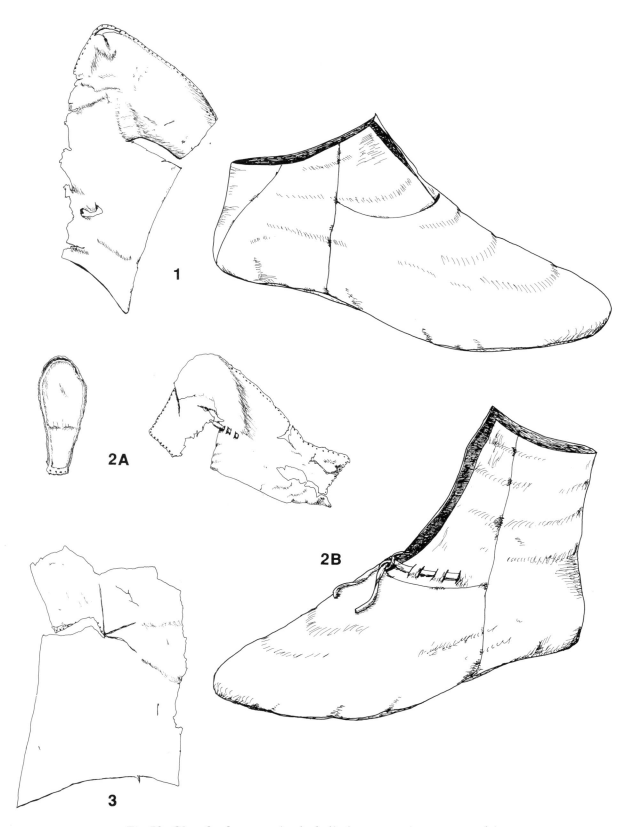

Fig. 78. Class 3a footwear (scale 1:4) (reconstruction not to scale)

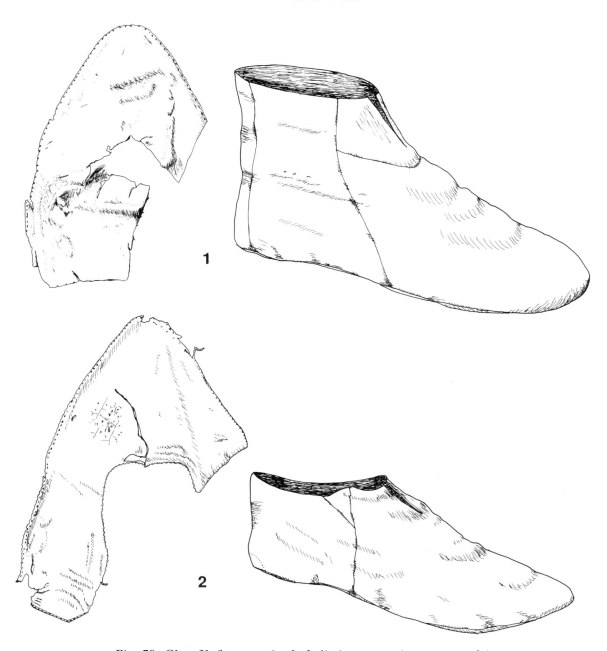

Fig. 79. Class 3b footwear (scale 1:4) (reconstruction not to scale)

boot to the above and dating to the same period was found in London (ibid., Fig. 9).

Two boot fragments, which are slightly different, are probably dated to the late 12th-early 13th century. E543:56:22 (Fig. 78, 3; Site B, level 1, late 12th century) is the remains of a low cut simple economy style wrap-around boot, which would have reached the lower calf. The economy style boot is also evident in the case of E543:225:401 (Fig. 78, 1; Site D, level 1, late 12th century). This boot upper is made from a single piece of leather which is wrapped around the foot and seamed at the side. Very occasionally a smaller piece of leather, such as an insert, would have been stitched between wing and quarter to complete the upper. These Dublin boots appear to have no fastening slits. The style was quite common across Britain and Europe. A similar boot was discovered in Durham, though this example has some slits for fastening (Carver 1979, Fig. 17).

A child's boot upper (E543:504:2; Fig. 78, 2; Site I, level 2, 12th century) is a simple wrap-around style with thong slits along the right hand quarter, with a piece of thong *in situ*. There are traces of thong holes on the left hand quarter where the leather is torn. It is made of very fine calf skin, just 1mm. thick.

Another boot, of which only one fragment was found, but which was common throughout the rest of the medieval world, is E543:714:10 (not illustrated; Site K, level 1, early 13th century). This upper differs from the others as there is a vertical line of slits along the quarters which would have accommodated leather thonging. This fragment is

169

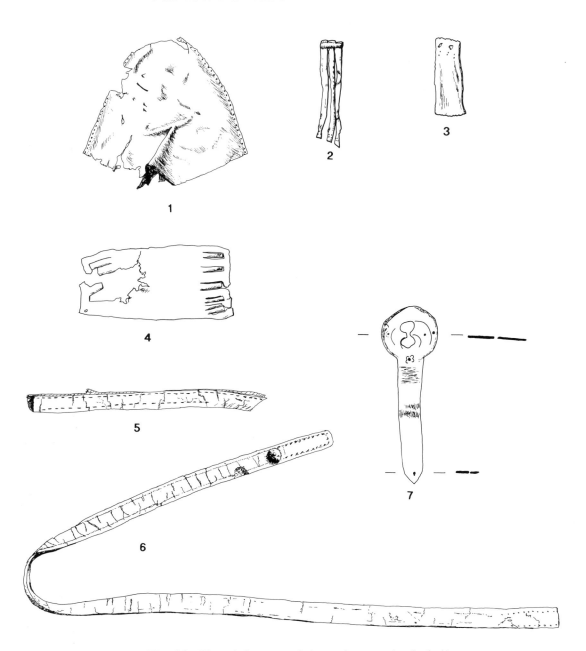

Fig. 80. Class 4 footwear, belts and straps (scale 1:4)

made from cattle hide and has parallels from High St, Dublin, King's Lynn (Clarke and Carter 1977, Fig. 165.19) and from Coventry (Thomas 1980, Fig. 5).

Class 3b (Fig. 79)

This simple wrap-around upper with no fastening thongs, while being present in boots, is also mirrored in two ankle boots. E543:48:8 (Fig. 79, 1; Site B, level 2, early 13th century) and E543:229:22 (Fig. 79, 2; Site D, level 1, late 12th century) both exhibit the simple economy style wrap-around technique. The former is very similar to E543:225:401 (Fig. 78, 1) except that the quarter is cut lower. The latter example is perhaps the simplest of all

footwear from Patrick St. In this instance a very small triangular insert would have been stitched at the top between the wing and quarter.

Class 4 (Fig. 80)

In the late 13th-early 14th century, a new style of upper was in vogue, where the vamp was detached from the heel and quarters and generally was front laced. There are two vamps which conform to this style. E543:32:1 (not illustrated; Site B, level 4, 14th century) is a torn, but intact vamp. The instep is slit, with two thong holes on either side for fastening. E543:102:17 (not illustrated; Site C, levels 1-2, late 12th-late 13th century) is similar to the piece above. Although the left hand wing is torn, it is feasible that the leather may have extended to the quarter. This style of front-laced upper is quite common in the 14th century, being found in similar dates in London (Grew and de Neergaard 1988, Fig. 98) and Coventry (Thomas 1980, Fig. 4). Examples where the front-laced upper is extended into a single-piece shoe are also found in London in the late 14th century (Grew and de Neergaard 1988, Fig. 99) and in Leicester in the 14th and early 15th centuries (Allin 1981, Fig. 56).

E543:3026:295 (not illustrated; Site G, level 3, 16th century) is a detached vamp and sole fragment which is torn at the seat. There is no indication of the fastening mechanism of this shoe, indicating that it was of the slip-on variety.

Two other detached vamps were also uncovered, one E543:29:4 (Fig. 80, 1; Site B, level 4, later 14th century) and E543:102:3 (not illustrated; Site C, levels 1-2, late 12th-late 13th century) are undiagnostic in their fastening arrangements, although they clearly indicate that they are not of the wrap-around variety.

One other style of upper, the latchet-fastened shoe, is present only in the guise of a single latchet. E543:216:158 (Fig. 80, 3; Site D, level 2, early 13th century) measures 82mm. x 28mm., and is stitched on all sides with a whip seam, having two thong holes at one end. This is a very early date for latchet-fastened uppers, as they are not generally seen until at least the mid-13th century.

An unusual thong fastening (E543:48:0; Fig. 80, 2; Site B, level 2, early 13th century) is made from sheep/goat skin, cut into three strips, the strips being folded in on themselves along the top. There appears to be three or four slits at the end of each strip. It is an interesting fastening device, though it is unclear how it would have been used to fasten any upper fragments found.

Binding strips (not illustrated)

Ten binding strips or top bands were uncovered. They may have been stitched to the top edge of the uppers to increase the height of the quarters, but as only one was found in association with an upper, this may not have been the case. Alternatively they may have been stitched to the edges/hems of clothing for protection or as trimmings. All are from 12th and 13th century levels. In all cases, they consist of a strip of leather folded in two and seamed along the length. One has a line of tiny slits along the top edge. This possibly belongs to a class 3 boot from the same context (Fig. 77).

Soles

Of the 161 soles recovered, 130 are medieval turnshoes. All are stitched with an edge/flesh seam along the edge. There is no evidence for any stitching material being left *in situ*. There are fifty-four soles or sole fragments from levels dating from the mid-12th century to *c*. 1300. Of

these, ten are complete. Most are waisted, though one (not illustrated) has straight sides. Where identifiable, five of these soles have pointed toes, the rest having rounded toes. The remainder are too worn and fragmentary to discern. Where complete enough, twelve of the twenty-four soles show evidence of being worn through or being patched in antiquity. Fifty-three soles are from 13th century levels. Of these five have pointed toes, and ten have more rounded toes. Twelve are relatively complete. Seven soles have evidence of holes being worn through and of being patched.

From the 13th-15th century levels, there are twenty-five soles/fragments, of which eight are complete. Four had very pointed toes, indicating either a late 12th-early 13th century date or a 14th century date – the ambiguity lies in the changeability of fashion. A possible pair of children's soles were recovered, one for the left foot and one for the right. They are very similar. Both have quite long treads and shorter narrowing waist and seat. The seat is squarely cut in both instances.

Cobbling (Fig. 81)

There is good evidence for cobbling from the leather finds. The cobbler repaired shoes or reused pieces of leather to make an article. From the 11th century onwards, in a charter from Henry II (1100-35) to the shoemakers of Rouen and another to the cobblers, the cobblers' trade was recognised as a distinct entity. Fourteenth century regulations stated that only new leather could be used by cobblers for soles, but only used leather could be incorporated into uppers (Richardson 1959, 63). Strict regulations were laid down as to the amount of new leather a cobbler was allowed to use. However, that these guidelines may not have been always strictly adhered to is seen in the number of times these regulations had to be enforced. The evidence for cobbling in this assemblage comes from nine patches, sixteen soles with evidence for patching and fourteen pieces of soles and other leather objects which have been cut up for reuse of the leather. There are also a number of offcuts. The quantity does not indicate that leather working was carried on or within the immediate vicinity of the sites.

Of the nine patches, where laminated, all are of quite thick cow hide and would have formed quite crude clumps. E543:224:13 (Fig. 81, 3; Site D, level 2, early 13th century) and E543:224:4 (Fig. 81, 2; as above) illustrate the clump quite well. A similar patch to E543:216:147 (not illustrated; Site D, level 2, early 13th century) was found in Durham from similarly dated deposits (Carver 1979, Fig. 19). Of the soles with evidence of patching, in all cases the patch is not extant, with evidence coming from the crude stitch holes around the offending part of the sole.

E543:40:7 (Fig. 81, 1; Site B, level 2, early 13th century) is a wide sole, which is not clearly waisted. There are a large number of crude thong holes for patching. It is

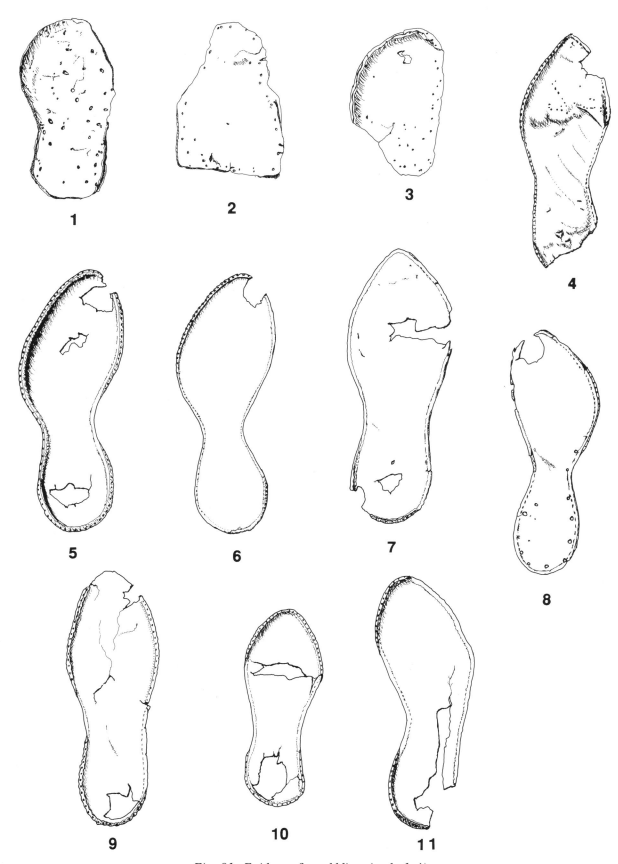

Fig. 81. Evidence for cobbling (scale 1:4)

almost completely delaminated and worn through and perhaps had been stitched on to a sole as a complete patch. Of the other soles, in three instances the tread has been patched as in E543:229:5 (Fig. 81, 4; Site D, level 1, late 12th century). In six instances, the seat is repaired as in E543:1137:6 (Fig. 81, 8; Site E, level 1, mid–13th century), and there are three examples where patching is evident over the entire sole, i.e., E543:56:10 (Fig. 81, 5; Site B, level 1, late 12th century), E543:56:11 (Fig. 81, 7; as before) and E543:48:5 (Fig. 81, 6; Site B, level 2, early 13th century).

Where soles are complete, in a number of instances where the sole may be completely worn through, no attempt was made to patch it. This is seen in a child's sole: E543:56:17 (Fig. 81, 10; Site B, level 1, late 12th century), and E543:225:402 (Fig. 81, 9; Site D, level 1, late 12th century). Such instances suggest that people may not have bothered to have soles repaired, perhaps preferring a new sole or maybe a new shoe! In the case of the latter, this sole is still in very good condition except for a hole worn near the back of the seat. Other evidence for cobbling comes in the guise of quite a large number of fragments which are cut away from the original piece.

Five soles have been cut up for reuse. E543:224:7 (Fig. 81, 11; Site D, level 2, early 13th century) shows clearly how an attempt has been made to cut up the existing sole for reuse of the leather. Three upper fragments show similar treatment. Sole E543:3041:2 (not illustrated; Site G, unstratified) has a V cut into the waist, indicating the reuse of the leather, while E543:3035:153 (not illustrated; Site G, level 1, 13th century) is a triangular piece of leather cut from a sole, with crude stitch holes along two sides.

A large number of stitching channels, comprising some rands and cutaway lasting margins, were also found. There are *c.* fifty from Site B, ten from Site C and eighteen from Site D. The pieces from Site B, while coming from a variety of contexts, are nonetheless interesting. Thus, while there is some evidence for cobbling from the sites, it is not present in sufficient quantities to indicate that in any one location repair work on leather was being undertaken.

Belts and straps (Fig. 80)

Nine belts/straps were recovered from the excavations. All are made from cow, calf or cattle leather. Two belt fragments have no distinct markings. E543:102:37 (not illustrated; Site C, levels 1–2, late 12th–late 13th century) consists of four or five fragments of a belt with a central line of perforations and a line of small decorative slits along either side. It is very torn and degraded, but is typical of a medieval belt, a number of similar ones coming from the Dublin Castle excavations (O'Rourke, forthcoming c). E543:1107:24 (Fig. 80, 6; Site E, level 2, 14th century) is a good example of a belt of this period. It is made from cow hide and measures 820mm. x 18mm. and is relatively complete. One end is cut so it may have been extended. There are a number of holes at the cut end which would

have been for the attachment of a buckle. There is an incised line running along each side, and a line of stitch holes finishing off the leather at the other end. There is one metal stud just before the stitch holes at this end, which was probably used in fastening. E543:718.2 (Fig. 80, 5; Site K, level 1, early 13th century) is a belt fragment of similar style. Several belts were recovered from the ditch fills of Site G. E543:3026:302a (not illustrated; level 3, 16th century) is probably medieval in date. It is made of cow/calf skin, and is in two pieces, torn at one end and cut at the other, where there are a number of perforations for attaching a buckle. Traces of leather thong are *in situ*. There is a double row of decorative slits along both sides, and a row of perforations for fastening along the centre.

Two further belts from the same context, E543:3026:302b (not illustrated; see above) and E543:3026:284 (not illustrated) are also of cow/calf skin. The former has no decoration, with three perforations along the length, while the latter has decorative stitch holes along the sides. This has a double line of faint stitch holes in a slight arc.

Miscellaneous worked leather (medieval)

A possible bag fragment (E543:504:1; not illustrated; Site I, level 2, 12th century) was recovered from the excavations. The leather is very much abraded and is torn and fragmentary. Along the top edge a strip of leather is folded from the grain to the flesh side where there are a number of crude thong holes and a piece of thong *in situ*.

E543:1012:3a (Fig 80, 4; Patrick St, unstratified river deposits) is an unusual piece. It is made from sheep/goat skin, and is rectangular in shape and torn at one end. There are a number of internal horizontal slits at one end and indications that this would have been the same at the other end. Its function is unclear although it may be a style of wrist band/guard. It measures 156mm. x 81mm. and just 1mm. in thickness. A somewhat similar piece of leather comes from a 13th century level in Waterford city (O'Rourke 1997). This consists of a piece of leather, which measured 120mm. x 62mm., and was cut to a scalloped edge at one end with five horizontal internal slits. One slit is pulled as if something has been threaded through here. The other end is torn.

E543:3026:288 and 296 (not illustrated; Site G, level 3, 16th century) are probably medieval in date. They comprise several pieces of calf skin, and derive either from clothing or a covering. There are double rows of decorative stitching along the edges, and one piece has a vertical double line of stitch holes. There is a hem where the leather was stitched from the grain on to the flesh side.

Two further fragments may have belonged to clothing fragments. Both have some evidence for stitching but are quite fragmentary. E543:48:254 (not illustrated; Site B, level 2, early 13th century) is made from sheep/goat skin and measures 327mm. x 98mm. The other, E543:29:147 (not illustrated; Site B, see above) is made from sheep skin and measures 301mm. x 136mm.

E543:3030:115 (Fig. 80, 7; Site G, level 3, 16th century) is unusual, and is probably a fastening from clothing. It is a circular piece with a leather latchet extension. The latchet has a small perforation, and within the circular piece is an 8-shaped perforation, perhaps to facilitate a toggle or button. A slight indentation of a quatrefoil object is apparent around a small perforation at one end of the latchet extension. There are no stitch holes along the edge to suggest how the leather may have been used.

E543:3026:283 (not illustrated; Site G, level 3, 16th century) are two scrap pieces of leather with open-work decoration consisting of a petalled motif.

Sheaths (Figs 82, 83)

Five sheaths were uncovered from the excavations. E543:717:30 (Fig. 82, 1; Site K, level 1, early 13th century) is a knife sheath measuring 207mm. x 42mm. and is made from calf skin. The use of calf skin in sheaths is ubiquitous at this time. In 1350 the London Guild of Furbishers forbade the use of any other type of leather in scabbards (Cowgill et al. 1987, 34). This sheath is seamed along the centre at the back. The decoration is in two panels, the uppermost panel measures one third of the length. The decoration is very worn but some diagonal lines are visible. The lower panel is defined by two sets of parallel lines, filled with a linear panel. The back also consists of two panels, the top one being very worn but the lower one consisting of slanting lines radiating from the central seam.

E543:48:244 (Fig. 83, 2; Site B, level 2, early 13th century) is a sheath fragment cut crudely along the top edge and torn at the tip. The decoration on the front is incised. The dots, where the pattern was laid out, are clearly visible and the decoration is both linear and plaited. The sheath is seamed in the centre along the back with slanting lines radiating from the central seam.

E543:48:8 (Fig. 83, 1; as above) is somewhat different in style. This sheath is cut to emphasise the difference between the handle and the blade. It is cut wider at the top to facilitate the handle, narrowing abruptly into the blade. By the 10th-11th century, the division of the sheath/scabbard into handle and blade with different motifs in each section is well catalogued (Russell 1939, 135). The decoration is clearly zoned with a panel in the handle area and another for the blade. The decoration, which is incised, is different in both zones, the top panel consisting of slanting lines with a lozenge in the centre and the lower panel consisting of a curvilinear design. This is the only sheath of the four which has slits for suspension. There are two crude slits along the right hand edge and across the top for suspension. The placing of slits seems to have been done by the owner of the sheath as they pay no heed to the lay-out of the decoration, cutting through it at random. The sheath is decorated at the back, with the uppermost panel consisting of a curvilinear motif and the lower one consisting of slanting lines radiating from the back seam.

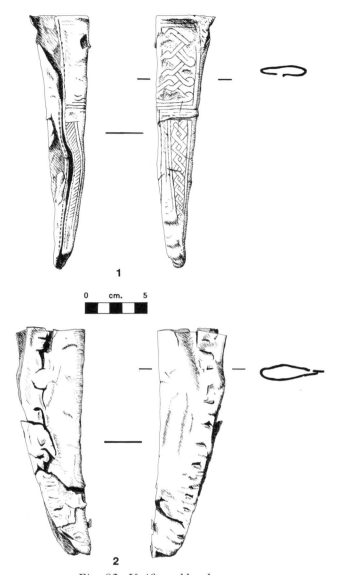

0 cm. 5

Fig. 82. Knife scabbards

E543:3032:142 (Fig. 83, 3; Site G, level 2, 14th-15th century) is a fragmentary sheath. It is seamed along the back, slightly to the left of centre. The decoration on the front is zoned in two panels. The uppermost is hatched, and the lower consists of lozenges. The panels are defined by double parallel lines. The back of the sheath is also decorated: the top panel is quite smooth, while the lower has four parallel vertical lines.

In all cases the back of the sheath is decorated as well as the front, with the most popular style being lines radiating from the central seam. This is a very common decorative motif and is seen in three sheaths from the London excavations which are dated slightly later, from the early to mid-14th century (Cowgill et al. 1987, Fig. 92.434 and Fig. 92.430).

Most leather work would have been painted or gilded to enhance the decoration or to brighten up the brown leather colour (Russell 1939, 133). To decorate a scabbard, it was held on to a last and then wetted, to enable decoration to

174

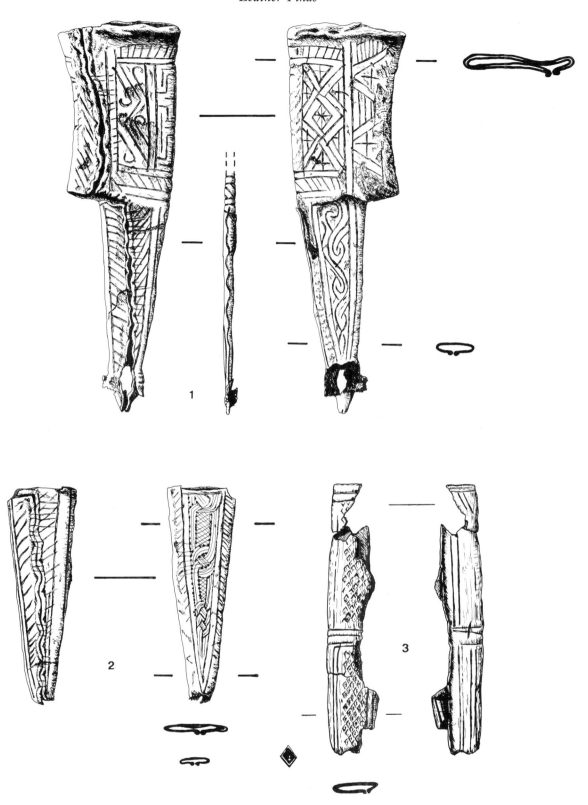

Fig. 83. Knife scabbards (scale 1:2)

be applied. After decoration the scabbard was moulded into shape. The back of the scabbard was deemed important enough to be also decorated. The position of the seam was therefore most important. If the seam was at the side then this gave a whole receptive surface to be decorated. If, however, as in the case of most later scabbards, the seam was in the centre, this greatly restricted the area for decoration. In this instance, lines extending from the seam was the easiest method of effective decoration, thus incorporating the seam into the ornamentation.

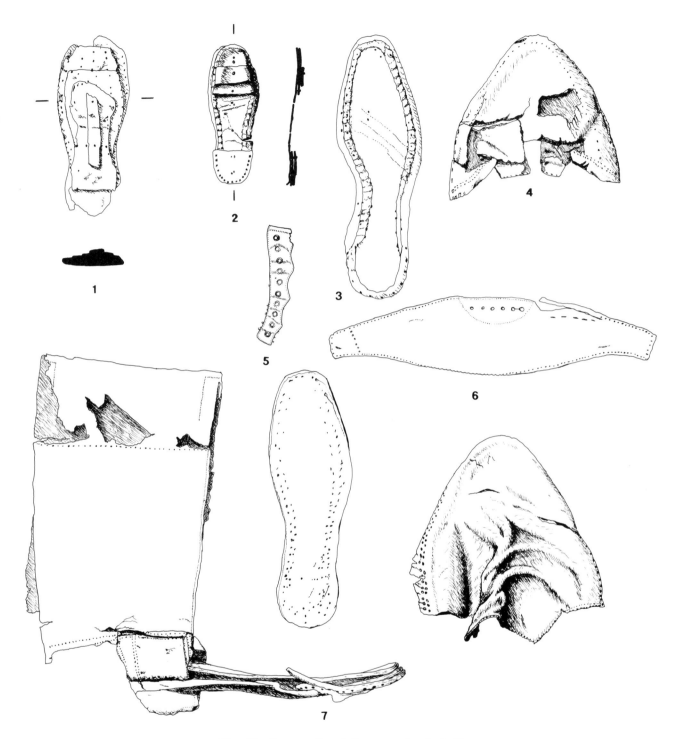

Fig. 84. Post-medieval footwear (scale 1:4)

E543:229:47 (Fig. 82, 2; Site D, level 1, late 12th century) is different from the other scabbards in that it is undecorated and is seamed crudely along the side with a leather thong. Three such scabbards were found in medieval layers at Dublin Castle, one of which had traces of decoration (O'Rourke, forthcoming c) while a similar sheath was uncovered from a mid-12th century context on the High St excavations (O'Rourke, forthcoming a). *Circa* 9mm. of leather along the top edge was folded over inside the sheath. Like the sheath from Patrick St, neither have any evidence for suspension slots, although they appear to be relatively complete.

Post-medieval leather (Figs 84, 85)

There are forty-one pieces of post-medieval leather, all except two pieces relating to footwear. Most of the pieces come from disturbed layers, with several retrieved from stratified post-medieval layers at Site G.

Footwear

The technology in footwear manufacture between the medieval and post-medieval periods differs considerably. During the medieval period, footwear was manufactured in the turnshoe technique, described above. However, *c.* 1500, manufacturing techniques were to alter considerably, giving rise to a heavier, more durable kind of footwear, the welted shoe.

In welted manufacture a strip of leather (a welt) is stitched to the upper and an insole. The welt is left to protrude around the edge of the shoe, allowing a heavier sole to be stitched here. Thus, this shoe could have a number of insoles and soles, making for a heavier, sturdier shoe. Initially, the welt was stitched in place when the shoe was reversed. However, eventually with the aid of a last the shoe did not need to be reversed. This style of footwear also enabled heels to be worn. By the late 16th-17th centuries, the heels were of two kinds: either stacked heels of layers of leather, held together by wooden pegs and/or nails (the use of nails is late 17th century in date) or wooden blocks which were protected by a leather cover which was often painted.

Soles

There are nineteen soles or insoles from the excavations, most of these from Site G. E543:1052:5 (Fig. 84, 1; Patrick St, unstratified find) is a tread fragment of a built-up sole. It consists of five insoles which all would have been nailed together. E543:32:2 (Fig. 84, 2; Site B, level 4, late 14th-mid-18th century) is a child's sole. Attached to the flesh side of the tread are two pieces of leather indicating a built-up sole and two lifts for a stacked heel.

E543:3009:29 (not illustrated; Site G, level 6, late 16th-mid-17th century) is comprised of a number of jumps. These are pieces of leather used to build up the heel of a sole. Several similar pieces were recovered.

Uppers

There are ten uppers of post-medieval date. E543:3010:75 (not illustrated; Site G, level 5, late 16th-mid-17th century), of cow hide, consists of a vamp, heel and quarters. Welts are extant, and the shoe is stitched with a leather thong. The vamp has been cut in antiquity so the fastening mechanism is unknown. There are very crude stitch holes at each wing, and the left hand wing extends to a point. The heel is cut to a point, and is stitched at each side.

E543:3008:8 and 9 (not illustrated; Site G, level 6, 17th-18th century) are both latchet-fastened shoes. The latter is of the most common post-medieval shoe type from the Dublin Castle excavations, where it was found to be 17th century in date (O'Rourke, forthcoming c). This piece consists of a sole, insole and welts stitched with leather thongs. Two latchets remain; these would have been stitched between wing and quarter and threaded through the tongue of the vamp to fasten the shoe. 3008:8 differs from the above in that the latchets are an extension of the quarters and not a distinct entity. The shoe is seamed to the left of the heel. There are two small perforations at the end of each latchet to facilitate fastening. As the latchet forms part of the upper and is not distinct it may imply that this shoe is an earlier development to 3008:9 (above).

Perhaps the best piece of post-medieval footwear is a gentleman's boot E543:1052:12 (Fig. 84, 7; Fig. 85; Patrick St, unstratified find from river silts), which is possibly 17th century in date. It is suede, i.e., the flesh side of the leather is on the outside. It is almost complete, with just the front part of the boot missing. The sole is stacked, consisting of three insoles and one non-continuous sole at the bottom. The stacked heel is nailed together, but is completely worn down on the right hand side indicating that the wearer never bothered to get the heel repaired. The vamp is in one piece, with quite a long instep extending up the ankle. The back of the boot is extant though it is delaminated in parts and is quite fragile. Towards the top there is a decorative row of stitch holes visible only on the flesh side. The back piece is a complete piece of leather while a front piece, now missing, was a separate piece of leather. A heel piece is *in situ*, which would have fitted inside the boot, to give support to the back of the foot. This extended slightly beyond each side of the back of the boot and would have been stitched to the inside of the vamp. It is an excellent example of a post-medieval boot. The height of the leg is 315mm., the sole is 262mm. in length and the heel measures 40mm. in height.

That the boot is suede implies that it would have been a gentleman's boot, as suede is not very practical for a working man. From the large amount of post-medieval footwear from the Dublin Castle excavations, it was unusual that no boots were amongst the footwear assemblage. Records of Thomas Pendleton and his company of thirteen shoemakers in Northampton show how he secured a contract for the manufacture of 600 pairs of boots as well as 4,000 pairs of shoes for the Cromwellian army's incursion into Ireland in 1642 (Swann 1986, 8). In Britain, the knee-high boot became very fashionable for men in the latter part of the 17th century (Swann 1975, 2). Thus, while there is good documentary and historical references to boots being very popular during this period, the archaeological record tells a different story. A Swedish boot, somewhat similar to above, is illustrated by Jafvert (Jafvert 1938, pl. 1.25.C).

Two detached vamps were uncovered, one (E543:216: 128; Fig. 84, 4) was found with a sole (Fig. 84, 3; Site D, clearance) and is fairly typical of the late 16th-17th

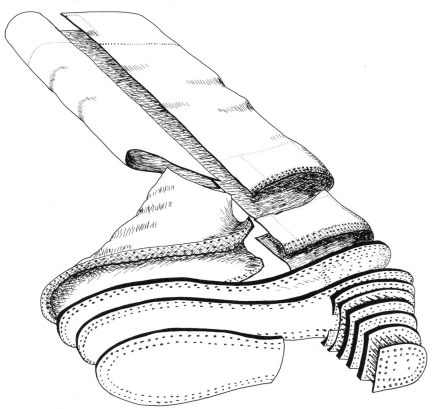

Fig 85. Exploded reconstruction of gentleman's boot (not to scale)

century. A number of similar styles were found during the Dublin Castle excavations. A central tongue would have extended from the instep partly up the ankle. There are stitch holes on each vamp wing indicating where the vamp would have been stitched to two quarters.

Other post-medieval worked leather

A strip of leather, E543:1100:239 (Fig. 85, 5; Site E, clearance), which may have been a shoe fastening, was uncovered. It is a long strip of leather measuring 119mm. x 23mm., cut straight along one side and cut to a curving pattern along the other side. There are ten perforations, lined with copper alloy eyes, along the length. A very fine seam runs along three sides. This piece probably functioned as a fastening.

The final leather artefact is E543:1052:43 (Fig. 85, 6; Patrick St, unstratified river silts). It is a very unusual piece and its function is indiscernible. An edge/flesh seam runs along each side. The piece is squarely cut but narrower at each end, being quite wide in the centre. The maximum width is 77mm. as opposed to 37mm. minimum width. It measures 319mm. in length. Along one side are six perforations which are surrounded by a seam. It may be some form of insole or some form of a front piece for a belt; its function is arbitrary. It is 4mm. in thickness, so while the grain pattern is completely smooth, it is probably made from cow/calf skin.

Conclusions

The leather finds from the excavations are fairly typical of this period. The vast majority of the finds are of footwear made from cattle, i.e., cow hide or calf skin. The most common style of footwear is a wrap-around shoe, seamed at the side with a row of slits just below the top edge. In all cases the leather at the instep and the heel is exaggerated and extended into a 'knobbed' effect. The side-laced ankle boot is also popular. Only one complete example of this style is extant, though there are several insert pieces which are consistent with this type. That these footwear pieces are fairly typical of the period is seen in the similarity with other footwear styles, both on Irish sites and abroad. Most of these styles are mirrored in London and other sites across England.

The non-footwear pieces are few, consisting of five sheaths, a number of belts and other miscellaneous pieces.

The post-medieval finds, while few in number, included a suede gentleman's knee length boot of the 17th century. This find is unique in the post-medieval record of this country. While it is well documented that the fashion for men's footwear in the 17th century was the knee-length boot, the archaeological evidence for such a boot, particularly from the rich post-medieval layers in Dublin Castle, was non-existent.

TEXTILES

Elizabeth Wincott Heckett

Four textiles were recovered from the sites. One piece (E543:524:1) dates to the early 12th century, while the second piece (E543:25:1 and 2) dates to the late 13th century. The third (E543:313:1) comes from a context with a date range from the 14th-17th centuries, while the fourth piece (E543:1052:53) most probably should be attributed to the early part of the 20th century.

Description

The 12th and 13th century pieces are woven cloth, the first a coarse tabby (or plain) weave, the second a 2/1 twill. E543:524:1, in plain weave, is an interesting variant of a type of cloth found very generally on medieval urban sites, mostly in conjunction with mercantile activities. In Ireland there are examples from High St, Dublin (Wincott Heckett, forthcoming a), Peter St, Waterford (Wincott Heckett 1997), and Tuckey St and Grand Parade, Cork (Janaway and Wincott Heckett, forthcoming; Wincott Heckett 1990, 81-82). The yarn for the textiles is made from wool or animal hair; the warp is generally Z-spun and then two strands are S-plied together. The weft is made from thick single Z-spun threads. The width of the cloth is c. 170mm., each edge being hemmed with two-ply wool thread. This width of 170mm. also occurred on 10th-11th century Viking age fine-weave wool textiles from Fishamble St/St John's Lane (Wincott Heckett 1987, 160). This is a narrower cloth than many of the other coarse-weave pieces referred to here and may suggest the use of a small upright loom.

Cloth

The cloth from Winetavern St, Site I, is, however, unlike these other pieces in that the weft system is not made from a spun yarn in the usual way. These weft picks have been made from loosely (S?) rolled pieces of wool that appear to be like those prepared for spinning. These are known as 'rovings' and are hanks of wool fibres that have been teased and combed out and loosely rolled into strips. A continuous rope-like roving can be made from a series of slivers of fibres (Lewis 1983, 53). However, before being used to weave this cloth the rolled pieces must have been subjected to a felting process so that they shrank and became firm enough to be used in weaving. The warp thread is a firmly Z-spun yarn which holds the soft, fat weft ends in place. The cloth is therefore quite thick, warm and waterproof.

The cloth appears to have been treated in some way, perhaps with grease or pitch. It may be that these felted rolls used in the weft system were made from unwashed wool so that the natural oils were retained. This would improve their water-repellent properties but would make the fibres more difficult to felt. It will be recalled that fishermen's gansies were knitted from unscoured or oiled wool to keep water out. It is also possible that some kind of pitch may have been put on to the cloth if it was used for a maritime industrial purpose. Similar rolls of wool have been found from medieval Waterford and from Newcastle in England (Wincott Heckett 1997; Walton 1988, 78). These were not incorporated into cloth and have been interpreted as caulking rolls used in shipbuilding or for waterproofing timber dock revetments. (Sheep's wool is still packed between planks as insulating material in modern Siberian houses).

It is interesting to see these unspun rolls used in cloth, and difficult to be precise as to the original function. If the narrow strips of cloth were sewn together, perhaps a cape or cloak could be made which would be effective against the rain. Alternatively the original use could have been industrial and, as already discussed, connected with ship or dock building.

E543:25:1, 2 is a medium quality 2/1 twill cloth very typical of the 12th-early 14th centuries. Examples are commonly found in Ireland, Britain and Continental Europe. In Ireland there are pieces from those levels in Dublin, Cork and Waterford (Wincott Heckett 1997 and forthcoming a). It seems to have been widely used for clothing. For example, garments in 2/1 twill have survived from 110-20 medieval graves from Herjolfnaes in Greenland (Ostergard 1982, 267) and in association with the murdered 14th century traveller known as the Bocksten man found in a Danish bog (Nockert 1985, 119). The density of threads per cm. of 10-12 warp 9-10 weft with thread diameters of 0.85mm.-0.89mm. (wa) and 1.12mm.-0.94mm. (we) mark the cloth as being of medium quality.

E543:313:1 is a fine quality wool tabby cloth of an open and balanced weave made from well combed and tightly spun yarn. Unfortunately it is not possible to date the textile very closely since its context dates from the 14th-17th centuries. With a cloth of this type it is not possible to be specific about its date from the actual weave since open-weave tabbies have certainly been found in Ireland from the 10th (Fishamble St/St John's Lane, Dublin; Wincott Heckett 1987, 159) to the 16th centuries (James St, Drogheda; Wincott Heckett, forthcoming b). In

Fishamble St this type of cloth was used for caps, bonnets and scarves. However, balanced open tabbies are not widely found in north-western European sites of the earlier period.

Hat

E543:1052:53, from unstratified levels of the river Poddle in Patrick St is a wool felt hat or bonnet of black colour. It is almost complete with a small torn area towards the crown. The felt has been shaped so that the crown is set in asymmetrically and one measurement from brim to crown is 130mm. and, opposite that, the crown to brim measurement is 100mm. This creates a 'bonnet' shape. There is a line of stitchholes 4mm. in from the edge of the hat 2mm.-4 mm. apart. It can be seen from the variation in wear between the lower and upper areas of the hat, and from a slight indentation in the felt, that some material must have trimmed the lower part. This material measured 60mm. at the longer side, presumably the front of the hat, and 35mm. at the presumed back. The diameter of the crown is 105mm.

The following description of hat making is excerpted from *The Pictorial Gallery* (1847, 139). The details relate to the manufacture of beaver hats so the process outlined is more complex than that of wool felt hats.

The fibrous wool that makes the hats must be disentangled and opened by the process of 'bowing'. 'The bower has a staff made of ash, with a cord of catgut stretched from end to end, and the bow thus formed is suspended by a string from the ceiling. The wool (and hair) are laid out flat on a bench, and the workman, plucking the cord by means of a piece of wood held in his right hand, causes it to vibrate against and among the wool, thereby working the fibrous mass into a light flocculent layer.'

This mass was separated into two parts, each part then shaped into a triangle by being pressed with a light wicker frame. The two triangles were then pressed together into a conical cap 'having just enough coherence to maintain its form'. After this the hats were processed around the 'hatter's kettle'. The various stages in the felting and shaping process were known as wetting, rolling, pressing, ruffing and blocking. 'The conical cap, measuring probably 20 inches in each direction, is dipped into a hot acid liquor, and then subjected for two hours to a most severe ordeal; it is beaten, pressed, rubbed, rolled and unrolled, twisted and turned about in every direction, wetted again and again; and such a constant agitation of the fibres kept up, that they become inextricably felted or interlocked one among another ... after the shrinkage occasioned by the felting, the cap presents itself under the form of Fig. 576; drab-coloured, flexible in substance, and measuring fourteen or fifteen inches each way.'

The conical hat was then pulled and shaped into a flat topped shape that was then put on to a wooden block and shaped still further to fit human heads. It was then artificially dried. After this, still on a block, the hat, along with many others, was attached to a cage which was then dipped into a cauldron containing a hot dye-liquor of logwood and other ingredients. After dyeing, the hats must again be steeped, washed and dried. Finally there is a process of steaming, pressing and rubbing over and around an oval block and is 'lastly shaped according to the fashion of the day by means of heated irons'.

Although the style of this hat suggests manufacture in the 18th century (M. Dunlevy, pers. comm.), dye analysis carried out on the hat presents another date. It is therefore possible that the hat is much later; indeed it may date to the 20th century. Colour-fast synthetic dyes such as seem to have been used on the felt came into use between 1904 and around 1929 (Morton 1929, 13). This interpretation would place the hat into the revolutionary period and the first years of independence.

Catalogue

Technical details listed in the catalogue are as follows:

The warp system (vertical threads) is listed first, then the weft (horizontal threads). Colour gradings according to the Munsell Color Charts are also given with the verbal description first and then the gradings for hue, value and chroma. Then the direction of spin, measurements of yarn diameter, densities of threads per cm. are given together with the thickness of cloth.

E543:524:1. Wool tabby, thick closely woven tabby with felted strips in weft system, black, 5YR 2.5/1 and dark reddish brown, 5YR 2.5/2; 260mm. x 125mm.; 2 selvedges (?) both hemmed; density of threads per cm., wa *c.* 3, we 1-2; yarn diameter 2-3mm.-5-10mm., combed wool in tight Z-spun warp, weft, felted strips; cloth thickness 5mm.; both edges hemmed with two-(S)ply, Z-spun yarn.

E543:25:1 and 2. Wool 2/1 twill, medium quality cloth, black, 5YR 2.5/1, carbonised; 1) 90mm. x 105mm. x 115mm.: 2) 95mm. x 115mm. x 130mm. (triangular), density of threads per cm., wa 10-12, we 9-10; yarn diameter 0.85-0.89mm. 0.94-1.12mm., combed wool in tight Z-spun warp and tight S-spun weft; thickness 1.45mm.; no selvedges or sewing.

E543:313:1. Wool tabby balanced weave, 10R 2.5/1 reddish black; 216mm. x 54mm.; density of threads per cm. wa *c.* 12, we 9; diameter wa 0.55mm.-0.69mm., we *c.* 0.41mm., combed wool yarn wa/we tight Z-spun; thickness 1.18mm.; one selvedge; no sewing.

E543:1052:53. Wool felt hat, 7.5YR N 2/0; diameter of brim *c.* 265mm., diameter of crown 105mm., brim to crown (front of hat) 130mm., brim to crown (back) 100mm.; stitch holes 4mm. in from brim at 2mm.-4mm. apart; mark of trimming 60mm. wide at front, 35mm. at back; thickness of felt 1.72mm.

Test for dye in samples of textile from Patrick Street, Dublin. *Penelope Walton*

E543:1052:53 black felt   20th century
E543:313:1   dark brown fine tabby 14th-17th century

The samples were exposed to our usual tests for natural dyes, that is, solvent extraction followed by absorption spectrometry. Sample 313:1 showed no trace of dye. Sample 1052:53, however, gave a strongly coloured red when extracted into the acid/alcohol mix used for mordant dyes. The extract was not ether-soluble and showed a broad area of absorption at 470mm.-490nm. with a shoulder at 530mm. This is similar to, but not the same as, cochineal. The spectrum was not identical with any of the usual natural dyes.

The apparent use of a red dye for a black colour seemed strange and further tests were therefore attempted. Ammonia solution added to the red extract turned it yellow, with absorption at 460nm.-470nm. This habit of changing colour in different conditions is often encountered in synthetic dyes and the sample was therefore exposed to the tests for synthetic dyes devised by Dr H. Schweppe (Schweppe 1979, 14-15). The Dublin dye extracted into glacial acetic acid, where it gave a strong yellow extract, but not into any other solvents. This suggests that the dye is a synthetic basic dye. A yarn dyed with cochineal was tested in parallel, but, as was to be expected with a natural dye, little colourant extracted, giving only a very pale pink in acid. This confirmed that the dye of the Dublin felt was not cochineal.

Synthetic dyes were developed in the second half of the 19th century. The early synthetics were rarely washfast, which the sample from Dublin appears to be; nor is the dye identifiable with any of the early synthetics characterised by Dr G. W. Taylor (Taylor 1988). The conclusion to be drawn is that this is a later synthetic dye, most probably of the 20th century.

ROPE

Alan Hayden and Brenda Collins

Four pieces of moss rope were recovered from the excavations. The moss used in all was *Polytrichum commune* var. *commune*, which is a common moss and grows in wet heaths, bogs and by streams in woodland. The stems are very strong and generally reach a height of 15cm.-20cm. although they can be taller. The length and strength of this species of moss made it suitable for rope making, and it was also found in the medieval and post-medieval deposits at Dublin Castle (Collins, forthcoming), Arran Quay, Dublin (identified by B. Collins), and from the medieval excavations in Perth (Robinson and Ford 1987, 208).

The largest piece of rope (E543:227.1a) measured 1.3m. in length. The ropes are composed of three or four plaited strands. The individual strands vary from 10mm.-20mm. in diameter. Some of the moss stems in the ropes are up to 250mm. in length.

E543:1002:1. Three-ply rope, 0.04m. in length, largely unravelled and in a number of small fragments.
Site F, level 3, 13th century.

E543:227:1a. Three-ply rope, 1.3m. in length, in a number of fragments.
Site D, level 2, early 13th century.

E543:227:1b. Four-ply rope, 1.1m. in length, in a number of fragments.
Site D, level 2, early 13th century.

E543:717:3. Four-ply rope, 0.80m. in length, in four fragments.
Site K, level 1, early 13th century.

CLAY PIPES

Joe Norton

Patrick Street

Thirty-nine bowls were recovered from clearance levels in Patrick St and they can be classified as follows:

17th-18th century pipes

Fourteen bowls, of which twelve are spurred and two are flat-heeled. Of the spurred pipes, three are mid-18th century Dutch, the remainder date from the mid to late-17th century and are either English or Irish pipes. The two flat-heeled pipes are incomplete but date to the late 17th century.

Illustrated are seven spurred pipes.

E543:1:61 (Fig. 86, 1). Small spur, bulbous bowl, milling at the rim, dates *c*. 1640-60.

E543:223:54 (Fig. 86, 2). Larger bowl, straight sides, no milling at rim, dates *c*. 1660-80.

E543:3:23 (Fig. 86, 3). Large plain spurred bowl, no milling at rim, dates *c*. 1670-90.

E543:3:15 (Fig. 86, 4). Small spur, plain bowl, dates *c*. 1680-1700.

E543:300:45 (Fig. 86, 5). Large late spurred type, unmarked, dates *c*. 1690-1710.

Dutch pipes
E543:300:44 (Fig. 86, 6). Typical Dutch pipe of mid-18th century date. It is well finished with fine milling at the rim; on the heel a stamp, a Crown over 'L'; on the side of the spur a faint mark, probably the arms of Gouda. The 'Crowned L' was in use from 1726 to around about 1900. This pipe dates *c*. 1740-60.

E543:201:7 (Fig. 86, 7). Similar bowl type to above; on the heel the 'Milkmaid' stamp, in use from *c*. 1600-1940 (Duco 1982). This pipe dates *c*. 1740-70.

19th century pipes

There are twenty-five of these, twenty complete and five incomplete. They range in date from *c*. 1850-1900. Illustrated are ten of these.

E543:202:36 (Fig. 87, 1). A small plain bowl, dating from *c*. 1850-1900.

E543:1100:75 (Fig. 87, 2). A large typically Irish pipe of the period, stamped 'United Trades Association Dublin', it dates from *c*. 1864 (when it was founded) to around 1900.

E543:202:41 (Fig. 87, 3). A large crude spurred type, stamped 'J. Byrne 144 Francis Street'. John Byrne was making pipes here from *c*. 1865-71.

E543:1100:144 (Fig. 87, 4). A large bowl, very small spur, stamped 'G. Brown, 3 Mullinahack, Dublin'. George

Brown worked here from *c*. 1871-86.

E543:201:2 (Fig. 87, 5). Similar pipe to 2:4, stamped 'Rory of the Hills', and dating from *c*. 1850-1900.

E543:1100:174 (Fig. 87, 6). A large forward sloping bowl, stamped 'The Parnell MP pipe'. The pipe style is also known as 'Parnell' and dates from *c*. 1875-1900, although this type of pipe continued to be made right up to the 1940s.

19th century decorated pipes
E543:1100:225 (Fig. 87, 7). A very ornate style pipe, showing a claw grasping an egg shaped bowl. It dates *c*. 1870-1900.

E543:201:1 (Fig. 87, 8). A large bowl, on one side a hand, on the other a heart. It dates *c*. 1880-1900.

E543:1100:74 (Fig. 87, 9). A large spurred type, on the back of the bowl a 'Crowned L' in a circular beaded frame. This is an Irish copy of the Dutch 'Crowned L' pipe, but of a much inferior quality. This stamp for some reason seems to have been very popular with Irish makers in the 19th century as it was much copied, but rarely with anything of the quality of the original. It dates *c*. 1850-1900.

E543:223:56 (Fig. 87, 10). A beautifully made pipe showing a hand clasping a beaker. It dates *c*. 1880-1900.

Of the remaining pipes the following is of interest: a pipe fragment (E543:100:11, not illustrated), made by William Daly, who worked in Francis St in the period 1870-77.

The remaining bowls or bowl fragments are all of late 19th century date and are typical pipes of this period.

Winetavern Street

There are seven pipes from Winetavern St, five complete and two incomplete. Two are flat-heeled, four are spurred and the seventh is a bowl fragment. Illustrated are five bowls, recovered from Site J cellar fills and clearance levels.

E543:605:21 (Fig. 86, 8). Flat-heeled, narrow oval base and forward sloping bowl, it dates *c*. 1690-1720.

E543:603:10 (Fig. 86, 9). A much larger bowl, a pinched splayed heel, dates *c*. 1700-40.

E543:612:1 (Fig. 86, 10). A large plain spurred type, it dates *c*. 1690-1730

E543:604:14 (Fig. 86, 11). A larger more elongated bowl, with a bigger spur, no markings, it dates *c*. 1710-50.

E543:603:9 (Fig. 86, 12). A spurred bowl, milling around the rim, a 'Clover Leaf' stamp on the base, and what seems to be the arms of Gouda on the side of the spur. A good quality, well-finished bowl, Dutch, date *c*. 1740-60.

Of the remaining two pipes, one is a bowl fragment only, probably of late 17th-early 18th century date. The other pipe is an incomplete bowl of late 18th century date. The date range for this group is from *c*. 1690-1750.

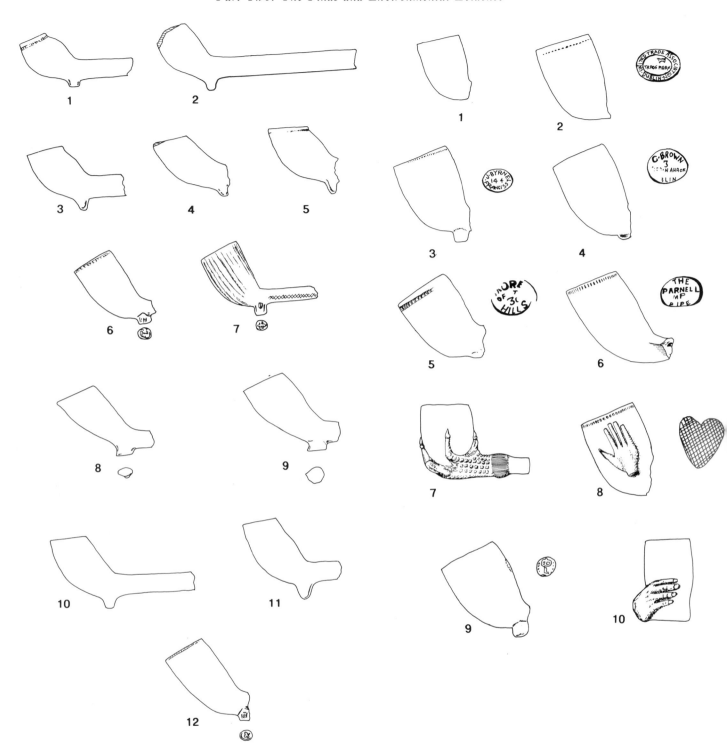

Fig. 86. 17th and 18th century clay pipes (scale 1:2)

Fig. 87. 19th century clay pipes (scale 1:2)

DENDROCHRONOLOGICAL REPORT
ON THE TIMBERS

David Brown

Apart from two timbers, both of which were subsidiary to the main structure of the Patrick St revetments, all were of oak. Fifty-seven samples were submitted for dendrochronological dating to the Paleoecology Centre, Queen's University, Belfast.

Patrick Street

There were fifty-one samples of timbers from Patrick St. These can be divided into seven structures.

1. Site D. Upstream of the mill. Upper revetment, west side. This consisted of one sample which was labelled Q8121 for reference.

QUB no.	Sample no.	Feature no.	Timber no.	Start year	End year
Q8121	1	203.1	baseplate	956	1221

This sample yielded 269 annual growth rings when measured. No sapwood or heartwood/sapwood boundary is present on the sample. The centre of the tree is not present. The ring pattern dated against the Dublin master chronology giving an end year date of 1221. The best estimated felling date for this tree will be 1256 +/- 9 or slightly later. This is calculated by adding the Belfast sapwood estimate of 32 +/- 9 to the end date obtained.

Site D. Upstream of the mill. Possible upper revetment, east side. One sample, E543:233, was submitted for dating (Q8215). The timber had 150 annual growth rings, and no sapwood or heartwood/sapwood boundary was present. The ring pattern dated against the Dublin master chronology giving an end year date of 1147. The best estimated felling date for this tree is 1179 +/- 9 or later.

(During excavation, it appeared that this timber was on the same level as the later revetment 203 at Site D. The dating suggests that it relates to the earlier structure. C.W.)

2. Site D. Upstream of the mill. Lower revetment. This structure consisted of eighteen samples, labelled Q8122 to Q8139 for reference.

QUB no.	Sample no.	Feature no.	Timber no.	Start year	End year
Q8122	11	220	1	997	1202
Q8123	11	220	4	1003	1160
Q8124	1	220	5	965	1157
Q8125	11	220	6	911	1157
Q8126	11	220	7	—	—
Q8127	11	220	8	961	1180
Q8128	11	220	9	942	1181
Q8129	11	220	x	907	1174
Q8130	11	220	11	888	1127
Q8131	11	220	12	994	1173
Q8132	11	220	13	1052	1159
Q8133	20a	220.3	plank	1031	1159
Q8134	77	220.18	baseplate	1009	1120
Q8135	78	220.16	vertical	1061	1160
Q8136	79	232.4	raft	972	1113
Q8137	80	232.2	brace ?	1009	1168
Q8138	82	232.2	brace ?	964	1155
Q8139	100	1404.1	baseplate	1015	1124

It is unnecessary to detail every individual sample from this structure. Two samples, Q8122 and Q8124, had complete sapwood. The tree-ring series from these samples date against the Dublin chronology, both giving an end year of 1202. Other samples with incomplete and crushed sapwood show, from their estimated felling ranges, that this date is likely to be the construction date for the whole structure. Other samples from the structure have been heavily squared. This makes it impossible to show repair phases or reuse of timbers.

3. Site F. Downstream of the mill. Upper revetment. This structure contained fifteen dendrochronological samples. Four of these samples had sapwood present and therefore a good estimated felling date can be obtained for the trees from this structure.

QUB no.	Sample no.	Feature no.	Start year	End year
Q8145	23	335.9	901	1110
Q8146	24	335.11	1049	1186
Q8147	26	335.6	910	1227
Q8148	27	335.3	1022	1165
Q8149	28	335.12	889	1049
Q8150	29	335.5	1008	1197
Q8151	30	335.14	1088	1177
Q8152	31	335.13	—	—
Q8153	58	370.3	1122	1199
Q8154	60	374	877	1026
Q8155	61	375	875	1104
Q8156	84	379.3	1072	1200
Q8157	85	379.1	—	—
Q8158	93	379.10	1083	1195
Q8159	94	379.9	1062	1201

The best estimated felling date for the trees in this structure will be 1209 +/- 9. This is calculated from four samples, Q8153, Q8156, Q8158 and Q8159, all of which have some sapwood present.

There is another possible construction or repair phase associated with samples with the context number (335). One sample, Q8147, has an end year date of 1227. The best estimated felling date for this tree will be 1259 +/- 9. Samples Q8146, Q8148, Q8150 and Q8151 have the same context number as Q8147. All are squared and all have end year dates in the late 12th century. This indicates a felling date range for these trees in the mid-13th century rather than in the early 13th century. The other samples from this structure are heavily worked and do not contribute to the estimation of the felling phases associated with this structure.

4. Site F. Downstream of the mill. Lower revetment. This structure provided three dendrochronological samples. Only on sample Q8160 was there some indication of the heartwood/sapwood boundary being present. The other two samples, Q8162 and Q8161, have been heavily squared.

QUB no.	Sample no.	Feature no.	Start year	End year
Q8160	49	360.1	978	1159
Q8161	50	360.3	925	1085
Q8162	51	360.2	1003	1133

The best estimated felling date for the trees from this structure will be 1181 +/- 9 or later. It is not impossible for this structure to be contemporary with the lower revetment upstream of the mill at Site D.

5. Site F. Downstream of the mill. Parallel lower revetment. Only one dendrochronological sample was received from this structure.

QUB no.	Sample no.	Feature no.	Timber no.	Start year	End year
Q8163	1	87	382.1	—	—

This sample yielded only 81 annual growth rings when measured. The ring pattern obtained did not date against any of the master chronologies or individual samples from the site.

6. Site E. The upper mill. This structure provided five dendrochronological samples. Samples Q8143 and Q8144 were very large but only yielded thirty-three and forty-three annual growth rings respectively. Sample Q8142 is ash. When measured it yielded 142 annual growth rings but could not be dated against the Dublin master chronology.

QUB no.	Sample no.	Feature no.	Timber no.	Start year	End year
Q8140	95	1102	—	1031	1321
Q8141	96	1113	—	1106	1314
Q8142	99	1122	Ash	—	—
Q8143	102	1132	—	—	—
Q8144	110	1114	—	—	—

The two ring patterns which cross date from this group, samples Q8140 and Q8141, have end year dates of 1321 and 1314 respectively. The best estimated felling date, based on these two samples, for the 'upper mill' structure will be 1349 +/- 9 or slightly later. This is calculated by adding the Belfast sapwood estimate of 32 +/- 9 years to the mean end date of the two samples.

7. Site E. The lower mill. Seven dendrochronological samples were obtained from this structure. None of the samples have sapwood or any indication of the heartwood/sapwood boundary being present.

QUB no.	Sample no.	Feature no.	Start year	End year
Q8177	104	1135	1008	1326
Q8178	106	1128	971	1154
Q8180	108	1127	956	1226
Q8181	109	1134	1142	1235
Q8182	113	1143.2	938	1148
Q8314	—	1143.1	938	1155

When measured, sample Q8177 yielded 319 annual growth rings. The ring pattern matched the master chronology, giving an end year date of 1326. The best estimated felling date for this tree will be 1358 +/- 9 or later. This sample is described as coming from the lower mill. If this is true, then a sample from the lower mill has the same estimated felling date range as two samples from the upper mill.

The four other dated samples from the lower mill, Q8178, Q8180, Q8181 and Q8182, look as if they have been heavily squared. It is unlikely but not impossible for these samples to have the same estimated felling date range as sample Q8177. The more probably explanation, from examination of the samples, is that samples Q8180 and Q8181 have not been as heavily squared as others. So the estimated felling date range would be in the mid-13th century rather than the mid-14th century.

Sample Q8314 comes from the same tree as sample Q8182. It gives a 't' value of 19.1 against the ring pattern from Q8182. The best felling date for this tree would be 1187 +/- 9 or later.

Interpretation

1. The single sample from the upper revetment, upstream of the mill at Site D, indicates that a mid-13th century date is the most likely felling date for the tree used in this structure.

2. The multiple samples from the lower revetment, upstream of the mill at Site D, indicate that a date of 1202 is the most likely felling date for the trees used in this structure.

3. The samples from the upper revetment, downstream of the mill at Site F, indicate that a date of 1209 +/- 9 is the most likely felling date for the trees used in this structure.

187

There is another construction phase for this structure indicating a mid-13th century date.

4. The samples from the lower revetment, downstream of the mill at Site F, indicate that an early 13th century date is the most likely felling period for the trees from this structure. It is not impossible for this revetment to be contemporary with the lower revetment upstream of the mill.

5. The single sample from the parallel lower revetment, downstream of the mill at Site F, did not match against the master chronology because of the short ring pattern obtained.

6. The two dated samples from the upper mill indicate that the best estimated felling date for these trees will be 1349 +/- 9 or slightly later.

7. One sample attributed to the lower mill falls into the dating range for the felling of trees from the upper mill. It is possible that this sample is part of the upper mill structure.

The four other dated samples from the lower mill structure are squared. It is improbable but not impossible for the felling dates for these trees to be in the mid-14th century. The more likely situation is that samples Q8180 and Q8181 are not as heavily truncated as samples Q8178 and Q8182. If this is so then samples Q8180 and Q8181 would indicate a mid-13th century date for the lower mill structure.

Winetavern Street

There were six samples of timber from Winetavern St. The samples were from two sites, J and K. They were labelled Q8164-Q8169 for reference. The two samples from Site J, Q8164 and Q8165, were noted as coming from the same tree.

Q8164, Site J. Sample number 55 (2). Context 621. Upright from jetty/walkway support.

This sample yielded 189 annual growth rings, including thirty-six sapwood rings when measured. The sapwood is complete. The centre of the tree is present. The ring pattern was compared against the standard Irish master. A significant correlation was found, giving an end date of 1188. The last ring on the sample had complete summer growth so the tree would have been felled between the autumn of 1188 and the spring of 1189.

Q8165, Site J. Sample number 56 (4). Context 621. Upright from jetty/walkway support.

This sample yielded 171 annual growth rings, including thirty-seven sapwood rings when measured. The sapwood is complete. The centre of the tree is not present. The ring pattern was compared against the standard Irish master. A significant correlation was found giving an end date of 1188. The last ring on the sample has complete

summer growth so the tree would have been felled between the autumn of 1188 and the spring of 1189.

Q8166, Site K. Sample number 64. Context number 719a. Baseplate.

This sample yielded 102 annual growth rings when measured. No sapwood or heartwood/sapwood boundary is present. The centre of the tree is present. The ring pattern obtained was compared against the standard Irish masters. Consistent correlation values were found, giving an end date of 1149. The best estimated felling date for this sample will be 1181 +/- 9 or slightly later. This is calculated by adding the Belfast sapwood estimate of 32 +/- 9 years to the date of the last heartwood ring of the sample.

Q8168, Site K. Sample number 66. Context number 720a. Post retaining baseplate 719.

This sample yielded 195 annual growth rings when measured. No sapwood or heartwood/sapwood boundary is present. The centre of the tree is not present. The ring pattern was compared against the standard Irish masters. Consistent correlation values were found, giving an end date of 1147. The best estimated felling date for this sample will be 1179 +/- 9 or later. This is calculated by adding the Belfast sapwood estimate of 32 +/- 9 years to the date of the last heartwood ring of the sample.

Q8169, Site K. Sample number 67. Context number 720b. Post retaining baseplate 719.

This sample yielded 137 annual growth rings when measured. No sapwood or heartwood/sapwood boundary is present. The centre of the tree is not present. The ring pattern was compared against the standard Irish masters. Consistent correlation values were found, giving an end date of 1161. The best estimated felling date for this sample will be 1193 +/- 9 or later. This is calculated by adding the Belfast sapwood estimate of 32 +/- 9 years to the date of the last heartwood ring of the sample.

Intepretation

The two samples from Site J, Q8164 and Q8165, are from the same tree and end in the same year. Felling occurred in the winter of 1188 or 1189.

The four samples from Site K have no sapwood or heartwood/sapwood boundary. Estimating the felling year for the timbers from this structure is difficult because it is impossible to know how many heartwood rings have been removed from the worked samples. The most likely felling date for the timbers from structure K would be early in the 13th century rather than the late 12th century. Sample Q8167 has an estimated felling date of 1204 +/- 9 or slightly later, which is the most likely date for felling.

STRUCTURAL TIMBERS

Claire Walsh

1191. *'John, Archbishop of Dublin, grants (to St Patrick's) tithes of his demense land of St. Kevin, and of the land of St Patrick's, and sufficient wood from that land for the oven of their commons and for fences...'* (McNeill 1950, 19).

The excavations and subsequent archaeological monitoring of machine work resulted in the retrieval of a large quantity of medieval timbers. Apart from the mill, over seventy adjoining baseplates, many in fragmentary condition, were recovered from the river Poddle, while two timbers forming a baseplate 17m. in length came from the structure at the foot of Winetavern St (Site K). Uprights, many of them tenoned to fit mortices in the baseplates, and plank shuttering placed on the landward side of the uprights, were also recovered in quantity.

Each timber was identified and recorded on site. Scale drawings were done, and details such as conversion, jointings and fixings, and tool marks were recorded on standard field sheets. All but two of the timbers recovered were of oak: the exceptions were of ash.

The purpose of this discussion is to place the timber working from Patrick St within the general framework of Irish carpentry of that period. Much of the carpentry is parallelled in the 13th century waterfront structures excavated at Wood Quay (Wallace 1982; Halpin 1994) and elsewhere (Hayden, forthcoming a; Swan 1992).

It should be stated that the carpentry of these Anglo-Norman waterfront structures, and perhaps even that of the Patrick St mill, may not be truly representative of the carpentry of that period, in terms of quality of work and sophistication of joinery. The methods used in the construction of the revetments are simpler and more direct than those used in the construction of buildings and furniture. Much of the work would have been done by eye, with the dimensions conditioned by the confines of the working environment, as these structures were surely carried through in the river itself. As such, they had to be completed reasonably quickly. Nonetheless, it can be convincingly stated (Milne 1992, 78, 79) that the woodworking techniques employed in such structures can reflect the contemporary traditions current in the vernacular buildings of those periods. The discovery also of reused timbers from vernacular and possibly other buildings contributes to the growing body of evidence indicating the structural use of timber in the Anglo-Norman period.

A glossary of the more common woodworking terms is given at the end of this chapter.

Woodworking: timber and tools

Excepting two timbers, oak was exclusively used. Oak was predominant in the late 12th-early 13th century waterfront structures at the Wood Quay and Usher's Quay sites in Dublin, and in those of Saxo-Norman London (Goodburn 1992, 108), while the baseplates from the early 14th century riverside revetment at Arran Quay, Dublin, were of ash (Hayden, forthcoming a). The use of oak in these arguably low-status structures at Patrick St contrasts with the dominance of ash as the main structural timber in houses of the pre-Norman period (Murray 1983, 3; Wallace 1992, 41; Hayden and Walsh, forthcoming). Boats of the earlier period, reused in the 12th century waterfront structures at Wood Quay, were almost all of oak (McGrail 1993, 87). These were straight grained, slow-grown oaks, most likely forest-grown, the largest of which was 5m.- 6m. in length. These would most probably have been worked while green (ibid., 88).

All the Patrick St timbers are converted from slow-grown oaks, with a mean ring count of less than 1mm. (D.

Brown, pers. comm.). Table 25 shows the span of ring sequences of the major timbers used in the structures at Patrick St. The timbers from Site D were converted from trees which had minimum annual growth rings ranging from 109 to 300 years. The timbers from the mill ranged in minimum age from 93-318 years, while the timbers from Site F ranged in minimum age from 77-317 years. These figures contrast with those from British medieval sites, where slow-growing oaks over 200 years old are unusual (Hillam and Morgan 1981). However, recent large-scale sampling of timbers from English excavations has indicated that previously established patterns of medieval timber usage are not always adhered to (see for example the report on the oak timbers from Dundas Wharf, Bristol; Nicholson and Hillam, 1987; also Goodburn 1992, 122; and Brown 1993). Diameters of individual timbers are given in tabular form and included with each site report.

The medieval carpenter normally selected the smallest trees to serve the purpose in hand, using them immediately without seasoning (Rackham et al 1978, 113). The lengths of the revetment timbers from Patrick St, complete

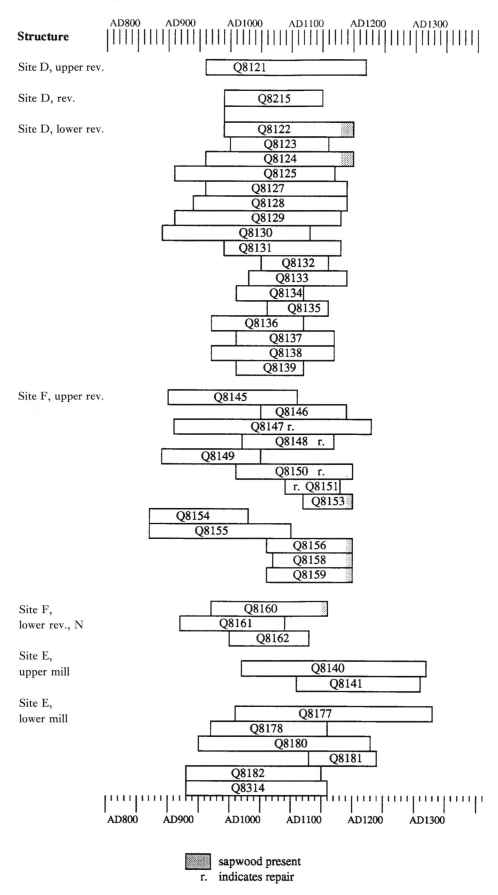

Table 25. Span of ring sequences, Patrick Street

190

Baseplate lengths, Patrick

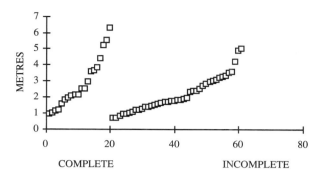

Chart 26. Baseplate lengths, Patrick Street

and otherwise, are given in Chart 26. Even within the limited sample of complete timbers there is a considerable range, from less than 1m. in length to over 6m., while one of the timbers from Winetavern St was a massive 10.60m. in length. It is noteworthy that this timber was straight-grained, indicating that the inferior upper parts of the tree were not utilised. In the medieval period, most trees were quite short, and a normal length for a timber is 6m. (Rackham 1982, 208).

Eighteen per cent of the timbers from the revetments showed evidence of reuse, and it was noticeable that these occurred in one particular stretch – that adjacent to the town defences (Site F), where presumably, the pickings from the scavenging of timber was richer. The timbers chosen for the lower revetment at Site D showed no evidence for reuse in the main structure, but considerable variation in length occurred here also.

All of the main structural timbers, excepting beam 1132 in the mill, which has insufficient rings for dating,

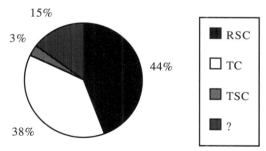

Chart 27. Baseplate timbers: conversion, Patrick Street

had the sapwood stripped from them, and all were heavily squared. Planks forming the shuttering at Site D (220), which were all radially split from the same tree, retained sapwood, giving a date in 1202 for the felling of the tree. Chart 27 gives the relative percentages of the conversion types used to convert the trees to timber.

Tools

Evidence for the tools used is indirect. All the timbers had been adze dressed, giving a relatively smooth finish. Few timbers showed evidence for sawing: this was used mainly in the formation of shouldered tenons, both for uprights, and in the subsidiary baseplate at Site F. Planks or boards were produced by radial cleaving. The use of the saw in medieval England dates to the late 12th century, with evidence for 13th century trestle-sawn planks recovered from the London waterfronts (Goodburn 1992, 114). Squared butts were generally axe trimmed.

Mortices were generally formed by drilling the corners with an auger and removing the intervening wood with a chisel. Both tools left their marks on many of the mortices, with auger holes particularly evident in several of the mortices of the mill. Dowel holes averaged 0.025m.-0.03m. in diameter – the standard size observed also in the Wood Quay timbers (Wallace 1982, 269).

Joinery: the revetments

The revetments on both sides of the channel were possibly built in parallel stretches - this is apparent from the location of timbers such as 379.12 and 1011.1, both of which had diagonally trimmed butts, and were reused from the same structure and placed on opposite sides of the river (Site F, level 3). Very basic techniques were employed in the construction of the Patrick St revetments, and these are all paralleled in the Wood Quay timbers. Where timbers were connected, the simple through-splayed scarf (Fig. 88, 1) was generally used, and these were laid from south to north. This joint has limited resistance to lateral pressure, but its use in the similar structures at Wood Quay as at Patrick St was dominant. Of the seventy timbers recovered, twenty-nine were jointed and facepegs were used in only four instances (Chart 28). Two timbers of the upper revetment at Site D were lightly nailed together. The Winetavern St revetment was more closely fitted, but no face pegs were used to hold the joint. A common failing here, as with several timbers at Patrick St,

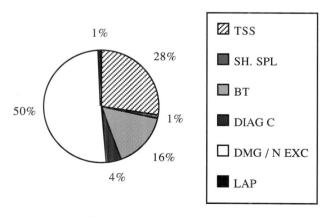

Chart 28. End joint types, Patrick Street

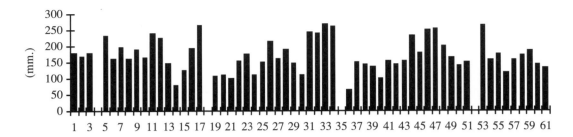

Chart 29. Average length of mortices, Patrick Street

Chart 30. Average width of mortices, by timber, Patrick Street

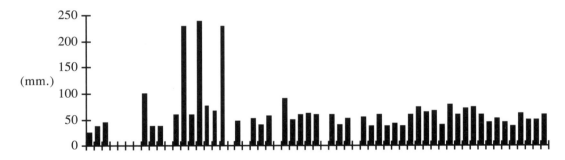

Chart 31. Average spacing of mortices by timber, Patrick Street

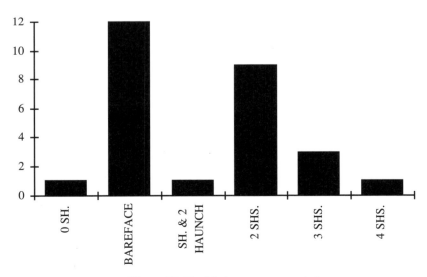

Chart 32. End joint types, uprights

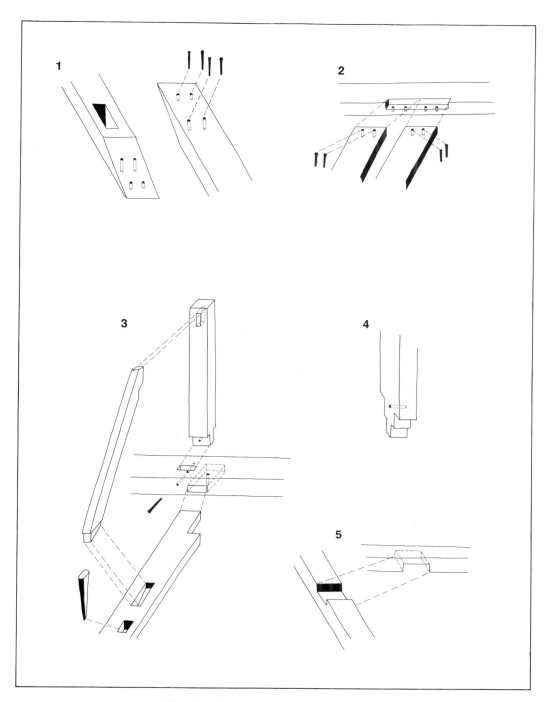

Fig. 88. Carpentry: joints and uprights

was to place a mortice at the joint. One stray timber from the river at Patrick St exhibited an edge-halved scarf, with a broken dowel hole at the extremity. This was probably reused from a different structure.

Mortices were generally rectangular (dimensions are given in Charts 29 and 30), but it is notable that the upper revetment at Site D had square mortices. Rigold (1975, 88) has argued for an early date for square mortices, the usual rectangular long mortice, more efficient in both directions, being a logical replacement for the square mortice. This was the case in the Bordesley Abbey mill races (Allen 1993, 83). In rough carpentry such as that at

Patrick St, however, little can be inferred from the occurrence of such an archaic feature.

Examples of mortices penetrating the timber and stopped mortices occur. Stopped mortices occur both on timbers with evident signs of reuse, and on those which appear to be in primary position. In a small number of instances, both types occur on the same timber. Almost 25 per cent of the mortices are stopped: this contrasts with the early 13th century revetment 1 at Wood Quay, where most of the mortices were cut through the timber (Wallace 1982, 279). Only one sloping or chase mortice was observed (Fig. 88, 3).

193

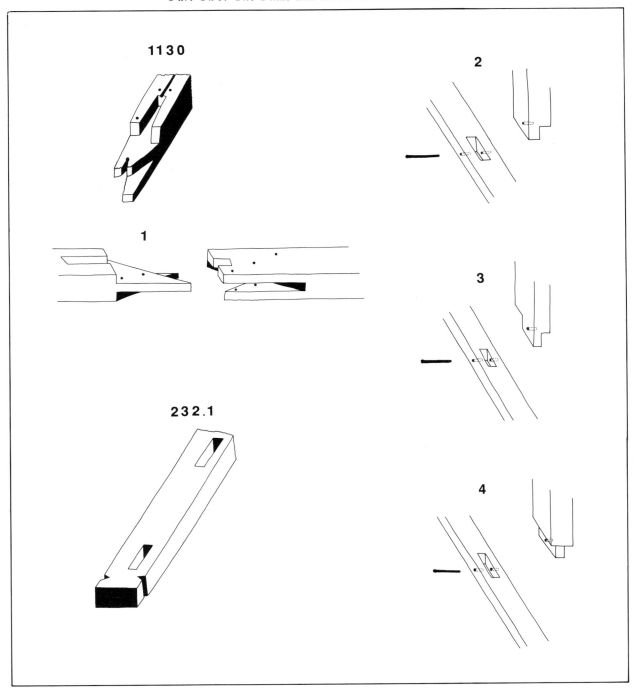

Fig. 89. Carpentry: joints and uprights

Average spacing of the mortices was calculated per timber (Chart 31). (The very widely spaced mortices refer to timbers 378 in the centre of the channel: Site F, level 3). Uprights *in situ* were poorly represented, with twenty-five survivals. Unshouldered, barefaced, two, three and four shouldered tenons occurred (Fig. 89, 2, 3, 4; Chart 32), with different examples occurring in the same baseplate. There is one example of a double-haunched and shouldered tenon in a reused context from the 'raft' structure at Site D (Fig. 8, 4). Tenons were occasionally secured into the mortices by circular dowels. Dowels of hazel, ash, birch and prunus occasionally occurred, but oak was more common. In several cases, oak dowel pegs survived in their position, while the upright did not. This may be due to the use of softer woods as uprights. It was otherwise apparent where uprights had been deliberately removed, leaving a broken dowel.

The baseplates of the revetments were not grooved to accommodate the lower boards of the shuttering, although one side of a surviving upright displayed a groove which was probably to fit planking: this element is likely to have been reused in the structure.

A baseplate of the wheelpit of the upper mill (Site E, level 2) though damaged, exhibited a centrally placed groove, aligned with the mortices. This would have provided a shallow seating for plank shuttering forming the sides of the wheelpit.

The mill timbers

There is little variation between the carpentry of the mill timbers and the other structures. The mortice and tenon is dominant: in the large parallel beams from the level 1 structure, the mortices are stopped, and the uprights were not pegged into position.

The dam or inlet of the level 1 structure exhibits rebating of the end and side baseplate timbers to accommodate plank flooring: this was dowelled into position at both ends. Rebating also featured in the end timbers of the feeder trough of both periods, where the plank flooring was dowelled into position in the first instance (Fig. 88, 2), and later iron nails were used. The lap joint, in rather crude form, was used in the fixing of two perpendicular timbers of the level 2 dam or inlet (Fig. 88, 5), while a corner halving joint occurred at the end of the same timber. An end-to-face lap was employed to attach the angled baseplate of the level 1 inlet. It was curious that the side timbers of the feeder trough were not in either structure jointed to the perpendicular beams at either end.

The one true piece of accomplished carpentry in the mill was the joining of the two parts of beam 1143, the end timber of the level 1 wheelpit. It was apparent only on dismantling the plank flooring of the feeder trough that the underlying beam was composed of two parts, so tightly were they fitted. The use of a splayed tongued and grooved pegged scarf joint (Fig. 90) is not usual in this position: I have not managed to find any exact parallel for it. The closest comparison for this joint is that used in roofing members in English architecture of the early 13th century (Rackham et al 1978, 110). At Gloucester Blackfriars, rafters in the choir were made from short lengths of timbers scarfed together by pairs of long tapering interlocking prongs, which were held with pegs and nails. However, a closer parallel is the scarf used in the top-plate of a late 13th century aisled hall in Hertfordshire which Hewett (1977, 294) describes as 'the most perfect scarf joint yet published'. The splay of that scarf was 0.724m., while the Patrick St join was 0.76m. in length. The scarf from Patrick St is not tabled, and has only two edge pegs. The joint would have been cut with a saw. The angled notch-lap housing with central dowel (Fig. 90, 1) is also paralleled in roofing members from English timber-framed buildings (Rackham et al 1978, 109). It is therefore suggested that this beam was reused as a ground beam in the mill from the roof of a large building, which was probably close to the site of the mill.

The western element of the baulk had 210 growth rings, giving an end date of 1148, and it is not impossible for it to have been used for some years in its original position before finishing its time in the mill. (The presence of a dowel in the notch-lap indicates that the timber

was assembled with another in its primary position). A suggested reconstruction of the timber as originally designed is given (Fig. 90, 2).

Timber 1130, which was reused as a joist to support the plank flooring of the feeder trough of the level 2a mill, also displays the start of a similar sort of scarf join (Fig. 89, 1), which was held with at least two spikes. This timber could have formed part of the superstructure of the earlier mill, which was 'thrown down and void' prior to its rebuilding in the later part of the 14th century. This timber had been used in two other positions before its final usage as a joist for the plank flooring of the feeder trough.

A subsidiary timber (1123; not illustrated) in the level 2 mill also exhibited two angled lap housings and a series of dowels on the underside - this timber appears to have been used in at least two different forms prior to its final use in the floor of the inlet. It too probably derived from the earlier mill on the site, where it may have formed part of the superstructure.

Other reused timbers

Of the baseplates from Patrick St, eleven showed evidence for reuse. In most cases, this was displayed by a non-functional dowel hole, or a mortice on the underside. A timber (232.1), which occurred in the 'raft' structure underlying the early 13th century revetment (Site D, level 2) had opposing V-shaped notches *c.* 0.04m. deep cut into either side, located 0.08m. from its square-trimmed butt (Fig. 89). This timber measured over 5.3m. in length, with no further anomalous markings evident upon it. The timber may have been used primarily as a floor joist.

Four timbers, reused from the top-plate of a timber-framed house, were recovered. None of these timbers was submitted for dendrochronological dating, but formed part of the structure of the lower revetment at Site F, dating to the early 13th century.

The timbers varied in length from 1.48m.-6.26m., and none was complete. Timber 378.2 measured 6.26m. in length, 0.13m. in width, and varied from 0.10m.- 0.12m. in thickness (Fig. 91). The other timbers were of similar dimension in girth. All three timbers had shallow recesses along one edge, and in several the shanks of iron spikes remained in the recesses. The recesses were shallow sloping cuts, between 0.02m.-0.04m. in depth. Timber 378.2, the most complete, had thirteen recesses spaced evenly at intervals of 0.45m. from each other (measurement taken from the centre of each recess), the intervening distance from the end of each recess to the next in most cases 0.33m. Common rafters to support the cladding were normally spaced at distances of 1 ft/*c.* 0.33m. (Hewett 1963, 267).

Two timbers exhibited a single lap dovetail housing (Fig. 91, 1). Saw marks were evident on the sides of these. A regular groove, *c.* 0.035m. long, 0.035m. in depth and up to 0.06m. in width, was cut into the underside of each

195

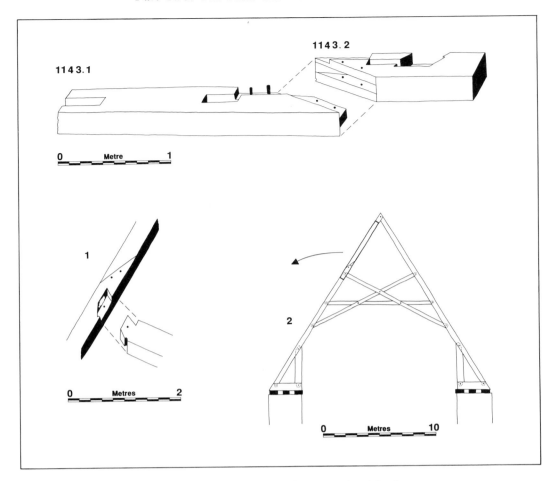

Fig. 90. Timber 1143, and suggested original use

beam: this was to accommodate the plank walling of the house. The tie beam housed in the lap dovetail would have been centrally placed. We do not know in what manner the ends of the top-plates were framed as these had been trimmed prior to the reuse of the timbers in the revetments. Each was cut through by large rectangular mortices. The suggested reconstruction of timber 378.2 in its primary use is given (Fig. 91, 2).

Usage of wattle

Wattle fences were uncovered at Sites A, C, D and F. The fences were invariably of simple weave, with the rods lying behind every alternate post. In each case, samples of the fence were randomly taken. Species used for both rods and uprights (sails) were identified, and where possible, annual growth ring counts of each piece were made. This work was carried out by Sarah Cross. The results are summarised in Charts 33 and 34.

Hazel produces strong, flexible rods and its predominance is evident. Hazel also dominated the species identified from 13th century wattle walled structures at Back Lane, Dublin (O'Sullivan and Deevy, forthcoming). Willow probably grew on the banks of the Poddle (Scannel 1988, 100) but is poorly represented among the rods. A wider variety of woods was employed for uprights.

Tabulation of the annual growth rings of the rods has shown concentrations in the span from three to ten rings (Chart 35), but evidence for woodland management, in particular coppicing, is not strong in this sample (S. Cross, pers. comm.). Counts of the growth rings of the sampled uprights has shown a fairly even distribution of annual growth rings from six to forty (not illustrated), and it could be suggested that the sails were chosen for their size, which ranged in size from 0.025m.-0.09m. from fence to fence, but with no noticeable variation of size within the same structure.

Identification of the charcoal from the limekiln at Site F *Donal Sinnott*

Percentages of sample (bulk or volume estimates) *Salix* (willow), twigs and young stems or branches, pieces 4mm.-15mm. diameter. The largest piece showed ten annual growth rings from pith to bark. 51 per cent.

The assumption is made that all the charcoal in this group is willow rather than poplar (*Populus*) based on the fact that all of the pith sections seen are circular rather than angular, the only practical character for separating the two genes in the charcoal state.

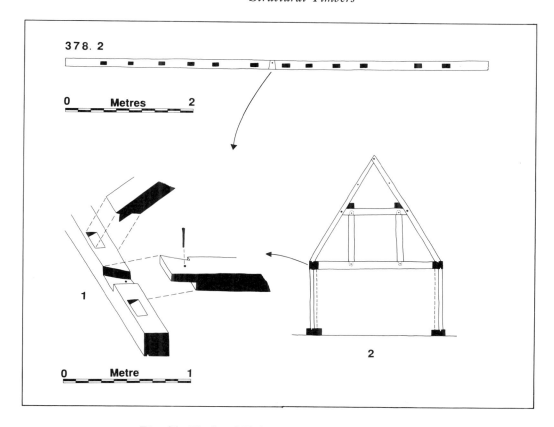

Fig. 91. Timber 378.2, and suggested original use

Corylus (hazel), twigs and young stems or branches. The largest piece, 17mm. diameter, showed nine annual growth rings from pith to bark. 42 per cent.

Fraxinus (ash), a few fragments of mature wood (i.e. tree trunk or large branch; the annual growth increments very narrow and linear, not wide and curved as in younger growth). 5 per cent.

Ilex (holly), a few fragments of mature wood. 2 per cent.

Proper names of woods:
Alder: *Alnus glutinosa*
Ash: *Fraxinus excelsior*
Birch: *Betula*
Hazel: *Corylus*
Holly: *Ilex aquifolium*
Oak: *Quercus*
Poplar: *Populus*
Prunus refers to fruitbearing trees
Willow: *Salix*

Glossary of woodworking terms (after Hewett 1963, 267-70; Milne 1982, 19-22).
Barefaced: a joint with only one shoulder, seen here in the tenons.
Brace: diagonally set member supporting a vertical member.
Butt: terminal point.
Cladding: external clothing of a structure – planks, tiles etc.
Common rafters: inclined roof members which support the cladding.
Groove: a furrow of square section which runs along the grain.

Housing: socket of identical shape to hold a timber in an end joint.
Lap joints: in which one part of the timbers overlaps part of the other.
Lap dovetail: lap joint in which member and housing are shaped like an extended dove's tail.
Notched laps: have a V-shaped notch which prevents withdrawal.
Mortice: a cavity chopped into a timber, usually rectangular.
Chase mortice: has one inclined end to accept the tenon of a member designed to run diagonally from the morticed timber.
Rebate: reduces the thickness of a timber along its edge.
Revetment: a facing of masonry or timber supporting or protecting a bank or embankment.
Sapwood: the outer or living part of a tree, usually removed by the carpenter as it is more prone to disease and decay.
Scarf: a joint making one long timber from two or more shorter lengths by joining their ends.
Through-splayed scarf: the timber ends are correspondingly sloped and overlapping, and occasionally fixed with dowels or facepegs.
Tenon: projection of rectangular section on the end of a timber to be fitted into the mortice.
Tongue and groove: any tenon greatly extended in one respect, generally lengthways, along, for instance, the edge of a plank. This fits into a groove (see above).
Top-plate: horizontal timber set along the top of a timber-framed wall, upon which the rafters rest at their lower ends.

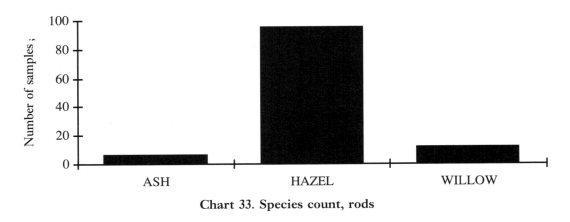

Chart 33. Species count, rods

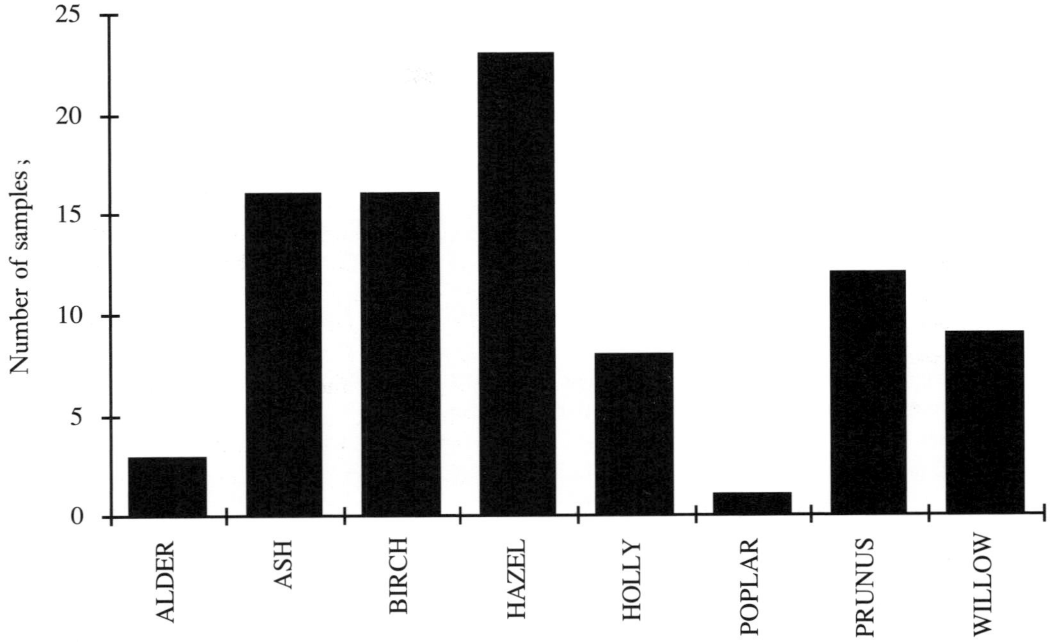

Chart 34. Species count, sails

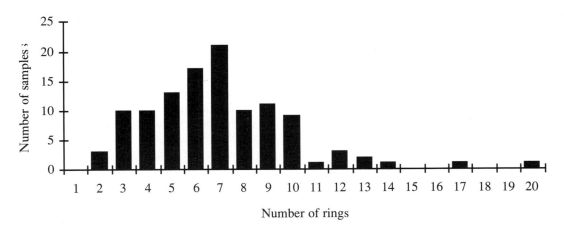

Chart 35. Annual growth rings, rods

MAMMAL BONES

Finbar McCormick and Eileen Murphy

Excavations on the Patrick St - Nicholas St - Winetavern St pipe line route uncovered five assemblages providing significant quantities of animal bone. Two of these were from Patrick St and are referred to as Sites B and C in the report. Site B consisted of dump deposits on the bank of the river Poddle, while Site C consisted of deposits which had been dumped into the same river. The presence of unfused epiphyses *in situ* indicated that the bones may not have suffered much water turbation after they were dumped. Pottery from these deposits indicate that the sites date from the late 12th to the mid-13th centuries. The three other assemblages came from the fill of the town moat at Site G. Site G, A is of late 12th-14th century date, Site G, B is of 14th-16th century date, while Site G, C is of mid-16th-early 18th century date.

Methodology

The minimum numbers of individuals (MNI) were calculated on the basis of the most frequent skeletal element present, taking left and right side into consideration. No attempt, however, was made to increase MNI on the basis of bone size or state of epiphyseal fusion and tooth eruption as this method is only valid for very small samples. The fusion data is based on Silver (1969) while the age of the state of tooth eruption is based on Higham (1967). The abbreviations used for cattle bone measurements are those of von den Driesch (1976).

Discussion

A list of the bones from the five assemblages is given in Tables 44 to 48. The species represented consist of cattle, horse, sheep, goat, pig, dog, cat, red deer, rabbit and cetacean (whale). A small quantity of mussel and oyster shells were also present. The great majority of the bones were from cattle, sheep/goat and pig. The remaining species were only occasionally represented.

The distribution of the three principal species from the sites are tabulated against those from other sites from Dublin in Table 36. These range in date between the 9th-10th centuries to the 18th century. It is interesting to note that although the Patrick St Site B and C samples are of the same date the distribution of the species differed greatly between the two sites. This is problematical as both are of the same general date and from relatively close proximity to each other. Before this problem is addressed the groups will be considered in the context of other samples from Dublin and related areas.

Table 36 clearly shows that the sample sizes from the different sites vary greatly. The results based on the smaller samples should therefore be treated with some caution. Some general trends can, however, be observed. Sheep/goat were of relatively low importance in the pre-Norman levels of Dublin, where they constituted between 10 per cent and 13 per cent of the MNI total. The diffi-culty of differentiating between sheep and goat is well documented but it can be shown that the majority of sheep/goat bones are of sheep (see below). In the 13th century deposits at Wood Quay, however, it is clear that the importance of sheep/goat had increased with a value of 36 per cent being recorded. The data from Site B in Patrick St, which are of 13th century date, show further development of this trend, although the sample from Site C deviates from this. The distribution from Site C will be considered in detail below. The increase in sheep is also reflected in samples from 13th-14th century levels in Drogheda and Waterford city where sheep/goat represent 55.6 per cent and 47.4 per cent, respectively (McCormick 1984a; 1997).

The reasons for the increase in the keeping of sheep in urban sites in the east and south-east of Ireland must be considered in the context of changing agricultural practices after the Anglo-Norman settlement in Ireland. Firstly, it must be recognised that sheep, unlike pig, could not be reared within the town but were instead supplied by outside producers. The Anglo-Normans established a manorial farming system which differed greatly from the preceding native system. Unlike the latter, the new system generated a cash economy as rents were generally paid in money rather than by labour and tribute (Down 1987, 463). The generation of money, by the selling of agricultural surplus, became the motivating force in agricultural production. In this context sheep had a distinct advantage over cattle or pig.

Firstly, the rural cash economy generated a great expansion in the production and export of grain (ibid. 460-61; O'Neill 1987, 20-29). The maintenance of productivity in arable farming necessitates continual manuring of the soil. Sheep dung is of higher quality than the dung of other domesticates being, for instance, richer in nitrogen, potassium and phosphorus than cattle dung (White 1970, 127-28). Thus, whenever there is an expansion in arable farming, there is often a corresponding increase in sheep rearing, as, for instance, in Iron Age England (Cunliffe 1974, 184). The Anglo-Normans in Ireland were aware of the qualities of sheep dung and the documentary sources

Site	Date	Cattle	Sheep/goat	Pig	No.
Fishamble St (Plots 2 and 3)	10–early 11 cen.	34.4	10.4	55.3	1062
Fishamble St (Bank to wall)	late 11–12 cen.	58.8	11.3	30.0	97
Ship St	late 12 cen.	47.8	13.0	39.1	23
Back Lane	12–early 13 cen.	43.2	13.6	43.2	44
Wood Quay	13 cen.	40.0	36.0	24.0	917
Site G, A	late 12–14 cen.	41.7	41.7	16.7	24
Patrick St, Site B	late 13–14 cen.	33.3	52.8	13.9	36
Patrick St, Site C	late 13–14 cen.	33.3	23.5	43.1	51
Arran Quay: Early	late 13–late 14 cen.	35.5	35.5	29.0	31
Arran Quay: Late	late 14–late 15 cen.	34.0	42.4	23.0	144
Site G, B	14–16 cen.	33.3	40.0	26.7	30
Site G, C	16–18cen.	41.9	48.4	9.7	31

Table 36. Relative percentages of the MNIs of the three principal domesticates from Dublin (McCormick 1987). The Wood Quay samples are after Butler (1984) and the MNI total is an estimate. The Fishamble St plot samples are from house sites while the bank to wall sample is from fill between the town bank and wall. Additional material from unpublished reports by McCormick and Murphy.

provide evidence for the high regard in which it was held. In the earl of Norfolk's Irish estates in the late 13th century the tenants were obliged to fold their sheep on the lord's land rather than their own, thus depriving their land of enrichment (Down 1987, 473).

Secondly, sheep were also of great 'cash crop' importance because of the value of wool which, unlike other hides or furs, and of course meat, could be repeatedly produced by the animal. Wool was one of the most important exports from medieval Ireland. Large herds were kept by the Cistercians, who became established in Ireland (1142) prior to the Norman arrival. The extent and mechanics of the trade are discussed by O'Neill (1987, 58-64) who notes that the production of wool also provided opportunities for the generation of money on a very small scale. He states (ibid., 61) that 'by no means did all the wool exported come from the estates of the monasteries or the lands of wealthy lords ... a great amount must have come from the smaller flocks of lesser farmers and peasants, who would have sold it to the nearest town'.

The high incidence of sheep noted in Site B in Patrick St does not necessarily reflect a preferential taste by the inhabitants for mutton. The food consumed in the town was not dictated by the tastes of the town inhabitants but, instead, by the preferences of the manorial farmers of the surrounding hinterland. As long as the export trade in wool and grain remained buoyant these farmers would maintain large sheep herds and more sheep than cattle would be sent to the Dublin meat market.

Cattle

Despite the greater numbers of sheep present in Site B and pig in Site C, cattle, in terms of weight, provided most of the meat consumed in the city. Medieval domes-

ticated animals were consistently smaller than their modern counterparts. Assuming a live animal weight of 450kg. for cattle, 23kg. for sheep and 80kg. for pig with a dressing-out weight of 50 per cent for cattle and sheep and 80 per cent for pig, the relative proportion of meat provided by the three main species is shown in Table 37.

The age at which the cattle were slaughtered was estimated on the basis of the tooth eruption and wear of the mandibulae. The sample was restricted to the larger group from Sites C and G, and a detailed breakdown of the data is presented in Table 52. Table 38 presents a summary of the data compared to the two Fishamble St samples of pre-Norman date and a large sample from Moynagh, Co. Meath, a rural Early Christian settlement.

The age-slaughter pattern from the two Dublin sites are in general agreement, with the great majority (70-85 per cent) being older than approximately two years at the time of slaughter. It is therefore clear that the outside producers found it more profitable to send semi-mature or fully grown beasts to the Dublin market. At Moynagh the distribution is quite different, with a peak in the slaughter of one to two year olds and with only 44 per cent being slaughtered in the age bracket outlined above.

The sex of cattle can best be determined on the basis of the metacarpals. Multivariate analysis of a large sample from Fishamble St, Dublin (McCormick 1987), indicated that metacarpals with distal widths (Bd) greater then 57.5mm. were definitely male while those of less than 55.5mm. were definitely female. On the basis of this 85 per cent, of a combined sample of twenty 12th-14th century bones from Patrick St and Nicholas St, Site G, could be attributed to cows. In the 14th-16th century levels 94 per cent (N=16) were cows while 100 per cent (N=9) of the 16th-18th century group were cows. The sex of an animal can only be determined when the distal end of the metacarpal has fused, i.e., in animals of greater than

Site	Date		Cattle	Sheep/Goat	Pig
Patrick St, Site B	13-14 cen.	MNI %	33.3	52.8	13.9
		Meat weight %	82.9	7.3	9.8
Patrick St, Site C	13-14 cen.	MNI %	33.3	25.3	43.1
		Meat weight %	71.1	2.8	26.2
Site G, A	12-14 cen.	MNI %	41.7	41.7	16.6
		Meat weight %	85.8	4.4	9.8
Site G, B	14-16 cen.	MNI %	33.3	40.0	26.7
		Meat weight %	77.6	4.8	17.7
Site G, C	mid 16-early 18 cen.	MNI %	41.9	48.4	9.7
		Meat weight %	88.9	5.2	5.8

Table 37. Relative MNI and meat weight values of the main meat-providing domesticates.

Approx. age (in months)	Moynagh	Fishamble St Plots 2-3	Fishamble St Bank to Wall	Patrick St Site C
	No.=195	No.=262	No.=27	No.=17
0-7	4.1	6.1	3.7	11.8
7-13	11.2	8.8	–	–
13-24	41.0	12.2	11.1	17.7
25-36	18.6	19.5	22.2	17.7
36+	25.1	53.4	62.9	52.9

Table 38. Cattle age distributions, after Table 52 and after McCormick (1987)

approximately 24-30 months of age at time of death (Silver 1969, 285). This distribution is higher than other urban samples from Dublin and also Waterford where 67-77 per cent were female. As the sample from Patrick St is small it is not known if the higher proportion of cows noted is significant. The farmer found it more profitable to rear females for the urban market because, firstly, they could replace themselves before being sent to slaughter and, secondly, because there is evidence that in primitive cattle females tended to fatten at a faster rate than males (Lisle 1957, 26).

Analysis of the cattle metrical data (Table 39) indicates no significant change in size between the Scandinavian and medieval period. The means from the Scandinavian levels from Fishamble St tend to be consistently larger than those noted at Patrick St but the difference is consistently less than one standard deviation, indicating that the difference is more apparent than real. The small numbers of long bones present indicate shoulder heights of between 104.0cm. and 111.6cm.

Only a small number of cattle bones display pathological changes. A single case of osteomyelitis is present on the shaft of a metacarpal shaft superior to the distal articular area (Patrick St, Site B). This is indicative of infec-

tion of the marrow. Site G, A produced two examples of pathology. Lytic activity on a right mandibular condyle indicates degenerative joint disease of the temperomandibular joint. An ossified haematoma on the inferior surface of the horizontal ramus of a mandible is indicative of bruising under the skin, possibly due to being struck/knocked on the jaw. Site G, B produced several examples of cattle skulls which had large foramina, situated behind the frontal and nuchal eminences on the occipital bone. The cause of these perforations is unknown, but it is considered to be related either to the use of yokes for draught purposes or to be congenital in nature (Brothwell, Dobney and Ervyack 1996). A large rib fragment, presumably bovine, displayed a well healed fracture. Site G, C contained two cattle bones which displayed degenerative joint disease. A butchered fragment from the left side of a first sacral vertebra exhibited lytic activity, osteophytes and eburnation on the superior surface of the vertebral body. The presence of eburnation and the fact that the eburnation had a grooved appearance indicates that the animal continued movement after the degenerative condition had developed. A fragment of a right proximal metatarsal displayed osteophytes along its anterior margin. Immediately inferior to the proximal epiphyses

Date	Fishamble St 10-11 cen.	Patrick St, Sites B, C, G 12-14 cen.	Site G 14-16 cen.	Site G 16-18 cen.
Horn length of outer curve	151.1	132.5	130.5	158.5
Radius Bp	75.7	71.9	70.8	69.1
Metacarpal Bp	53.4	51.3	48.9	49.4
Bd	54.6	53.1	52.4	52.7
Tibia Bd	57.0	54.8	55.3	53.9
Calcaneus GL	125.5	121.5	121.5	118.6
Metatarsal Bp	44.0	41.7	49.1	—
Bd	50.6	48.0	48.0	48.4

Table 39. **Mean dimensions (mm.) of cattle measurements from Scandinavian levels from Fishamble St and the present samples from Patrick St, Sites B, C and G (after McCormick 1987 and Tables 49-51)**

there was an area of new bone on all surfaces of the shaft which extended to the inferior margin of the fragment (*c.* 5.5cm.). The new bone consisted of a plaque of grey, woven bone. It is probable that the animal had an active infection or area of trauma on its lower leg when it died.

A single scurred horncore was present in the Site G, B sample.

Sheep/goat

The difficulty of differentiating between sheep and goat bones is well attested to in the literature. Geraldus Cambrensis noted as early as the 12th century that Welsh diviners had difficulty in differentiating between the shoulder blades of sheep and goat (Thorpe 1978, 146). The species can be most convincingly differentiated on the basis of the horns and metapodia. Table 40 indicates that in most cases the majority of the horns present could be identified as goat, but that the majority of post-cranial bones are those of sheep. In a case where an attempt was made to identify the humeri (Site G, B), all of a sample of four were sheep. The under-representation of sheep horns can partly be accounted for by the presence of polled animals but it is unlikely that this would fully account for the pattern. This general dichotomy between horns and post-cranial bones has been consistently noted in Irish medieval urban sites such as Waterford and Limerick and also abroad, e.g., Lund, Sweden (Ekman 1973, 25). It is generally thought that the extra horns are representative of trade in horns, as the straight horn sheath of goats was more suitable for horn-working than that of sheep. McCormick (1984a, 211) used this as an explanation for the high incidence of goat horn, compared with post-cranial bone, at Drogheda. The fact that this pattern is becoming the norm in virtually all urban contexts containing the two species would appear to make this explanation

untenable in some, if not most, cases. It seems more likely that differential preservation accounts for the difference. The horn core of sheep, especially ewes, is very fragile, while that of goat is one of the strongest and most dense of all animal bones. The high incidence of goat horn cores may simply be attributed to the durability of the goat horn-core. The absence of 'meat' on the horn core, unlike post-cranial goat bones, also reduced its potential for destruction by the gnawing of dogs. On the basis of this it can be assumed that the great majority of caprovine bones present at Patrick St were those of sheep. The proportion of goat present (5 per cent) was slightly less than that noted in the Scandinavian levels in Fishamble St where goat accounted for between 9 and 15 per cent of the two species.

Goat were almost certainly kept in the town primarily as dairy animals as cow's milk would not have been readily available. This is reflected in the fact that the great majority of the horns from Patrick St, Sites B and C (88 per cent N=16) were female. This pattern was also reflected in all levels at Site G. A comparable bias towards females was also noted on the Scandinavian levels at Fishamble St. The keeping of goat on a large scale tends to be an urban phenomenon as they are rarely found on rural Early Christian period sites (McCormick 1991).

In order to attempt to reconstruct an age/slaughter pattern for sheep it is assumed that the great majority of caprovine mandibulae are sheep. Table 41 compares the data from various Irish sites using the ageing data provided by Higham (1967).

It is interesting to note that the age/slaughter distribution of rural Early Christian sites, such as Moynagh, differs little from that noted from the Scandinavian levels in Dublin. From the 13th century onwards few lambs are present and if one ignores the small sample from Site G, B, the proportion killed in the 12-26 month age bracket tends to increase with time. It is interesting that in a late

Site	Bone	Date	Sheep	Goat
Patrick St, Site B	Horn	13-14 cen.	3	8
	Metacarpal		7	0
	Metatarsal		6	0
Patrick St, Site C	Horn	13-14 cen.	12	8
	Metacarpal		6	0
	Metatarsal		7	1
Site G, A	Horn	12-14 cen.	4	0
	Metacarpal		7	1
	Metatarsal		5	3
Site G, B	Horn	14-16 cen.	1	7
	Metacarpal		5	1
	Metatarsal		1	2
Site G, C	Horn	16-18 cen.	2	9
	Metacarpal		1	2
	Metatarsal		7	0

Table 40. Identifiable sheep and goat bones, Patrick Street

Site	Date	Approximate age			No.
		0-11 months	12-26 months	26+ months	
Moynagh	E. Christian	12.8	59.8	27.4	117
Fish. St: Plots	10-11 cen.	16.5	51.3	32.2	115
Site B	13 cen.	3.1	50.0	46.9	32
Site C	13 cen.	0	70.0	30.0	20
Site G, A	12-14 cen.	0	58.3	41.7	12
Site G, B	14-16 cen.	4.2	70.8	25.0	24

Table 41. Sheep/goat age distribution, Patrick Street and other Irish sites (after McCormick 1987 and Table 58)

Bone	Site	Date	No.	Min.	Max.	Mean	SD
Metacarpal	Fish. St	10-11 cen.	25	101.9	123.5	114.3	5.90
	Patrick St	12-14 cen.	19	112.5	132.2	122.0	6.62
Metatarsal	Fish. St	10-11 cen.	13	102.7	129.9	119.0	7.0
	Patrick St	12-14 cen.	14	114.5	146.3	130.2	9.92
	Site G	16-18 cen.	6	108.6	129.0	120.7	7.64

Table 42. Comparison between sheep metapodial greatest lengths (GL) from the Scandinavian levels at Fishamble Street and Patrick Street

13th-early 14th century context from Waterford (F2003) the emphasis has changed to the 26+ month group with 73 per cent being in that age bracket. O'Neill (1987, 61) has stated that the wool trade seems to have been concentrated in the south-east of the country. The presence of such a high proportion of older animals in the sample may represent old animals, passed their wool-bearing best, being sent to the urban meat market.

Little can be said of the type of sheep present. In the Patrick St samples (N=18) 17 per cent of the sheep were polled (hornless). This is similar to patterns noted in the Scandinavian levels at Fishamble St (18 per cent) and High St, Waterford (20 per cent). Polled sheep are very rarely found on Early Christian rural sites. Multi-horned sheep are relatively common in the pre-Norman period compared with later periods. They accounted for 7.5 per cent of all sheep in the Scandinavian levels at Fishamble St, and are absent from Patrick St. In Waterford also, multi-horned sheep, while occasionally present in the earlier levels, were absent from the 13th century deposits. The metrical data for sheep and goat is presented in Tables 55, 56 and 57 and compared with the Scandinavian period data in Table 42.

Table 42 clearly shows an improvement in sheep size between the two periods and probably indicates that new breeds of sheep were being introduced into the country, possibly better wool-bearing types. There is documentary evidence for the importation of French sheep in the *Vision of Mac Conglinne*, which dates probably to the early 12th century (Meyer 1892, 154). The apparent decline in sheep size during the 16th-18th centuries is probably an aberration due to the small size of the sample. Evidence from other Irish sites have, in fact, shown a clear increase in sheep size during the post-medieval period (McCormick 1984b, 329).

The only pathological anomaly noted was an ossified haematoma on the horizontal ramus of a left mandible.

Pig

The high incidence of pig at Site C is an aberrant phenomenon for a context in Dublin of such a date. Pig, however, was consistently the dominant species present in 10th and 11th century Dublin, but the reasons for this can be summarised as follows. Pig, unlike sheep or cattle, can be bred within a town and therefore reduce the dependence of the town population on outside producers. The presence of pig pens at Fishamble St behind the houses provide evidence for the breeding of pigs in Scandinavian Dublin (Wallace 1992, 124). Several neonate pig bones present at Site G, B, also attest to the occurrence of pig rearing. The negative aspect of pig rearing is that they are difficult to control, and being omnivorous are in competition with humans, as much of the food they eat is also consumed by humans. Maintaining large herds of pigs within a town is therefore only justified if meat supplies from outside are unreliable. While this may have been the case for Scandinavian Dublin, surrounded by an often hostile hinterland, it was not the case in the 13th and 14th centuries.

Pig are a specialised meat animal producing no other useful by-product either when alive or dead (the use of pig leather is generally a modern development). They are also much more prolific than other domesticated animals. Pigs were therefore commonly used for the provisioning of military garrisons: 3,200 pigs, for instance, being shipped to the Anglo-Norman armies in Ireland in the years 1170-71 (Sweetman 1875, 1-3). It is this factor that possibly accounts for the high incidence of pig at Clough Castle motte and bailey, Co. Down (Jope 1954), where they constituted 61 per cent of the MNI total, compared with 27 per cent in the case of cattle and 12 per cent in the case of sheep/goat (McCormick 1991).

Neither of these explanations, however, adequately account for the high incidence of pig in Site C. An alterna-

| | | *Approximate age in months* | | | | |
Site	Date	0-12	12-23	23-29	30+	No.
Moynagh	E. Christian	10.3	73.4	12.0	4.1	241
Fish. St: Plots	10-11 cen.	29.2	45.1	22.6	3.1	965
Fish. St: Ditch-wall	11-12 cen.	11.8	64.4	23.4	–	51
Site C	13 cen.	31.2	37.5	31.2	–	32
Site G, A	12-14 cen.	11.1	66.7	11.1	11.1	9
Site G, B	14-16 cen.	25.0	25.0	25.0	25.0	8

Table 43. Pig age-slaughter distributions from three Patrick Street and other Irish sites (after McCormick 1987 and Table 54)

tive explanation must therefore be proposed. It is possible that the deposits that produced this sample accumulated within a very short period of time. A sudden increase in the incidence of pig might reflect a sudden killing of a large proportion of the pigs kept within the town rather than representing an actual expansion in pig-keeping. This could be caused by a sudden outbreak of food shortage or famine. A shortage of meat from outside suppliers might necessitate the killing off of pig herds within the city, not only in order to compensate for the loss of outside meat supplies, but more importantly because there was no longer food available within the town to feed the pigs. Such an occurrence is implied in the *Annals of Kilronan* in 1203 when it states that 'A great famine in Ireland this year, so that priests used to eat flesh meat in Lent' (Wilde 1856, 76). A sudden increase in the incidence of pig can, therefore, reflect the sudden onset of food shortage. Site C is not, however, the only post-Norman Dublin context to have produced such a high incidence of pig. A similar level of pig was noted in a 12th-early 13th century context at Back Lane (Table 36).

The age-slaughter pattern of pig is shown in Table 43 and shows a more even age-slaughter of pig at Site C than on the other sites. A more detailed breakdown of the age-slaughter pattern is given in Table 54.

The only pathological anomaly observed among the Patrick St pig bones was a successfully repaired broken mandible which had left the jaw malaligned. A right pig tibia from Site G, A, appears to have a fracture on the distal third of the shaft. There is hypertrophy at the point of fracture and a considerable amount of callus has formed on the medial side of the shaft. The complete unification of the shaft with callus indicates that the fracture was in an advanced stage of healing when the animal died. A right pelvis from Site G, C, displays a possible osteochondroma. This is one of the most common types of benign bone tumours and it occurs as a result of the faulty differentiation of the inner layer of the periosteum into cartilage. This cartilage undergoes enchondral ossification and the resulting exostoses enlarges continuously (Ortner and Putschar 1985, 371). The lesion has a cauliflower-like appearance and it obscures the entire acetabulum. Slight eburnation on the infero-lateral area of the acetabulum implies that the animal continued to use the joint despite the condition. A right distal femur had exostoses on its medial epicondyle. It is possible that these are associated with muscle strain as the medial epicondyle is the origin of the flexor muscles. The pig measurements from the site are shown in Table 53

Other domesticates

Only small numbers of horse, dog and cat remains were present, the measurements of which are presented in Table 61. None of these remains displayed butchery marks.

A complete horse radius from Site G, C, provided an estimated shoulder height of 131.7cm. which equals about 13 hands. This corresponds to the modern Connemara pony which generally measure between 13 and 14 hands (Miller 1935, 485). All the horse present are adult individuals. Two mandibles from Site G, B, show some slight wear at the anterior end of the second premolar which may be indicative of wear from a bit.

Dog remains were present during all phases and represented a wide range of sizes. The measurements and estimated shoulder heights of the dogs are shown in Table 59. Both the 12th-14th and 14th-16th century levels have produced examples of small lap-dogs. These had shoulder heights of 22-27cm. and are similar in size to the smallest dogs known from Irish archaeological sites (McCormick 1991). Most of the dogs present were mature, but the recovery of radii with unfused proximal and distal ends from Site G, A, may represent the deliberate killing of immature dogs for their skins. None of the dog bones, however, displayed butchery marks.

Nearly all of the cat bones present were mature individuals, a pattern that contradicts the usual urban pattern where a large proportion of the cats tend to be immature individuals (McCormick 1988). The cats included both small and medium sized types (ibid.) No butchery marks were noted.

Wild animals

The red deer bones were confined to Sites B and C and consisted of antler fragments and a single metacarpal. One of the antler pieces was sawn, indicating that it was being used as an industrial raw material. Antler can be imported on to a site as a separate commodity but the presence of the metacarpal suggests that venison, at least occasionally, was being consumed although it is possible that this, too, represents industrial waste.

Small quantities of rabbit bones were noted during all phases.

A skull of an immature pilot whale (*Globicephala melaena*) was recovered from Site D. The skull displayed butchery marks. Adult pilot whales can grow up to 28ft long, but are generally about 20ft in length. They shoal in large groups, sometimes consisting of many hundreds of individuals (Frazer 1976, 25). Pilot whales also have a tendency to become beached, and the Patrick St specimen may represent such a stranding. It is very tempting to suggest that it is one of the whales recorded as having become stranded in Dublin Bay in June 1331. The context in which it was found dates to this period and the possibility of famine in Dublin at this time has already been discussed. The record of the beaching is as follows:

'A great famine afflicted all Ireland in this and the foregoing year; and the city of Dublin suffered miserably. But the people in their distress met with an unexpected and providential relief: for about the 24th of June a prodigious number of large sea-fish, called Turlehydes, were brought in to the bay of Dublin, and cast on shore at the mouth of the river Dodder; they were 30-40 feet long, and so bulky

	Cattle	Horse	Sheep/goat	Pig	Dog	Cat	Red deer
Horn/Antler	21	0	12	0	0	0	2
Skull	29	0	18	6	2	0	0
Mandible	24	2 *	51 *	11 *	0	0	0
Teeth	13	0	5	3	0	0	0
Atlas	8	0	0	0	0	0	0
Axis	6	0	0	0	0	0	0
Scapula	31 *	0	13	2	1	0	0
Humerus	13	0	6	5	0	0	0
Radius	14	0	7	4	0	0	0
Ulna	11	0	0	0	1	0	0
Metacarpal	15	0	20	1	0	0	1
Pelvis	28	0	6	1	0	0	0
Femur	4	0	5	2	1	0	0
Tibia	22	0	8	4	0	1	0
Fibula	0	1	0	2	0	0	0
Astralagus	7	0	0	0	0	0	0
Calcaneus	13	0	1	2	0	0	0
Metatarsal	14	0	26	1	0	0	0
Carpal/Tarsal	2	1	0	0	0	0	0
Phalanx 1	15	1	2	0	0	0	0
Phalanx 2	3	0	0	0	0	0	0
Phalanx 3	2	0	0	0	0	0	0
TOTAL	295	5	180	44	5	1	3
TOTAL %	55.3	0.9	32.5	7.9	0.9	0.2	0.5
MNI	12	2	19	5	1	1	1

Table 44. Distribution of mammal bones, 13th century, Patrick Street, Site B
The asterisk in this and the following tables denotes the bone in each species with
the highest MNI value. Horns were not used for calculations of overall MNI.

that two tall men placed one on each side of the fish could
not see one another. The Lord Justice, Sir Anthony Lucy,
with his servants and many of the citizens of Dublin,
killed above 200 of them, and gave leave to the poor to
carry them away at their pleasure (*Harris's Dublin* quoted
in Wilde 1856, 84).

A slightly different description of the beaching recorded in *Camden's Annals* (quoted ibid.) states that there
were above 500 whales beached of which 200 were killed.

Acknowledgement

The writers would like to thank Jerry Herman of the
Natural History Department of the Royal Museum of
Scotland for identifying the whale bone.

Mammal Bones

	Cattle	Horse	Sheep/ goat	Pig	Dog	Red deer	Cetacean
Horn/Antler	17	0	20	0	0	1	0
Skull	109	1	27	32	0	0	0
Mandible	47	0	21	41	0	0	0
Teeth	0	0	3	15	1	0	0
Hyoid	0	0	0	0	0	0	0
Atlas	4	0	0	1	0	0	0
Axis	5	1	1	0	0	0	0
Sacrum	0	0	0	0	0	0	0
Scapula	20	1	13	4	0	0	0
Humerus	27	1	10	3	1	0	0
Radius	52	0	8	10	0	0	0
Ulna	25	1	0	21	0	0	0
Metacarpal	26	0	22	6	0	0	0
Pelvis	32	0	3	16	0	0	0
Femur	20	0	12	3	1	0	0
Patella	0	0	0	0	0	0	0
Tibia	34	0	25	17	1	0	0
Fibula	1	0	0	1	0	0	0
Astralagus	13	0	0	0	0	0	0
Calcaneus	16	0	1	4	0	0	0
Metatarsal	49	1	22	8	0	0	0
Carpal/Tarsal	5	0	0	0	0	0	0
Phalanx 1	23	0	1	0	0	0	0
Phalanx 2	8	0	0	0	0	0	0
Phalanx 3	8	0	0	0	0	0	0
TOTAL	541	6	189	182	4	1	2
TOTAL %	58.9	0.6	20.2	19.5	0.4	0.1	0.1
MNI	17	1	12	22	1	1	1

Table 45. Distribution of mammal bones, 13th century, Patrick Street, Site C

	Cattle	Horse	Sheep/goat	Pig	Dog	Cat	Rabbit
Horn	32 **	0	15	0	0	0	0
Skull	34	0	16	8	4	0	0
Mandible	17	1	25	13	0	0	0
Teeth	6	0	2	7	0	0	0
Atlas	2	0	0	0	0	0	0
Axis	2	0	0	0	0	0	0
Scapula	28	1	9	4	0	0	0
Humerus	15	0	10	1	0	0	2
Radius	15	0	19	13 *	1	2	0
Ulna	9	0	3	6 *	2	2	0
Metacarpal	23	0	26	3	0	0	0
Pelvis	43	0	8	4	1	0	0
Femur	16	0	7	1	1	0	0
Tibia	20	0	24	5	3 *	2	0
Astralagus	6	0	0	0	0	0	0
Calcaneus	8	0	0	1	0	0	0
Metatarsal	21 *	0	32 *	2	0	0	0
Phalanx 1	7	0	0	0	0	0	0
Phalanx 2	1	0	0	0	0	0	0
Phalanx 3	6	0	0	0	0	0	0
TOTAL	311	2	196	68	12	6	2
TOTAL %	52.1	0.3	32.8	11.4	2	1	0.3
MNI	10	1	10	4	3	1	1
MNI %	33.3	3.3	33.3	13.4	10.1	3.3	3.3

** Cattle horncore MNI – 13

Table 46. Distribution of animal bones, late 12th – 14th century, Site G, A

Mammal Bones

	Cattle	Horse	Sheep/goat	Pig	Dog	Cat	Rabbit
Horn	37 **	0	16	0	0	0	0
Skull	13	0	15	15	1	0	0
Mandible	13	3 *	44	16	3	0	0
Teeth	10	2	12	14	2	0	0
Atlas	10	0	0	0	0	0	0
Axis	5	0	0	0	0	0	0
Scapula	46	0	21	12	0	0	0
Humerus	34	0	8	17	1	1	0
Radius	29	0	15	12	1	1	0
Ulna	10	0	2	7	0	1	0
Metacarpal	36	0	32 *	2	0	0	0
Pelvis	49	1	12	14	2	0	0
Femur	24	0	11	17	1	1	1
Tibia	26	0	27	25 *	3	2	0
Fibula	0	0	0	1	0	0	0
Astralagus	7	0	0	1	0	0	0
Calcaneus	13	1	1	0	0	0	0
Metatarsal	40 *	0	24	0	0	0	0
Carpal/tarsal	0	1	0	0	0	0	0
Phalanx 1	14	0	0	1	0	0	0
Phalanx 2	3	0	0	0	0	0	0
Phalanx 3	5	0	0	0	0	0	0
TOTAL	424	8	240	154	14	6	1
TOTAL %	50.1	1	28.3	18.2	1.7	0.7	0.1
MNI	10	2	12	8	2	1	1
MNI %	27.7	5.6	33.3	22.2	5.6	2.8	2.8

** Cattle horncore MNI – 18

Table 47. Distribution of animal bones, 14th – 16th century, Site G, B

	Cattle	Horse	Sheep/goat	Pig	Dog	Cat	Rabbit
Horn	84 **	0	11	0	0	0	0
Skull	14	0	4	4	0	1	0
Mandible	6	0	21	7	0	0	0
Teeth	2	0	1	5	0	0	0
Atlas	11	0	0	0	0	0	0
Axis	4	0	1	0	0	0	0
Scapula	66	0	16	5	1	0	0
Humerus	30	0	16	4	2	0	0
Radius	33	1	38	5	0	1	0
Ulna	24 *	1	3	7	0	0	0
Metacarpal	30	0	44	0	0	0	1
Pelvis	60	0	4	4	0	0	0
Femur	25	0	10	3	1	0	1
Tibia	26	0	37 *	5	0	0	0
Astralagus	1	0	0	0	0	0	0
Calcaneus	15	0	0	1	0	0	0
Metatarsal	19	0	50	2	0	0	0
Carpal/tarsal	0	0	0	0	0	0	0
Phalanx 1	8	1	0	1	0	0	0
Phalanx 2	2	0	0	0	0	0	0
Phalanx 3	2	0	0	0	0	0	0
TOTAL	465	3	256	53	4	2	2
TOTAL %	59.2	0.4	32.5	6.8	0.5	0.3	0.3
MNI	13	1	15	3	1	1	1
MNI %	37.2	2.8	42.9	8.7	2.8	2.8	2.8

** Cattle horncore MNI – 45

Table 48. Distribution of animal bones, mid-16th – early-18th century, Site G, C

Bone/measurement	Date	No.	Min.	Max.	Mean	SD
Horncore						
Length outer curve	12–14 cen.	18	90	165	132.5	22.46
	14–16 cen.	12	97	164	130.5	47.38
	16–18 cen.	55	85	232	158.5	103.94
Basal circumference	12–14 cen.	19	103	190	131.7	20.51
	14–16 cen.	15	106	170	129.0	19.80
	16–18 cen.	62	97	182	125	39.6
Max. basal diameter	12–14 cen.	19	39.2	65.7	46.7	6.19
	14–16 cen.	15	38.1	63.2	46.5	5.02
	16–18 cen.	62	33.1	63.5	42.9	13.86
Min. basal diameter	12–14 cen.	19	25.3	51.5	35.8	5.86
	14–16 cen.	15	29.4	46.0	38.8	9.99
	16–18 cen.	62	25.0	52.7	36.8	11.67
Radius						
Greatest length (GL)	12–14 cen.	1	–	–	241.9	–
Prox. width (Bp)	12–14 cen.	13	62.0	80.9	71.9	5.26
	14–16 cen.	3	67.2	74.3	70.8	3.55
	16–18 cen.	2	66.0	72.2	69.1	4.38
Metacarpal						
Greatest length (GL)	12–14 cen.	3	177.2	182.9	179.3	3.13
	14–16 cen.	1	–	–	190.0	–
Prox. width (Bp)	12–14 cen.	26	44.6	62.2	51.3	3.70
	14–16 cen.	15	46.0	52.2	48.9	1.99
	16–18 cen.	5	48.6	50.4	49.4	0.75
Dist. width (Bd)	12–14 cen.	20	48.8	64.9	53.1	4.32
	14–16 cen.	16	49.8	59.0	52.4	2.30
	16–18 cen.	9	51.0	54.8	52.7	1.18
Min. shaft width (SD)	12–14 cen.	3	26.2	29.1	27.3	1.55
	14–16 cen.	3	26.2	29.1	27.3	1.55
Tibia						
Distal width (Bd)	12–14 cen.	8	52.5	60.1	54.8	2.61
	14–16 cen.	2	54.4	56.1	55.3	–
	16–18 cen.	5	51.1	56.4	53.9	2.18
Calcaneus						
Greatest length (GL)	12–14 cen.	14	117.2	124.0	121.5	4.43
	14–16 cen.	6	115.9	128.7	121.5	4.61
	16–18 cen.	4	112.3	122.6	118.6	4.44
Astralagus						
Greatest lateral length (GLl)	12–14 cen.	16	55.4	63.1	59.4	1.99
	14–16 cen.	2	56.0	60.1	58.1	–
Distal width (Bd)	12–14 cen.	16	35.5	40.5	37.6	1.44
	14–16 cen.	2	35.1	36.4	35.8	–
Metatarsal						
Greatest length (GL)	12–14 cen.	3	194.9	204.9	199.8	5.01
	14–16 cen.	1	–	–	199.4	–
	16–18 cen.	1	–	–	207.5	–
Proximal breadth (Bp)	12–14 cen.	20	37.1	47.9	41.7	2.36
	14–16 cen.	17	37.2	47.2	41.9	2.20
	16–18 cen.	1	–	–	46.0	–
Distal breadth (Bd)	12–14 cen.	24	40.0	56.9	48.0	3.62
	14–16 cen.	13	46.0	52.9	48.0	1.81
	16–18 cen.	9	45.0	51.4	48.4	2.25
Min. shaft width (SD)	12–14 cen.	3	23.6	28.8	25.7	2.76

Table 49. Cattle measurements (in mm.) after von den Driesch (1976), Patrick Street

Bone	Date	GL height (cm)	Bp	Bd	SD	Sex	Estimated
Radius	12–14 C	241.9	66.2	57.1	32.0	?	104.0
Metacarpal	12–14 C	177.2	55.1	59.9	33.9	M	110.0
		177.8	50.9	51.9	27.7	F	106.7
		182.9	–	51.5	23.7	F	109.7
	14–16 C	190.0	52.2	53.5	29.1	–	–
Metatarsal	12–14 C	194.9	40.2	46.4	24.6	?	106.2
		204.9	40.1	45.1	23.6	?	111.6
		199.5	47.9	46.9	28.8	?	108.7
	14–16 C	199.4	41.4	46.8	22.1	?	–
	16–18 C	207.5	46.0	49.7	25.0	?	–

Table 50. Cattle measurements (mm.) with estimated shoulder heights (cm.) after Fock and Matolchi in von den Driesch and Boessneck (1974, 336), Patrick Street

Date	Length along outer curve	Basal circumference	Max. basal diameter	Min. basal diameter
12–14 cen.	90	110	39.2	27.6
12–14 cen.	100	103	45.4	36.6
12–14 cen.	105	190	65.7	51.5
12–14 cen.	115	110	44.7	25.3
12–14 cen.	115	122	44.4	32.0
12–14 cen.	116	117	41.5	31.0
12–14 cen.	120	120	40.9	31.8
12–14 cen.	120	110	40.2	30.9
12–14 cen.	140	130	43.1	34.9
12–14 cen.	140	150	53.6	41.9
12–14 cen.	145	135	47.2	37.9
12–14 cen.	145	125	43.4	34.2
12–14 cen.	151	126	46.2	35.1
12–14 cen.	153	131	45.7	35.7
12–14 cen.	155	140	47.3	36.2
12–14 cen.	155	155	52.3	40.2
12–14 cen.	155	135	45.5	36.4
12–14 cen.	165	145	47.1	40.0
14–16 cen.	164	143	50.0	45.3
14–16 cen.	160	165	61.9	46.0
14–16 cen.	160	170	63.4	44.0
14–16 cen.	134	128	44.2	37.0
14–16 cen.	130	115	38.3	30.6
14–16 cen.	130	126	45.3	32.0
14–16 cen.	125	121	41.8	36.5
14–16 cen.	120	116	44.0	29.4
14–16 cen.	115	106	38.1	30.8
14–16 cen.	110	135	49.1	36.2
14–16 cen.	104	114	39.1	33.5
14–16 cen.	97	133	45.5	39.0
16–18 cen.	232	153	52.7	45.0
16–18 cen.	215	182	63.5	52.7
16–18 cen.	197	152	55.5	45.0

Date	Length along outer curve	Basal circumference	Max. basal diameter	Min. basal diameter
16–18 cen.	192	144	50.1	41.1
16–18 cen.	183	140	52.0	36.5
16–18 cen.	181	130	45.7	39.0
16–18 cen.	177	140	52.0	40.1
16–18 cen.	175	165	60.0	44.0
16–18 cen.	175	161	55.6	46.0
16–18 cen.	170	138	47.5	39.9
16–18 cen.	170	155	51.3	45.5
16–18 cen.	166	140	49.3	41.0
16–18 cen.	165	154	54.8	40.5
16–18 cen.	165	136	50.0	25.0
16–18 cen.	165	164	56.0	48.2
16–18 cen.	163	127	46.6	34.2
16–18 cen.	160	147	49.0	44.3
16–18 cen.	155	137	50.8	37.5
16–18 cen.	150	154	53.1	45.0
16–18 cen.	145	119	42.7	35.2
16–18 cen.	145	120	45.0	33.1
16–18 cen.	145	116	40.9	33.5
16–18 cen.	145	130	48.6	35.7
16–18 cen.	142	128	46.0	33.6
16–18 cen.	142	155	52.0	38.0
16–18 cen.	140	128	45.6	35.5
16–18 cen.	140	120	43.0	34.4
16–18 cen.	140	126	46.1	34.0
16–18 cen.	140	120	41.4	33.0
16–18 cen.	138	144	49.1	41.5
16–18 cen.	137	120	42.5	34.8
16–18 cen.	135	130	47.0	35.7
16–18 cen.	130	125	44.1	35.0
16–18 cen.	130	135	47.4	37.0
16–18 cen.	128	134	47.2	36.1
16–18 cen.	128	121	44.1	33.1
16–18 cen.	127	115	39.1	34.2
16–18 cen.	127	113	40.1	30.5
16–18 cen.	126	115	42.0	31.5
16–18 cen.	125	142	47.1	44.4
16–18 cen.	125	148	52.5	42.0
16–18 cen.	125	116	40.0	35.0
16–18 cen.	125	120	43.9	33.4
16–18 cen.	118	142	49.0	41.0
16–18 cen.	115	108	39.1	29.0
16–18 cen.	115	122	43.8	35.0
16–18 cen.	111	110	38.5	30.8
16–18 cen.	110	131	47.5	37.6
16–18 cen.	110	108	35.4	33.8
16–18 cen.	100	111	42.6	30.0
16–18 cen.	100	107	37.6	30.0
16–18 cen.	96	100	33.9	27.6
16–18 cen.	95	115	40.0	30.9
16–18 cen.	95	126	41.6	34.1
16–18 cen.	85	97	34.5	31.0

Table 51. Cattle horn measurements, Patrick Street

Higham eruption stage	Approx. age (in months)	12–14 cen. No.	14–16 cen. No.	16–18 cen. No.
0– 3	0–5	0	0	1
4– 5	5–7	2	0	0
6– 7	7–13	0	2	0
8–10	13–18	2	0	0
11–12	18–24	1	0	0
13	24–30	1	1	0
14–18	30–36	2	0	0
19+	36+	10 *	0	2?

* The 19+ third molar had the following wear patterns after Grant (1982): Gx3, Jx4, Kx1, Lx2.

Table 52. Cattle age distribution after Higham (1967), Site A and Site G

Bone measurement	Date	No.	Min.	Max.	Mean	SD
Humerus (Bd)	12–14 cen.	0	0	0	0	0
	14–16 cen.	4	33.6	37.7	35.8	1.69
	16–18 cen.	3	36.4	37.9	37.1	0.75
Humerus (Bt)	12–14 cen.	3	28.9	30.5	29.8	0.83
	14–16 cen.	0	0	0	0	0
	16–18 cen.	3	29.6	29.9	29.7	0.17
Radius (Bp)	12–14 cen.	11	21.7	29.4	25.7	1.94
	14–16 cen.	4	26.3	28.3	27.3	1.02
	16–18 cen.	3	24.6	26.8	25.7	1.1
Tibia (Bd)	12–14 cen.	6	25.6	29.1	26.8	1.23
	14–16 cen.	4	28.0	30.5	29.1	1.04
	16–18 cen.	2	26.8	28.0	27.4	0
Pelvis (LAR)	12–14 cen.	10	26.5	29.5	28.0	1.03
	14–16 cen.	3	21.9	27.8	25.3	3.05
	16–18 cen.	1	0	0	23.2	0

Table 53. Pig measurements, Patrick Street

Higham eruption stage	Approx. age (months)	Site C 13 cen. No.	Site G 12–14 cen. No.	Site G 14–16 cen. No.	Site G 16–18 cen. No.
7	5–6	0	1	0	0
8	6–7	1	0	0	0
9	7–8	3	0	0	0
19	8–9	2	0	1	0
11	9–10	2	0	0	0
12	10–11	0	0	1	0
13	11–12	2	0	0	0
14–17	12–17	1	1	0	0
18	17–19	5	0	0	0
19	19–21	5	2	2	1
20	21–23	1	3	0	1
21	23–25	9	1	1	1
22	25–27	1	0	1	0
23	27–29	0	0	0	0
24+	30+	0	1	2	3

Table 54. Pig age slaughter distributions based on mandibulae using data of Higham (1967), Patrick Street

Bone/measurement	No.	Min.	Max.	Mean	SD
Sheep Metacarpal					
12–14 cen.					
Greatest length (GL)	19	112.5	132.2	122.0	6.62
Proximal breadth (Bp)	19	19.1	26.1	21.8	1.71
Distal breadth (Bd)	19	21.9	26.0	24.1	1.13
Min. shaft width (SD)	18	11.2	15.1	13.7	1.18
Sheep metatarsal					
12–14 cen.					
Greatest length (GL)	14	114.5	146.3	130.2	9.32
Proximal breadth (Bp)	14	16.5	21.5	18.7	1.45
Distal breadth (Bd)	14	20.0	24.9	22.4	1.52
Min. shaft width (SD)	14	10.0	14.2	11.8	1.27
16–18 cen.					
Greatest length (GL)	6	108.6	129.0	120.7	7.64
Proximal breadth (Bp)	6	16.7	18.8	17.9	0.71
Distal breadth (Bd)	6	19.4	23.0	21.8	1.30
Min. shaft width (SD)	6	9.8	12.0	10.8	0.81
Goat horn – female					
12–14 cen.					
Length outer curve	5	138.0	190.9	177.2	13.41
Basal circumference	6	82.0	117.0	93.8	12.29
Max. basal diameter	6	30.9	46.5	35.4	25.2
Min. basal diameter	6	20.8	30.1	25.2	3.09
Goat horn – male					
12–14 cen.					
Length outer curve	3	170.0	234.0	196.3	33.47
Basal circumference	5	120.0	135.0	126.2	6.14
Max. basal diameter	5	48.2	53.0	49.8	2.00
Min. basal diameter	5	31.6	35.4	33.4	1.78
Goat horn – female					
16–18 cen.					
Length outer curve	4	140.0	230.0	173.8	39.02
Basal circumference	4	83.0	120.0	101.8	15.02
Max. basal diameter	4	31.3	48.4	39.2	7.04
Min. basal diameter	4	19.9	31.0	26.5	4.72

Table 55. Summary of sheep and goat measurements, Patrick Street

Species and sex	Date	Length along outer curve	Basal circumference	Max. basal diameter	Min. basal diameter
Goat (f)	12–14 cen.	158	82	30.9	20.8
Goat (f)	12–14 cen.	173	90	32.6	24.7
Goat (f)	12–14 cen.	175	117	46.5	30.1
Goat (f)	12–14 cen.	190	95	35.3	26
Goat (f)	12–14 cen.	190	86	31.1	23.5
Goat (f)	12–14 cen.	–	93	35.7	25.9
Goat (m)	12–14 cen.	170	123	48.2	31.9
Goat (m)	12–14 cen.	185	135	53	35.1
Goat (m)	12–14 cen.	234	130	50.4	35.4
Goat (m)	12–14 cen.	–	123	49.2	32.9
Goat (m)	12–14 cen.	–	120	48.2	31.6
Goat (f)	14–16 cen.	–	91	33.7	22.9
Goat (f)	14–16 cen.	191	95	33.9	23
Goat (f)	16–18 cen.	140	83	31.3	19.9
Goat (f)	16–18 cen.	160	104	39.1	27
Goat (f)	16–18 cen.	165	100	38	28.2
Goat (f)	16–18 cen.	230	120	48.4	31
Sheep (?)	14–16 cen.	83	95	32	26
Sheep (m)	14–16 cen.	220	128	44.8	33.8
Sheep (m)	14–16 cen.	–	126	46.7	33
Sheep (m)	16–18 cen.	–	131	48.6	33

Table 56. Sheep and goat horncore dimensions, Patrick Street

Species	Bone	Date	GL	Bp	Bd	SD	Estimated shoulder height
Sheep	Metacarpal	12–14 cen.	112.5	19.8	21.9	11.8	55.0
Sheep	Metacarpal	12–14 cen.	112.5	20.8	23.5	11.9	55.0
Sheep	Metacarpal	12–14 cen.	114.0	20.8	22.7	11.2	55.7
Sheep	Metacarpal	12–14 cen.	114.5	20.5	24.1	14.1	56.0
Sheep	Metacarpal	12–14 cen.	115.1	20.1	22.9	13.6	56.3
Sheep	Metacarpal	12–14 cen.	115.8	20.5	24.1	14.1	56.6
Sheep	Metacarpal	12–14 cen.	119.1	19.1	23.4	–	58.2
Sheep	Metacarpal	12–14 cen.	119.6	22.9	24.3	15.1	58.5
Sheep	Metacarpal	12–14 cen.	120.9	20.0	22.9	12.3	59.1
Sheep	Metacarpal	12–14 cen.	121.5	23.0	26.0	14.2	59.4
Sheep	Metacarpal	12–14 cen.	123.5	22.5	23.2	14.5	60.4
Sheep	Metacarpal	12–14 cen.	124.9	26.1	24.9	14.6	61.1
Sheep	Metacarpal	12–14 cen.	125.5	21.2	24.2	13.6	61.4
Sheep	Metacarpal	12–14 cen.	127.2	22.1	25.3	14.8	62.2
Sheep	Metacarpal	12–14 cen.	128.4	21.9	25.3	13.1	62.8
Sheep	Metacarpal	12–14 cen.	128.9	22.9	25.8	14.9	63.0
Sheep	Metacarpal	12–14 cen.	130.5	23.1	24.2	14.0	63.8
Sheep	Metacarpal	12–14 cen.	130.5	23.1	24.2	14.0	63.8
Sheep	Metacarpal	12–14 cen.	132.2	23.5	25.4	14.9	64.6
Sheep	Metacarpal	14–16 cen.	112.1	21.0	22.1	11.4	54.8
Sheep	Metacarpal	14–16 cen.	118.1	20.6	24.0	13.0	57.8
Sheep	Metacarpal	14–16 cen.	119.4	20.1	22.2	11.1	58.4
Sheep	Metatarsal	12–14 cen.	114.5	17.1	21.5	11.8	52.0
Sheep	Metatarsal	12–14 cen.	118.6	16.5	20.5	11.5	53.8
Sheep	Metatarsal	12–14 cen.	122.9	17.6	21.1	10.0	55.8
Sheep	Metatarsal	12–14 cen.	124.6	17.2	20.0	10.4	56.6
Sheep	Metatarsal	12–14 cen.	124.9	18.4	21.9	10.9	56.7
Sheep	Metatarsal	12–14 cen.	125.8	18.4	21.2	10.5	57.1
Sheep	Metatarsal	12–14 cen.	129.3	19.2	23.7	12.7	58.7
Sheep	Metatarsal	12–14 cen.	130.1	17.9	22.1	10.7	59.1
Sheep	Metatarsal	12–14 cen.	130.3	19.2	22.9	11.9	59.2
Sheep	Metatarsal	12–14 cen.	133.1	18.9	22.0	11.5	60.4
Sheep	Metatarsal	12–14 cen.	140.1	21.5	24.3	14.2	63.6
Sheep	Metatarsal	12–14 cen.	141.4	20.0	23.9	13.4	64.2
Sheep	Metatarsal	12–14 cen.	141.4	19.6	24.9	13.1	64.2
Sheep	Metatarsal	12–14 cen.	146.3	20.9	23.9	12.9	66.4
Sheep	Metatarsal	14–16 cen.	134.0	18.6	23.2	11.2	60.8
Sheep	Metatarsal	16–18 cen.	108.6	16.7	19.4	9.8	49.3
Sheep	Metatarsal	16–18 cen.	114.5	18.0	23.0	10.1	52.0
Sheep	Metatarsal	16–18 cen.	123.5	18.8	22.9	11.4	56.1
Sheep	Metatarsal	16–18 cen.	123.5	17.7	22.1	12.0	56.1
Sheep	Metatarsal	16–18 cen.	125.5	18.4	21.8	10.9	57.0
Sheep	Metatarsal	16–18 cen.	129.0	17.7	21.7	11.0	58.6
Goat	Metacarpal	12–14 cen.	110.1	23.6	27.5	16.5	63.3
Goat	Metacarpal	14–16 cen.	105.0	21.4	26.0	14.0	60.4
Goat	Metacarpal	16–18 cen.	110.0	19.2	21.5	11.1	63.3
Goat	Metacarpal	16–18 cen.	113.3	20.6	26.2	13.6	65.1
Goat	Metatarsal	12–14 cen.	117.9	19.1	24.1	12.8	63.0
Goat	Metatarsal	12–14 cen.	118.8	18.0	22.2	10.9	63.4
Goat	Metatarsal	12–14 cen.	126.8	18.4	21.4	10.5	67.7
Goat	Metatarsal	12–14 cen.	130.5	17.6	21.4	11.5	69.7
Goat	Metatarsal	14–16 cen.	124.0	19.4	24.0	12.0	66.2
Goat	Metatarsal	14–16 cen.	134.0	21.0	25.1	14.0	71.6

Table 57. Complete sheep and goat metapodia with shoulder height multiplication heights after Teichert (sheep) and Scramm (goat), quoted in von den Driesch and Boessneck (1974, 339 and 341)

Higham eruption stage	Approx. age (in months)	Site B	Site C	Site G 12–14 cen.	Site G 14–16 cen.	Site G 16–18 cen.
2	birth–six weeks	0	0	0	0	1
4	3	1	0	0	0	0
5	4	0	0	0	0	0
6	5	0	0	0	0	0
7	5–7	0	0	0	0	0
8	7–9	0	0	0	1	0
9	9–10	0	0	0	0	0
10–11	10–12	0	0	0	0	0
12	12–21	1	9	4	12	5
13	21–24	9	3	1	2	2
14	25–26	6	2	2	3	0
15	26+	15	6	5	6	1

Table 58. Sheep/goat age distribution based on Higham (1967), Patrick Street

Species	Bone	Date	GL	GL1	Bp	Bd	SD	Estimated shoulder height (cm.)*
Cat	Humerus	12–14 cen.	81.0	–	16.5	(Dp)14.9	4.9	–
		14–16 cen.	96.6	–	19.5	(Dp)17.2	6.1	–
	Radius	12–14 cen.	86.7	–	7.4	12.0	5.0	–
	Tibia	12–14 cen.	94.9	–	16.0	11.5	4.2	–
		12–14 cen.	113.9	–	18.4	12.7	6.6	–
	Femur	12–14 cen.	98.9	–	19.1	18.0	7.1	–
Dog	Humerus	16–18 cen.	135.8	–	35.1	(Dp)25.5	10.4	43.9
		14–16 cen.	72.9	–	20.1	(Dp)17.9	5.6	22.3
	Ulna	12–14 cen.	205.3	–	–	–	–	57.6
	Femur	12–14 cen.	114.5	–	29.9	25.5	10.5	34.7
		12–14 cen.	156.7	–	32.6	24.5	11.6	47.9
		16–18 cen.	174.0	–	37.2	30.1	13.0	53.3
	Tibia	12–14 cen.	88.1	–	22.1	16.1	9.0	26.6
		12–14 cen.	209.0	–	37.9	24.7	12.1	62.0
		12–14 cen.	187.0	–	22.7	13.0	55.5	–
		14–16 cen.	115.2	–	23.3	9.8	7.2	34.5
		14–16 cen.	90	–	23.1	15.8	9.0	27.2
Horse	Metacarpal	12–14 cen.	46.5	–	–	–	–	–
	Radius	16–18 cen.	319	303.5	74.9	69.8	37.5	131.7
	Calcaneus	14–16 cen.	103.1	–	–	–	–	–
Red deer	Metacarpal	12–14 cen.	204.9	–	29.6	30.5	20.9	–

* Shoulder heights of dog use multiplication factors of Harcourt (1974, 154), while those for horse are of Vitt quoted in von den Driesch and Boessneck (1974, 331).

Table 59. Cat, dog, horse and red deer measurements (in mm.), Patrick Street

Report on the Bird Bones from Site C

Tanya O'Sullivan

Thirty bones were submitted for examination. Two of these were identified as rabbit. The remainder were examined, measured and identified to species where possible.

The small size of the sample, combined with the fact that the bones were recovered from 13th-14th century dump material, ruled out any attempt at an economic interpretation of the bird material.

At least five species of bird were represented by the sample (Table 60), showing a minimum number of two domestic geese (*Anser anser*), three pink footed geese (*Anser brachyrhynchos*), two fowl (*Gallus gallus*), one raven (*Corus corax*) and one herring gull (*Larus argentus*). All specimens were mature and butchery marks were evident on only two bones. These occurred across the proximal bicippital surface of one fowl humerus, and on the right distal condyle of a fowl tibia. Cut marks in these areas are consistent with the removal of the lower limbs and wings of a bird before cooking (O'Sullivan 1990).

The majority of goose bones in the sample were complete upper limb bones. This would normally be an indication that goose feathers were being imported on the wing to the site. However, because of the size of the sample examined from Patrick St it can only be tentatively suggested that goose wings were imported. Goose feathers were widely sought after for fletching arrows and for use as quills.

Ravens are a common occurrence in urban archaeological deposits. They were primarily scavengers but occasionally exploited (ibid.). The herring gull has always been a popular bird on the east coast of Ireland, and bones have turned up in urban deposits in Dublin as early as the 10th century.

	No. of fragments	MNI	MNI %
Domestic goose	7	2	22
Pink footed goose	4	3	33
Fowl	6	2	22
Raven	2	1	11
Herring gull	1	1	11
Unidentified	8	–	–

Table 60. Birdbones, Site C

BIRDS, FISH AND MARINE INVERTEBRATES FROM SITE G

Sheila Hamilton-Dyer

The methods used for identification and recording were based on the FRU (Faunal Remains Unit, Southampton) method 86 system, with some modifications (see FRU archive, and SH-D archive file BONESTRU). Identifications were made using the modern comparative collections of S. Hamilton-Dyer. Fish nomenclature follows Wheeler (1978). A small number of bones have been counted as one where they are broken parts of the same element. Archive material includes metrical and other data not in the text and is kept on paper and floppy disk. Measurements of the bones are in millimetres. In general these follow the methods of von den Driesch (1976) for birds and Morales and Rosenlund (1979) for fish.

Birds

Bird bones numbered eighty-six fragments, of which twenty-eight were identified as domestic fowl and thirty-nine as goose, probably also domestic. Other species identified were domestic duck (or mallard), raven, herring gull (or lesser black-backed) and turkey. There were also nine fragments not identified to species. Group 1 (12th-14th century) material contained only fowl and goose bones while Group 2 (14th-16th century) also contained a complete raven tibia. Group 3 contained all species identified. The presence of a turkey femur in Group 3 (16th-18th century) is consistent with the late date of this group as this species was introduced from North America to Britain from about 1520, probably initially in the Bristol region.

Several bones, particularly goose, showed signs of gnawing. In one case this was rodent damage but most of the tooth marks were compatible with cat.

Butchery marks were observed on twelve bones. Although most were consistent with disjointing, a chopped goose furcula indicates a carcass divided lengthwise, and the gull ulna may have been cut while removing the flight feathers.

The fragment numbers are too small to detect any real difference in the sizes of the fowl from the different phases. They are comparable with the larger group of medieval bones at Back Lane (Hamilton-Dyer, forthcoming).

Fish

Seventy-seven fish bone fragments were examined. These were from eight species: ling (*Molva molva*), cod (*Gadus*

Phase	Fowl	Goose	Duck	Raven	Gull	Turkey	Bird frags	Total
Group 1	7	16	0	0	0	0	2	25
Group 2	10	4	0	1	0	0	6	21
Group 3	11	19	6	1	1	1	1	40
Total	28	39	6	2	1	1	9	86
Total %	36.4	50.6	7.8	2.6	1.3	1.3	11.7	

Phase	Conger	Cod	Ling	Haddock	Hake	Gadidae	Other	Frags	Total
Group 1	2	0	10	1	3	0	1	8	25
Group 2	0	3	29	1	0	4	1	0	38
Group 3	0	8	1	1	0	3	1	0	14
Total	2	11	40	3	3	7	3	8	77
Total %	2.6	14.3	51.9	3.9	3.9	9.1	3.9	10.4	

Table 61. Species distribution, Site G

220

morhua), conger eel (*Conger conger*), haddock (*Melano-grammus aeglefinus*), hake (*Merluccius merluccius*), gurnard (*Triglidae*), sea-bream, probably the red sea-bream, (*Pagellus bogeraveo*), and plaice (*Pleuronectes platessa*). Eight fragments were not identified to species but are likely to be of *Gadidae*.

Most of the fish bones are of ling with only a few fragments of the other species. In contrast with Groups 1 and 2, only one bone of ling was recorded for the late Group 3 material. The fragment numbers are too small to indicate whether this is likely to be significant.

Many of the bones are of large fish, over 1m. for most ling bones. The haddock cleithrum is larger than a recent speciment of 70cm. total length and weighing 3kg. This is considered large for modern stocks.

The distribution of anatomical elements is biased in favour of the sturdier of the head bones; only one vertebra was recovered. It is difficult to establish whether the lack of small species is genuine or due to a lack of sieving or to differential preservation. Similarly the absence of verte-brae may be due to butchery and disposal practises or to poor preservation.

None of the bones showed butchery marks.

Ling, particularly large ones, are usually found at depths of 200-600m. on the Atlantic side of the British Isles. These large fish are therefore unlikely to have been caught in the immediate vicinity of Dublin.

Invertebrates

A small number of marine invertebrate remains were also in the assemblage. These were shells of whelk, buckie, mussel and razorfish and part of the claw of a large edible crab. All were of commercial size and are likely to have been food waste rather than incidental finds.

fow	domestic fowl
goo	domestic goose or greylag (*Anser anser*)
anas/d	domestic duck or mallard (*Anas platyrhynchos*)
turkey	turkey (*Meleagris gallopavo*)
lar arg	herring gull (*Larus argentatus*) (or lesser black-backed)
raven	raven (*Corvus corax*)
con con	conger eel (*Conger conger*)
cod	cod (*Gadus morhua*)
lin	ling (*Molva molva*)
mel aeg	haddock (*Melanogrammus aeglefinus*)
gad fam	cod family (*Gadidae*)
hake	hake (*Merluccius merluccius*)
tri fam	gurnard species (*Triglidae*)
spa fam	sea-bream family (*Sparidae*), probably red sea-bream (*Pagellus bogaraveo*)
flat	flatfish, cf. plaice (*Pleuronectes platessa*)
fis	unidentified fish fragments, probably *Gadidae*
whelk	whelk (*Buccinum undatum*)
buckie	buckie (*Neptunae antiqua*)
mussel	common mussel (*Mytilus edulis*)
razor	razorfish (*Ensis siliqua*)
crab	edible crab (*Cancer pagrus*)

Table 62. Species list and archive codes

Human Remains

Catryn Power

The partial remains of seven individuals were recovered from the excavations. Several skulls were retrieved from dumped material outside the town wall at Winetavern St, while skull and other human fragments came from the Poddle river at Site B and from the backfill of a disused limekiln at Site F.

E543:48:4 (river silts, Site B)

These remains consist of the skull of an individual, probably male, aged in the late 20s to early 30s. This well preserved skull was reconstructed and is complete except for small fragments of the frontal, temporal, occipital and nasal bones which were lost post-mortem. The mandible (56:53) was recovered from a short distance away.

All the teeth had erupted during life and ten are lost post-mortem. Dental pathology is evident. Occlusal attrition has resulted in severe exposure of dentine on the first molars; smaller amounts of dentine are exposed on the occlusal surfaces of the canines, left mandibular premolars and right maxillary premolars. Attrition is confined to the enamel on the wisdom teeth (or third molars), left maxillary premolars and right mandibular premolars. Deposits of calculus occur on all teeth; these are moderate on two teeth and mild on the remainder. Incipient periodontal disease is evident around 87 | 6.

Hypoplastic defects occur on the following teeth:

$$\frac{8\ 7\quad 3|\ 4\quad 7\ 8}{7\quad 4\ |34\quad 7}$$

These occur as faint grooves and crinkling on the crowns. These defects indicate that a recurring illness or nutritional deficiency occurred intermittently between the age of 3-7/8 years and again between 10-12/16 years. An interradicular extension of enamel is present on the palatal surface of |8. These are usually found on the buccal surface. There is slight rotation of 3|.

E543:300:62 (unstratified, Site F)

These remains consist of a fragment of the left parietal from the skull of an adult.

E543:322:1 (fill of limekiln, Site F)

These remains consist of part of a fragmented cranium of a mature adult, which was reconstructed. The frontal bone, part of the parietals, the left temporal and occipital bones are present. The supra-orbital ridges and mastoid process are suggestive of a male. Traces of the metopic suture on the frontal bone are still visible.

E543:340 (fill of limekiln, Site F)

These remains consist of part of the skeleton of a female aged at least 40-50 years. Preservation of the bones is good. The following bones are lost post-mortem: left radius, right clavicle, three ribs, left hand, some phalanges and carpals of the right hand, parts of the sternum, ulnae and humerii, the coccyx, the tibiae, patellae, feet, left fibula and distal parts of the femora. The left humerus, left ulna, left femur and right fibula were also recovered The metopic suture remains open. Incipient osteoarthritis occurs on the right thumb of the right hand and on the palmar surface of three proximal phalanges and on the articular parts of the tubercles of six left ribs and those of seven right ribs. Osteophytosis occurs on the edge of the sacroiliac joints and on the edge of the apex of the sacrum. Osteoarthritis occurs on C.3-C.7, T.1-T.12 and L.1-L.5. Mild osteophytosis occurs on C.3-C.7, T.4-T.12 and L.2-L.5. Osteoarthritis occurs from the third cervical vertebra through to the sacrum; it is incipient on most but severe on the articulations between C.5-C.7.

Dental

Occlusal attrition has resulted in severe dentine exposure on six teeth - mainly premolars and molars. Here three or more islands of dentine are exposed and some of these islands have coalesced; smaller amounts of dentine are exposed on 17 teeth while attrition is confined to the enamel on one tooth. The wisdom teeth failed to erupt probably due to insufficient space in the jaws. Two maxillary right premolars are lost post-mortem. The mandibular first molars were lost during life: the right at least 6-12 months prior to death; its socket is completely resorbed, while the left, where resorption is irregular and incomplete, was lost shortly before death.

Hypoplastic defects are present on the following teeth:

$$\frac{1|1\ \ 3}{5\ \ 3\ \ |\ \ 3\ \ 5}$$

These are evident as faint grooves and crinkling, and

occurred intermittently between the age of 2-6/7 years. One carious cavity is present on the buccal surface of the cervical margin of 7.

Periodontal disease is present; bone loss has occurred around

$$\begin{array}{c|c} 6 \quad 2 & 2 \quad 4567 \\ \hline 7 \quad 5432 & 6 \end{array}$$

It has resulted in exposure of almost the entire roots of 6 | 6. Mild deposits of calculus occur on twenty teeth while moderate amounts occur on four teeth. Hypercementosis is present on the root apex of 6 | . The lingual surface of | 3 has rotated mesially. Two minute tori are present on the lingual surfaces of 43 | 34.

E543:505:3

These remains consist of part of the cranium of a mature adult, probably male. The skull vault and part of the occipital and right temporal were found. It was possible to reconstruct these fragments. A trace of the metopic suture is still obvious on the frontal bone.

Two weapon injuries to the skull are evident (Fig. 92). One injury is on the back of the skull. The blow was dealt horizontally and cut cleanly through the bone resulting in a fracture 8.2cm. in length which curved upwards from immediately above the nuchal crest on the occipital through the left parietal. The second injury was to the base of the skull; it sliced through the left temporal truncating the mastoid process and then cut through the left occipital condyle. The cut is 5cm. in width and sliced through 5.5cm. in length of bone. It also cut off the left styloid process and finally the left zygomatic process. This last injury would have been fatal, resulting in the left carotid artery and jugular vein being severed. These two injuries were probably produced by a sword, used by a right handed person; they are well defined, clean cut, and smooth and have parallel scratch marks on polished surfaces. Brothwell (1981) indicates that bone injuries of a clean-cut appearance can be produced only when the bone has its full organic matrix, i.e., when the person is alive or recently dead.

There is a third fracture on the skull but it is most probably post-mortem. It is 3.8cm. in length and sliced vertically through the centre of the occipital at the nuchal crest; it runs perpendicular to another fracture on the occipital (Injury No. 1). The edges of this fracture do not show the characteristic features of an injury produced by a weapon during life.

E543:505:4

These remains consist of the cranium of a mature adult, probably male; most of the facial bones and fragments of the temporals and frontal bone are lost post-mortem. It was possible to reconstruct these remains.

Three injuries to the skull are evident (Fig. 93 left). The first blow to be delivered was probably one to the left side of the frontal bone. It left a curved fracture (6cm. in length), above the left supra orbital ridge. This wound was probably caused by a sword. It is smooth, well defined and clean cut and also affects the edge of the left parietal. The blow was dealt at an oblique angle cutting downwards into the forehead, and removing a slice of bone which is lost post-mortem.

There are two injuries to the base of the head which represent two further attempts to slay this individual; most probably after he had been knocked to the ground by the first blow to the forehead, he was then slain from behind. The second blow to the head grazes the inferior curved line of the occipital and measures 20mm. x 25mm. The third and final injury to the skull (measuring 23mm. x 19mm.) occurs on the edge of the foramen magnum, at the crest of the occipital ridge; this blow probably severed the spinal canal but may not have resulted in decapitation because it does not follow through the entire foramen magnum. However, this final blow was certainly fatal. Part of the left mastoid process is lost, probably post-mortem. These injuries to the base of the skull are clean cut and smooth with parallel striations. The direction of the striations on each cut would indicate that they resulted from two separate blows. The three injuries on this skull were delivered by a right-handed person using a sharp edged weapon, probably a sword, as the curvature of the first fracture would suggest. The injuries were sustained perimortal, or at the time of death, and resulted in the death of this individual.

E543:517:1

These remains consist of the well preserved skull of a male aged in his late 20s to early 30s. Part of the occipital bone is lost post-mortem. There are two injuries to the skull, both probably produced in a single blow which cut cleanly into the back of the head and resulted in instant death (Fig. 93 right). There is a single linear injury (6cm. long) to the base of the skull. The plane of this injury is horizontal and cuts across the nuchal crest and results in the loss of part of the occipital. The blade may also have passed through the left ramus of the mandible. The left ramus is completely severed: this fracture, however, may be due to post-mortem damage. These injuries were produced by an edged weapon; the fractures are linear, well-defined and clean-cut, showing a flat almost polished surface, though there is a jagged edge on the mandibular cut. A small sliver of bone is lost from the mandible below the ramus, perhaps removed when the weapon was pulled out. There are no signs of healing on these wounds. The injury to the occipital would have resulted in decapitation and severance of the brainstem. If the cervical vertebrae were present these would almost certainly show some sign of injury. During executions by decapitation a blow deliv-

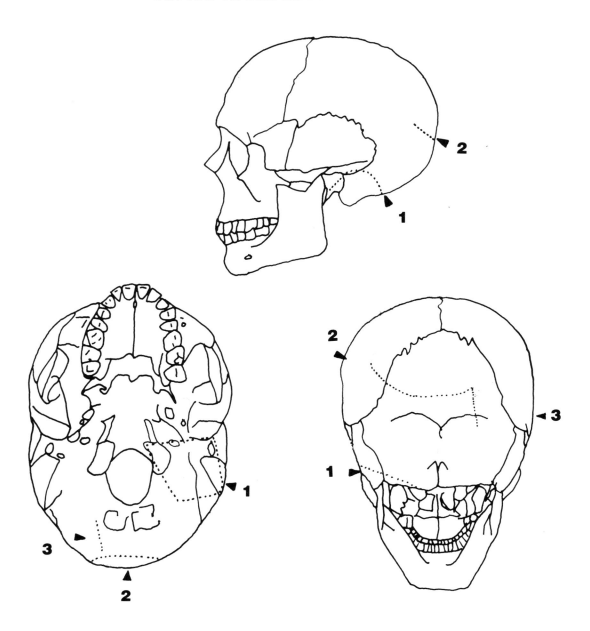

Fig. 92. Human skull showing injuries of victim 505:3

ered upon the back of the neck follows through sometimes to the jaw. These fracture lines were probably produced by a sharp-edged weapon at least 6cm. long, such as a sword. The victim may have been lying on the ground when attacked, or perhaps his skilled assailant was on horseback when he was struck from behind or from above.

All thirty-two teeth had erupted during life but two teeth were lost post-mortem. Occlusal attrition has resulted in exposure of islands of dentine on twenty-two teeth; it is most severe on the first and second molars. Attrition is confined to the enamel on eight teeth. Deposits of calculus, mostly mild, are present on all teeth. $\overline{3\,|\,3}$ have rotated distally, $\underline{|\,3}$ is slightly crowded. Incipient periodontal disease has resulted in loss of bone as well as flattening of the septae around

$$\frac{8 \qquad\qquad 1|\qquad\qquad 8}{76 \qquad\qquad | \qquad\qquad 67}$$

Hypoplasia occurs on the following teeth:

$$\frac{8 \qquad 3\,2\,1\|1\,2\,3 \qquad 8}{3\,2\,1\| \quad 3}$$

It occurs in the form of horizontal lines and grooves which occurred between the age of 2-6/7 years and again between 10-12 years, probably as a result of a specific illness or nutritional deficiency.

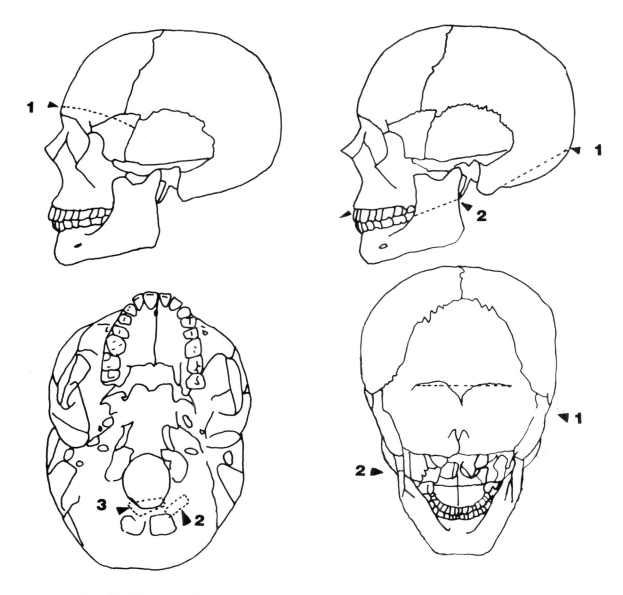

Fig. 93. Human skulls showing injuries of victim 505:4 [left] & 517:1 [right]

Discussion

The skeletal remains of seven adults are represented. Six consist of cranial remains only and one is an incomplete skeleton of a female (E543:340). Without complete skeletal remains sex and age are difficult to determine. However, from the cranial remains four were identified as being probably male while the sex of the remaining three could not be determined. An estimate of age was achieved from a comparison of molar attrition in the three individuals with dental remains (48: 4; 340 and 517:1) while postcranial criteria were also used to age Skeleton 340. An age of at least 40-50 years was estimated for Skeleton 340 and the cranial remains of 48:4 and 517:1 belong to individuals aged in their late 20s-early 30s. Sufficient skeletal remains were not present to determine the ages of five individuals (300:62; 322:1; 357:1; 505:3 and 505:4). They were, however, mature adults.

Pathology

Osteoarthritis
Osteoarthritis is a degenerative joint disease and the articulations of the vertebrae are the commonest areas to be affected. During life the cartilage is destroyed and later the bone surfaces which form a joint: subsequently a reactionary bone formation (osteophytosis) occurs at the articular margins. The postcranial remains of one person only are present post-mortem.

Osteoarthritis affects the entire spinal column of Skeleton 340. It is most severe on the lower neck vertebrae and is mild on the other vertebrae. This disease probably represents the wear and tear from manual labour, as well as age related stress and strain. This woman may have carried loads across her shoulders and on her head, and the neck or cervical vertebrae would take the strain of these loads. She also had mild osteoarthritis on her hands, including her right thumb, as well as on her ribs; these would indicate other strains during life, either work related or as a result of minor injuries.

Injuries

Three of the male skulls show multiple injuries; all were probably produced by swords and all were fatal. None of these injuries show evidence of healing or infection and therefore they certainly occurred perimortal. One male was decapitated (517:1) (Fig. 93 right). There was an attempt at decapitation on another man (505:4) (Fig. 93 left), resulting in his spinal cord being severed, while the third victim (505:3) (Fig. 92) had his left carotid artery and jugular vein cut.

Victim 505:4 probably died during single combat with a swordsman, first receiving a blow to the front of the left side of his head, the easiest blow to the head from a right-handed attacker (Wenham 1989), and finally being finished off when he lay on the ground. If he was not involved in single combat then perhaps he was ill-defended.

The other two victims (505:3 and 517:1) were attacked by assailants from behind. One of these was also attacked from a blow to the side of his head. Perhaps when these men had fallen (from postcranial injuries), they retreated and were then struck from behind, or the assailants may have been on horseback. The injury on 517:1 indicates that he was slain by a skilled swordsman in one single blow. The likelihood also exists that perhaps these skulls which had fallen from battle victims were displayed on the walls of the medieval town, hence the lack of any postcranial bone.

Dental pathology

Attrition

Attrition is the mechanical wearing down of the occlusal (biting) surfaces of the teeth as a result of the mastication of food. It occurred more frequently in the prehistoric and historic periods than in modern times. In those days the nature of the food, such as cereals, was coarse and tough and took longer to masticate; the food also probably contained gritty impurities, included during the grinding of corn with millstones or quernstones. Wear is most severe in the oldest individual, Skeleton 340. Considerable wear is seen in all three individuals with dental remains, indicating that a large part of their diet contained tough and abrasive food, such as coarse breads and meal. This type of wear is seen in other Irish populations from the Early Christian and medieval periods (Power 1985/86, Power forthcoming a & b).

Caries

Caries is a localised process of decay which results from bacterial action on the remains of food, especially carbohydrates, in the mouth, and results in the formation of a cavity. Caries occurs in one of the three individuals with dental remains, Skeleton 340. It occurs on the cervical margin (neck of the tooth) of a second molar. The cervical margin is a common location for caries to occur. With lack of hygiene, food debris becomes trapped in stagnation areas around the necks of the teeth long enough for acids from the carbohydrates to form.

Calculus

Calculus is a deposit of calcified plaque which is attached to the teeth. It results from the consumption of large amounts of soft foods, especially porridge or the *bán bíd*, or 'white foods', consisting of cheese, milk and curds which formed a large part of the Irish diet up to the 17th century (Lucas 1960). Deposits of calculus are mild on the three individuals with dental remains but moderate deposits do occur on a few teeth from each subject. These mild deposits would suggest that some soft foods were a regular part of their diet along with large amounts of coarse food, which produced the attrition. All three individuals had periodontal disease, which was probably exacerbated by deposits of calculus.

Periodontal Disease

Periodontal disease is an infection which leads to inflammation and the destruction of the supporting structures of the tooth, so that the tooth becomes loosened in its socket, and may ultimately be shed. Periodontal disease is evident in the three individuals with dental remains. It is incipient in the two individuals aged in their late 20s-early 30s (48: 4; 517:1), involving some bone loss around the molar teeth. Periodontitis is severe in the older individual, Skeleton 340, and has resulted in bone loss around most of the teeth.

Antemortem Tooth Loss

Skeleton 340 has lost two mandibular molars during life: these may have been lost as a result of periodontal disease or caries, both of which were present in this woman.

Hypoplasia

Hypoplasias are abnormalities in the structure of the teeth which occur during development. The position of the defect on the tooth or teeth affected makes it possible to tell the age at which the disturbance occurred. Hypoplasias are commonly due to some dietary disturbance, infection or trauma. The more common causes are vitamin and mineral deficiencies. The three individuals with dental disease display hypoplastic defects. They appear as faint grooves and crinkling on two individuals and as lines and grooves on the third individual.

They occurred in two of the individuals between the age of 2-6/7 years and in the third person between 3-7/8 years. In one of these individuals hypoplasia recurred between the age of 10-12 years. These defects may have been caused by one of the specific fevers such as measles, chicken pox or scarlet fever or by some nutritional deficiency, which in turn may have been associated with an inadequate weaning diet, between the age of 2-4 years, the most natural time for weaning to occur (Raphael 1977).

Hypercementosis

Hypercementosis is the overdevelopment of cementum on tooth roots. It usually occurs on the apical third of the roots and is often associated with infection. It occurs on the root apices of 6⌋ in Skeleton 340: this tooth is associated with periodontal disease.

Hereditary anomalies

Crowding

Slight crowding occurs in the three dentitions all involving canines, some resulting in rotation. In Skeleton 340 there was insufficient space for the wisdom teeth to erupt.

Interradicular Extension of Enamel

This is one of the so-called 'Mongoloid' dental characteristics found in Europe during prehistoric and historic times, and even today, though less frequently (Brabent and Twiesselmann 1964). One interradicular extension of enamel is present on a maxillary wisdom tooth of Skeleton 48:4. These have been recorded from other Irish sites including Anglo/Norman Wood Quay and 16th century Tintern, Co. Wexford (Power 1986).

Torus

The torus mandibularis is a benign growth of bone on the internal surface of the lower jaw and is genetic in origin. Two minute tori occur bilaterally in the region of the canines and first premolars of Skeleton 340.

Metopism

Metopism is the persistence of the metopic suture in an adult. The metopic suture divides the frontal bone into two halves and usually disappears between the first and second years of life. This anomaly is one of many non-metrical variants which are genetically controlled. Its incidence is high among these individuals: it persists in three of the six skulls with frontal bones present (322:1; 340 and 505:5/505:3) and may suggest a familial or racial link. This anomaly has also been recorded by the author in two individuals from the Early Christian site at Cathedral Hill, Co. Down (Power, forthcoming a) and in two individuals from Iron Age/ Early Christian Betaghstown, Co. Meath (Power, forthcoming b).

PLANT REMAINS

Brenda Collins

Method

A subsample of 500ml. was disaggregated in hot water and washed through a bank of Endecotts sieves (2mm., 1mm., 0.5mm. and 0.30mm.). The retent was sorted using a binocular microscope. Seed identification was carried out using reliably identified reference material and the manuals of Beijerinck (1947) and Bertsch (1941). The term 'seed' is used as a general term for the fruiting bodies of plants.

Eleven samples were examined.
1. Site C, F106, F117, F124
   Natural deposits deliberately embanked. Late 12th century in date.
2. Site B, F37
   Sample associated with hearthstone. 13th century in date.
3. Site B, F11
   Mid-14th century sample from behind staves of a possible tanning pit.
4. Site F, F345
   Drain fill. Later 12th century in date.
5. Site E, F1148 and F1136
   Associated with Mill. Mid-14th century in date.
6. Site J, F618
   Silty clay thought to have been deposited naturally. Deposits of organic material throughout. Mid to late-12th century in date.
7. Site I, F505
   Dump deposit immediately outside the town wall. Early 12th century in date.
8. Sample from Barrel 3050e, Dean St. Late medieval.
9. Site G, ditch fill F3026
   14th century.
10. Site G, F3017
    Pit fill of late 16th-early 17th century date.
11. Site G, F3002
    Upper fill from early 18th century barrel (F3001). Lower fill of barrel (F3003) was also analysed (see Appendix 3).

Results

The seeds identified from all samples are given in Tables 63, 64 and 65.

1. Site C, F106, F117, F124 (natural deposits deliberately embanked)
The sample from F106 was unproductive and contained a lot of unrolled stones, two blackberry seeds (*Rubus fruticosus*) and a small amount of charcoal.

The preservation of plant material in the other two samples varied considerably, indicating the mixed nature of the deposits. Some seeds were very well preserved but in general preservation was quite poor. The deposits contained small quantities of poorly preserved food waste such as blackberry (*Rubus fruticosus*), bilberry (*Vaccinium myrtillus*), mussel shells and one charred grain of oat (possibly cultivated oat, *Avena sativa*). Weeds of disturbed ground were well represented. Most of these were annuals, producing large quantities of seeds, and could have grown on or close by the deposits. A small number of plants associated with grassy places and wet/damp environments were present. They are plants consistently present in Dublin archaeological deposits (Geraghty 1996; Mitchell 1987; Collins, forthcoming) and some of them, like ribwort plantain (*Plantago lanceolata*), selfheal (*Prunella vulgaris*), buttercup (*Ranunculus acris/repens*), gipsywort (*Lycopus europaeus*) and rushes (*Juncus* spp.) undoubtedly grew in the medieval town as they do today (Wyse Jackson and Sheehy Skeffington 1984). The river Poddle, now underground, accommodated riverside and riverbank plants, while to the north, just beyond the town wall, lay marshland and sandbanks on the edge of the river Liffey (Mitchell 1987).

Corncockle (*Agrostemma githago*) and corn marigold (*Chrysanthemum segetum*) were weeds, which prior to the modern use of herbicides grew and were threshed with the crop, and would have been removed and thrown out with other refuse when the crop was being cleaned. Two hemp seeds (*Cannabis sativa*) were present. Hemp is a cultivated Asiatic plant and provides fibre for ropes and fabrics. The drug marijuana comes from hemp and its seeds are used for culinary purposes and as an animal feed (Catling and Greyson 1982). The seeds were probably imported with the fibre as contaminants and came into the deposit with domestic refuse.

2. Site B, F37 (associated with hearthstone)
A small number of seeds was present. Food remains included charred grains of wheat and oat, hazelnut shells, some of which were charred, and blackberry seeds. They represent the accidental or deliberate inclusion of human refuse into the fire. Lots of charcoal was present. Corn marigold (*Chrysanthemum segetum*), a crop contaminant, came in with the cereals and was burnt with them. Dock (*Rumex* spp.), sedge (*Carex* spp.) and other seeds were probably wind blown and accidentally incorporated into the ashes.

3. Site B, F11 (from behind staves of a possible tanning pit)
This was a black, silty wet deposit with dark grey clay mottles. Preservation was very poor and no significant material was extracted. A small amount of charcoal was present.

4. Site F, F345 (drain fill)

This was dark brown in colour and fairly organic. Preservation seemed to vary and some seeds were better preserved than others.

Compared to the other samples looked at, a greater range of food and useful plants were represented. Haw, hazelnuts, apple, sloe, blackberry, raspberry, rowan and bilberry could have been eaten fresh, cooked to make jams, etc., and used to flavour drinks. A hazelnut shell and one sloe fruitstone showed signs of gnawing, probably by mice, although the teeth marks on the hazelnut shell were considerably larger, indicating a larger animal, possibly a rat. One seed of black mustard (*Brassica nigra*) was present. These seeds could be ground into a mustard. Apparently, medieval mustard had not the same consistency as the mustard we use today and was more like a salad dressing (Maybe 1972).

Cultivated flax (*Linum usitatissimum*) seeds have been found in Viking, medieval and post-medieval archaeological deposits from Dublin (Mitchell 1987; Geraghty 1996). *Linum usitatissimum* is cultivated either for its strong fibre, which when processed produces linen thread and yarn, or for its seeds which were used as a source of linseed oil, as a medicine, or as animal feed.

Plants of disturbed ground, grassland, wet/damp places and arable weeds were again present. A significantly large amount of fragmented corncockle seeds (*Agrostemma githago*) were noted. In the past, corncockle and other arable weeds were cut with the crop, and seeds were either removed as contaminants, or eaten with it. When found in archaeological material, they could represent crop processing waste and/or seeds consumed and deposited with excrement. The seeds are poisonous and contain a poisonous glucoside (Salisbury 1964). The deposit was a breeding ground for flies and hundreds of unidentified fly puparia (not the common house fly, *Musca domestica*) were present. Sanitation in the area must have been quite poor.

5. Site E, F1148 and F1136 (associated with mill)

The samples relate to activities in the area after the mill had fallen into disuse. Both deposits contained small amounts of food and other waste indicating how waste was casually dumped around the town. Fruits like fig, grape, apple, blackberry and raspberry were represented. Parsley, flax seeds and one charred grain of oat were also identified. Small quantities of moss, hazelnut shells, mussel shells, pottery sherds, wood chips, charcoal and herring fishbone, some of which were burnt, were also present. Arable weeds, like corn marigold and corncockle were fairly well represented and would have been dumped as waste.

The samples were packed with seeds of plants which grow in damp/wet places, e.g., common spike-rush (*Eleocharis palustris*) and rushes (*Juncus* spp.). Watercress (*Nasturtium officinale*) and water crowfoot (*Ranunculus batrachium*) were also present, and the area was certainly close to or submerged in water. Perennials like common spike-rush, sedge and many of the rushes, all of which are represented by hundreds of seeds in the samples, are rhizomatous plants. This means that they have underground rhizomes which produce new plants at intervals along their lengths. As a result they tend to dominate, forming dense cover and competing successfully against other species by their network of shoots. The hundreds of buttercup seeds in the sample from F1148 indicate the presence of grassy waste-ground in the area.

6. Site J, F618 (silty clay of probable natural deposition)

This was a deposit of mixed origin streaked with organic material throughout. A small amount of small, smooth, rolled pebbles were present, although the majority were unrolled stones of varying sizes. The excavator's opinion is that the deposit was laid down naturally. The organic inclusions seem to represent dumped human refuse which was incorporated into the naturally laid down deposit.

Preservation was very poor. The few well preserved biological remains came from the organic deposits. Two blackberry seeds and corncockle fragments indicate that the organic matter relates to the dumping of human waste. Animal bone, cockle and mussel shells, hazelnut shells, charcoal, moss and fishbone vertebrae were also present. Vegetable matter, which was abundant in the organic sample, was extracted and sent for identification to Jan Peter Pals (IPP, Amsterdam). These were *Gramineae* (grass family) stalks and were possibly purple moor-grass (*Molinia caerulea*), although positive identification was impossible on the basis of epidermis characteristics alone. *Molinia caerulea* forms dense tussocks, has wiry stems and grows on wet moors and heaths on acid soils. In the post-medieval period, purple moor-grass stems were used as pipe-cleaners (Maybe 1979) and, providing that the tentative identification is correct, it is likely that they had been collected for some useful purpose, particularly given their association with human refuse in the sample.

7. Site I, F505 (dump deposit immediately outside the town wall)

This was an organic deposit. Preservation was good, although there was a low concentration of seeds in the subsample analysed. Food remains included sloe, raspberry, blackberry, bilberry, hazelnut shells, herring and thornback ray fishbones. Cultivated flax seeds and capsules were identified and are waste products in the processing of flax to linen. Fragments of corncockle (*Agrostemma githago*), a cornfield weed and a crop contaminant, would have been dumped with the rubbish.

There is a smattering of seeds from disturbed ground, grassy places and wet places, all habitats in or within close proximity to the town.

8. Sample from Barrel F3050e

This was an organic sample with little or no mineral content. It contained wood chip and bark which was 'sawdust-like' in appearance. One nail was present. The absence of weed seeds in the sample suggests that the barrel was covered over. It also suggests, particularly in the absence of any kind of refuse which might have accumulated had the empty barrel been discarded, that the contents are associated with the original use of the barrel. This was one of many such barrels uncovered in the immediate area, all of which were described as having similar type fills. Cattle horncores were present in all of the barrels.

Possibly the barrels were used for tanning, although in the excavator's opinion, they are too small for soaking even medium sized hides. Part of the final tanning process involved the immersion of the hides in solutions of oak bark and water (D. O' Rourke, pers. comm.). The very finely fragmented wood chip and bark could well be part of the residue following this final stage of the tanning process. As in the barrels from Patrick St, the tanning pits excavated at Northampton contained large quantities of cattle horncores (Shaw 1984).

9. Site G, Ditch fill F3026

A small amount of bone, including small mammal bone, fishbone (including herring), mussel and cockle shells, charcoal, strips of leather and animal teeth were present. Seeds identified are given in Table 64.

Food debris was evidently being dumped into the ditch and included bilberry, blackberry, fig and charred cereal grain. Hemp seeds (*Cannabis sativa*) were present. This is a cultivated Asiatic plant, whose stems provide a tough fibre for ropes. The seeds of the plant can be used for culinary purposes. They could however have been accidently imported as contaminants with the fibre.

The large number of watercress seeds indicate that shallow water flowed in the bottom of the ditch, while species like celery-leaved buttercup would have thrived along its muddy edges. Disturbed conditions encouraged annuals like nipplewort, while species like common nettle persisted from year to year.

10. Site G, Fill F3017 of Pit F3019

This was an organic sample with no mineral content. The sample contained twigs, cut branches and straw. Hundreds of lentils were present. Other food plants found in the sample were blackberry and grape. Small scraps of leather and the occasional cockle shell were also noted. Seeds identified are given in Table 65.

Lens culinaris (lentil) is an erect annual with seeds which are green, greenish brown or reddish, sometimes mottled in colour. They require a light, warm sandy soil and are cultivated as a field crop in southern Europe and in hot summers in eastern Europe (de Rougemont 1989). They can be grown in southern England in the right conditions, but are susceptible to frost. Lentils have been found on early farming sites in the Near East (Renfrew 1973) and were known to the ancient Egyptians and Greeks. They are recorded from Neolithic sites in Europe (Grieg 1983) and occur in small amounts in Britain in the Roman period when they were most likely imported. There is evidence that lentils were grown in a small way

in the post-medieval period in England (Green 1983) although they were more usually imported from the Continent where it was easier to grow them.

Lentils are high in protein (on average they contain 25 per cent protein) and are easily digested. They were a protein supplement in Catholic countries during Lent when the consumption of meat was forbidden. The seeds can be used in soups and stews or ground to a meal and mixed with cereal flour. The husks, bran and vegetative parts provide fodder and manure (de Rougemont 1989). The seeds in this sample were whole and had not been ground or chewed. They measured approximately 3mm. in diameter and fall into the sub-species *microspermae* which has small to medium sized convex pods and seeds which measure 3mm.-6mm. in diameter. Most of the prehistoric finds of lentil are of this sub-species (Renfrew 1973). When thoroughly cooked, lentils disintegrate and lose their shape. The seeds in the sample were readily identified and had been dumped prior to cooking. Any number of reasons might account for the large quantity of lentils in the pit, including accidental spillage, contamination, or even sheer dislike of the vegetable. It is also possible that the protein rich lentils were assigned as fodder and ultimately were thrown into the pit with animal bedding and litter (straw and twigs were abundant in the sample).

An interesting find was the presence of serradella in the sample, which would have arrived as an imported crops. It is a native of Portugal, coastal Spain and Morocco, and adapted to moist sandy soils and cool, Mediterranean type climates. It is cultivated for grazing (it is a rich source of protein), soil cover and soil improvement (nitrate enrichment) on light acid soils and for hay and silage (Allen and Allen 1981). It is thought that the cultivation of serradella did not take place in the Iberian peninsula prior to 1800, although it was used as fodder for nomadic sheep flocks on the Portugese and Spanish highlands (Schofield 1950). Its presence, however, in a lentil crop dating to the late 16th-early 17th century is significant, and indicates that serradella was being cultivated earlier than this, probably as a green manure crop (a plant crop, like clover, ploughed under while green to enrich the soil).

11. Site G, Sample F3002 from Barrel F3001 (upper fill)

The sample contained wood chip, charcoal, tiny fragments of cockle and mussel shell, fragments of bone, one animal tooth, two lentil seeds and one seed each of redshank and black nightshade, both common annual weeds of disturbed ground. Lime was also present. The sample contained a mixture of rubbish, probably from a number of sources, which could have accumulated there when the barrel was abandoned. The upper fill does not appear to have been associated with the original use of the barrel (see also Appendix 3).

Conclusions

The samples analysed came from a variety of contexts and included naturally laid down fluvial deposits, the fill of a ditch and barrel fills, a hearth deposit and material associated with a disused mill. Preservation varied from sample to sample. Small quantities of food refuse were present in practically all of the samples, regardless of archaeological context. In some instances this reflects deliberate dumping, for example, the ditch fill sample (F345) and the mill samples (F1148 and F1136). On the other hand in F106, F117 and F124 the food refuse probably represents secondary deposition and derives from primary dump deposits elsewhere. Fig and grape, both present in the 14th century mill samples, would have been imported and have not been found in Dublin samples prior to the 13th century. The lentils and serradella from F3017 were an interesting find.

When preservation was not a problem, weeds and plants of disturbed ground were abundant. Practically all of these would have been growing in the town. The majority of species were annuals, producing lots of seed with efficient dispersal mechanisms, and their predominance in the samples is to be expected. Many of the weeds represented in the medieval town can still be found on waste land, car parks and along the canals in Dublin today, while others like stinking chamomile and herbore are absent (Wyse Jackson and Sheehy Skeffington 1984). The reasons why there is continuity and decline of species through time are varied and often complex and is an interesting topic worth consideration and research.

Acknowledgments

I would like to acknowledge Jan Peter Pals and Henk van Haaster, IPP, Amsterdam, and Allan Hall, EAU, York, for their time and expertise in the identification of plant material, particularly Jan Peter Pals for his help in the identification of *Ornithopus sativus* and cf. *Molina caerula*.

Feature Number: Volume: (ml.)	106 500	117 500	124 500	37 500	11 500	345 500	1148 500	1136 500	618 1000	505 1000	
Corylus avellana L.	0	0	0	P	0	P	P	P	P	P	Hazel
Ficus carica L.	0	0	0	0	0	0	P	0	0	0	Fig
Cannabis sativa L.	0	P	0	0	0	0	0	0	0	0	Hemp
Urtica dioica L.	0	P	P	0	0	0	0	P	0	P	Common nettle
Urtica urens L.	0	P	0	0	P	0	P	P	0	P	Small nettle
Polygonum aviculare L.	0	P	P	0	P	P	P	P	0	P	Knotgrass
Polygonum persicaria L.	0	P	0	P	0	P	P	P	P	P	Redshank
Polygonum lapathifolium L.	0	0	0	0	0	P	0	0	0	0	Pale persicaria
Polygonum sp.	0	0	0	0	0	0	P	P	0	0	Various
Fallopia convolvulus (L.) A. Love	0	0	0	0	0	0	P	0	0	0	Black-bindweed
Rumex acetosella L.	0	P	0	0	0	P	P	P	0	P	Sheep's sorrel
Rumex spp.	0	P	P	P	0	P	0	P	0	P	Dock
Chenopodium album L.	0	P	0	0	0	P	P	P	0	P	Fat-hen
Chenopodium rubrum L.	0	P	P	0	0	0	0	P	0	P	Red goosefoot
Atriplex cf. *patula* L.	0	P	P	0	P	P	P	P	0	P	? Common orache
Montia fontana L. subsp. *chondrosperma* (Fenzl.) Walters	0	0	P	0	0	P	0	0	0	P	Blinks
Stellaria media (L.) Vill.	0	P	P	0	0	P	P	P	0	P	Common chickweed
Stellaria holostea L.	0	0	0	0	0	0	0	0	0	P	Greater stitchwort
Stellaria cf. *graminea* L.	0	P	0	0	0	P	P	0	0	P	? Lesser stitchwort
Stellaria sp.	0	0	0	0	0	0	P	P	0	0	Chickweed/Stitchwort
Cerastium sp.	0	0	0	0	0	0	0	0	0	0	Mouse-ear
Spergula arvensis L.	0	0	0	0	0	P	P	P	0	0	Corn spurrey
Agrostemma githago L.	0	P	0	0	0	0	0	P	P	P	Corncockle
Silene vulgaris (Moench) Garcke subsp. *vulgaris*	0	P	0	0	0	P	0	0	0	0	Bladder campion
Ranunculus acris L./*repens* L.	0	P	P	0	P	P	P	P	P	P	Meadow/Creeping buttercup
Ranunculus sceleratus L.	0	0	0	0	0	0	P	P	0	P	Celery-leaved buttercup
Ranunculus flammula L.	0	P	0	0	0	P	0	P	0	P	Lesser spearwort
Ranunculus Subgenus *Batrachium*	0	0	0	0	0	0	0	P	0	0	Water-crowfoot
Papaver rhoeas L./*dubium* L.	0	0	P	0	0	P	P	0	0	0	Common/Long-headed poppy
Fumaria officinalis L.	0	0	0	0	0	0	0	0	0	0	Common fumitory
Nasturtium officinale R. Br.	0	0	0	0	0	0	P	P	0	0	Watercress
Thlaspi arvense L.	0	0	0	0	0	0	P	0	0	0	Field penny-cress
Brassica nigra L.	0	0	0	0	0	P	0	0	0	0	Black mustard

P means present.   (Nomenclature follows Scannell and Synnott 1987)

Table 63. Botanical Remains from Selected Contexts, Patrick Street

Scientific name	Common name	106 (500)	117 (500)	124 (500)	37 (500)	11 (500)	345 (500)	1148 (500)	1136 (500)	618 (1000)	505 (1000)
Brassica sp.	Various	0	0	0	0	0	P	P	P	0	0
Sinapis arvensis L.	Charlock	0	0	0	0	0	0	0	P	0	P
Rubus idaeus L./*fruticosus* L.	Raspberry/Blackberry	P	P	P	P	0	P	0	P	P	P
Potentilla anserina L.	Silverweed	0	0	0	0	0	0	P	P	0	P
Aphanes arvensis L.	Parsley-piert	0	0	0	0	0	0	0	0	0	P
Malus sp.	Apple	0	0	0	0	0	P	P	0	0	0
Sorbus aucuparia L.	Rowan	0	0	0	0	0	P	0	0	0	0
Crataegus monogyna Jacq.	Hawthorn	0	0	0	0	0	P	0	0	0	0
Prunus spinosa L.	Sloe	0	0	0	0	0	P	0	P	0	P
Oxalis acetosella L.	Wood-sorrel	0	0	0	0	0	0	P	0	0	0
Linum usitatissimum L.	Cultivated flax	0	P	0	0	0	P	P	P	0	P
Linum catharticum L.	Fairy flax	0	P	0	0	0	P	0	0	0	P
Euphorbia helioscopia L.	Sun spurge	0	P	0	0	0	0	0	0	0	0
Vitis vinifera L.	Grape	0	0	0	0	0	0	P	0	0	0
Lythrum sp.	Various	0	0	0	0	0	P	0	P	0	P
Scandix pecten-veneris L.	Shepherd's needle	0	0	0	0	0	0	0	P	0	0
Oenanthe sp.	Water-dropwort	0	0	0	0	0	0	0	P	0	0
Aethusa cynapium L.	Fool's parsley	0	0	P	0	0	0	P	0	0	0
Conium maculatum L.	Hemlock	0	0	P	P	0	0	0	P	0	0
Apium graveolens L.	Wild celery	0	0	0	0	0	0	0	P	0	0
Petroselinum crispum (Miller) A.W. Hill	Garden parsley	0	P	0	0	0	0	0	P	0	0
Torilis sp.	Hedge-parsley	0	0	0	0	0	0	0	0	0	0
Daucus carota L.	Wild carrot	0	0	0	0	0	0	0	0	0	0
Vaccinium myrtillus L.	Bilberry	0	0	0	0	0	0	0	P	0	P
Vaccinium sp.	Various	0	0	0	0	0	0	0	0	0	0
Galeopsis sp.	Hemp-nettle	0	0	0	0	0	0	0	0	0	0
cf.*Ballota nigra* L.	? Black horehound	0	0	P	0	0	P	0	0	0	0
Stachys cf. *palustris* L.	Marsh woundwort	0	0	0	0	0	0	0	P	0	0
Prunella vulgaris L.	Selfheal	0	0	0	0	0	P	P	P	0	P
Lycopus europaeus L.	Gipsywort	0	0	0	0	0	P	0	P	0	0
Solanum nigrum L	Black nightshade	0	0	0	0	0	P	0	P	0	0
Plantago major L.	Greater plantain	0	0	0	0	0	P	0	0	0	P
Plantago lanceolata L.	Ribwort plantain	0	0	0	0	0	P	0	0	P	0
Sambucus nigra L.	Elder	0	0	0	0	0	0	0	0	P	P

P means present. (Nomenclature follows Scannell and Synnott 1987)

Table 63. (cont.) Botanical Remains from Selected Contexts, Patrick Street

233

Feature Number:	106	117	124	37	11	345	1148	1136	618	505	
Volume: (ml.)	500	500	500	500	500	500	500	500	1000	1000	
Valerianella dentata (L.) Pollich	0	0	0	0	0	P	0	0	0	0	Narrow-fruited cornsalad
Bellis perennis L.	0	0	0	0	0	0	P	0	0	P	Daisy
Anthemis cotula L.	0	0	0	0	0	P	P	P	0	P	Stinking chamomile
Chrysanthemum segetum L.	0	P	0	P	0	P	P	P	0	0	Corn marigold
Senecio cf. *jacobaea* L.	0	0	0	0	0	0	0	0	0	P	? Common ragwort
Senecio sp.	0	0	0	0	0	0	P	0	0	P	Ragwort/Groundsel
Carduus/Cirsium spp.	0	P	P	0	0	P	0	P	P	P	Thistle
Leontodon sp.	0	0	P	0	0	0	P	P	P	P	Hawkbit
Sonchus asper (L.) Hill	0	P	P	0	0	P	P	P	P	P	Prickly sow-thistle
Sonchus oleraceus L.	0	0	0	0	0	0	0	0	0	P	Smooth sow-thistle
Sonchus arvensis L.	0	P	0	0	0	0	0	0	0	P	Perennial sow-thistle
Lapsana communis L	0	P	P	0	0	P	P	P	P	P	Nipplewort
Triglochin maritima L	0	0	0	0	0	0	0	0	P	P	Sea arrowgrass
Juncus spp.	0	P	P	0	0	0	P	P	P	P	Rush
Luzula sp.	0	0	0	0	0	0	P	0	0	0	Wood-rush
Gramineae	0	0	0	0	0	P	0	0	0	P	Grasses
Triticum sp.	0	0	0	P	0	0	0	0	0	0	Wheat
Avena sp.	0	P	0	P	0	P	P	0	0	0	Oat
Scirpus setaceus L.	0	P	P	0	0	0	0	0	0	0	Bristle club-rush
Eleocharis palustris (L.) Roemer & Schultes	0	P	0	0	0	P	P	P	0	0	Common spike-rush
Carex rostrata Stokes/*vesicaria* L.	0	0	P	P	0	0	P	0	0	P	Bottle sedge/Bladder-sedge
Carex spp.	0	P	0	P	0	P	0	P	P	P	Sedge

P means present   (Nomenclature follows Scannell and Synnott 1987)

Table 63. *(cont.)* Botanical Remains from Selected Contexts, Patrick Street

Ficus carica L. (fig)
Cannabis sativa L. (hemp)
Urtica dioica L. (common nettle)
Urtica urens L. (small nettle)
Polygonum persicaria L. (redshank)
Atriplex cf. *patula* L. (? common orache)
Ranunculus acris L./*repens* L. (meadow/creeping buttercup)
Ranunculus scleratus L. (celery-leaved buttercup)
Barbarea vulgaris R. Br. (wintercress)
Nasturtium officinale R. Br. (watercress)
Rubus sp. (bramble/blackberry)
Umbelliferae (various)
Conium maculatum L. (hemlock)
Apium graveolens L. (wild celery)
Apium nodiflorum (L.) Lag. (fool's watercress)
Vaccinium myrtillus L. (bilberry)
Lamium album L. (white dead-nettle)
Lamium cf. *purpureum* L. (red dead-nettle)
Lamium sp. (dead-nettle)
Sambucus nigra L. (elder)
Compositae (various)
Hyoscyamus niger L. (henbane)
Chrysanthemum segetum L. (corn marigold)
Carduus/Cirsium sp. (thistle)
Sonchus asper (L.) Hill (prickly sow-thistle)
Sonchus cf. *oleraceus* L. (? smooth sow-thistle)
Lapsana communis L. (nipplewort)
Juncus sp. (rush)
Triticum cf *aestivum* type (wheat – ? bread wheat)
cf. *Lemna* sp. (? duckweed)
Eleocharis palustris (L.) (common spike-rush) Roemer & Schultes
Carex spp. (sedges)
Unidentifiable charred cereal grains (3 poorly preserved grains)

(Nomenclature follows Scannell and Synnott 1987)

Table 64. Plant remains from ditch fill F3026

Urtica dioica L. (common nettle)
Urtica urens L. (small nettle)
Polygonum aviculare L. (knotgrass)
Polygonum sp. (various)
Agrostemma githago L. (corncockle)
Silene sp. (various)
Ranunculus flammula L. (lesser spearwort)
Rubus sp. (bramble/blackberry)
Ornithopus sativus Brot. (serradella)
Lens culinaris Medicus (lentil)
Vitis vinifera L. (grape)
Hypericum sp. (St. John's Wort)
Anagallis arvensis L. (scarlet pimpernel)
Sherardia arvensis L. (field madder)
cf. *Marrubium vulgare* L. (? white horehound)
Lamium sp. (dead-nettle)
Bidens cernua L. (nodding bur-marigold)
Chrysanthemum segetum L. (corn marigold)
Leucanthemum vulgare Lam. (oxeye daisy)
Hieracium sp. (hawkweed)
Gramineae (grasses)

(Nomenclature follows Scannell and Synnott 1987)

Table 65. Plant remains from pit fill F3019

APPENDIX 1
LIST OF LAYERS AND FEATURES BY LEVEL

Site B

Level 1	Level 2	Level 3	Level 4	Level 5
54	27=28=29=34	24	5	1
55	40	25	7	2
56	45	31	8	3
57	48	35	9	4
58	49	37/37a	11	6
59	50-51	38	12	10
53	39	13	16	
		41/41b	14	18
		42/26	15	
		43=30	17	
		44	19	
		46	20	
		47	21	
			22	
			23	
			32	
			33	
			36	
			52	
			60	

Site C

Level 1	Level 2	Level 3
102=108	107	100
103=110=111=113	120	101
104	121	
105		
106		
109		
112		
114		
115		
116		
117		
118		
119		
122		
123		
124		

Site D

Level 1	Level 2	Level 3	Level 4	Miscellaneous
205	206	203	201	211
208	207	213	202	212
219	216	217		204
221	218	233		
225	220	209		*Contaminated*
229	223			215
	224			209
	226			
	227			*Unstratified*
	228			231
	232			
	234			

Site E

Level 1	Level 2	Level 3
1110	1101	1110
1115	1102	1106
1121	1103	1111
1125	1104	
1127	1105	
1128	1107	
1129	1108	
1134	1109	
1135	1112	
1136	1113	
1137	1114/1117	
1139	1116	
1140 – 1152	1118 – 1120	
	1122	
	1123	
	1124	
	1126	
	1130	
	1131	
	1132	
	1133	
	1138	

Appendix 1

Site F

Level 1	Level 2	Level 3	Level 4	Level 5	Level 6
322	329	313	335	301	300
331	337/328/	343		303	302
332	333/336	344/376/381		304	311
340	338	352		305	385
334	339	360		306	
342	341	364		307	
346	345	366		308	
347	359	367		309	
348	362	369		310	
349	363	370/373/374		312	
350	365	371		314	
351	368	372		315	
353/356	388	375		316	
354	1003/1008	377		317	
358	1113/1004/	378/384/		318	
361	1009	392/393		319	
394		379		320	
1005		382		321	
		383		323	
		386		324	
		391		325	
		1000		326	
		1001		331	
		1002			
		1007			
		1011			

Site clearance: 311
Contaminated: 313
Unstratified finds: 327, 357, 377, 391, 1010 & 1052.
Pottery between Levels 3 & 4: 355
Loose timber: 1006
Finds: 364 & 390

Site G

Level 1	Level 2	Level 3	Level 4	Level 5	Level 6
3038	3039	3030	3015	3023/3010	3009
	3035	3026	3025	3020	3001
	3037	3031	3014	3021	3004
	3033	3012	3003		
	3034	3016	3002		
	3036	3022	3005		
	3032	3006			
					3007/3008
					3013
					3028
					3019
					3018
Clearance:	3000				3017
	3029				3011

Site I

Level 1	Level 2	Level 3
506	500	501
509	504	502
511	505	503
512	510	507
513	514	508
525	515	526
	516	
	517	
	518	
	519	
	520	
	521	
	522	
	523	
	524	

Site J

Level 1	Level 2	Level 3	
5606	613	601	
616	615	602	
617	623	603	
618		604	*Disturbed*: 605
619		605	*Sewer*: 607
620		607	*Borehole*: 614
621		608	
622		609	
624		610	
625		611	
626		612	
627		614	
628			
629			
630			
631			

Site K

Level 1	Level 2	Level 3	Level 4
713	703	704	700
714	705	706	701
716	709	707	702
717	710	708	736
718	711	735	
719	712		
720	715		
721	722		
724	723		
725			
726			
727			
728			
729			
730			
731			
732			
733			
734			
737			

Appendix 2
Analysis of Samples from Limekiln, Site F
John Fortune

Two samples, one of lime or mortar, the other of firestone, were submitted for thin-section and chemical analysis to Irish Cement Ltd. The process of cement production during the 11th-17th centuries was briefly as follows:

'The stones or clay were first broken into small fragments, then burnt in a kiln or furnace with a heat nearly sufficient to vitrify them, then reduced to powder by any mechanical or other operation. This method was used during Roman times with gradual decline in the quality of cement throughout the middle ages. The mineral assemblage of this cement comprised calcium aluminates, calcium aluminium silicates; B_2CAO, S_{102} and unreacted silica' (Viollet-le-Duc 1863, 402).

In this particular case it is likely that we are dealing with a limekiln only, and that the limestone used has become aggregated with the clay walls of the kiln over the years. For this reason, the chemical analysis indicates a blend of limestone and clay, with the former predominating. The analysis is in Table 66.

Based on our microscopic analysis, there is very little evidence of burning. A visual examination of the bulk of the material does point to a composite of burnt limestone with some burnt clay. It is not clear whether the clay had been added as part of the process or not.

	Sample 20 Lime or mortar	Sample 13 Firestone
S102	29.47	20.82
AL203	2.95	1.39
FE203	2.35	1.29
CAO	37.4	42.62
MGO	0.95	1.02
K20	0.52	0.25
LOI	32.1	36.3
TOTAL	105.7	103.7
LOI (1200 DEG. C)	29.024	34.3
S102	44.34	33.08
AL203	4.69	2.35
FE203	2.5	1.72
CAO	45.39	62.43
MG0	1.39	1.78
K20	1.2	0.51
TOTAL	99.5	101.9

Table 66. Chemical Analysis of Samples 16 and 20

APPENDIX 3
REPORT ON SAMPLE F3003
David Doff

The soil sample (F3003) from the post-medieval barrel at Site G was looked at using both x-ray diffraction and x-ray spectroscopy. The sample consists almost entirely of calcite $CaCo_3$. The residue remaining after dissolution of the calcite in dilute hydrochloric acid consists of:

    (a) coarse (*c.* 3mm.) grains of coal
    (b) finely divided quartz
    (c) organic matter
    (d) iron oxides

There is no sign of any clay minerals.

ABBREVIATIONS

Cal. Close Rolls Hen. VIII. *Calendar of the Patent and Close Rolls of Chancery in Ireland in the Reigns of Henry VIII, Edward IV, Mary and Elizabeth*, ed. J. Morrin, Dublin, 1861

C.D.I. *Calendar of Documents Relating to Ireland, 1171- 1307*, ed. H.S. Sweetman, 5 vols, London, 1875-76

Cal. Just. Rolls. *Calendar of the Justiciary Rolls of Ireland 1295-1314*, ed. J. Mills and M.C. Griffith, 3 vols, Dublin, 1905-14

C.A.R. *Calendar of the Ancient Records of Dublin*, ed. J.T. Gilbert, 19 vols, Dublin, 1889-1944

C. of St M. *Chartularies of St Mary's Abbey, Dublin, and Annals of Ireland, 1162- 1370*, ed. J.T. Gilbert, 2 vols, London, 1884-86

Court Lib. *Court Book of the Liberty of St Sepulchre*, ed. H. Wood, Dublin, 1930

D.K.R. *Reports of the Keeper of the Public Records, Ireland*, Dublin, 1903-21

Dub. Assem. R. *Dublin Assembly Rolls*

Exp. Hib. *Expugnatio Hibernica: the Conquest of Ireland by Geraldis Cambrensis*, ed. A.B. Scott and F.X. Martin, Dublin, 1978

Griffith Val. *Griffith's Valuation*

Hist. Municip. Doc. *Historic and Municipal Documents of Ireland*, ed. J.T. Gilbert, London, 1870

Kend. Sur. 1749, *Kendrick's Survey of 1749*, Marsh's Library

L.A. *Liber Albus* (in C.A.R. Vol. 1)

P.R.M. *Poddle River Minutes*

Reg. St J. *Register of the Hospital of St John the Baptist*, ed. E. St John Brooks, Dublin, 1936

Thomas Reg. *Register of the Abbey of St Thomas the Martyr*, Dublin, ed. J.T. Gilbert, London, 1889

W.S.C. *Reports of the Wide Street Comissioners*

Journals and Periodicals

Arch. Ir. *Archaeology Ireland*

Arch. J. *Archaeological Journal*

B.A.R. *British Archaeological Reports (British and International series)*

C.B.A. *Council for British Archaeology*

J. Co. Louth Arch. Soc. *Journal of the County Louth Archaeological Society*

Current Arch. *Current Archaeology*

D.H.R. *Dublin Historical Record*

Ir. Eng. J. *Irish Engineering Journal*

Indust. Arch. *Industrial Archaeology*

J. Cork Hist. and Arch. Soc. *Journal of the Cork Historical and Archaeological Society*

J. Co. Kildare Arch. Soc. *Journal of the Kildare Archaeological Society*

J. Roy. Soc. Ant. Ir. *Journal of the Royal Society of Antiquities of Ireland*

Med. Arch. *Medieval Archaeology*

Post-Med. Arch. *Post-Medieval Archaeology*

Proc. Roy. Ir. Acad. *Proceedings of the Royal Irish Academy*

Proc. Prehist. Soc. *Proceedings of the Prehistoric Society*

Proc. Soc. Ant. Scot. *Proceedings of the Society of Antiquaries of Scotland*

Trans. Bristol and Glouc. Arch. Soc. *Transactions of the Bristol and Gloucestershire Archaeological Society*

U. J. Arch. *Ulster Journal of Archaeology*

BIBLIOGRAPHY

Alexander, J. and Binski, P. (eds), *The Age of Chivalry – Art in Plantagenet England 1200-1400*, London, 1987.

Allan, J. and Perry, I. 'The Pottery and the Tiles' in 'Okehampton Castle: Part 2, The Bailey,' *Proceedings of the Devon Archaeological Society* 40, 1982.

Allan, J.P. 'The Importation of Pottery to Southern England *c*. 1200-1500' in P. Davey and R. Hodges (eds), *Ceramics and Trade*, Sheffield, 1983.

Allan, J.P. *Medieval and Post-Medieval Finds From Exeter 1971-1980*, Exeter, 1984.

Allen, O.N. and Allen, E.K. *Leguminosa*, London, 1981.

Allen, S.J. 'The Mill Structural Timber Sequence' in G.C. Astill, *A Medieval Industrial Complex and its Landscape: the Metal Working Watermills and Workshops of Bordesley Abbey*, York, 1993.

Allin, C.E. 'The Leather' in J.E. Mellors and T. Pearce, *The Austin Friars, Leicester*, C.B.A. Research Report No. 35, 1981.

Andrews, J.H. 'The Oldest Map of Dublin,' *Proc. Roy. Ir. Acad.* 83C, 1983.

Astill, G. 'Monastic Research Designs. Bordesley Abbey and the Arrow Valley' in R. Gilchrist and H. Mytum (eds), *The Archaeology of Rural Monasteries*, B.A.R. British Series 203, 1989.

Bagniewski, Z. and Kubow, P. 'Sredniowieczny Mlyn Wodny y Ptakowic na Dolnym Slasku,' *Kwartalnik Historii Kultury Materialnej*, 1977.

Barker, D. 'North Staffordshire Ceramics – a Type Series. Part 1: Cistercian Wares,' *Staffordshire Archaeological Studies* No. 3, 1986.

Barry, T. B. *The Archaeology of Medieval Ireland*, London, 1987.

Barton, K.G. 'The Medieval Pottery of the Saintonge,' *Arch. J.* 1963a.

Barton, K.G. 'A Medieval Pottery Kiln at Ham Green, Bristol,' *Trans. Bristol and Glouc. Arch. Soc.* 82, 1963b.

Barton, K.G. 'Medieval Pottery at Rouen,' *Arch. J.* 1965.

Barton, K.G. 'The Medieval Pottery of Dublin' in G. Mac Niocaill and P. Wallace (eds), *Keimelia*, Galway, 1988.

Bedwin, O. 'The Excavation of Ardingly Fulling Mill and Forge,' *Post.-Med. Arch.*, 1976.

Bedwin, O. 'The Excavation of Batsford Mill, Warbleton, East Sussex, 1978,' *Post-Med. Arch.* 1980a.

Bedwin, O. 'The Excavation of a Late 16th Century Blast Furnace at Batsford, Herstmonceux, East Sussex 1978,' *Post.-Med. Arch.* 1980b.

Beijerinck, W. *Zadenatlas der Nederlandsche Flora*, Wageningen, 1947.

Bennet, R. and Elton, J. *A History of Cornmilling* (4 vols), London and Liverpool, 1898-1904.

Bernard, J. H. 'Calendar of Documents Contained in the Chartulary Commonly Called "Dignitas Decani of St. Patrick's Cathedral",' *Proc. Roy. Ir. Acad.* 25C, 1905.

Berry, H. F. 'The Water Supply of Greater Dublin,' *J. Roy. Soc. Ant. Ir.* 21, 1891.

Berry, H. F. 'Notes on an Unpublished Manuscript of the Dublin Watercourse From the Muniments of the Earl of Meath,' *Proc. Roy. Ir. Acad.* 24C, 1904.

Berthelot, M. 'Pour des Arts mechaniques et de l'Artillerie vers la Fin du Moyen Age,' *Annales de Chemie et de Physique*, 6e Serie, 1891.

Bertsch, K. *Fruchte und Samen: Ein Bestimmungsbuch zur Pflanzenkunde der Vorgeschichtlichen Zeit*, Stuttgart, 1941.

Brabant, H. and Twiesselmann, F. 'Observations sur l'Evolution de la Denture Permanente Humaine en Europe Occidentale,' *Bulletin de Group International Recherche Scientifique de Stomatologie* 7, 1964.

Bradley, J. (ed.), *Viking Dublin Exposed – The Wood Quay Saga*, Dublin, 1984.

Bradley, J. 'The Interpretation of Scandinavian Settlement in Ireland' in J. Bradley (ed.), *Settlement and Society in Medieval Ireland*, Kilkenny, 1988.

Brett, G. 'Byzantine Watermill,' *Antiquity* 13, 1939.

Brewster, T.C.M and Hayfield, C. 'Cowlam Deserted Village: a Case Study of Post-Medieval Village Desertion,' *Post-Med. Arch.* 1988.

Brooks, E. St J. (ed.), *The Register of the Hospital of St John the Baptist Without the Newgate, Dublin*, Dublin, 1936.

Brothwell, D.R. 'Forensic Aspects of the So-Called Skeleton Q1 From Maiden Castle, Dorset,' *World Arch.* 3, 1971.

Brothwell, D.R. *Digging up Bones*, London, 1981.

Brown, D. 'Dendrochronological Analysis' in G.C. Astill, *A Medieval Industrial Complex and Its Landscape: the Metal Working Watermills and Workshops of Bordesley Abbey*, York, 1993.

Burns, R. 'Post-Medieval Ceramics From Guernsey' in E. Lewis (ed.), *Custom and Ceramics*, Wickham, 1991.

Butler, V. *Cattle in Thirteenth Century Dublin*, unpublished M.A. thesis, the National University of Ireland, 1984.

Campbell, 'A Medieval Tile Kiln Site at Magdalene St, Drogheda,' *J. Co. Louth Arch. and Hist. Soc.* 21 No.1, 1985.

Campbell, K. 'The Archaeology of Medieval Drogheda,' *Arch. Ir.*, No. 2, 1987.

Carroll, F. 'The Ancient Name of the Poddle,' *D.H.R.* 13, 1954.

Carver, M.O.H. 'Three Saxo-Norman Tenements in Durham City,' *Med. Arch.* 23, 1979.

Catling, D. and Grayson, J. *Identification of Vegetable Fibres*, London, 1982.

Clarke, H. and Carter, A. *Excavations at King's Lynn 1963-1970*, London, 1977.

Clarke, H. B. 'The Topographical Development of Early Medieval Dublin,' *J. Roy. Soc. Ant. Ir.* 107, 1977, reprinted in H.B. Clarke (ed.), *Medieval Dublin: the Making of a Metropolis*, Dublin, 1990.

Clarke, H. B. *Dublin c. 840-1540, the Medieval Town in the Modern City*, Dublin, 1978a.

Clarke, H. B. (ed.), 'Focus on Medieval Dublin,' *Dublin Arts Festival*, Dublin, 1978b.

Clarke, H. B. 'The Medieval Liffey – Fresh Water and Barehaven,' *Dublin Arts Festival*, Dublin, 1979.

Clarke, H. B. (ed.), *Medieval Dublin: the Making of a Metropolis*, Dublin, 1990a.

Clarke, H. B. (ed.), *Medieval Dublin: the Living City*, Dublin, 1990b.

Clay, P. 'Castle Donnington,' *Current Arch.* 102, IX, 1986.

Cloe, E.J. 'The Bailiff's Account for the Manor of Kingsland, 1389-90,' *Trans. Woolhope Nature Field Club* 35, 1955.

Collins, B. 'Botanical Remains From the Dublin Castle Excavations,' forthcoming.

Cosgrove, A. (ed.), *Dublin Through the Ages*, Dublin, 1988.

Cowgill, J. et al. *Knives and Scabbards: Medieval Finds From Excavations in London*, London, 1987.

Crossley, D.W. *The Bewl Valley Iron Works, Kent*, c. *1300-1730*, London, 1975a.

Crossley, D.W. 'Canon Manufacture at Pippingford, Sussex: the Excavation of Two Iron Furnaces of c. 1717,' *Post.-Med. Arch.* 9, 1975b.

Crossley, D.W. (ed.), *Medieval Industry, C.B.A. Research Report* No. 40, 1981.

Cunliffe, B. W. *Iron Age Communities in Britain*, London, 1974.

Curtis, E. and McDowell, R.B. (eds), *Irish Historical Documents 1171-1922*, London, 1943.

Davey, N. *A History of Building Materials*, London, 1961.

de Courcy, J.W. 'Medieval Banks of the Liffey Estuary' in J. Bradley (ed.), *Viking Dublin Exposed*, Dublin, 1984.

de Courcy, J.W. 'The Engineering of Dublin,' *Ir. Eng. J.* 41, No. 9, 1988.

Dembrinska, M. *Przetworstwo Zbozowe w Polsce Sredniowiecznej X-XIV Wiek*, Gdansk, 1973.

de Rougemont, G.M. *A Field Guide to the Crops of Britain and Europe*, London, 1989.

Dick, W. 'The Back of the Pipes and James Harbour,' *Indust. Arch.* 37, 1974.

Down, M. 'Colonial Society and Economy in the High Middle Ages' in A. Cosgrove (ed.), *A New History of Ireland*, Vol 2, Oxford, 1987.

Drew, T. 'The Surroundings of the Cathedral Church of St Patrick's *in Insula*,' *J. Roy. Soc. Ant. Ir.* 21, 1891.

Drew, T. 'A Further Note on the Surroundings of St Patrick's *in Insula*, Dublin,' *J. Roy Soc. Ant. Ir.* 29, 1899.

Drew, T. 'The Ancient Chapter-house of the Priory of the Holy Trinity, Dublin,' in H.B. Clarke (ed.), *Medieval Dublin: the Making of a Metropolis*, Dublin, 1990.

Driesch, A. von den, and Boessneck, A.J. 'Kritische Anmerkungen zur Widderisthoherberechnung aus Langermassen vor- und fruhgeschtlicher Tierknoke,' *Saugetierkundliche Mitteilungen* 22, 1974.

Driesch, A. von den, *A Guide to the Measurement of Animal Bones From Archaeological Sites, Peabody Museum Bulletin*, Harvard, Cambridge, MA, 1976.

Duco, D.H. *Merken van Goudse Pijpenmakers 1660-1940*, Lochem, 1982.

Duco, D.H. 'The Crowned L: the History of a Famous Gouda Pipemaker's Mark' in R. Jackson and P. Jackson (eds), *Clay Pipe Research* 1, 1988.

Dudley Edwards, R. 'The Beginnings of Municipal Government in Dublin' in H.B. Clarke (ed.), *Medieval Dublin: the Living City*, Dublin, 1990.

Dunlevy, M. 'A Classification of Early Irish Combs,' *Proc. Roy. Ir. Acad.* 88C, 1988.

Dunning, G.C. 'The Pottery Louver From Goosegate, Nottingham,' *Trans. Thoroton Soc. Nottinghamshire* LXVI, 1962.

Dunning, G.C. 'A Pottery Louver From Great Easton, Essex,' *Med. Arch.* 10, 1966.

Dunning, G.C. 'The Trade in Medieval Pottery Around the North Sea' in J.G. Renaud (ed.), *Rotterdam Papers* 1, Rotterdam, 1968.

Dunning, G.C. 'Roof-fittings' in C. Platt and R. Coleman-Smith, *Excavations in Medieval Southampton 1953-1969*, Leicester, 1975.

Eames, E.S. and Fanning, T. *Irish Medieval Tiles*, Dublin, 1988.

East, K. 'The Shoes' in R.L.S. Bruce-Mitford (ed.), *The Sutton-Hoo Ship Burial* Vol. 3, London, 1983.

Egan, G., and Pritchard, F. *Dress Accessories* c. *1150*-c. *1450*, London, 1991.

Elliot, A.C. 'The Abbey of St Thomas the Martyr, Near Dublin' in H.B. Clarke (ed.), *Medieval Dublin: the Living City*, Dublin, 1990.

Evans, E.E. *Irish Folk Ways*, London, 1976.

Fahy, E.M. 'A Horizontal Mill at Mashanaglass, Co. Cork,' *J. Cork Hist. and Arch. Soc.* 61, 1956.

Ford, B. and Walsh, A. 'Iron Nails' in P. Holdsworth (ed.), *Excavations in the Medieval Burgh of Perth*, Aberdeen, 1987.

Frazer, F.C. *British Whales, Dolphins and Porpoises*, London, 1976.

Gahan, A. and McCutcheon, C. 'The Medieval Pottery' in M.F. Hurley, O.M.B. Scully and S.W.J. McCutcheon, *Late Viking Age and Medieval Waterford*, Waterford, 1997.

Gahwiler, A. 'Romische Wasserader aus Hangendorn,' *Helvitia Archaeologia* 15, 1984.

Galhano, F. *Moinhos e Azenhaus de Portugal*, Lisbon, 1978.

Geraghty, S. *Viking Dublin: Botanical Evidence From Fishamble Street*, Dublin, 1996.

Gilbert, J.T. (ed.), *Historical and Municipal Documents of Ireland 1172-1320*, London, 1870.

Gilbert, J.T. (ed.), *Register of the Abbey of St. Thomas the Martyr, Dublin*, London, 1889.

Gilbert, J.T. (ed.), *Chartularies of St. Mary's Abbey, Dublin, and Annals of Ireland 1162-1370* (2 vols), London, 1884-86.

Gilbert, J.T. (ed.), *Crede Mihi: the Most Ancient Register Book of the Archbishop of Dublin Before the Reformation*, London, 1897.

Gilbert, J.T. *The Streets of Dublin*, London, 1852.

Gilbert, J.T. *A History of the City of Dublin* (3 vols), Dublin, 1854-59.

Gilbert, J.T. and Gilbert, R.M. *Calendar of Ancient Records of Dublin in the Possession of the Municipal Corporation of that City* (19 vols), Dublin, 1889-1944.

Gillespie, E. (ed.), *The Liberties of Dublin*, Dublin, 1973.

Goodburn, D. 'Woods and Woodland: Carpenters and Carpentry' in G. Milne, *Timber Building Techiques in London c. 900-1400*, London, 1992.

Gowen, M. 'Excavations at St Michael le Pole,' Dublin, forthcoming.

Graham, A.H. 'The Old Malthouse, Abbotsbury, Dorset: the Medieval Watermill of the Benedictine Abbey,' *Proc. Dorset Nat. Hist. and Arch. Soc.* 108, 1986.

Grant, A. 'The Use of Tooth Wear as a Guide to the Age of Domestic Ungulates' in B. Wilson, C. Grigson and S. Payne (eds), *Aging and Sexing Animal Bones From Archaeological Sites*, B.A.R. British Series 109, 1982.

Grant, A. *North Devon Pottery: the Seventeenth Century*, Exeter, 1983.

Green, F.J. 'The Archaeological and Documentary Evidence For Plants From the Medieval Period in England' in W. Van Zeist and W.A. Casparie (eds), *Plants and Ancient Man*, Rotterdam, 1983.

Greig, J. 'Plant Foods in the Past: a Review of the Evidence From Northern Europe,' *Journal of Plant Foods* 5, 1983.

Grew, F. and de Neergaard, M. *Shoes and Pattens: Medieval Finds From Excavations in London*, London, 1988.

Gwynn, A. 'The Early History of St Thomas Abbey, Dublin,' *J. Roy. Soc. Ant. Ir.* 84, 1954.

Gwynn, A. and Hadcock, R.N. *Medieval Religious Houses of Ireland*, Dublin, 1970.

Halpin, A. 'Winetavern St, Dublin' in I. Bennet (ed.), *Excavations 1993*, Dublin, 1994.

Hamilton-Dyer, S. 'Bird, Fish and Marine Invertebrates From Back Lane, Dublin,' forthcoming.

Hand, G.J. 'The Rivalry of the Cathedral Chapters in Medieval Dublin' in H.B. Clarke (ed.), *Medieval Dublin: the Living City*, Dublin, 1990.

Harcourt, RA. 'The Dog in Prehistoric and Early Historic Britain,' *Journal of Archaeological Science* 1, 1974.

Hayden, A.R. 'Excavations at Arran Quay, Dublin,' forthcoming a.

Hayden, A.R. 'Excavations at Werburgh St, Dublin,' forthcoming b.

Hayden, A.R. 'Excavations at Cornmarket and Bridge St Upper, Dublin,' forthcoming c.

Hayden, A.R. 'Patrick St/Nicholas St, Dublin' in I. Bennett (ed.), *Excavations 1991*, Dublin, 1992.

Hayden, A.R. and Walsh, C. 'Excavations at Christchurch Place and Werburgh St, Dublin', forthcoming.

Healy, P. 'The Town Walls of Dublin' in H.B. Clarke (ed.), *Medieval Dublin: the Making of a Metropolis*, Dublin, 1990.

Hewett, C. 'Structural Carpentry in Medieval Essex,' *Med. Arch.* 6 and 7, 1963.

Hewett, C.A. 'Scarf Jointing During the Later 13th and 14th Centuries and a Reappraisal of the Origins of Spurred Tenons,' *Arch. J.* 134, 1977.

Higham, C.F.W. 'Flock Rearing as a Cultural Factor in Prehistoric Europe,' *Proc. Prehist. Soc.* 33, 1967.

Holt, R. *The Mills of Medieval England*, Oxford, 1988.

Hurley, F. 'Patrick St, Dublin' in I. Bennet (ed.), *Excavations 1992*, Dublin 1993.

Hurley, M.F. 'Excavations at Grand Parade, Cork 11, Part 1,' *J. Cork Hist. and Arch. Soc.* 90, 1989.

Hurst, J. 'The Dating of Late 12th and Early 13th Century Pottery in Ireland,' *U. J. Arch.* 48, 1985.

Hurst, J. 'Medieval Pottery Imported into Ireland' in G. Mac Niocaill and P.F. Wallace (eds), *Keimelia*, Galway, 1988.

Hurst, J, Neal, D, van Beuningen, H.J.E. *Pottery Produced and Traded in North-west Europe 1350-1650*, Rotterdam, 1988.

Jackson, V. 'The Glib Water and Colman's Brook,' *D.H.R.* 11, 1950.

Jackson, V. 'The Palace of Sepulchre,' *D.H.R.* 28, 1975.

Jackson, V. 'The Inception of the Dodder Water Supply' in H.B. Clarke (ed.), *Medieval Dublin: the Making of a Metropolis*, Dublin, 1990.

Jacono, L. 'La Ruota Idraulica di Venafro,' *L'Ingegnere* 12, 1938.

Jafvert, E. *Skomod Och Skotillverkning Fran Medeltiden Till Vara Dagar*, Stockholm, 1938.

Janaway, R. and Wincott Heckett, E. 'The Textiles From Tuckey St, Cork,' forthcoming.

Jennings, S. *Eighteen Centuries of Pottery From Norwich*, Norwich, 1981.

Jones, R.H. 'Industry and Environment in Medieval Bristol' in G.L. Good, R.H. Jones and M.W. Ponsford (eds), *Waterfront Archaeology: Proceedings of the 3rd International Conference*, London, 1991.

Jope, E.M. and Seaby, W.A. 'A New Document in the Public Record Office: Defensive Houses in Medieval Towns,' *U. J. Arch.* 22, 1959.

Jope, M. 'Animal Bones From Clough Castle' in D.M. Waterman, 'Excavations at Clough Castle,' *U. J. Arch.* 17, 1954.

Keene, D.J. 'Rubbish in Medieval Towns' in R.A. Hall and H.K. Kennard (eds), *Environmental Archaeology in the Urban Context*, *C.B.A. Research Report* No. 43, 1982.

King, D. 'Currents of Trade: Industry, Merchants and Money' in J. Evans (ed.), *The Flowering of the Middle Ages*, London, 1966.

Langer, R.H.M. and Hill, G.D. *Agricultural Plants*, Cambridge, 1982.

Lawlor, H.J. *Fasti of St Patrick's*, Dundalk, 1930.

le Patourel, J. (ed.), 'Documents Relating to the Manor and Borough of Leeds 1066-1400,' *Public. Thoresby Soc.* 45, No. 104, 1956.

Lewis, J. *From Fleece to Fabric*, London, 1983.

Lisle, L. *Observations on Husbandry* (2 vols), London, 1957.

Little, G.A. *Dublin Before the Vikings – An Adventure in Discovery*, Dublin, 1957.

Liversage, G.D. 'Excavations at Dalkey Island, Co. Dublin, 1956-1959,' *Proc. Roy. Ir. Acad.* 66C, 1968.

London Museum Catalogues. No. 7, *Medieval Catalogue*, London, 1940.

Lucas, A.T. 'The Horizontal Mill in Ireland,' *J. Roy. Soc. Ant. Ir.* 83, 1953.

Lucas, A.T. 'A Horizontal Mill at Ballykilleen, Co. Offaly,' *J. Roy. Soc. Ant. Ir.* 85, 1955.

Lucas, A.T. 'Irish Food Before the Potato,' *Gwerin* 3, 1960.

Lungescu, O. and Godea, J. 'Die Wassermuhlen im Rosia-Tal,' *Cibinium, 1960-73*, 1978.

Lydon, J. 'The Mills at Ardee in 1304,' *J. Co. Louth Arch. and Hist. Soc.* 4, 1981.

Lydon, J.F. 'Edward I, Ireland and the War in Scotland 1303-1304' in J. F. Lydon (ed.), *England and Ireland in the Later Middle Ages*, Dublin, 1981.

Lydon, J.F. 'The Medieval City' in A. Cosgrove (ed.), *Dublin Through the Ages*, Dublin, 1988.

Lynch, W. *The Law of Election in the Ancient Cities and Towns of Ireland*, London, 1831.

Lynn, C. 'The Excavation of Rathmullan, a Raised Rath and Motte in Co. Down,' *U. J. Arch.* 44-45, 1982.

MacGregor, A. *Bone, Antler, Ivory and Horn*, London, 1985.

MacGregor, A. 'Bone, Antler and Horn Industries in the Urban Context' in D. Serjeantson and T. Waldron (eds), *Diet and Crafts in Towns*, B.A.R. British Series 1989.

Maltese, C. (ed.), *Francesco di Giorgio Martini: Trattati di Architettura Ingegneria e Arte Militaire* (2 vols), Milan, 1967.

Manning, C. 'Excavations at Kilteel Church, Co. Kildare,' *J. Co. Kildare Arch. Soc.* 16, No. 3, 1982.

Martin, J. *The Liberties* 1, No. 4, 1969.

Maybe, R. *Food for Free*, Glasgow, 1972.

McCarthy, M. and Brooks, C. *Medieval Pottery in Britain AD 900-1600*, Leicester, 1988.

McCormick, F. 'The Animal Bones From Ditch 1' in J. W. Barber, 'Excavations at Iona,' *Proc. Soc. Ant. Scot.* 111, 1981.

McCormick, F. 'The Mammal Bones From Drogheda,' in D. Sweetman, 'Archaeological Excavations at Shop St, Drogheda, Co. Louth,' *Proc. Roy. Ir. Acad.* 84C, 1984a.

McCormick, F. 'The Animal Bones' in A. Lynch, 'Excavations of the Medieval Town Defences at Charlotte's Quay, Limerick,' *Proc. Roy. Ir. Acad.* 1984b.

McCormick, F. *Stockrearing in Ancient Ireland*, unpublished Ph.D. thesis, Queens University, Belfast, 1987.

McCormick, F. 'The Domesticated Cat in Early Christian and Medieval Ireland' in G. Mac Niocaill and P.F. Wallace (eds), *Keimelia*, Galway, 1988.

McCormick, F. 'The Effect of the Anglo-Norman Settlement on Ireland's Wild and Domesticated Fauna' in P.J. Crabtree and K. Ryan (eds), *Animal Use and Cultural Change*, MASCA Research Papers in Science and Archaeology, Supplement to Vol. 8, 1991.

McCormick, F. 'Animal Bones' in M.F. Hurley, O.M.B. Scully and S.W.J. McCutcheon, *Late Viking Age and Medieval Waterford*, Waterford, 1997.

McGrail, S. *Medieval Boat and Ship Timbers From Dublin*, Dublin, 1993.

McMahon, M. 'Winetavern St' in I. Bennett (ed.), *Excavations 1989*, Dublin, 1990.

McMahon, M. 'Excavations at Bride St, Dublin,' forthcoming.

McNeill, C. *Calender of Archbishop Alen's Register* c. *1172-1534*, Dublin, 1950.

McNeill, C. 'The Hospital of St John Without the Newgate, Dublin' in H.B. Clarke (ed.), *Medieval Dublin: the Living City*, Dublin, 1990.

Meenan, R. '20-23 Merchant's Quay, Dublin' in I. Bennett (ed.), *Excavations 1990*, Dublin, 1991.

Meenan, R. '27-30 Merchants Quay, Dublin' in I. Bennett (ed.), *Excavations 1989*, Dublin, 1990.

Meenan, R. 'A Survey of Late Medieval and Early Post-Medieval Iberian Pottery From Ireland' in D. Gaimster and M. Redknap (eds), *Everyday and Exotic Pottery From Europe*, Exeter, 1992.

Meyer, K. *The Vision of Mac Conglinne*, London, 1892.

Miller, W.C. *Black's Veterinary Dictionary*, London, 1935.

Mills, J. 'Notices of the Manor of St Sepulchre in the 14th Century,' *J. Roy. Soc. Ant. Ir.* 9, Series 4, Parts 1, 2, 1889.

Mills, J. (ed.), *Account Roll of the Priory of the Holy Trinity, Dublin, 1337-46*, Dublin, 1891.

Mills, J. 'Norman Settlement in Leinster: the Cantreds Near Dublin,' *J. Roy. Soc. Ant. Ir.* 24, 1894.

Mills, J. and Griffith, M.C. (eds), *The Calender of Justiciary Rolls of Ireland 1295-1314* (3 vols), Dublin, 1905.

Milne, G. and Hobley, B. (eds), *Waterfront Archaeology in Britain and Northern Europe*, London, 1981.

Milne, G. and Milne, C. 'Excavations at Trig Lane, London, 1974-77,' *Med. Arch.* 22, 1978.

Milne, G. and Milne, C. 'The Making of the London Waterfront,' *Current Arch.* 66, Vol. VI, No. 7, 1979.

Milne, G. 'Recording Timber on the London Waterfront' in S. McGrail (ed.), *Woodworking Before 1500 AD*, B.A.R. British Series 129, 1982.

Milne, G. *Timber Building Techniques in London* c. *900-1400*, London, 1992.

Mitchell, G.F. *Archaeology and Environment in Early Dublin*, Dublin, 1987.

Mitchener, M. *The Medieval Period and Nuremberg*, Vol. 1, London, 1988.

Monck Mason, W. *Antiquities of the Collegiate and Cathedral Church of St Patrick's, Near Dublin*, Dublin, 1818.

Morales, A. and Rosenlund, K. *Fish Bone Measurements*, Copenhagen, 1979.

Morrin, J. (ed.), *Calendar of the Patent and Close Rolls of Chancery in Ireland in the Reigns of Henry VIII, Ed IV, Mary and Elizabeth*, Dublin, 1861.

Morton, J. *Fast Dying and Dyes*, Edinburgh, 1929.

Murray, H. *Viking and Early Medieval Buildings in Dublin*, B.A.R. British Series 119, 1983.

Murtagh, M. 'Walking Around the Liberties' in E. Gillespie (ed.), *The Liberties of Dublin*, Dublin, 1973.

Nice Boyer, M. 'Watermills: a Problem for the Bridges and Boats of Medieval France,' *History of Technology* 7, 1982.

Nicholson, R. and Hillam, J. 'Tree-ring Analysis of Medieval Oak Timbers From Dundas Wharf, Redcliff St, Bristol,' *Trans. of the Bris. and Glouc. Arch. Soc.* 105, 1987.

Nockert, M. *Bockstensmannen och hans Drakt*, Varberg, 1985.

Ó Conbhuidhe, C. 'The Land of St Mary's Abbey,' *Proc. Roy. Ir. Acad.* 62C, 1952.

O'Connor, P. 'Hurdle Making in Dublin 1302-03,' *D.H.R.* 13, 1952.

Ó Cuilleain, L. 'Tráchtáil is Bainceareacht i nGaillimh san 18iú Céad,' *Galvia* 5, 1958.

Ó Floinn, R. 'Handmade Medieval Pottery in S.E. Ireland – Leinster Cooking Ware' in G. Mac Niocaill and P.F. Wallace (eds), *Keimelia*, Galway, 1988.

O'Kelly, M.J. 'A Wooden Bridge on the Cashen River, Co. Kerry,' *J. Roy. Soc. Ant. Ir.* 91, Part 2, 1961.

Ó Lochlainn, C. 'Roadways in Ancient Ireland' in J. Ryan (ed.), *Essays and Studies Presented to Professor Eoin Mac Neill on the Occasion of his Seventieth Birthday*, Dublin, 1983.

O'Neill, T. *Merchants and Mariners in Medieval Ireland*, Dublin, 1987.

Ortner, D.J. and Putschar, W.G.J. *Identification of Pathological Conditions in Human Skeletal Remains*, Washington, 1985.

O'Rourke, D. 'The Leather Finds From High St, Dublin,' forthcoming a.

O'Rourke, D. 'The Leather Finds' in R.M. Cleary, M.F. Hurley, and E. Shea Twohig (eds), *Excavations by D.C. Twohig at Christ Church and Skiddy's Castle, Cork 1974-77*, forthcoming b.

O'Rourke, D. 'The Leather Finds from the Dublin Castle Excavations,' forthcoming c.

O'Rourke, D. 'Leather Artefacts' in M.F.H. Hurley, O.M.B. Scully and S.W.J. McCutcheon, *Late Viking Age and Medieval Waterford*, Waterford, 1997.

Ostergard, E. 'The Medieval Everyday Costumes of the Norsemen in Greenland' in Bender, L. Jorgensen and K. Tidow (eds), *Textilsymposium Neumunster*, 1982.

O'Sullivan, T. '*The Exploitation of Birds in Viking Dublin: an Avi-faunal Analysis of a Sample From Fishamble St*,' unpublished M.A. thesis, National University of Ireland, 1995.

O'Sullivan, A. and Deevy, M. 'Trees, Woodland and Woodmanship in Anglo-Norman Dublin: the Back Lane evidence,' forthcoming.

Orton, C. and Tyers, P. 'Slicing the Pie – a Framework for Comparing Ceramic Assemblages,' *Medieval Ceramics* 14, 1990.

Otway-Ruthven, A.J. *A History of Medieval Ireland*, London, 1980.

Papazian, C. *The Medieval Pottery From the Dublin Castle Excavations*, unpublished M.A. thesis, National University of Ireland, 1989.

Papazian, C. 'The Medieval Pottery From High St, Dublin,' forthcoming a.

Papazian, C. 'The Medieval Pottery From Christchurch Place, Dublin,' forthcoming b.

Papazian, C. 'The Medieval Pottery From Back Lane, Dublin,' forthcoming c.

Papazian, C. 'The Medieval Pottery From Cornmarket and Bridge St Upper, Dublin,' forthcoming d.

Pearce, J.E., Vince, A.G., and Jenner, M.A. *A Dated Type Series of London Medieval Pottery Part 2: London Type Ware*, London, 1985.

Petchey, M. and Giggins, B. 'The Excavation of a Late Seventeenth Century Watermill at Caldecotte, Bow Brickhill, Bucks,' *Post.-Med. Arch.* 17, 1983.

Platt, C. and Coleman-Smith, R. *Excavations in Medieval Southampton 1953-69* (2 vols), Leicester, 1975.

Ponsford, M. 'Dendrochronological Dates From Dundas Wharf, Bristol, and the Dating of Ham Green and Other Medieval Pottery' in E. Lewis (ed.), *Customs and Ceramics. Essays Presented to Kenneth Barton*, Wickham, 1991.

Power, C. 'Anthropological Studies on the Dental Remains From Some Irish Archaeological Sites,' *OSSA* 12, 1986.

Power, C. 'Report on the Human Skeletal Remains From the Early Christian Site at Cathedral Hill, Armagh, Co. Down,' *U. J. Arch.*, forthcoming a.

Power, C. 'Report on the Human Skeletal Remains From Betaghstown, Co. Meath,' forthcoming.

Prager, F.D. and Scaglia, G. *Mariano Taccola and His Book* De Ingeneis, Massachussetts, 1972.

Rackham, O, Blair, W.J. and Murray, J.T. 'Roofs and Floors of Blackfriars Priory,' *Med. Arch.* 22, 1978.

Rackham, O. 'The Growing and Transport of Timber and Underwood' in S. McGrail (ed.), *Woodworking Before 1500 AD*, B.A.R. British Series 129, 1982.

Rahtz, P. 'Excavation of the Town Wall, Baldwin St, Bristol,' *Trans. Bristol and Glouc. Arch. Soc.* Vol. 74, Part 2, 1960.

Rahtz, P.A. and Bullough, D. 'The Parts of an Anglo-Saxon Mill,' *Anglo-Saxon England* 6, 1977.

Rahtz, P.A. 'Medieval Milling' in D.W. Crossley (ed.), *Medieval Industry*, C.B.A. Research Report No. 40, 1981.

Raphael, D. *The Tender Gift: Breast-Feeding*, New York, 1977.

Reed, R. *Ancient Skins, Parchments and Leathers*, 1972.

Reindl, C. 'Ein Romisches Wasserad,' *Wasserkraft und Wasserwirtschaft* 34, 1939.

Renfrew, J.M. *Paleoethnobotany: the Prehistoric Food Plants of the Near East and Europe*, London, 1973.

Reynolds, T.S. *Stronger Than a Hundred Men: a History of the Vertical Waterwheel*, London, 1983.

Richardson, K.M. 'Excavations in Hungate, York,' *Arch. J.* 116, 1959.

Rigold, S.E. 'Structural Aspects of Medieval Timber Bridges,' *Med. Arch.* 19, 1975.

Robinson, D. and Ford, B. 'Moss' in P. Holdsworth (ed.), *Excavations in the Medieval Burgh of Perth*, Aberdeen.

Roche, G. 'The Animal Bones' in M.J. O'Kelly, 'Church Island Near Valentia, Co. Kerry,' *Proc. Roy. Ir. Acad.* 59C, 1958.

Rogerson, A. and Adams, N. 'A Saxo-Norman Pottery Kiln at Bircham' in D.W. Crossley (ed.), *Medieval Industry*, London, 1981.

Romeuf, A.M. 'Un Moulin a Eau Gallo-Romain aux Martres de Veyre,' *Revue d'Avergne* 92, 2, 1978.

Ronan, M.V. 'The Poddle River and Its Branches,' *J. Roy. Soc. Ant. Ir.* 57, 1927.

Ronan, M.V. 'Stone Circles in St Patrick's Cathedral,' *J. Roy. Soc. Ant. Ir.* 71, 1941.

Russell, J. 'English Medieval Leatherwork,' *Arch. J.* XCVI, 1939.

Ryan, J. *Irish Monasticism – Origins and Early Development*, Dublin, 1931.

Ryan, J. 'Pre-Norman Dublin,' *J. Roy. Soc. Ant. Ir.* 79, 1949.

Rynne, C. *The Archaeology and Technology of the Horizontal-Wheeled Watermill, With Special Reference to Ireland*, unpublished Ph.D. thesis, National University of Ireland, 1988.

Rynne, C. 'Archaeology and the Early Irish Watermill,' *Arch. Ir.* 3, No. 3, 1989a.

Rynne, C. 'The Introduction of the Vertical Watermill Into Ireland: Some Recent Evidence,' *Med. Arch.* 33, 1989b.

Rynne, C. 'Some Observations on the Production of Flour and Meal in the Early Historic Period,' *J. Cork Hist. and Arch. Soc.* 95, 1990.

Salaman, R.A. *Dictionary of Leatherworking Tools c. 1700-1950*, London, 1986.

Salisbury, E. *Weeds and Aliens*, London, 1964.

Salzman, L.F. *Building in England Down to 1540: a Documentary History*, Oxford, 1952.

Scannell, M.J.P. 'Handlist of Species of Wood Identified' in J. Lang, *Viking Age Decorated Wood*, Dublin, 1988.

Scannell, M.J.P. and Synnott, D.M. *Census Catalogue of the Flora of Ireland*, Dublin, 1987.

Schweppe, H. 'Identification of Dyes on Old Textiles,' *Journal of the American Institute for Conservation* 19/1, 1979.

Schofield, J.L. 'Serradella: a Legume for Light Acid Soils,' *Journal of the British Grassland Society* 5, 1950.

Scott, A.B. and Martin, F.X. (eds), *Expugnatio Hibernica: the Conquest of Ireland, by Geraldis Cambrensis*, Dublin, 1978.

Seaby, W. *Sylloge of Coins of the British Isles,* Vol. 32, London, 1984.

Serjeantson, D. 'Animal Remains and the Tanning Trade' in D. Serjeantson and T. Waldron (eds), *Diet and Craft in Towns*, B.A.R. British Series 199, 1989.

Shaw, M. 'Northampton – Excavating a 16th Century Tannery,' *Current Arch.* 8 No. 91, 1984.

Sheppard, A.O. *Ceramics for the Archaeologist*, Washington, 1976.

Silver, I.A. 'The Aging of Domesticated Animals' in D. Brothwell and E. Higgs, *Science in Archaeology*, 2nd ed., London, 1969.

Simms, A. 'The Topography of Medieval Dublin' in H.B. Clarke (ed.), *Focus on Medieval Dublin*, Dublin, 1978.

Simms, A. 'Medieval Dublin in a European Context: From Proto-Town to Chartered Town' in H.B. Clarke (ed.), *Medieval Dublin: the Making of a Metropolis*, Dublin, 1990.

Singer, C. et al. (eds), *A History of Technology*, Vol. 2, Oxford, 1956.

Spain, R.J. 'The Second Century Romano-British Watermill at Ickham, Kent,' *History of Technology* 9, 1984a.

Spain, R.J. 'Romano-British Watermills,' *Archaeologia Cantania* 100, 1984b.

Swan, D.L. '6-8 Usher's Quay, Dublin' in I. Bennet (ed.), *Excavations 1991*, Dublin, 1992.

Swann, J.M. *A History of Shoe Fashions*, Northampton, 1975.

Swann, J.M. *Shoemaking*, Bucks, 1986.

Sweetman, H.S. (ed.), *Calendar of Documents Relating to Ireland 1171-1307* (5 vols), London, 1875-86.

Sweetman, P.D. 'Archaeological Excavation at Shop St, Drogheda, Co. Louth,' *Proc. Roy. Ir. Acad.* 84C, 1984.

Taylor, G.W. 'Natural Testing of Synthetic Dyings,' *Dyes in History and Archaeology* 7, 1988.

Thomas, S. *Medieval Footwear From Coventry*, Coventry, 1980.

Thorpe, K (ed.), *The Journey Through Wales and the Description of Wales*, London, 1978.

Thun, E. 'Die Wassermuhlen, ein Okonomischer Entwicklungsfactor der Mittelalterlichen Stade Schonen,' *Meddelanden fran Lunds Universitet Historisked Museum* 1962-1963, 1963.

Usher, A.P. *A History of Mechanical Inventions*, Massachussetts, 1954.

Veale, E.M. *The English Fur Trade in the Later Middle Ages*, Oxford, 1966.

Verriest, L. (ed.), *Le Polyptque Illustre dir 'Veil Rentier' de Messire Jehan de Pamele-Audenarde (c. 1275)*, Gembloux, 1950.

Vince, A.G. 'Some Aspects of Pottery Quantification,' *Medieval Ceramics* 1, 1977.

Vince, A.G. *The Medieval Pottery Industry of the Severn Valley (*3 vols), unpublished Ph.D. thesis, University of Southampton, 1983.

Vince, A.G. 'The Saxon and Medieval Pottery of London: a Review,' *Med. Arch.* 29, 1985.

Vince, A.G. 'Early Medieval English Pottery in Viking Dublin' in G. Mac Niocaill and P.F. Wallace (eds), *Keimelia*, Galway, 1988.

Viollet-le-Duc, E.E. *Dictionnaire Raisonnede L'Architecture Française*, Vol. VI, 1863.

Walker, P. 'The Tools Available to the Medieval Woodworker' in S. McGrail (ed.), *Woodworking Before 1500 AD*, B.A.R. British Series 129, 1982.

Wallace, P.F. 'Dublin's Waterfront at Wood Quay AD 900-1317' in G. Milne and B. Hobley, *Waterfront Archaeology in Britain and Northern Europe*, C.B.A. Research Report No. 41, 1981.

Wallace, P.F. 'Carpentry in Ireland AD 900-1300, The Wood Quay Evidence' in S. McGrail (ed.), *Woodworking Before 1500 AD*, B.A.R. British Series 129, 1982.

Wallace P.F. 'North European Pottery Imported Into Dublin 1200-1500' in P. Davey and R. Hodges (eds), *Ceramics and Trade*, Sheffield, 1983.

Wallace, P.F. 'A Reappraisal of the Archaeological Significance of Wood Quay' in J. Bradley (ed.), *Viking Dublin Exposed*, Dublin, 1984.

Wallace, P.F. 'The Archaeology of Viking Dublin' in H.B. Clarke and A. Simms (eds), *The Comparative History of Urban Origins in Non-Roman Europe*, B.A.R. International Series 255, ii, 1985a.

Wallace, P.F. 'Archaeology and the Emergence of Dublin as the Principal Town of Ireland' in J. Bradley (ed.), *Settlement and Society in Medieval Ireland*, Kilkenny, 1988.

Wallace, P.F. 'The Origins of Dublin' in H.B. Clarke (ed.), *Medieval Dublin: the Making of a Metropolis*, Dublin, 1990.

Wallace, P.F. 'The Archaeological Identity of the Hiberno-Norse Town,' *J. Roy. Soc. Ant. Ir.* 122, 1992.

Wallace, P.F. *The Viking Age Buildings of Dublin*, Dublin, 1992.

Walsh, C. *Excavations at Back Lane, Dublin*, forthcoming.

Walsh, M. 'A Watermill at Ballyine, Co. Limerick,' *J. Cork. Hist. and Arch. Soc.* 70, Part 1, 1965.

Walsh, P. 'Leaves From a Retrospective Photo Album' in J. Bradley (ed.), *Viking Dublin Exposed*, Dublin, 1984.

Walton, P. 'Caulking, Cordage and Textiles' in C. O'Brien et al (eds), *The Origins of Newcastle Quayside*, Newcastle, 1988.

Webb, J.J. *The Guilds Of Dublin*, Dublin, 1929.

Wedlake, W.J. 'The Excavation of the Shrine of Apollo at Nettleton, Wilts. (1957-71),' *Reports of the Research Committee*, No. XI, Soc. of Antiquaries, London, 1982.

Wenham, S.J. 'Anatomical Interpretations of Anglo-Saxon Weapon Injuries,' in S. Chadwick Hawkes (ed.), *Weapons and Warfare in Anglo-Saxon England*, Oxford, 1989.

Went, A.E.J. 'Fisheries of the River Liffey' in H.B. Clarke (ed.), *Medieval Dublin: the Living City*, Dublin, 1990.

Wheeler, A. *Key to the Fishes of Northern Europe*, London, 1978.

White, K.D. *Roman Farming*, London, 1970.

White, N.B. *Dignitas Decani of St Patrick's*, Dublin, 1957.

White, N.B. (ed.), *Extents of Irish Monastic Possessions 1540-1541, From Manuscripts in the Public Record Office, London*, Dublin, 1943.

Whitelaw, J., Walsh, R. and Warburton, J. *The History Of Dublin*, Dublin, 1818.

Whittow, J.B. *Geology and Scenery in Ireland*, Dublin, 1974.

Wikander, O. 'Archaeological Evidence for Early Water Mills – an Interim Report,' *History of Technology*, 1985.

Wilde, W. 'Tables of Deaths,' *Census of Ireland For the Year 1851*, Part 5, Vol. 1, Dublin, 1856.

Williams, J.H. *St Peter's Street, Northampton, Excavations 1973-1976*, Northampton, 1979.

Wincott Heckett, E. 'Some Hiberno-Norse Headcoverings From Fishamble Street and St John's Lane, Dublin,' *Textile History* 18, 1987.

Wincott Heckett, E. 'Report on Textiles. Grand Parade II and Grand Parade I, 1984,' *J. Cork Hist. and Arch. Soc.* XCV, 254, 1990.

Wincott Heckett, E. 'Textiles, Cordage, Basketry and Raw Fibre' in M.F.H. Hurley, O.M.B. Scully and S.W.J. McCutcheon, *Late Viking Age and Medieval Waterford*, Waterford, 1997.

Wincott Heckett, E. 'The Textiles From High St, Dublin,' forthcoming a.

Wincott Heckett, E. 'The Textiles From James's St, Drogheda,' forthcoming b.

Wood, H. (ed.), *The Court Book of the Liberty of Saint Sepulchre Within the Jurisdiction of the Archbishop of Dublin, 1586-1590*, Dublin, 1930.

Wood, M. *The English Medieval House*, London, 1965.

Wren, J. *Crested Ridge-tiles From Medieval Towns in Leinster 1200-1500 AD*, unpublished M.A. thesis, National University of Ireland, 1987.

Wren, J. 'The Roof-tiles From Arran Quay, Dublin,' forthcoming a.

Wren, J. 'The Roof-tiles From Tintern Abbey, Wexford,' forthcoming b.

Wren, J. 'The Roof-tiles From the Dublin Castle Excavations,' forthcoming c.

Wren, J. 'The Roof-tiles From Washington St, Cork,' forthcoming d.

Wren, J. 'The Roof-tiles From the Excavations at the Southern Portion of the City Wall, Waterford,' forthcoming e.

Wright, G.N. *An Historical Guide to Ancient and Modern Dublin*, Dublin, 1821.

Wyse Jackson, P. and Sheefy Skeffington, M. *The Flora of Inner Dublin*, Dublin, 1984.

Young, C. 'The Late Roman Mill at Ickham and the Saxon Shore' in A. Detsicas (ed.), *Collectanea Historica: Essays in Memory of Stuart Rigold*, Gloucester, 1982.

Young, S.M. et al, 'Medieval Britain and Ireland in 1984,' *Med. Arch.* 28, 1985.

Zeven, A.C., and Zhukovsky, P.M. *Dictionary of Cultivated Plants and Their Centres of Diversity*, Pudoc Wageningen, 1975.